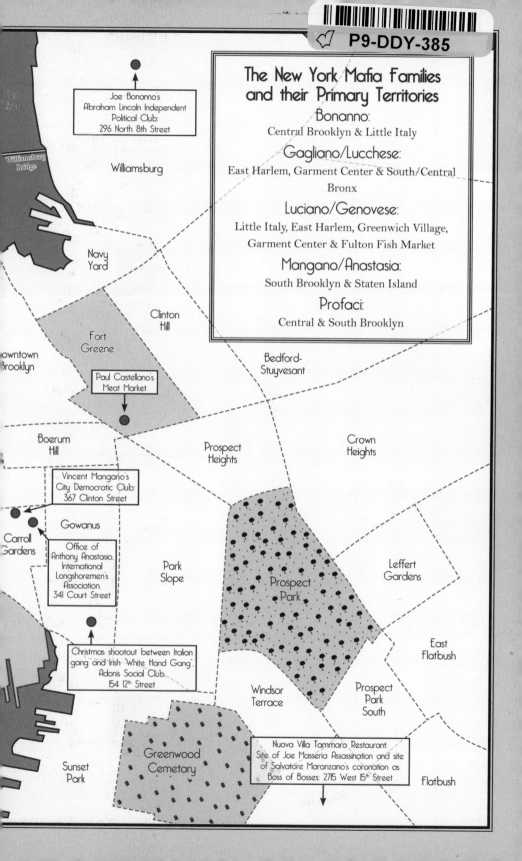

The New York Mafia Families and their Primary Territories

Bonanno:
Central Brooklyn & Little Italy

Gagliano/Lucchese:
East Harlem, Garment Center & South/Central Bronx

Luciano/Genovese:
Little Italy, East Harlem, Greenwich Village, Garment Center & Fulton Fish Market

Mangano/Anastasia:
South Brooklyn & Staten Island

Profaci:
Central & South Brooklyn

Joe Bonanno's Abraham Lincoln Independent Political Club: 296 North 8th Street

Paul Castellano's Meat Market

Vincent Mangano's City Democratic Club: 367 Clinton Street

Office of Anthony Anastasio, International Longshoremen's Association. 341 Court Street

Christmas shootout between Italian gang and Irish "White Hand Gang". Adonis Social Club. 154 12th Street

Nuova Villa Tammaro Restaurant: Site of Joe Masseria Assassination and site of Salvatore Maranzano's coronation as Boss of Bosses: 2715 West 15th Street

East River

Williamsburg Bridge

Williamsburg

Navy Yard

Clinton Hill

Fort Greene

Downtown Brooklyn

Boerum Hill

Bedford-Stuyvesant

Gowanus

Carroll Gardens

Park Slope

Prospect Heights

Crown Heights

Prospect Park

Leffert Gardens

East Flatbush

Windsor Terrace

Prospect Park South

Greenwood Cemetery

Sunset Park

Flatbush

THE MOB AND THE CITY

THE MOB AND THE CITY

THE HIDDEN HISTORY OF HOW
THE MAFIA CAPTURED NEW YORK

C. ALEXANDER HORTIS

Foreword by JAMES B. JACOBS
Coauthor of *BREAKING THE DEVIL'S PACT*

Prometheus Books
59 John Glenn Drive
Amherst, New York 14228

Published 2014 by Prometheus Books

Cover photo of Paul "The Waiter" Ricca, Sylvester Agoglia, Charles "Lucky" Luciano, and Meyer Lansky used by permission of the John Binder Collection

Jacket design by Grace M. Conti-Zilsberger

Inquiries should be addressed to
Prometheus Books
59 John Glenn Drive
Amherst, New York 14228
VOICE: 716–691–0133
FAX: 716–691–0137
WWW.PROMETHEUSBOOKS.COM

18 17 16 15 14   5 4 3 2 1

Library of Congress Cataloging-in-Publication Data

Hortis, C. Alexander, 1972–
   The mob and the city : the hidden history of how the mafia captured New York / by C. Alexander Hortis.
      pages cm
   Includes bibliographical references and index.
   ISBN 978-1-61614-923-9 (hardback)
   ISBN 978-1-61614-924-6 (ebook)
   1. Mafia—New York (State)—New York—History. 2. Organized crime—New York (State)—New York—History. I. Title.

HV6452.N72H67 2014
364.10609747'1—dc23

                                                                    2013049314

Printed in the United States of America

CONTENTS

Foreword by Dr. James B. Jacobs   7

Acknowledgments   9

Introduction: *The Godfather* vs. New York History   11

PART 1. NEW YORK CITY THROUGH PROHIBITION

1. A City Built for the Mob   17

2. Prohibition and the Rise of the Sicilians   41

PART 2. TAKING GOTHAM: THE 1930s AND '40s

3. The Mafia Rebellion of 1928–1931 and the Fall of the Boss of Bosses   71

4. The Racketeer Cometh: How the Mob Infiltrated Labor Unions   99

5. The Mafia and the Drug Trade   125

6. The Mob Nightlife   155

PART 3. THE MOBBED-UP METROPOLIS: THE 1950s

7. The Lives of Wiseguys   177

8. Mouthpieces for the Mob: Crooked Cops, Mob Lawyers, and Director Hoover   207

9. The Assassinations of 1957   225

10. Apalachin   249

Conclusion: New York's Mafia   283

Notes   285

Select Bibliography   357

Index   361

FOREWORD

The book you are about to read is an important contribution to New York City history and, given New York's importance, to the urban history of the United States. I take much delight in it because Alex Hortis was my student and coauthor at New York University School of Law in the late 1990s.

Much has been written about the Mafia and about New York City's Mafia families. However, Hortis shows that much of what has been written is wrong. Perhaps the greatest contribution of this highly readable tome is its debunking of many Mafia myths, for example, that Mafia members did not deal in drugs and did not inform on one another. His revisionist history of the so-called Castellammarese War is one of the most impressive achievements of this meticulous primary-source-based history.

In attempting to integrate New York City's Mafia history with the city's demographic, social, economic, and political history, Hortis is absolutely on the right track. He begins by showing that the evolution of the Mafia in New York is very much a story of ethnic succession. The Italians did not invent organized crime, but they brought it to a new level. Italian immigration followed both Jewish and Irish immigration, and Italians followed both of those groups into rackets like drugs, gambling, and labor racketeering. But the Italian mobsters were not nearly as monolithic and ethnocentric as other writers have assumed. Their intra- and intergroup relations were complex and important. Their ability to forge coalitions and overcome factionalism was utterly necessary for their remarkable successes.

Hortis presents a fascinating look at Mafia members' social lives, particularly their participation in New York's nightlife at the most famous nightclubs like the Copacabana (owned by Frank Costello), where they rubbed shoulders with famous sports figures, entertainers, businessmen, and politicians. People went to the Copa to meet and be seen with the Mafia bosses; this tells us much about how Mafia members were regarded by and integrated with the city's elite. Also fascinating and new (at least to me) are Hortis's accounts of Mafia members' ownership of gay bars and clubs and the participation of some mobsters in the gay scene.

The Mafia carried on the role of its Jewish and Irish predecessors, connecting the underworld (especially the world of vice) with the upperworld (business and labor). Hortis does a great job documenting and explaining how Italian-American organized crime members infiltrated or strong-armed their way into many New York City union locals. They used labor power to attract employer bribes or to extort employer payoffs. They then leveraged their union power to create and police employer cartels. And they took business interests in many companies that participated in the racketeer-ridden industries. The history of New York City's economy, especially in construction, seaborne and airborne cargo, and wholesale food markets is thoroughly permeated by the influence of the Mafia.

Hortis also provides some tantalizing clues as to the influence of the Mafia in politics. There is no question about the fact that the Mafia was highly integrated into Tammany Hall. Mob bosses contributed money and other forms of support to their favored politicians. In return, they obtained a good deal of immunity from interference with their illegal activities. Even after the demise of Tammany, mob bosses continued to be power brokers who exercised influence over politicians and political events. Much of their power stemmed from their positions in the unions.

The beginning of the Mafia's decline can be traced back to the early 1970s. After the 1972 death of FBI director J. Edgar Hoover, the FBI reinvented itself, changing from an internal security (anti-subversives, anti-Communist) agency to a modern-day law enforcement agency. By the late 1970s and early 1980s, the FBI had settled on control of organized crime as a target worthy of the attention of the nation's most important and competent law enforcement agency. Since then, federal, state, and local law enforcement agencies have decimated the Mafia's ranks. Yet remnants of the Mafia continue to exist and continue to engage in many of the rackets that Hortis documents in this tome.

James B. Jacobs
Warren E. Burger Professor of Law
New York University School of Law

ACKNOWLEDGMENTS

Researching this book was terrific fun. The book was built on primary sources, so I must first acknowledge the archivists. I am particularly grateful to Leonora Gidlund, Marcia Kirk, Kenneth Cobb, and Dwight Johnson of the New York Municipal Archives; William Davis of the National Archives in Washington, DC; Michael Desmond of the John F. Kennedy Presidential Library; Keith Swaney of the New York State Archives; Ellen Belcher of the John Jay College of Criminal Justice; Mattie Taormina of Stanford University; George Rugg of the University of Notre Dame; Lori Birrell of the University of Rochester; Michael Oliveira of the ONE National Gay & Lesbian Archives; and Patrizia Sione and Kathryn Dowgiewicz of the Kheel Center for Labor-Management Documentation and Archives. Special thanks to Chris Magee for locating cases at the National Archives at Kansas City. I also appreciate the help of the staffs of the Enoch Pratt Free Library in Baltimore, Maryland, and the Library of Congress in Washington, DC.

New and old friends contributed to this book. Christina M. Gentile was my Italian-language translator, and Ted Pertzborn was the graphics artist for the maps. I received support and assistance from Ryan Artis, John Binder, David Critchley, Josh Dowlut, Mario Hortis, Jacqueline Janowich, Meirong Liu, Will Meyerhofer, Arthur Nash, Lennert van't Riet, and Nathan Ward. I would also like to thank Greg Cross, Chris Mellott, and Colleen Mallon, my former colleagues, for allowing me to work part-time while completing the book. My agent Scott Mendel is the best *consigliere* anyone could have in the publishing world.

Prometheus Books is a wonderful place for authors. Editor-in-Chief Steven L. Mitchell improved the book with his editing. Grace M. Conti-Zilsberger designed the beautiful cover. Thanks also to Brian McMahon, Lisa Michalski, Mark Hall, and Melissa Raé Shofner.

My high school teacher Mr. Gerald Gerads first turned me on to history, and Professor Peter Rachleff introduced me to primary-source research. Professor James Jacobs of New York University School of Law, the nation's foremost scholar on the mob, started me on the path to this book back in 1998. He has been extraordinary generous over the years. This book could not have been finished without Thomas Hunt and Richard Warner. Tom Hunt contributed his eye for detail and shared sources from his own book *DiCarlo: Buffalo's First Family of Crime*. My honorary coauthor Rick Warner read the entire manuscript and offered invaluable suggestions.

Above all, I thank my parents, Bati and Linda, Mom and Kent. They have shown me the meaning of unconditional love.

INTRODUCTION
THE GODFATHER VS. NEW YORK HISTORY

W hen the cell doors clanged shut on Giuseppe Morello, Ignazio Lupo, and dozens of their men in the Atlanta Federal Penitentiary in 1910, their gang *should* have just dissolved into the streets of New York City. The Morello Family was just another struggling band of rogues, its modest numbers cut in half by convictions for a reckless counterfeiting scheme that had drawn the ire of the United States Secret Service.[1] The Sicilians were small fish in New York's underworld. The Irish mob enjoyed natural ties to the docks and police force; African-American gangsters held sway in black Harlem and San Juan Hill; and Jewish organized crime was far stronger throughout the city.

Then, improbably, the *mafiosi* reconstituted themselves and returned with a vengeance. By the late 1930s, they evolved into the Cosa Nostra ("Our Thing"), the top syndicate in Gotham. By the 1950s, the Mafia families had grown to include two thousand "made men" and thousands more criminal associates entrenched throughout the economy, neighborhoods, and nightlife of New York.[2]

The remarkable story of how the modern Mafia actually took power on the streets of New York remains largely hidden. Mob books gloss over this formative era with superficial "rise of" chapters that rehash dubious anecdotes from secondhand sources about the purported machinations of the bosses. Telling the Cosa Nostra's early history, however, requires digging up primary sources in archives. Moreover, the narrow obsession with the bosses (the "godfathers") neglects the soldiers (the "button men") who ran the rackets on the streets.

Mob history has been blurred by eighty years of Mafia mythology as well. America's greatest filmmakers have created indelible images of the mob, from Howard Hawks's *Scarface* to Martin Scorsese's gangster epics to Francis Ford

Coppola's *The Godfather* trilogy. They have been joined by "prestige dramas" such as *The Sopranos* and *Boardwalk Empire*. *Mafiosi* themselves have influenced the narrative. Al Capone in the 1920s, Joey Gallo in the 1970s, and John Gotti in the 1980s all manipulated the media. In his 1983 autobiography *A Man of Honor* (a bestseller that's still in print), Joseph Bonanno painted a romanticized portrait of himself as a benevolent "Father" who fought Americanized mobsters trying to pervert his noble "Tradition."[3]

This is the first full-length book devoted specifically to uncovering the hidden history of how the street soldiers of the modern Mafia captured New York City during the 1930s, 1940s, and 1950s. While discussing the Prohibition era of the 1920s, this book argues that the key formative decade for the Mafia was actually the 1930s. The book covers such hot topics as: Who actually founded the modern Mafia? Who shot Albert Anastasia at the Park Sheraton barbershop? And who exactly was present at the 1957 meeting of the Mafia in the town of Apalachin, New York? At the same time, the book goes beyond traditional mob topics as well. It not only documents who shot who, but explores *how* and *why* the Cosa Nostra emerged in Gotham.[4]

This revisionist history cuts through thickets of Mafia mythology with a machete of primary sources. It draws on the deepest collection of primary sources—many newly discovered—of any history of the modern Mafia. The primary sources include, among others, trial transcripts, investigative hearings, mayoral papers, personal memoirs, labor union records, and surveillance reports of the Federal Bureau of Narcotics. These are complimented by internal files of the Federal Bureau of Investigation from the National Archives or obtained via the Freedom of Information Act. All of the quoted conversations in these pages are real and taken directly from primary sources. I supply extensive endnotes that allow readers to see the evidence for each chapter. This is an authentic history.[5]

Contrary to its image, the Mafia was *not* primarily the product of Sicilian intrigue among the godfathers. As we will see, mob bosses had limited control over these lucrative crime franchises. Rather, the Cosa Nostra was forged by the street soldiers as they adapted to the unique conditions of twentieth-century Gotham. They captured New York City by becoming part of it.

This approach places the Mafia squarely back into New York history. It shows how the infamous "French Connection" heroin case was merely an off-shoot of Mafia narcotics trafficking dating back to the dawn of America's drug war. It describes how the Cosa Nostra rode labor unions and business cartels to power during the New Deal. It shows why the Stonewall riots of 1969 were the culmination of the mob-run system of gay bars that dated to the 1930s. By replacing gauzy myths with historical evidence, we can see this extraordinary crime syndicate in a whole new light.

PART I

NEW YORK CITY THROUGH PROHIBITION

I

A CITY BUILT FOR THE MOB

The scale and variety of New York City's economic activity makes it unique among the cities of America. . . . Its 7,835,000 residents occupy only 300 square miles and thus comprise the largest and most concentrated consumer market in the country. . . . It is the major gateway to America with almost half the country's exports and imports flowing through its harbor. . . . Although it has few giant industrial establishments, the city's multiplicity of small firms makes it the leading manufacturing city in the United States . . . exceeding those of Philadelphia, Detroit, Los Angeles and Boston combined.

—New York State Department of Commerce (1951)

Is it not a fact that because New York is an island it is particularly vulnerable to pressure on the docks and trucking, with a great many people in a concentrated area? There is an enormous amount of money involved. . . . If you fail to deliver to a large store in New York, if no trucks deliver to them, you can pretty well squeeze them down in a couple of days and cause losses of hundreds of thousands and millions of dollars. Therefore, this is probably the most vulnerable area in the country to that type of pressure.

—Senator John F. Kennedy,
McClellan Committee (1958)

Lost in books about the New York Mafia is New York City itself. Gotham has been reduced to an operatic backdrop for epic clashes between mob bosses, the FBI, and prosecutors.[1] Although these conflicts are important, these books are missing half the story.

It is impossible to understand the rise of the Mafia without understanding historic New York City—a city very different than it is today. For the Cosa Nostra was in many ways a testament to New York's exceptionalism: to its tremendous economy and unique geography; to its voracious appetites and almost natural corruption. This book then is as much about New York and its peoples as it is about organized crime.

The Mafia saw unparalleled opportunities in New York City. New York had five thriving families, with another across the river in northern New Jersey. Although the Sicilian Mafia was powerful in the villages of Sicily, it never achieved the economic successes of the New York Mafia. The Sicilian *cosche* (clans) had few industrial rackets or labor unions because there was not much industry on their island. By contrast, the New York Mafia always had a bounty of goods and services ripe for the picking.

Our story begins in another city. When Gotham was a place that built things, between the 1890s and the 1950s, Lower Manhattan was the center of skilled manufacturing in the Atlantic world. Before SoHo became gleaming storefronts, its cast-iron buildings were filled with dirty factories, leather tanneries, and trucking companies. It was a city where nighthawks smoked in jazz clubs owned by gangsters who were paying off the police, and where entire neighborhoods spoke Sicilian or Yiddish, or with Irish lilts, or in the southern drawls of African-American migrants.

This chapter explores why *this city* fueled the rise of the Mafia in America.

THE PORT OF NEW YORK

It all began with the port. When ships entered the placid waters of Upper New York Bay, their crews marveled at one of the finest natural harbors on earth. Sheltered from storm swells by Long Island and Staten Island, it was an ideal haven. Its waters were deep enough for transatlantic vessels; its weather temperate enough to allow the harbor to be open year round with little ice or fog. From the open ocean to the Manhattan piers was only seventeen miles, compared to the hundred-odd miles ships had to travel inland to reach Baltimore or Philadelphia. The building of the Erie Canal in the 1820s linked the Great Lakes to the Hudson River, drastically reducing shipping costs for New York City. It made a superb port.[2]

As craft industries sprang up around the harbor, and the population mushroomed, New York City became an international center of commerce. The ambitious immigrants who made it to New York in the mid-to-late nineteenth century—principally the Germans and the Irish, then later the Jews and the Italians—filled the workshops and factories in Manhattan, making it a manufacturing powerhouse. The exploding population became a huge consumer market. "The consuming power of the population of the harbor, that is of New York, Brooklyn, Bayonne, Hoboken, Jersey City, and Newark, was an important fact making for commerce and further growth," said a shipping expert.[3]

These competitive advantages made the Port of New York the busiest port in the world. In old maps, Manhattan resembles a centipede, with wooden wharves and piers jutting out on all sides into the water. Nearly *half* of all the imports and exports of the United States went through the Port of New York. Moreover, the *kind* of cargo moving through it was exceptionally valuable. While Baltimore and Philadelphia were handling low-price commodities like iron ore, New York was taking in valuable raw materials for skilled manufacturing, and huge amounts of "general cargo" for finished consumer goods. By 1939, the Port of New York received 82 percent of the nation's imports of raw silk, 70 percent of the gums and resins, and 61 percent of the animal furs. Meanwhile, New York's consumers and food companies took in 72 percent of the nation's imports of cheeses, 64 percent of the wines, and 51 percent of the cocoa beans. The per-ton value of imports coming through New York was *double* that of any other port in the United States.[4]

The bottom line: lots of valuable goods were coursing through the New York harbor.

I–I: Removing cargo from a banana boat on a New York pier, ca. 1900. Gangsters controlled the piers on the New York waterfront. (Photo courtesy of the Library of Congress Prints and Photographs Division)

THE PORT'S VULNERABILITIES TO RACKETEERING

The port's magnificence helped to mask its vulnerabilities. Its problems with racketeering were first widely exposed by the famous waterfront investigations of the early 1950s later immortalized by the 1954 film *On the Waterfront*, in which Marlon Brando portrays a gritty longshoreman.

Close observers of the harbor, however, had been issuing quiet alarms since the previous century. The port had developed haphazardly along the narrow streets and piers of Lower Manhattan and Brooklyn, with only a single railroad freight line for waterborne cargo, and little warehouse space along the harbors. Ships floated in frustration in the harbor, waiting for openings on the narrow, overburdened piers. As early as 1871, an engineer warned: "From this insufficient breadth of the majority of the piers, the lack of width in the river streets, and the consequent difficulty of access, this quarter of the city is entirely too crowded, and it is impossible to transact the shipping business satisfactorily."[5] Calls for improvements to the shoddy wooden wharves and bulkheads were persistently ignored. "The port, by its great natural advantages, has reached its present position among the ports of the world, in spite of the mismanagement of the docks," warned another report in 1922.[6]

During the 1800s, waterfront squatters and thugs took dominion over these precious spaces to extract payoffs from ships. As early as 1874, the Department of Docks noted the "opposition in the removal of the obstructions on the wharves and bulkheads" by people "who, from long occupancy of public property, have supposed themselves entitled to exclusive possession."[7] The New York City Police Department (NYPD) could *not* be relied on to maintain law and order; waterfront cops were among the most corrupt in the city. In 1875, the City Council lamented that waterfront streets were "reduced to forty feet by squatters or corrupt police supervision," which exacerbated the "daily gorges of vehicles now witnessed, lasting frequently for hours, and obstructing commerce."[8] Police corruption on the docks became systemic over time. "Steamship companies, who require police service on their docks . . . have to contribute in substantial sums to the vast amounts which flow into the station-houses, and which, after leaving something of the nature of a deposit, then flow on higher," described the Lexow Committee's report on police corruption in 1895.[9]

Racketeers perfected these extortion tactics through the "public loader." Unique to the Port of New York, the "public loaders" were *not* public employees, nor did they perform a public service; they often did not even do the loading. Rather, they were thugs who muscled in on key docks and assumed territorial control over them. They then demanded payoffs from shippers simply for the right to have their cargo loaded onto a delivery truck. Those who resisted found their shipments of Cuban tomatoes or Honduran bananas rotting on a pier. Shippers paid about $50,000 (in current dollars) more in port charges out of New York than other ports—one of the mysterious fees that came to be called the "mob tax."[10]

Fed up, a shipper denounced public loaders who "with the banner of God and their union in one hand, and an iron pipe in the other, stand between merchants and their trucks and defy them to take away their freight."[11] Privately, shippers lamented that they could not clear away the public loaders "without assistance in the way of police protection," which they said "has never been forthcoming."[12] As an investigative report concluded, "By merely controlling these bottlenecks and jammed conditions, underworld scum can exact tribute from those who will pay to avoid long lines and excessive waiting time in loading and unloading."[13]

Pilferage was massive as well. Before steel containerization and electronic checking, cargo was shipped in wooden crates and tracked by paper, making it vulnerable to theft. A stevedore could sign a phony signature on a delivery slip indicating that cargo had "short-landed" (never arrived). By the time an overseas shipper learned of the theft, the cargo was missing for weeks. "When a whisky ship came in . . . it seemed like everybody on the waterfront would descend on the ship. Talk about stealing!" recalled Sam Madell, a waterfront organizer. So why didn't the shippers call the police? "It was pretty widely known among the longshoremen that the maritime police were involved with the stealing," explained Madell. When stolen cargo turned up in the pier superintendent's office it was clear no one watched the watchmen.[14]

Irish and Italian gangsters controlled the labor force using the International Longshoremen's Association (ILA). The ILA's president during the Mafia's ascendancy was Joseph P. Ryan. Bestowed the title "president for life" of the ILA by his cronies, Ryan collected an annual salary of $1.7 million while representing longshoremen who made $20,000 (both in current dollars). Behind the scenes, "King Joe" did the opposite: he collaborated with shippers to quell strikes. Most galling was his defense of the "shape-up" system of hiring in which longshoremen became permanent temp workers; each morning they shaped into a horseshoe crowd around a foreman who collected kickbacks from longshoremen to pick them. In 1916, public reports warned that these "conditions of hiring are degrading in the extreme [and] are open to the danger of graft." Yet Ryan consistently, and absurdly for a union leader, defended the shape-up system.[15]

Joe Ryan's real job was to oversee the smooth running of the rackets. He used his blarney and connections with Irish politicians, from Mayor Jimmy Walker to Mayor Bill O'Dwyer, to fend off scrutiny of the docks. For those resistant to his charm—rank-and-file rebels, naïve shippers, Communist Party agitators—Ryan could call on the many convicts he kept on staff (a third of the ILA staff had criminal records) to drop the hook on troublemakers.[16]

THE IRISH AND ITALIAN RIVALRY
ON THE WATERFRONT

The Mafia gradually took over rackets as the ethnic makeup of the waterfront changed from Irish to Italian. In 1880, fully 95 percent of the longshoremen were Irish; but after 1910, one-third of the longshoremen were Italians, and their numbers were surging. A 1916 report found that the Irish "still are predominant in trade union councils and general harbor politics" even as "Sicilians and other South Italians, are rapidly approaching them in number." Even as the Italians surpassed them in numbers in the 1930s, there was still a "strong feeling of superiority of the Irish-Americans" because "in times past the Irish were dominant on all New York piers." This hostility was also due to the nebulous "racial" status of South Italians: foremen complained that it was "impossible to get 'white men' and that they were obliged to take Italians."[17]

While the West Side was still contested, the Brooklyn waterfront was overwhelmingly Italian by the 1930s. Entire neighborhoods revolved around the hard life of longshoring. "Red Hook, Carroll Gardens, South Brooklyn—I can remember when those waterfront areas used to be like a company town. Most of the longshoremen left their houses and walked five minutes to the pier," recalled Frank Barbaro, a longtime resident of Brooklyn. These rough neighborhoods were breeding grounds for gamblers, hoodlums, and loansharks. A young teenager named Al Capone began life as a hard-fighting "wharf rat" on the Brooklyn waterfront.[18]

THE MAFIA MOVES ON THE DOCKS

The first Italian gangster to gain power on the docks was Paolo Vaccarelli, who rode the wave of Italian longshoring on the East Side piers of Manhattan. Diminutive, dapper, and intelligent (he spoke four languages), he took the Irish name "Paul Kelly" and formed the Paul Kelly Association, the strongest street gang on the Lower East Side in the late 1800s.

Ever the opportunist, he changed his name back to "Paul Vaccarelli" as Italian immigration surged, and he organized the Italian "scow trimmers," who sorted garbage on waterborne barges, into an ILA charter by appealing to their ethnic solidarity. After rising to vice president of the ILA in 1912, he lost a power struggle with a young Joe Ryan, and formed a breakaway union of Italian longshoremen, which was a thorn in the side of the ILA. Meanwhile, the rising force of the Mafia built ties with Vaccarelli.[19]

From his nineteenth-floor office on West 14th Street, on the border between Irish Chelsea and the Italian South Village, the newly installed ILA president Joseph P. Ryan tried to straddle the divide through a grand bargain between the Irish and the Italian syndicates. Scarred by his battles with Paul Vaccarelli, upon becoming president in 1927, Ryan embraced a "non-interference" policy (in reality, anything goes) with the Italian ILA locals along the waterfront.[20] The Mafia quickly gained footholds in these locals.

By the late 1920s, Emil Camarda, Camarda's brother, and two cousins had become the patriarchal rulers of six huge ILA locals on the Brooklyn waterfront. Emil came from a unionist background; his father organized Local 338 in Brooklyn before the First World War. Brooklyn's locals became so identified with his family that they were known as "the Camarda locals." But during Emil's own rise to the office of vice president of the ILA, he brought in his childhood friend Vincent Mangano, a mobster on the Brooklyn waterfront. Camarda and Mangano knew each other "from the other side," having grown up together in Palermo, Sicily. The two formed the City Democratic Club, supposedly to represent Italian Americans in Brooklyn. It was a cynical appeal. "They often said the organization existed merely to help many deserving Americans of Italian extraction find their rightful place in the sun of our city," explained Vincent Mannino, former attorney for the Camarda locals. "I felt that the reason why they were interested in this organization was to help and promote their own personal interests, politically."[21]

Unknown to the public at the time, in 1931, Vince Mangano had become one of the five bosses of the Mafia families in New York City. The Camarda locals quickly deteriorated into tools for racketeering. These paper locals were *not* really unions at all: they conducted no elections, rarely held meetings of the rank-and-file, and never went on strike. In 1941, Emil Camarda was shot dead under murky circumstances in the office of a stevedoring company during an argument about putting a crony on the payroll.[22]

Stalking the Camarda locals like the four horsemen of the Mafia were the brothers Anastasio. Jumping ship from freighters between 1917 and 1924, the four teenagers from Calabria disappeared into the Italian longshore gangs for a time only to reemerge with a vengeance in the 1920s. Anthony Anastasio became a feared hiring boss on the Red Hook piers and a liaison to Joe Ryan. As master of the shape-up, the man they called "Tough Tony" controlled the daily bread of thousands of longshoremen. Anthony Anastasio was secretly also a *caporegime* (captain) in the Mangano Family. His brother Joseph Anastasio, a pier official for the ILA, reportedly stole cargo "by the ton" according to a shipping association. Meanwhile, the youngest brother, Gerardo "Jerry" Anastasio, a convicted bookie and ILA business agent, demanded shippers put him on their payrolls as a phantom employee or "there would be trouble."[23]

The brothers' threats were terrifying because everyone knew that their oldest brother, Umberto, was Albert "The Executioner" Anastasia, the psychopathic underboss of the Mangano Family. The compact, pigeon-chested Anastasia possessed a ferocity that shocked even fellow mobsters. Albert worked briefly on the Brooklyn docks, but the job bored him, and he quit after meeting *mafiosi* Philip and Vincent Mangano in 1920. In 1923, gunmen fired four bullets into Albert's stomach as he sat in an automobile as wheelman on a bootlegging run in Red Hook; he survived what doctors thought were fatal wounds. Prosecutors charged Anastasia with four different murders (one victim stabbed to death by an ice pick) only to see key witnesses change their stories or vanish.[24]

Across the East River in Manhattan, what became the Genovese Family gradually took over the smaller East Side piers. As a kid on the docks, Joseph "Socks" Lanza saw how anxious fishing boat skippers were to get their perishable fish unloaded and put on ice quickly in the nearby Fulton Fish Market. Fish-worker unions in New York sometimes refused to unload "non-union" fish, letting it decompose in the barrel. Around 1923, while barely in his twenties, Lanza organized a new union, the United Seafood Workers, which began demanding that all skippers and fishmongers pay a $50 tribute just for the right to have their fish unloaded and "protected" from sabotage and thievery in the market.[25]

After Lanza's convictions on federal antitrust charges in the 1930s, his lieutenant Michelino Clemente rose to power. As a young man, Clemente was just another lean Italian longshoreman who worked in his underwear on the docks. But the smooth-talking Clemente's fortunes changed when he became one of the "public loaders" on the East Side piers, where he picked up the nickname

"Loader Mike." In 1941, he set down his cargo hook for good and became the secretary-treasurer and business agent for ILA Local 856, the twelve-hundred-member local encompassing Manhattan's East Side. In 1953, Clemente came under fire when a stevedoring company president testified that he picked up the $97,000 tab for Clemente's daughter's lavish wedding at the Biltmore Hotel. The reception had several *mafiosi* as invited guests, including Albert Anastasia. It was an open secret that the now dough-faced, nattily dressed Clemente had become the "racket boss of East River piers" for the Genovese Family.[26]

1–2: Anthony "Tough Tony" Anastasio talking to ILA president Joe Ryan, 1953. Ryan upheld a "non-interference" policy with the Mafia-controlled Brooklyn ILA locals. (© Bettmann/CORBIS)

Out on the Richmond docks (Staten Island), Alex "The Ox" Di Brizzi took control of the ILA locals in the early 1930s. Unlike most early *mafiosi*, Di Brizzi was born in America in 1892 and was a professional boxer before turning to a life of crime.[27] The pugilist made himself president of ILA Local 920 in the early 1930s, and he was later appointed vice president of the ILA's commanding

Atlantic Coast District by Joe Ryan. Di Brizzi was caught taking thousands of dollars in cash from stevedoring companies while supposedly representing their unionized employees. "I haven't taken no money outside of gifts," he insisted. Di Brizzi was in fact the Mangano Family's "top man" on Staten Island, overseeing loansharking and gambling operations.[28]

This was only the beginning of Mafia rule of the waterfront. As we will see, the mob's stranglehold on the harbor tightened in the 1940s, until it sparked a public backlash that would test its strength. For now, let us step back and scan the city from the vantage point of the Mafia.

SKIMMING SEVEN MILLION NEW YORKERS

The sheer enormity of Gotham was a catalyst for organized crime, though for reasons that have not been fully appreciated. Ever since federal census records were kept, New York City was the most heavily populated—and most *densely* populated—city of the republic. Between 1900 and 1930, Gotham's population doubled from 3,400,000 people, to 6,900,000 people. After 1940, its population never fell below seven million people. As of World War II, one of every eighteen Americans lived within the five boroughs of New York City.[29]

These seven million New Yorkers lived and worked disproportionately in crowded neighborhoods and industrial districts in Manhattan and Brooklyn. During the early 1900s, the Lower East Side had a higher population density than Bombay, Calcutta, or London. In Little Italy, 3,500 people lived on a single block of Elizabeth Street.[30] Immigrants who grew up in these neighborhoods recall them with astonishment. "The block at 112th Street between First and Second avenues was lined with six-story buildings with families that had twelve or thirteen children. You could imagine how many people," marveled Joseph Verdiccio of Italian East Harlem.[31]

To the Mafia, these were seven million pockets to pick. The mob did *not* make money by engaging in gratuitous orgies of violence. In 1912, an assistant district attorney noted that even with extortion, while Italian syndicates might threaten bombing, they drew the line at "child-snatching" because "America will not stand for kidnapping."[32] The Cosa Nostra preferred schemes where money was quietly skimmed or handed over without any immediate physical force. Mafia soldier Joe Valachi distinguished the common American criminal who "usually stole" and was "taking a chance for his money" from the Italian *mafioso* (member of the Mafia) who "has racketeering on his mind."[33] Mafia boss Joe Bonanno likewise eschewed violent extortion in favor of collecting surplus profits through monopolies: "In my world, there was a distinction between what constitutes extortion and what does not," explained Bonanno. "One must remember that in the economic sphere one of the objectives of a Family was to set up monopolies as far as possible."[34]

The Mafia's desire for racketeering was logical: the victims were diffuse and it generated less heat from law enforcement. Rob a million dollars by gunpoint from a bank in Manhattan and soon the Federal Bureau of Investigation is on your trail. Skim a dollar off the budgets of a million New Yorkers through a racketeering scheme and hardly anyone notices. A new phrase arose: the "mob tax." The Cosa Nostra "made sure people anted up their Mafia 'taxes,'" said John Manca, a cop involved with the mob.[35] The ability to "tax" so many people in so many different ways concentrated in one city enabled generations of mob soldiers to live off New York City.

NEW YORK'S ECONOMIC ENGINES: SMALL MANUFACTURERS AND INDUSTRY CLUSTERS

It was not only the size of Gotham that mattered; New York's tremendously productive economy, and the *kinds* of industries it attracted, fostered industrial racketeering.

The Mafia followed the money. Recent studies show that "men of honor" in Sicily were concentrated in the areas with the highest production of lemons and sulfur—the island's most valuable exports. The *cosche* (clans) were entrenched in Sicily's villages before modern industry could take hold. Their omnipresence retarded economic development on Sicily. In essence, the Sicilian Mafia cannibalized the rural island.[36]

By comparison, the New York families thrived by skimming only a small portion of the profits generated by the economic engines of Manhattan and

Brooklyn. Although New York was famous for its mighty banks, it was also a place that built things and fed people.[37]

New York City had an enormous number of small, value-added manufacturers. In 1954, there were approximately 37,500 manufacturing establishments within the five boroughs. The industrial heartland states of Ohio and Pennsylvania put together had fewer manufacturers (32,000 total). New York's manufacturing firms were incredibly small though: more than 70 percent had fewer than twenty employees.[38] The garment industry was particularly famous for its tiny shops—and its racketeers. The muckraker Jacob Riis observed that the garment subcontractor was simply "a workman like his fellows . . . with the accidental possession of two or three sewing machines, or of credit enough to hire them, as his capital, who drums up work among the clothing-houses." Nevertheless, collectively, they produced the large majority of the women's cloaks and men's suits in the United States.[39]

1–3: Men moving racks of clothes in Manhattan's garment district, 1955. (Photo by Al Ravenna, courtesy of the Library of Congress Prints and Photographs Division, New York World-Telegram and Sun Newspaper Photograph Collection)

New York's small manufacturers crowded together in hives that were extraordinarily productive. "Is it not going too far to assume that congestion is an evil?" asked Edgar Levey, president of a title insurance company, at a municipal hearing. "Each trade is apt to huddle together in one center in as concentrated a manner as possible, the dry goods trade in one district, the machinery trade in another, the leather trade in another, and so on," Levey explained. "Business people do this because it is to their advantage to do so."[40] Abe Feinglass, a union leader, made similar observations: "The fur industry was concentrated in a small area of 26th, 27th, 28th, 29th, 30th Street, 31st Street, and the whole area was fur because there is a need for being together, the auction, the lining people, the skin people, the fur people." As Feinglass explained, there was "a unity of purpose that forces them together." These men were describing, in their own words, what economists call "industry clusters" (famous examples include Hollywood's film industry, Napa Valley's wine industry, and New Jersey's pharmaceutical industry).[41]

New York's huge, concentrated consumer market supported a multitude of locally based, small service businesses and food companies. In the 1820s, Manhattan imported the modern restaurant in the form of a French establishment called Delmonico's. Middle-class and wealthy New Yorkers supported thousands of restaurants, cafés, and lunch counters. Moreover, less than 2 percent of New York's restaurants belonged to national chains.[42]

Southern and Eastern European immigrants collectively consumed large amounts of highly perishable foods, especially fresh fish, kosher meats, fruits, and vegetables. "Nearly 1 out of every 8 carloads of fruits and vegetables produced in the United States ... finds its way to the markets of New York City to meet the needs of its millions of consumers," reported the Department of Agriculture.[43] Restaurants and retailers purchased most raw foods at centralized, wholesale markets within the city. As we will see, these became rich targets for racketeers.

NARROW STREETS AND BRIDGES

The proliferation of these kinds of industries and services within the environs of mid-twentieth-century Manhattan and Brooklyn led to widespread racketeering. New York City's seven million people and clustered industries overwhelmed its streets and bridges. Gangsters soon learned the importance of controlling the trucking and shipping of goods and materials.

As industries and workers gravitated to Lower Manhattan and the Brooklyn waterfront, they created transportation chokepoints. In 1875, the City Council warned that the "over-crowding of all the streets in this section of the city, with both pedestrians and vehicles, directly and indirectly connected with commerce, has become a grievous public evil, disastrously affecting all public and private interests." After 1910, fully half the factory workers in the city toiled in firms located below 20th Street in Manhattan.[44]

In addition, by the 1920s, three hundred thousand automobiles were registered in New York City. Manhattan's outdated streets and bridges were inadequate for motorized traffic on this scale. The garment center between West 34th and 42nd Streets was chronically congested as trucks loaded piecework for contractors, and unloaded finished clothes bound for distribution.[45]

1–4: Traffic congestion on West 35th Street, 1927. Mobsters controlled trucking vital to New York's small manufacturers. (Used by permission of the NYC Municipal Archives)

Fast and reliable shipping through the city became critical for time-sensitive industries, especially clothing (as fashions go out of style) and food (as it spoils). Virtually all of the city's 37,500 manufacturers needed shipping companies to transport their goods to retailers. "The cost of transportation of merchandise of any and all characters, is a very sensitive point in the financing of virtually all of the most important business enterprises," noted a police report.[46] The Mafia leveraged these problems to its advantage. As we will see, the Cosa Nostra gained influence over the teamsters and longshoremen who moved goods through the city.

BULLYING THE LITTLE GUY

The small, locally owned businesses that proliferated in New York City were also much more vulnerable to gangsters than were large, distant corporations. For all their *machismo*, mobsters liked to pick on the little guys. They were easier to push around.

Small business owners were intimidated by the Mafia. New York's non-chain, independent stores were typically owned by families who still lived in the neighborhood and survived on thin profit margins. The Cosa Nostra could delay shipments of supplies, engineer labor problems, scare off customers, or physically threaten the owner and his or her family. When John Montesano got into a dispute with a mobster over his family-owned waste-hauling business, he quickly learned not to mess with *mafiosi*. "Don't you realize that they could put you out of business and they can hurt you in other ways?" warned a connected guy. "Don't forget, you have got kids." Montesano quickly relented.[47] "It was common knowledge that if you offended the Mafia you were dead," explained Frank DiTrapani, a small businessman.[48]

Big business could counter the gangsters by pulling strings and hiring its own thugs. When the labor racketeer Max "The Butcher" Block was organizing for the Amalgamated Meat Cutters Union, he found that "it was big businessmen ... who tried to get tough guys." He complained that "cops gave us trouble because they were being paid off by the bosses." So Block always started with the small, independent butcher shops. "The industries now have chain operations, and they're spread out all over," Block later lamented.[49]

Nor was it just a matter of muscle. In the $60 million racketeer-plagued kosher chicken market, the A. L. A. Schechter Poultry Corporation was the single biggest company and, not coincidentally, the last holdout from the price-fixing cartel. With $1 million in annual revenues, the Schechter brothers could endure harassment, as when emery powder was poured into their trucks' engines. When the industry was legally cartelized under the National Industrial Recovery Act during the New Deal and the Schechters were prosecuted for such new crimes as cutting prices, their lawyers could litigate the law's constitutionality all the way up to the Supreme Court, where they won a 9–0 decision striking down the law in 1935.[50]

It is no accident that the Detroit Mafia never gained control over the Big Three auto plants. On the one side stood Walter Reuther, president of the United Autoworkers of America, a strong union with a well-deserved reputation for integrity. On the other side stood three of the most powerful corporations in the world. *Mafiosi* had little desire to confront either of them. To the contrary, it was Harry Bennett, the head of Ford Motor Company's Internal Security Department, who retained convicts to act as union busters on occasion.[51]

CONSPIRING AGAINST "RUINOUS COMPETITION"

Along with the stick of violence, the Mafia held out the carrot of restricting competition. Joe Bonanno was candid about his aim of limiting competition: "If two Family members are bakers, they are not allowed to own bakeries on the same block, for that would be bad for both their businesses. They would be competing against each other," he explained.[52]

Bonanno's views fit comfortably with the prevailing sentiments of the business community at the time. From World War I through the New Deal, business leaders orchestrated a campaign to reduce competition throughout the economy. They often singled out the "ruinous competition" or "cut-throat business" in New York City. Businesses commonly used "trade associations" as fronts for efforts to restrict competition.[53]

Joining the chorus of the captains of industry were their counterparts in the labor unions. Though adversaries on other issues, business and labor agreed on the need to "stabilize" industries by artificially limiting competition. The International Ladies' Garment Workers' Union (ILGWU) declared that "only the strong and responsible associations of employers can be of assistance in stabilizing the industry." The ILGWU decried the "situation that permits an easy entry into the business, and makes for the chaotic competition that has been the source of so many evils."[54]

The Cosa Nostra engineered collusive agreements between trade associations and labor unions to limit competition. Bonanno boasted of his "connections" in the garment merchants association *and* the International Ladies' Garment Workers' Union *and* the trucking companies. "By putting all my connections in touch with one another, I could harmonize our activities in a mutually advantageous way," Bonanno asserted.[55] What Bonanno left out from his rosy account (and the collusive arrangement) are the would-be competitors shut out of the industry and the consumers who would have benefitted from lower prices. Nor does Bonanno mention the rank-and-file workers whose interests were often sold out by corrupt union leaders.

Trade associations with respectable names like the Brooklyn Fish Dealers Association, the Metropolitan New York Dry Wall Contractors Association, and the Boxing Managers Guild sprung up around the city. These were each fronts for organized crime.

RACKETLAND

By the time Sicilian "men of honor" arrived in New York City, there already existed an entire underworld of professional criminals. Gotham had long had a subculture of *gonifs*, confidence men, and extortion artists. Supporting them were professional fences for stolen goods, and the new specialty of criminal defense lawyers of varying degrees of ethics (more later on these "mouthpieces for the mob"). A popular booklet dubbed it all "racketland." But the members of this criminal fraternity proudly called themselves "Good Fellows," which *mafiosi* shortened to "goodfellas."[56] Indeed, many of the rackets that we now associate with the Cosa Nostra were actually variations of schemes used by earlier criminals.

The Cosa Nostra "bust-out" operation had its origins in arson scams of the early 1900s. Torching businesses to collect insurance was so prevalent on the Lower East Side that the press dubbed it "Jewish lightning." In 1912, the New York City Fire Commissioner issued a report titled *Incendiarism in Greater New*

York, which estimated that fully 25 percent of fires were due to arson. It called the area of East Harlem the "fire-bug" district where "more fires of a suspicious origin occur than [*sic*] in any other single territory in Manhattan."[57]

The Mafia "protection racket" was a refined version of extortion ploys. In early Italian neighborhoods, "Black Handers" mailed letters to businessmen threatening harm unless they paid money. On the Lower East Side, merchants found their horses poisoned unless they paid tribute to Jewish gangsters.[58] Extortion artists became subtle over time. "The fellow would go in there and simply remove his hat. It was understood that if the businessman didn't hand it over, they would retaliate," said Peter Rofrano of East Harlem.[59]

Before *mafiosi* perfected them, "price-fixing territories" were organized by other groups. At the turn of the century, Chinatown tongs (quasi-fraternal organizations) helped to enforce a scheme to raise prices among Chinese laundries. When dissident laundrymen tried to cut their prices or encroach on the territories of other Chinese laundries, Chinese businessmen and their allies in the tongs sent agents to "persuade" the dissidents to honor the unwritten code of competition.[60]

THE POLICE DEPARTMENT

Crime syndicates flourished because the New York City Police Department (NYPD) as a whole did little to stop them. It was often difficult to separate the cops from the crooks.

The NYPD's large, decentralized patrol force became a font of corruption in the city. With sixteen thousand patrolmen by 1930, the NYPD was described as a "vast and complicated machine maintained in the City of New York." Before computerized oversight tools like CompStat, supervision over this sprawling force was weak, and the opportunities for graft were vast. The police had authority to enforce any of the array of state and municipal regulations. Any cop on the beat could shut down a business for supposed regulatory violations, large or small, real or contrived.[61]

Patrolmen shook down small businesses for petty infractions. In 1894, the Lexow Committee investigation on corruption found that "men of business were harassed and annoyed in their affairs, so that they too, were compelled to bend their necks to the police yoke, in order that they might share that so-called protection which seemed indispensable to the profitable conduct of their affairs." The Committee described the myriad ways small businesses were extorted:

> Boot-blacks, push-cart and fruit venders, as well as keepers of soda water stands, corner grocerymen, sailmakers with flag-poles extending a few feet beyond the place which they occupy, boxmakers, provision dealers, wholesale drygoods merchants and builders, who are compelled at times to use the sidewalk and street, steamboat and steamship companies, who require police service on their docks, those who give public exhibition, and in fact all persons, and all classes of persons whose business is subject to the observation of the police, or who may be reported as violating ordinances, or who may require the aid of the police, all have to contribute in substantial sums to the vast amounts which flow into the station-houses.[62]

Seventy years later, the Knapp Commission (made famous by Frank Serpico) identified similar patterns. "The heart of the problem of police corruption in the construction industry is the dizzying array of laws, ordinances, and regulations governing construction in the City."[63]

GANGSTER DOMINION OVER PUBLIC PLACES

The Mafia also learned how to game New York's sprawling, opaque, and unaccountable bureaucracy. By World War I, the city had 85,000 municipal employees; the number ballooned to 200,000 by the 1950s. Efforts by good-government progressives (derided as "goo goos") to reform city agencies were frequently thwarted or backfired. In 1919, reformers lamented that "the effort to protect employes [sic] from removal for political reasons has resulted in giving them so much security of tenure that they have little or no motive to fear losing their jobs."[64] A later study found that "neither the city's civil servants nor Mayor . . . possessed much influence over the city's personnel system. In a sense, nobody did."[65]

Perhaps the biggest failure of the city agencies toward organized crime was losing control over public property. On a congested island, taking dominion over public spaces was a means of power in itself. Time after time, the city lost control of public properties to gangsters. In 1922, a legislative committee lambasted the Department of Docks for issuing berthing permits to companies that did not own any ships. Shippers had to make extortionate payments to shady companies just to berth on the docks. Issuance of permits to sell on city streets and marketplaces was a source of abuse, too. "It has been the apparently arbitrary power, which they give to the Commissioner to revoke permits and to approve transfers, which has facilitated the collection of graft and the attempts to do so," concluded a committee on the wholesale food markets. Between 1930 and 1933, not a *single* person who applied for a newsstand license in the legal manner ever received one.[66]

NEW YORK'S FRAGILE INDUSTRIES IN SERVICES

All of these factors conspired to create fragile industries throughout New York City. Fragile industries can be defined as sectors of small businesses with characteristics that make them vulnerable to extortion and racketeering.[67] Gotham had a wide spectrum of fragile industries that were preyed upon by gangsters. Small, local-service businesses were frequently targeted.

The most fragile was the pushcart peddler, who everyday fought for a spot on the street. An 1875 report warned that peddler overcrowding was "a great source of political corruption." Pushcart owners paid graft to police to overlook regulatory violations and paid tribute to thugs to leave them alone.[68] *Mafioso* Joe Valachi remembered the extortion of his own father by neighborhood thugs: "They would shake down the push cart peddlers . . . my father used to pay a dollar a week."[69]

Manhattan's many small bars and restaurants were sitting targets for extortionists. Racketeers would toss "stink bombs" into lunchtime crowds to drive off customers and bring resistant owners into line. In the mid-1930s, the mobster Dutch Schultz and union leaders forced restaurants into the Metropolitan Restaurant and Cafeteria Owners Association; the owners paid $1,500 in "associational dues" to protect themselves against sham strikes.[70]

Mafiosi also liked to acquire hidden interests in restaurants through coercive partnerships. While Tommy Morton was the owner of record of a restaurant called The Azores, his silent partner was mob boss Thomas Lucchese. "[Tommy] must have fronted for lots of wiseguys. But he also had to pay back a certain amount every week to his partners," explained Henry Hill, a Lucchese associate. "That's the way it is with a wiseguy partner. He gets his money, no matter what. You got no business? Fuck you, pay me."[71]

The taxicabs that drove the restaurant goers back to their apartments or hotels were easy targets for gangsters as well. Roughly 5,600 cabs in New York belonged to single-cab companies, where the owner was typically the driver himself. "Mobsters try to bully you and order you around," complained a cabbie during the 1940s.[72] *Mafioso* Frankie Carbo actually killed a taxi driver.[73] Racketeers were so pervasive that even the International Brotherhood of Teamsters refused to issue union charters to taxis. The Teamsters' top official in New York warned that the industry was full of "all sorts of gorillas."[74]

NEW YORK'S FRAGILE INDUSTRIES IN FOOD

Many of the foods supplied to those restaurants, and to the dinner tables of New Yorkers, were subject to illegal cartels. Nearly all their food was grown elsewhere, shipped by freight trains, and trucked through the narrow streets of the city. In 1913, a report cautioned that New York's food-distribution facilities were misplaced and outdated, but "the downtown terminals have developed into well recognized markets."[75]

Trade associations, teamsters, and gangsters schemed to fix food prices in New York City. In 1909, members of the Milk Dealers' Protective Association conspired to raise the price of milk about eight cents a quart by cutting off independent dealers from milk supplies. The gangster Louis "Lepke" Buchalter was convicted of using the Flour Truckmen's Association to extort payoffs from bakeries during the 1930s. Racketeers even organized the ice business, vital before refrigeration, into price-fixing conspiracies.[76]

The wholesale meat markets in Brooklyn and the Bronx were beset by labor racketeers connected to the Mafia. Max Block of the Amalgamated Meat

Cutters union explained how he exploited the timing of the kosher meat market. "We stopped the trucks on a Monday, a busy day when they normally slaughtered about two hundred steers. Meanwhile, because it had to be fresh, they were supposed to move the kosher meat every day. But now they couldn't move the meat," bragged Block. When he was organizing the wholesale market in Fort Greene, Brooklyn, Block reached an understanding with the Gambino Family. "Fort Greene was all wholesalers. You had mostly Italians hanging out there. Mostly the tough guys. That's where I met Carlo Gambino," Block explained. "So when the bosses went to the tough guys, the Italian fellows, they already knew us. We were buddies."[77] Later, the McClellan Committee uncovered evidence that Block sold out his union's interests by cutting collusive deals with companies. The Gambino Family continued to hold interests in New York's meat markets into the 1980s.[78]

Humble vegetables became the objects of racketeering, too. Each day, five hundred carloads of produce grown in California and the Midwest arrived by train at the Bronx Terminal Market and a few other smaller terminals. Teamsters then maneuvered the produce through the canyons of Lower Manhattan to the twelve-block-long Washington Street Fruit and Vegetable Market, the largest wholesale market in the country. Gangsters went after weak links in the food chain.[79]

Mafioso Ciro Terranova of the Morello Family made his name with the miniature artichoke, a favorite of southern Italian cooking. In the 1910s, Terranova used strongarm tactics to gain control of artichoke shipments into the city. Eyeing his success, the Brooklyn-based Camorra (mainland Italy's equivalent of Sicily's Mafia) moved in on the artichoke racket, leading to a bizarre vegetable war on the streets of New York in 1916.[80]

After prevailing over the Camorra, Terranova expanded his control by going to the source. He used his front corporation, the Union Pacific Produce Company both to purchase artichokes as soon they arrived at the Bronx Terminal Market and to scare off other potential buyers from the market. After monopolizing the artichoke supply, he jacked up the price to wholesalers, who passed it on to retailers and consumers. In December 1935, Mayor Fiorello La Guardia shrewdly targeted "the Artichoke King" as a brazen monopolist of a popular food. La Guardia publicly suspended the sale of artichokes until all dealers agreed not to deal with the Union Pacific Produce Company, and he had the police literally drive Terranova out of the city. Within days, the retail price of artichokes dropped 30 percent, unveiling the size the "mob tax."[81]

This was a city built for the mob. But there were many people vying for the rackets. Next, we will look at Prohibition, and the rise of the Sicilian gangs during the 1920s.

2

PROHIBITION AND THE RISE OF THE SICILIANS

I am not rich.

—Joe Masseria, on trial for burglary in
People against Masseria, May 15, 1913

The police declare that both [Umberto] Valenti and [Joe]
Masseria were millionaires.
—*New York Evening Telegram*, August 11, 1922

SUNDAY, APRIL 13, 1913, HOLDING CELL, POLICE STATION HOUSE, MULBERRY STREET, MANHATTAN: JOE MASSERIA'S BURGLARY RING

"What was I to do? Shoot?" said the burglar, in Italian, to his three partners. They were stewing in the holding cell of the Twelfth Precinct Station House in Little Italy, Manhattan.[1]

"Yes, you should have taken a—" responded one of the men.

"Why, they only found one gun," the burglar said.

"No, they found two," corrected the other man.

"No, I know positive he only found one," the burglar insisted defensively.

The leader of the ring tried to calm everyone down. "We were to get diamonds and we get backhouse," he lamented, referring to the poor man's toilet. He then sounded a note of unity: "Four we were and four we are."[2]

Joe Masseria and his three partners in crime had been arrested that Sunday morning, April 13, 1913, on the charge of the burglary of Simpson's pawnbrokers at 146 Bowery Street in Lower Manhattan. With him in the cell were Pietro "Pete the Bum" Lagatutta and the brothers Salvatore and Giuseppe Ruffino of Brooklyn. None of the "four we are" would flip and give evidence to the police about anyone else in the hope of reducing their charge. They would soon go on trial for first-degree burglary.[3]

Looking at him in the prison cell that Sunday, no one would have predicted that Joe Masseria would someday become the *capo di capi* or "boss of bosses" of the Mafia. It would have not been considered much of a title anyway. In the 1910s, the Italian gangs were near the bottom of the underworld. Within a decade, however, Joe Masseria would be one of New York's most powerful gangsters, and the Mafia families were on their way to becoming the dominant crime syndicates in Gotham.

This chapter begins with an overview of the dismal state of the Italian gangs in the 1910s. It looks at the rather sad early "careers" of three gangsters: Joe Masseria, Charles "Lucky" Luciano, and Giuseppe Morello. Next, it looks at how the Prohibition era (1920–1933) helped fuel their ascents and that of the Mafia generally. The chapter then presents three other large-scale factors that accelerated the Mafia's growth beginning in the 1920s. These include: the surge of South Italian immigration to New York, the development of the Mafia franchise system, and the advent of new technologies like the telephone and automobile.

THE HUMBLE BEGINNINGS OF GIUSEPPE "JOE THE BOSS" MASSERIA

Giuseppe Masseria had been looking for a big score since coming to America. Born January 17, 1886, in the southwest province of Agrigento, Sicily, he immigrated to New York City as a teenager in 1902 and lived in the rough-and-tumble Mulberry Bend on the Lower East Side.

A natural leader, Masseria was aggressive, fearless, and physically agile. A stout 5 feet, 4 inches, Masseria had black hair, puffy cheeks, and several gold teeth. Good work in the rackets was sparse for young Italians, however, and he struggled to make it on high-risk, strongarm crimes. He racked up arrests for assault and extortion; in 1909, he was convicted of burglary and given a suspended sentence.[4]

Masseria had his sights on Simpson's pawnbroking establishment near Little Italy. Simpson's was no low-rent pawnshop. It was a three-story building with a Holmes electric security system and a safe deposit vault holding $300,000 worth of diamonds and other valuables (about $7 million in present dollars).[5] Pietro Lagatutta rented an apartment that shared a backyard with Simpson's. During a rainstorm on the night of Saturday, April 12, 1913, the burglars used a ladder to scale a dugout behind the Simpson's building and drilled a hole in the rear brick wall. Once inside, they planned to crack the vault.

Unfortunately for them, a beat cop saw a blanket stuffed in the wall of Simpson's. Early Sunday morning, police on surveillance stopped the men as they tried to leave Lagatutta's apartment. While Masseria was dressed in a brown suit and derby hat, the other men had raincoats with wet brick dust. They were all arrested and charged with burglary.[6]

MAY 15, 1913, COURT OF SPECIAL SESSIONS, MANHATTAN: THE TRIAL OF MASSERIA

Masseria testified on his own behalf at trial. Although his English was good enough for the judge to dispense with the interpreter, Masseria was out of his element in the staid courtroom. "Before I speak to you and Mr. District Attorney I want to tell something to the judge," said Masseria, bursting with energy. "Now, you sit perfectly still and just answer questions," the judge instructed.[7]

"I am not rich," Masseria later testified. This was embarrassingly true. Masseria lived with his mother until she passed away, then he moved his wife and children into a room in a tenement owned by his brother-in-law and sister at 217 Forsythe Street on the Lower East Side. Masseria was the barkeep for his sister's saloon across the street.[8]

The trial went badly. The prosecutor had a lot of physical evidence, including the new technology of a "finger-print" impression of Lagatutta inside Simpson's. Masseria tried to explain his presence at Lagatutta's apartment at 7:00 Sunday morning, testifying that he stopped by looking for help "to work in the saloon on Sunday." The jury convicted after only ninety minutes of deliberation. The judge sentenced Masseria to the maximum-security prison at Ossining, New York—the infamous Sing Sing—where he would spend the next four-and-a-half years. On January 17, 1916, Masseria reached the age of thirty in prison. He had two felony convictions, three young children, and few prospects in sight.[9]

SALVATORE LUCANIA: PETTY CROOK LIVING AT HOME, 1910–1919

Another young Sicilian immigrant was struggling to get by as a petty crook in New York during the 1910s. Born Salvatore Lucania on November 24, 1897, Charles Luciano was the middle child of a family from Lercara Friddi, a depressed mining town southeast of Palermo. His father was among the waves of Sicilian men who left for work in the manufacturing metropolis of New York City, bringing over nine-year-old Salvatore and the rest of the family in 1907. They lived in a tenement on East 10th Street, a polyglot area of Russian Jewish, Southern Italian, and other later-arriving immigrants.[10]

Recently rediscovered prison reports, which were based in part on interviews with Luciano himself, provide insight on his "formative years." Luciano's parents were a respectable, working-class married couple with no history of criminality, mental illness, or major alcoholism. Nevertheless, they found themselves with an incorrigible son, who was sent to reform school for truancy and juvenile delinquency. He dropped out of school permanently at the age of fourteen in 1912.[11]

Charlie then went through jobs like a tour of Manhattan's manufacturing industries. He stuffed dolls in a doll factory, labored alongside his father in a brass factory, pressed dresses in a garment shop, worked in the fish market, and prepared shipments for the Goodman Hat Company. "He admits he did not like to work so never held a job for any length of time," read a prison report. Luciano would learn how to extract money from such industries through racketeering.[12]

But for now, he simply wanted to find easier ways to make money. Luciano's psychiatric evaluations found he was an "egocentric, antisocial type," and "rather a socio-path than a psychopath," who chose the criminal life. Aptitude tests found him to have "bright intelligence," and a report noted his "calmness at times of stress" and "reserve and strength." (Essentially, the exact opposite of his portrayal as a hotheaded buffoon in HBO's *Boardwalk Empire*). These traits eventually brought him respect in the underworld.[13]

There was something else: Luciano's coolly indifferent, nihilistic view of life. "He manifests a peasant-like faith in chance and has developed an attitude of nonchalance."[14]

This good-time Charlie said he "liked luxury," spending freely on high-class hotels and nightclubs, platinum jewelry, and beautiful women. Unlike most *mafiosi*, he never married or had children. At age fourteen, he lost his virginity and caught gonorrhea, the first of seven cases of gonorrhea and two cases of syphilis. Luciano did have common-law relations for six years with a special woman, but they never married because he "couldn't get along with the girl."[15]

2–1: Charles Luciano, 1928. (Courtesy of the National Archives and Records Administration)

Luciano's drooping right eye, caused by a vicious cutting of his face by assailants, reinforced this appearance of indifference. His nickname "Charles Lucky" was a play on his surname and his fortunes. Luciano later admitted to a psychiatrist that he had been arrested dozens of times (including several never made public) but was able "to free himself from most of these charges and because of this was nicknamed Lucky."[16]

"Charles Lucky" saw himself as a gambler. Though he would later become a bootlegger and labor racketeer, controlling trucking in the Garment Center, when Luciano was asked about his profession, he usually said "bookmaker" or "gambling." He would purchase a place in upstate New York, and he spent summer months at the Saratoga Springs racetrack betting on the ponies. To avoid the fate of Al Capone, Luciano's lawyers filed federal income tax returns in which he listed "miscellaneous" income. "I'm a gambler. That's my profession," he brashly told IRS examiners. Like any good gambler, Luciano was at ease taking huge, calculated risks in the underworld.[17]

These traits would come in handy in the years to come. But that was all in the distant future. Through the late 1910s, Salvatore Lucania was just another petty crook with a record. At age twenty-two, he was still living at home with his parents on East 10th Street.[18]

THE MORELLO FAMILY IN SHAMBLES, 1910–1919

Meanwhile, the small Mafia of New York City was in shambles as well. The first substantial Sicilian *cosca* (or clan) in New York was led by Giuseppe "The Clutch Hand" Morello, his brother-in-law Ignazio "The Wolf" Lupo, and Morello's three half-brothers Ciro, Nick, and Vincenzo Terranova. The Morello Family barely survived on petty extortion, horse thievery, and insurance fraud. A few of its leaders graduated to early racketeering by using threats and extortion to control shipping and access to the wholesale vegetable markets in early 1900s.[19]

Then, the Morellos made a disastrous mistake: in 1909, they got caught counterfeiting US currency. Disastrous because, while the Morellos might be able to bribe local officials, counterfeiting fell under the federal jurisdiction of the US Secret Service. In 1910, the Morello Family, which never totaled more than 110 men, including its associates, saw 45 of its men convicted and sentenced to lengthy prison terms in the Atlanta Federal Penitentiary. All their legal appeals failed, and their convictions were affirmed.[20]

The hardest fall was Giuseppe Morello. Besides being the head of his own family, Morello held the title of *capo di capi* or "boss of bosses" of the American Mafia. After being sent to prison, Morello lost that title to Salvatore D'Aquila, a former confidence man and gang leader in East Harlem. Morello's underboss Ignazio Lupo went away with him, too. With their leadership decimated, the remnants of the Morello Family came under attack from a Brooklyn-based Camorra gang (whose members were from the Naples area of Italy), which began trying to kill off the Morello's remaining men and poach their territories.[21]

The Morello Family prisoners grew increasingly desperate as their sentences wore on at the Atlanta Federal Penitentiary. Mislead by their ability to pay off local police, they convinced themselves that influence might spring them from federal prison. They banked their hopes on an Italian politician from the Lower East Side who apparently promised them that "an attempt will be made to pass a law in Congress" to help them. When that fizzled out, they next retained a lawyer who claimed he was "cousin of the President's Secretary," and put $5,000 in deposit "for the lawyer after Morello is released." It did not work. Giuseppe Morello wasted away in the Atlanta federal prison for a full decade, until he was finally released in 1920, a gaunt and penniless man.[22]

PROHIBITION NEW YORK, 1920–1933

Then came Prohibition. At 12:01 a.m., Saturday, January 17, 1920, the Eighteenth Amendment to the Constitution went into effect, prohibiting "the manufacture, sale, or transportation of intoxicating liquors within . . . the United States." The new Prohibition Unit was given the task of enforcing the federal law, with only fifteen hundred enforcement agents initially for the entire United States. "Detailed plans have been made to carry out the law in cities, such as New York," the *New York Times* reported. "Fifty men are said to have been assigned to New York."[23]

New Yorkers rejected Prohibition in massive numbers by continuing to buy beer and booze. Law enforcement was quickly overwhelmed. The federal court in Manhattan held "cafeteria court" hearings where two hundred defendants at a time were brought before a judge to plead guilty and pay fines averaging $25. Responding to the public backlash, the New York State Legislature repealed its state "dry" law in June 1923. Gotham thus became the symbolic capital of drinking in America. As a Prohibition report said, "New York is considered the most conspicuous example of a wet city."[24]

Prohibition agents, and some local police, arbitrarily enforced the federal law just enough to keep the liquor trade underground.[25] By the late 1920s, the NYPD was still making over eight thousand arrests a year for violation of the National Prohibition Act. Manhattan speakeasies were especially vulnerable to shakedowns from corrupt cops. A report on Prohibition noted the NYPD's peculiar practice of wholesale arrests of "bartenders in speak-easies and waiters in night clubs, cabarets, and so-called restaurants."[26] It was in this environment that gangsters thrived.

2–2: Deputy police commissioner and agents dump illegal beer during Prohibition, 1921. (Courtesy of the Library of Congress Prints and Photographs Division, New York World-Telegram and Sun Newspaper Photograph Collection)

MOONSHINERS AND BASEMENT BREWERS

Moonshining and basement brewing was a phenomenon common in immigrant neighborhoods. "I think that about twenty minutes after Prohibition started, my father made a deal with the tinsmith to make him a still," recalled Tom Geraghty, who grew up in Hell's Kitchen.[27] In the South Village, Italian immigrants had long produced homemade wines. Now that it became a premium product, Italian grocers and barbershops sold it out the back door. When *mafiosi* started converting their basements into distilleries, they looked no different than the innumerable other makeshift stills throughout Italian neighborhoods.[28]

Over time, bootleggers built large and sophisticated brewing operations. Gangsters learned that they could increase profits by producing quality beer and achieving economics of scale. "I set out to make a superior product," said Roger Touhy, a Chicago bootlegger who sparred with Al Capone. "At peak production, we had ten fermenting plants, each one a small brewery in itself."[29] The Irish gangsters William "Big Bill" Dwyer and Owney "The Killer" Madden operated secret breweries in buildings on the West Side of Manhattan.[30]

The Italian gangs were an emerging force in bootlegging during Prohibition. A study of New York's top bootleggers in the late 1920s found that about 50 percent were Jewish, 25 percent were Irish, and 25 percent were Italians. Most were young and ambitious. They scrambled to make it in the cut-throat world of bootlegging.[31] In Williamsburg, Brooklyn, future mob boss Joe Bonanno and his relative Gaspar DiGregorio started out with a basement distillery. They had a tunnel to a garage where they loaded their booze onto delivery trucks. Bonanno later went to work for a major bootlegger named Salvatore Maranzano, a Sicilian *mafioso* who like Bonanno came from Castellammare del Gulfo ("Castle by the Sea") in northwestern Sicily. Barely in his twenties, Bonanno was an overseer of Maranzano's huge brewery operations in upstate New York.[32]

Gangsters made money in related businesses, too. *Mafioso* Nicola Gentile sold raw materials to bootleggers. Gentile conspired with Italian barbershops to divert their licensed supplies of alcohol meant for perfumes. He later ran a general store to supply "bootleggers with corn sugar for alcohol distillation and the jars and tin for the contraband of alcohol."[33]

RUM RUNNERS

"Rum runners" smuggled name-brand liquors from foreign countries into America. While bathtub gin was (usually) drinkable, Manhattan's connoisseurs started clamoring for the finest brand liquors from Europe and the Caribbean. Gangsters circulated "flyers and price lists with recognizable brands—Johnny Walker scotch, Martell cognac, Booth's gin, Bacardi rum, and Veuve Cliquot champagne—catering to customers who refused to settle for anything else," explains historian Michael Lerner.[34]

Rum running involved sophisticated smuggling operations. Rum runners would purchase crates of liquor from foreign ports like London then travel across the ocean, stopping just outside a three-mile perimeter of the East Coast (the United States Coast Guard agreed not to search British ships outside three miles). Speed boats then smuggled the crates to clandestine landing points on Long Island or the New Jersey shore. There, the crates would be loaded onto waiting trucks. So many boats were anchored off the coast that it came to be known as "Rum Row." Although Jewish and Irish gangsters had the biggest rum-running operations, there were major Italian smugglers, too.[35]

FRANK COSTELLO, BUSINESSMAN SMUGGLER

The leading Italian rum runner was Frank Costello. Born Francesco Castiglia in a mountain village in Calabria, Italy, he grew up in a ghetto in Italian East Harlem. "It is important, very important, to put in evidence the education received by Frank in the streets of 108th and 109th," said a lifelong friend. "There is Frank, a very intelligent boy, whose aim was to arrive higher, to get revenge." He took on the Irish surname of Costello to try to gain more respect. But like Joe Masseria and Salvatore Lucania, he struggled to make it on petty crimes. In 1915, the newly-wedded Costello was sentenced to a year in prison for illegal possession of a revolver.[36]

2–3: Frank Costello, 1915. (Courtesy of the New York Police Department)

Then came Prohibition. Costello learned that he was very good at bootlegging and rum running. He soon opened a "real estate" front office at 405 Lexington Avenue, from which he managed sophisticated smuggling operations with employees responsible for police payoffs, logistics, and distribution. He did business with such luminaries as Arnold Rothstein, the Jewish gangster, and Samuel Bronfman, the Canadian owner of the Seagram's liquor conglomerate. As we will see, Costello gained additional street protection under a new Mafia family.[37]

In 1926, Frank Costello was indicted along with sixty other defendants of a conspiracy to smuggle liquor from Newfoundland, Canada, in boats to Rum Row off the coast of New York. Among those indicted were Irish gangster William "Big Bill" Dwyer and thirteen sailors of the United States Coast Guard. While William Dwyer was convicted of the conspiracy at trial, a hung jury could not reach a verdict on Frank Costello. Observers believed that the involvement of Coast Guard sailors turned the case into something of a referendum on Prohibition.[38]

Frank Costello later admitted to the New York State Liquor Authority (NYSLA) that he had, in fact, imported foreign whiskey during Prohibition:

> NYSLA: What years were you engaged in bootlegging during prohibition?
> Costello: From 1923 to 1926.
> . . .
> NYSLA: You brought whisky into the United States?
> Costello: That is right.

NYSLA: From places outside the country?

Costello: That is right.[39]

Costello admitted making at least $305,000 during Prohibition (about $5.2 million in 2013 dollars). He invested his bootlegging profits in slot machines and real estate, and he became a powerbroker in Gotham, finally getting the respect he had so badly wanted.[40]

LIQUOR DISTRIBUTION

The most dangerous part of bootlegging was not making beer, or even smuggling in foreign liquor, but distributing it without getting robbed or killed. Much of the violence associated with Prohibition was due to truck hijackings and territorial disputes.

Bootleggers had to move high-premium, illegal goods on back roads and through dark alleys. Liquor trucks became prime targets for hijackers. "Four armed 'hijackers' yesterday morning forced four truckmen waist deep into the [water canal], and then sped off with two trucks containing 320 cases of whisky, valued at about $30,000," reported a typical news story from August 1924.[41] "A common occurrence was the hijacking of delivery trucks by rival bootlegging groups," recounted Joe Bonanno. To protect Maranzano's operations, Bonanno began carrying a pistol and hunting down stolen liquor trucks.[42]

Rival bootleggers fought fiercely over territories around the city as well. Bootleggers would muscle in on neighborhoods and require all the speakeasies to buy booze only from them. "There were guys going around selling beer, and you had to buy it. You just couldn't switch outfits. They may blow you away," explained John Morahan, who ran speakeasies in Hell's Kitchen. "Owney Madden's beer would come and the guy would say, 'You take this beer,' and you didn't have much choice."[43] Arthur Flegenheimer (a.k.a. Dutch Schultz) had fleets of trucks shipping beer from the Bronx down to areas of Harlem he had taken over. He did battle with Jack "Legs" Diamond and his lieutenant Benjamin "Bugsy" Siegel over beer territories. A neighborhood study of the South Village found that while alcohol makers were plentiful during Prohibition, "selling liquor was still a rough proposition" and the "deliveries were a dangerous business."[44]

Since their product was illegal, bootleggers could not resolve their disputes by calling the police or bringing a civil suit in court. This added up to an extremely dangerous business: roughly one thousand bootleggers would be killed on the streets of New York City during Prohibition. "The scramble for bootlegging revenue was far more vicious and complex in New York than in any other American city," concluded historian Humbert Nelli.[45] It was within this violent context of Prohibition that many *mafiosi* made their names.

THE MAKING OF "JOE THE BOSS" DURING PROHIBITION

Joe Masseria had perhaps the most dramatic reversal of fortune during Prohibition.[46] When Masseria got out of Sing Sing prison a couple years before Prohibition, he went back to his sister's saloon on Forsythe Street. Masseria was in the right place at the right time: he was working at the Forsythe Street saloon just before Prohibition went into effect. The saloon was located near the Curb Exchange, an underworld marketplace for illicit alcohol wholesaling on the Lower East Side. Masseria's traits of aggressiveness, fearlessness, and persistence found an outlet as a leader of bootleggers in Prohibition New York. Masseria and his men could assure that shipments of whiskey and other spirits made it through to the thirsty residents of Gotham. His underworld reputation grew amid wild shootouts in 1922.[47]

MONDAY EVENING, MAY 8, 1922, GRAND STREET, MANHATTAN: THE STREET SHOOTOUT

Around 5:45 p.m. on Monday, May 8, 1922, three well-dressed Italian men were milling in front of a cheese dealer's shop on Grand Street in Little Italy, a block east of the headquarters of the New York City Police. The sidewalks were bustling with people returning from work on the Lower East Side. Joe Masseria and his partner were among those walking up Grand Street. Spotting Masseria, the three men pulled out semiautomatic handguns and fired at their targets.[48]

With bullets flying at him, Masseria grabbed his .32 caliber Colt pistol and returned fire. Pandemonium ensued as sixty bullets crisscrossed the air. Masseria stood firm on the street, pushing back his would-be killers with his gunfire. As the gunmen ran off, Masseria realized police were now on the scene. Masseria tossed his Colt and tried to disappear into Little Italy, but he was apprehended. Even though five innocent passersby had been shot, Joe Masseria escaped unscathed. Masseria had a gun permit, and there was no proof he shot any pedestrians: steel bullets were found in the wounded, while his gun was loaded with lead bullets.[49]

TUESDAY AFTERNOON, AUGUST 8, 1922, SECOND AVENUE, MANHATTAN: DUCKING BULLETS

Joe Masseria's rivals were still lurking. On Tuesday, August 8, 1922, a Hudson Touring car dropped off two men at a restaurant across the street from Masseria's brownstone at 80 Second Avenue. At 2:00 p.m., they saw Masseria leave his front stoop and walk north on the sidewalk.

This time, Masseria was unarmed and defenseless. Spotting the gunmen, he made a dash for his home, but they cornered him on the sidewalk. As Masseria dodged and weaved at point-blank range, "four bullets passed through his straw hat and two passed through his coat" yet none struck his head or torso. The police found a stunned Masseria "sitting on the edge of his bed, shot-punctured hat still on." Newspapers reported how Masseria's "astonishing agility in ducking bullets from automatics saved his life."[50]

These shootouts enhanced Masseria's standing in the underworld. But he had enough near-death experiences. As an insurance policy, he built an armored sedan with steel plates and inch-thick windows. He would later have a penthouse on the Upper West Side, too. Within a decade, he would go from staring at grey prison walls in Ossining, New York, to a view of Manhattan's Central Park.[51]

2–4: Giuseppe "Joe the Boss" Masseria, ca. 1922.
(Courtesy of the New York Police Department)

A NEW MOB: THE MASSERIA FAMILY

Giuseppe "Joe the Boss" Masseria's real innovation was creating a mob meritocracy in his new Masseria Family. Rivals such as the Castellammarese clan of Brooklyn limited their membership to men who came from the town of Castellammare del Golfo on the northwestern coast of Sicily. By contrast, Masseria did not particularly care if his men were from his village or were even Sicilians. Rather, Joe the Boss recruited the best bootleggers and racketeers he could find. Masseria was aided by his *consigliere* (counselor) Giuseppe Morello, the former *capo di capi* or "boss of bosses," who had been released in 1920 after a decade in

Atlanta federal prison. Joe the Boss benefitted from Morello's deep experience and connections. The remnants of the old Morello Family were reconstituted as part of the Masseria Family. Masseria also recruited young new talent like Charles Luciano, who proved himself to be a savvy and cool-headed bootlegger on the Lower East Side.[52]

Along with able Sicilians like Morello and Luciano, Masseria welcomed into his ranks Neapolitans like Vito Genovese and Joe Adonis; Calabrians (from mainland Italy's southernmost province) such as Frank Costello and Frankie Uale; and American-born men like Anthony "Little Augie Pisano" Carfano. Although Charles Luciano is often said to have "Americanized" the Mafia, the seeds were actually planted by his boss Joe Masseria.[53]

By the late 1920s, the Masseria Family became a thriving, multifaceted crime syndicate. By swallowing or forcing out competitors, it became the "A & P of bootleggers" in New York. And the Masseria Family was not limited to bootlegging. Masseria's broad confederation held interests in everything from the Italian numbers lottery to the Brooklyn waterfront labor-union locals taken over by mobsters Vincent Mangano and Albert Anastasia (see chapter 1). New York police detectives identified "Joe the Boss" as the gangster who was "the biggest of 'em all."[54]

THE END OF PROHIBITION

Prohibition officially ended with ratification of the Twenty-First Amendment on December 5, 1933. It was a major blow to bootleggers. "We made $400,000 in one year, and we thought we had something going on forever," said an Irish bootlegger. "But when Prohibition ended, that was the end of the empire. We had to go to work and find a way to make a living."[55]

The thirteen-year boom of Prohibition masked longer-term trends among the gangs. The Prohibition era would be the swan song for the Irish gangsters, the high point for the Jewish syndicates, and the coming-out party for the Italian Mafia. The following sections examine other trends fueling the rise of the modern Mafia.

TRENDS IN THE 1920s: ITALIAN IMMIGRATION, MAFIA FRANCHISES, AND NEW TECHNOLOGIES

Prohibition was not the only factor behind the ascent of the Cosa Nostra. Throughout the 1920s, others forces were having transformative effects on the New York underworld. These included south Italian immigration to New York, Mafia family franchising, and new technologies like the telephone and automobile.

DEMOGRAPHY AS DESTINY: IMMIGRATION TO NEW YORK CITY

"Demography is destiny," is a truism of population experts.[56] In the early twentieth century, New York City was not so much a giant melting pot as a series of overlapping, immigrant enclaves. In 1910, 41 percent of its residents had been born outside America. While Germans and Irish were the largest immigrant groups in the 1800s, Jews and Italians were the largest groups by the early 1900s. "Within the brief span of less than a generation the ethnic composition of the metropolis altered radically," explains demographer Ira Rosenwaike. "Persons of Jewish and Italian background had become numerically superior to those of Irish and German descent."[57]

Table 2–1: Demographic Trends in New York City, 1890–1940 ~ Total Numbers and Percentages of New York City Population[58]					
Census Year	Irish	Jewish	Italian	Black	NYC Total Population
1890	624,000 (26%)	175,000 (7%)	67,000 (2%)	35,000 (<2%)	2,321,000
1900	710,000 (20%)	510,000 (14%)	216,000 (6%)	60,000 (<2%)	3,437,000
1910	676,000 (14%)	1,050,000 (22%)	544,000 (11%)	91,000 (<2%)	4,766,000
1920	616,000 (10%)	1,600,000 (28%)	802,000 (14%)	152,000 (2%)	5,620,000
1930	613,000 (8%)	1,800,000 (25%)	1,070,000 (15%)	327,000 (4%)	6,930,000
1940	518,000 (6%)	1,785,000 (23%)	1,785,000 (23%)	458,000 (6%)	7,454,000

In chapter 4 "The Racketeer Cometh" we will see how these demographic trends bolstered the Mafia's labor racketeering. Now, let us look at their social effects on the underworld.

THE SOUTH ITALIAN *COLONIAE* IN NEW YORK CITY

South Italians especially favored living among fellow *paesani*. "No other nationality in New York City is so given over to aggregation as the Italians," observed a writer. Settlement patterns bear out this observation. Gotham was home to large-scale Italian enclaves. The two largest were Italian East Harlem and the Little Italy along Mulberry Street; each was home to about 110,000 Italians. There were also major settlements in the South Village (70,000 Italians) below West 4th Street in Manhattan; in Belmont (35,000 Italians) in central Bronx; on the northern tip of Staten Island (15,000 Italians); and in Williamsburg (40,000 Italians), Bushwick (30,000 Italians), and Red Hook (20,000 Italians) in Brooklyn.[59]

These were intensely insular, family-centric enclaves. "Our Italian neighborhood was a ghetto. Italian was the spoken language. People built this wall around them to keep the outside world from coming in," said Jerry Della Femina.[60] Italians from the same regions, and even same villages, flocked to the same streets. "Most people from Sicily settled on Elizabeth Street, the people from Mott Street were from mixed cities in Italy, and the people from Mulberry Street were mostly Neapolitans," recounted a man who grew up in Little Italy.[61] Italians married fellow Italians, too. As late as 1920, only 6 percent of south Italians married outside their national origin, rarer than every major immigrant group except Jews.[62]

THE CORNER WISEGUY AND THE CONNECTED UNCLE

Only a tiny fraction of the residents of these neighborhoods were ever involved with the mob, and many more resented the gangsters. At the Mafia's height, it constituted less than one-half of one percent of New York's Italian population. Nevertheless, the creation of south Italian enclaves around New York indirectly facilitated the emergence of the Cosa Nostra.[63]

Mafiosi exploited the insularity of these enclaves. South Italians placed a strong primacy on the Italian home and had a deep mistrust of government outsiders. The Mafia played on these cultural traditions. Robert Orsi, the author of an award-winning study of Italian East Harlem, explains the mythology he found: "The racketeers, in the community's mythical restatement of their identity, were the enforcers of the values of the domus [the Italian home]," Orsi explained. "Of course, no one talked about what these men might have done outside the community."[64]

The mob relied on social pressure and intimidation, too. "We never asked what they did for a living," said Clara Ferrara, a resident of East Harlem. "We never knew what Joey Rao did. His wife was a lovely woman."[65] It was hard for outsiders to penetrate the wall of silence. "The coroner's office in New York found itself handicapped whenever we had a case involving members of the Mafia," said the chief coroner. "Respectable and hard-working Italians, some of whom I knew personally, would become evasive or refuse to answer questions."[66]

Wiseguys were an everyday presence in many neighborhoods. The unofficial headquarters of the early Mafia was East 107th Street in Harlem. "The tenements gave the block the appearance of a walled medieval town somehow replanted in New York City," said Salvatore Mondello, who grew up along 107th Street.[67] Goodfellas gravitated there for decades. "They used to hang on the corner. There was the Artichoke King, Rao, Joe Stutz, Joe Stretch," said Pete Pascale of East Harlem. "They think nothin' of breakin' your legs."[68]

Ronald Goldstock, former director of the New York State Organized Crime Task Force, has pointed out that these Little Italies were recruiting grounds for young members.[69] "When you were brought up in the neighborhood, East Harlem in New York City, you always looked up to the wiseguys," said Vincent "Fish" Cafaro.[70] "In Italian neighborhoods, priests and gangsters were held in virtually the same esteem," echoed Tony Napoli. "Both were loved and feared, and most of all, respected."[71]

Kinship ties further drew young men into a "Mafia family." When FBI agent Joseph Pistone infiltrated the Bonanno Family, he found there was often "some type of family bond, real family, not Mafia family, a father, an uncle, a cousin," between them.[72] Anthony "Gaspipe" Casso was influenced to join the mob by his (lowercase *g*) godfather Sally Callinbrano, whom young Anthony saw as "a class act" and a "man of respect."[73] Vincent "Fat Vinnie" Teresa was drawn to his mobster uncle Dominick Teresa who "seemed to have everything."[74]

MAFIA FRANCHISING: WHY THE COSA NOSTRA WAS LIKE A BURGER FRANCHISE

The Sicilian *mafiosi* who settled in Gotham brought with them the organizational structure of the *cosche* or "clans." In New York, these became known as the Mafia families.[75] Mafia families have been inaccurately compared to a traditional corporation, with managers and employees.[76]

Rather, the Mafia families most closely resembled franchise companies.[77] Franchise companies (that is, burger chains and hotels) allow the use of their trademark by franchisees in exchange for a fee or percent of profits. The franchise company controls minimum standards, guarantees exclusive territories, and arbitrates disputes among franchisees. Franchises are economically efficient because they let the franchisees reap the benefits of a trademark, while the franchisees put up their own capital and know-how to operate on a daily basis.[78]

Similarly, the Mafia families, rather than paying salaries, simply allowed its members to operate under their names to make money in the underworld. Of course, the Cosa Nostra did not produce any (legal) goods or services, and it was a parasitic enterprise in general. Nonetheless, as the Mafia families expanded in the 1920s, they took on the characteristics of franchise companies.

MAFIA FRANCHISES: THE MAFIA TRADEMARK AND FRANCHISE FEE

Like a franchise company, the New York Mafia developed a valuable "trademark" in the underworld. The Cosa Nostra developed a reputation for reliability, for protection from police and other criminals, and for its capacity for violence.[79]

The Mafia was known for its ability to offer reliable immunity from local cops. "You had to be allied with somebody like Paulie [Vario] to keep the cops off your back," believed Henry Hill, an associate of the Lucchese Family. "Wiseguys like Paulie have been paying off the cops for so many years," explained

Hill. "They developed a trust, the crooked cops and the wiseguys."[80] The Mafia became an elite slice of the underworld. When NYPD detective Frank Serpico joined the plainclothes division, he was bluntly told by a fellow officer that while he could arrest black and Puerto Rican criminals, "the Italians, of course, are different. They're on top, they run the show, and they're very reliable, and they can do whatever they want."[81]

The Cosa Nostra's underworld reputation was so ferocious that it shielded its members from *other* crooks. "That's what the FBI can never understand—what Paulie and the organization offer is protection for the kinds of guys who can't go to the cops. They're like the police department for wiseguys," described Hill. "The only way to guarantee that I'm not going to get ripped off by anybody is to be established with a member, like Paulie."[82] Mob connections could shield non-mobsters, too. "When a businessman is 'with' someone, it means he has a godfather, a gladiator who will protect him," explained Michael Franzese, a prominent ex-*mafioso*. "That status made him 'hands off' to anyone on the street." The Mafia's preeminent reputation in the underworld was such that it often served as a kind of master arbiter of disputes among other criminals well into the 1970s.[83]

Ultimately, the Mafia's "brand" was based on its reputation for extreme violence. The scholar Diego Gambetta noted how many *mafiosi* demonstrated "the ability to use violence" early in their careers to enhance their reputations.[84] New York's mob bosses commanded authority based on "a reputation for savagery and a history of settling disputes by shedding blood," confirms undercover FBI agent Joseph Pistone.[85]

The Mafia's *reputation* for violence was so intimidating, that it only had to resort to actual violence sparingly.[86] As an FBI informant stated, "a 'button guy' received a lot of respect in the neighborhood and was able to use this position to obtain money without getting himself involved in a lot of problems."[87] When Jimmy Fratianno became a "made man," the *mafioso* John Roselli explained its reputational benefits: "The fact that you're a member gives you an edge. You can go into various businesses and people will deal with you because of what you represent," said Roselli. "Nobody fucks with you. We're nationwide. . . . And that means you can make a pretty good living if you hustle," counseled the veteran wiseguy.[88]

The Mafia trademark was valuable enough that there was even some "licensing" and "passing off" of the mark in the underworld. Trademark owners sometimes license their mark to nonaffiliated companies (for example, "[trademark] Diet™-Approved" for food companies). In Manhattan, an Irish gang named "the Westies" entered into a virtual licensing agreement with the Gambino Family. As a federal court explained, the Gambino Family "permitted the Westies to use the Gambino name and reputation in connection with their own illicit business," and in exchange "the Westies paid the Gambino Family ten percent of the proceeds from various illegal activities."[89] Others occasionally tried to "pass off" the mob's trademark by pretending to be affiliated. "Because of my ethnic background, they thought I was mob-connected and it worked to my advantage. It gave me some leverage to keep bettors in line," said Anthony Serritella, a Chicago bookie. "I really wasn't connected, but never admitted or denied it."[90]

In exchange for operating under a Mafia family, the members paid something resembling a franchise fee and percentage of the profits. Joseph Valachi testified before Congress that each of the five-hundred-odd soldiers in the Genovese Family of which he was a member paid $25 monthly "dues" (about $2,300 annually for each soldier). In the mid-1950s, an Anastasia Family underboss named Frank Scalise was selling mob memberships for $40,000—an express franchise fee. Soldiers were also expected to split some of their profits with their *caporegimes* (captains) who in turn sent some up to the bosses of the family. "Usually the split is half with your captain," explained FBI agent Joseph Pistone, who infiltrated the Bonanno Family. "The captain in turn has to kick in, say, ten percent upstairs, to the boss."[91]

MAFIA FRANCHISES: TERRITORIAL RIGHTS

Franchise companies often guarantee each franchisee an exclusive territory and prohibit encroachments by their other franchisees (for example, no two coffee shops of the same trademark may open on the same block).[92] Similarly, the Cosa Nostra upheld territorial rights for wiseguys.

The Mafia's recognition of territorial rights can be traced all the way back to Sicily. An investigative report from Sicily in the 1890s stated:

Among the canons of the mafia there is one regarding the respect for the territorial jurisdictions of other [*cosche*]. The infraction of this canon constitutes a personal insult. Hence the encroachments . . . were perceived by the Siino family as an atrocious personal insult.[93]

This carried over to New York, albeit in a narrower form. Gotham was too dense to grant exclusive rights to *all* criminal activities in a neighborhood. In the 1920s, East Harlem was divided up between the Masseria Family and the Reina Family. Later, the New York Mafia protected rights to specific rackets. For example, the Lucchese Family controlled shipping at Kennedy Airport, and different families controlled specific factories in the garment district.[94]

Soldiers were conversely limited by the territorial rights of other members. The Profaci Family had to suppress a dissident crew lead by the brothers Larry Gallo, Joseph "Crazy Joe" Gallo, and Albert "Kid Blast" Gallo. An FBI informant reported that the Gallo brothers believed that once they were "made" they "would come into sudden wealth." They grew angry when they discovered the rackets "were already under the control of someone else, and the GALLOS were not allowed to move in on anyone else's operation."[95]

MAFIA FRANCHISES: MAINTAINING STANDARDS AND ARBITRATING DISPUTES

To preserve the trademark, franchise companies retain the right to enforce standards or step in when a franchisee is harming the brand (for example, running a shoddy motel under their trademark). Similarly, the Mafia families had the authority to maintain rules to protect the organization and its trademark. Among the most serious rules were that a member could not betray secrets of the Cosa Nostra, he could not physically attack another member, and he could not "fool around . . . with another *amico nostra*'s [made man's] wife."[96] Although the Mafia talked about these rules in terms of "honor," they also served the business rationale of protecting the organization. "In New York we step all over each other. What I mean is there is a lot of animosity among the soldiers," Joe Valachi explained. "So you can see why it is that they are strict about the no-hands rule."[97] The Mafia also sought to protect the reputation of its "brand."

Publicly, at least, the Mafia disavowed any involvement with prostitution, pornography, and drugs (much more on that later), which were viewed negatively by the public.[98]

Like mainstream franchises, the Mafia even had something resembling arbitration panels to resolve disputes among its members. In his memoirs on the 1920s, *mafioso* Nicola Gentile describes a "council" in which bosses from different Mafia families met to hear charges of wrongdoing and resolve disputes.[99] Later, the Cosa Nostra created "the Commission" as a forum to resolve major disputes. As Joe Bonanno explained, "The Commission, as an agent of harmony, could arbitrate disputes brought before it."[100] In chapter 3 we will look at how the Commission came into being in 1931.

THE NEW TECHNOLOGIES OF TELEPHONES, AUTOMOBILES, AND PLANES

New technologies have been described as waves that roll through society. At the same time that new technologies were changing New York, they were transforming organized crime as well.[101]

In the nineteenth and early twentieth centuries, New York gangsters had relatively limited reach. Groups like the "Eighteen Street Gang" or the "Bottle Alley Gang" rarely controlled more than a couple blocks.[102] They were hampered by unreliable communication and transportation. The early Mafia families actually communicated by mail. Men of Honor would even carry with them "letters of recommendation" from their mob bosses when they traveled to new cities.[103] Communicating through hard documents proved risky: in the early 1900s, the United States Secret Service seized letters of members of the Morello Family and used the letters to build cases against them.[104]

The advent of the modern telephone system gave organized crime a valuable new tool to communicate efficiently across regions and the United States. As service grew, New Yorkers developed the habit of using the telephone regularly on massive levels from the 1910s onward.[105] Professional criminals were relatively free to use phones in this time, too. The Federal Communications Act of 1934 prohibited the interception and disclosure of wire communications, rendering any wiretapped phone conversations inadmissible in federal court. This remained the law until 1968.[106] Although local law enforcement was not so restricted, it was often compromised by corruption from investigating organized crime. From the 1920s through the mid-1950s, there was something of a golden era for gangsters to use phones. Los Angeles goodfella Jimmy Fratianno used pay phones to have conversations about loansharking and casino operations through the 1960s. Asked why he did not take more precautions, Fratianno, referring to his 1970s conviction, explained: "Well, later years we did, but like see, I was the first person that ever went to jail on a wiretap in Los Angeles."[107]

The telephone expanded the reach and efficiency of organized crime starting in the 1920s. New York *mafioso* Frank Costello regularly phoned his partner Phillip "Dandy Phil" Kastel in New Orleans to coordinate their joint gambling operations. During the 1940s, state police discovered that *mafioso* Joseph Barbara was calling gangsters throughout the East Coast (he kept his conversations short and veiled to avoid incrimination). Despite the growing risks, the efficiencies from telephones were so great that *mafiosi* were still communicating over pay phones (using coded words) well into the 1970s. As Judge Richard Posner points out, phones are so efficient and attractive that they are *still* used by many gangsters despite the risks.[108]

Mass-produced automobiles opened up new territories and criminal enterprises as well. By 1927, a majority of America households owned a car.[109] Gangsters likewise started using automobiles for criminal activities. Joe Valachi got his start as a "wheelman" for burglaries, driving his careening Packard car through the streets after heists.[110] Bootlegging operations depended on fleets of trucks. The Mafia began relying on cars to smuggle narcotics, too.[111]

These new technologies enabled gangsters to forge cross-country links during Prohibition. As historian Mark Haller describes, "Bootleggers east of the Mississippi were wintering in Miami and occasionally vacationing in Hot Springs, Arkansas," they met "in Nova Scotia or Havana, to which they traveled to look after their import interests," and those with joint ventures were in "continual contact by telephone" to coordinate activities.[112] Las Vegas's casino industry, in which mobsters conducted skimming operations, would not have developed without modern cars and airplanes.[113]

TECHNOLOGY AND GAMBLING:
THE NUMBERS LOTTERY AND SPORTS BOOKMAKING

Technology had its most direct impact on illegal gambling operations. Although gambling had been around forever, it was boosted by new communications in the 1920s. The Mafia families specialized in two different forms of gambling: the numbers lottery and sports bookmaking.

During the 1920s, the numbers lottery took off in New York City. Historians have shown that New York's illegal lotteries nearly disappeared in the early 1900s, following revelations that paper drawings were being fixed by their operators. In the early 1920s, African-American gangsters in black Harlem built a new numbers lottery based on an unimpeachable public source of randomly generated numbers: the New York Clearing House. Each morning at 10:00 a.m., as the clearings numbers were announced in Lower Manhattan, numbers runners would telephone the winning digits throughout Gotham. "Once the Clearing House numbers became known in Harlem, the game spread like wildfire," describes a history of the numbers lottery.[114]

Numbers lotteries were highly territorial in areas of New York City. Numbers lotteries required "banks" and numbers "shops" (such as liquor stores that sold numbers under the counter) in neighborhoods to enable a large customer base of numbers purchasers. For banks and numbers shops to operate, pay-offs to the police and protection from others were required.[115] As a result, the Mafia held interests in numbers lotteries around New York. In the 1930s, the lucrative Harlem numbers lottery was taken over by members of the Luciano family, and it was passed down for decades from Michael "Trigger Mike" Coppola to Anthony "Fat Tony" Salerno.[116] Likewise, Joe Bonanno recalled how when he became a boss in central Brooklyn, he "also inherited the 'rights' to the neighborhood lottery."[117] Later, his son Bill Bonanno described how "a member could run numbers within a designated four-block area of the neighborhood," and "if someone else interfered by encroaching on his territory," the family would intervene.[118]

Bookmaking was revolutionized by wire services, telephones, radio, and later television. Bookmaking involved handling wagers on sporting events like horse races and boxing matches. During the 1930s and '40s, "wire rooms" became tools to obtain instant sports results. The Chicago Outfit muscled in on a major wire service to gain an informational advantage on sporting results. This advantage, however, faded with television. "Wherever there was a television set, there was a new type of sports wire service," described a history of bookmaking. Unlike numbers lotteries, bookmaking could be handled largely over the phone and with "runners," and did not require as many brick-and-mortar locations.[119]

Gambling, and bookmaking in particular, has sometimes been called the "life blood" of organized crime. This is somewhat misleading. The ease of bookmaking made it commonplace among low-level wiseguys. However, since it was so easy to become a bookie, the market was fairly competitive and the profits limited.[120] Mob soldiers tended to use bookmaking as everyday "work" income and to raise capital for more lucrative activities.[121] Few wiseguys relied *solely* on bookmaking to make money.[122]

Prohibition reversed the fortunes of the Italian gangsters in New York City. But they were also bolstered by historical trends that were accelerating in the 1920s. The Italian gangsters were very much in the right place at the right time. The profits from bootlegging and other rackets, however, would soon lead to internal conflicts among the Mafia families. In our next chapter, we will look at a series of gang fights that have been shrouded in Mafia mythology.

PART 2

TAKING GOTHAM

The 1930s and '40s

THE MAFIA REBELLION OF 1928-1931 AND THE FALL OF THE BOSS OF BOSSES

He wanted something more terrible than money: power.
And he had decided to carry out any action in order to
obtain absolute power and to become the boss of bosses.
—Nicola Gentile, *Vita di Capomafia* (1963)

Al Capone was causing trouble for the Sicilians in New York. Capone had been on a meteoric rise since his teenage days as a wharf rat on the Brooklyn waterfront. Barely in his thirties, he was vying to become boss of Chicago during Prohibition. Except now Joseph Aiello, a Sicilian *mafioso*, was ominously calling Capone an "intruder" in Chicago. As the son of immigrant parents from Naples on mainland Italy, Capone was sneered at by many in the Sicilian Mafia who had thrown their support behind Aiello.[1]

The wild card was Joe Masseria, the new *capo di capi* or "boss of bosses" of the Mafia. Had Giuseppe "Joe the Boss" Masseria gotten different press, he might today be as well-known as Alphonse "Scarface" Capone or Charles "Lucky" Luciano. Joe Masseria built a sprawling Mafia syndicate, the largest in New York during Prohibition. He was less concerned with Sicilian lineage than with recruiting the toughest, shrewdest bootleggers he could find. Could Al Capone the Neapolitan gangster make a deal with Joe the Boss?

What followed next has been called the "Castellammarese War of 1930–1931," a conflict which, it is said, created the modern Mafia. In his bestselling autobiography *A Man of Honor*, Joseph Bonanno, who participated on the winning side, paints a romanticized portrait of the "war." Under Bonanno's conventional telling of the story, the noble Castellammarese clan of Brooklyn—the true "Men of Honor"—rally to defend themselves against the greedy, low-class Giuseppe "Joe the Boss" Masseria. This so-called Castellammarese War is the source of many myths about the Cosa Nostra. Even its title is misleading. This was hardly a "war"; it was *not* only about the Castellammarese clan of the Mafia; and it originated back in the 1920s.[2]

Another set of myths paints this as a generational conflict in which younger "Americanized" mobsters pushed aside the older Sicilian *mafiosi*. The conventional history suggests that Italian-American gangsters like Charles "Lucky" Luciano were impatient with the more tradition-minded, Sicily-born "Moustache Petes" for failing to modernize to the times in New York City. But as we will see, the historical facts do not square with this popular myth of "Americanization."[3]

Rather, the conflicts were simply gang fights over money and power. Different *mafiosi* with self-interested motives were rebelling against overreaching by three successive boss of bosses: Salvatore D'Aquila, Joe Masseria, and Salvatore Maranzano. Let us call it simply the *Mafia Rebellion of 1928–1931*. This chapter tells a revisionist history of this conflict and explores what it actually meant for the New York Mafia. It dismantles the myths presented by the winners of the "war" and perpetuated by subsequent writers on the mob.

CAPO DI CAPI: SALVATORE "TOTÒ" D'AQUILA

As we saw in the previous chapter, Joe Masseria rose to power as the leader of bootleggers and professional criminals during Prohibition. The Masseria Family became the largest mob syndicate in Gotham. By 1928, Joe the Boss had one obstacle standing in his way.

The *capo di capi* of the American Mafia between 1910 and 1928 was an extraordinarily secretive man by the name of Salvatore "Totò" D'Aquila. He spent the majority of his life in Palermo, Sicily, when that city was swarming with rival clans. Barely 5 feet, 2 inches tall, D'Aquila had a penchant for dressing well and speaking smoothly. Soon after disembarking, he became a confidence man in Manhattan, talking his marks out of their money. D'Aquila gradually established himself as a gang leader with a base of power in East Harlem.[4]

When Giuseppe Morello went to the Atlanta Federal Penitentiary for counterfeiting in 1910, Salvatore D'Aquila became *capo di capi* at the nadir of the Sicilian Mafia in the second decade of the twentieth century, only to see its fortunes reverse during Prohibition. Flush with cash, Totò D'Aquila moved his family to an elaborately furnished house across from the Bronx Zoo. By outward appearances, D'Aquila was a quiet family man with successful business ventures in real estate, olive oil, and cheese importing.[5]

Behind the scenes, it was a different story. According to Nicola Gentile, a kind of freelance consultant to *mafiosi* in the 1920s, D'Aquila significantly expanded the reach of the *capo di capi*. D'Aquila became "very authoritative," enlisted a "secret service" of spies, and brought trumped-up charges against rivals. Other informants confirm that D'Aquila presided over trials of *mafiosi* who allegedly broke rules of the mob. With D'Aquila acting like a kind of judge, the trials were held before the "general assembly" of Mafia representatives from clans across America.[6]

6:20 P.M., OCTOBER 10, 1928, 13TH STREET & AVENUE A, LOWER EAST SIDE, MANHATTAN: THE DEATH OF SALVATORE D'AQUILA

In October 1928, the fifty-year-old D'Aquila and his wife were consulting a cardiologist on the Lower East Side. During the drive from the Bronx, Totò D'Aquila noticed something wrong with his sedan. After ushering his wife and children into the doctor's office, he went back outside and lifted the hood of the engine.

Three men came up to D'Aquila on the sidewalk. They engaged him in a conversation that turned into a heated argument. Suddenly, the trio pulled out guns and started blasting away. The autumn dusk was shattered by gunfire as nine bullets ripped through D'Aquila's heart, left lung, pancreas, and other vital organs. D'Aquila collapsed on the sidewalk drenched in blood as his killers escaped on foot.[7]

JOE THE BOSS . . . OF ALL BOSSES

The death of D'Aquila paved the way for Masseria to become the boss of bosses. He was the obvious replacement: his Masseria Family was by far the largest in Prohibition New York. So, in the winter of 1928, the general assembly of the Mafia elected Giuseppe "Joe the Boss" Masseria to be *capo di capi*. Previously, the boss of bosses title was more honorary and consultative. The boss of bosses was seen as a kind of wise mediator among the Mafia families. But under D'Aquila, more and more authority had built up in the position. Masseria intended to take advantage of this to expand his interests in New York and westward to mob enclaves in Detroit and elsewhere.

The timing of Masseria's accession later fueled suspicions that he was secretly behind D'Aquila's murder. To this day, it is *not* at all clear that D'Aquila was, in fact, killed by men sent by Masseria.[8] But conflicts are sometimes launched on misinformation, and the underworld eventually came to *believe* that Masseria was behind it. "Masseria managed to kill Totò D'Aquila, becoming himself boss of the bosses," summarized Nicola Gentile.[9]

For now though, Joe the Boss of Bosses stood astride the Cosa Nostra. From the winter of 1928 through early 1930, the Masseria Family sought to expand its interests across the United States and to generate more revenues from New York. The general assembly of the Mafia supported him.

Then, like D'Aquila before him, Masseria began to overreach. Masseria's one-time ally Nicola Gentile said Joe the Boss started "bullying" Mafia representatives; further, his top lieutenants did "not permit objections" and "would command with the force of terror." Joe the Boss's real problems began when he started to meddle with other Mafia families.[10]

NEW YORK'S OTHER MAFIA FAMILIES, 1929–1931

When Joe Masseria became boss of bosses, in addition to his Masseria Family, there were four other Mafia families in New York City. As a brief overview, they were as follows:

- The second Mafia family was based in South Brooklyn, which as we saw was full of lucrative waterfront rackets (see chapter 1). This family was headed by Alfred Mineo, an ally of Joe Masseria. But this South Brooklyn waterfront family would really be defined by Mineo's successors as boss, Vincent Mangano and Albert Anastasia.[11]

- The third was the Castellammarese clan of central Brooklyn, headed by Nicola "Cola" Schiro. These men haled from the port village of Castellammare del Gulfo ("Castle on the Sea of the Gulf") on the northwestern coast of Sicily. This lawless village was thick with *mafiosi* known for their ferocity. The Castellammarese, who liked to boast that they were "Men of Honor," were among the most insular and chauvinistic *mafiosi* in Sicily.[12]

- The fourth was the Joseph Profaci Family, also based in Brooklyn. Joseph Profaci and his clan mostly came from a suburb outside Palermo, Sicily. With his relative Joseph Magliocco as his underboss, the Profaci Family held a mix of bootlegging interests, the numbers lottery, and some legitimate businesses. Profaci would later secretly ally himself with the Castellammarese clan.[13]

- And fifth, but not least, there was the Gaetano Reina Family. The Reina Family had its base in central Bronx and East Harlem. Gaetano Reina took control over much of north New York City's wholesale ice business (a valuable business before refrigeration) by muscling out competitors and taking over routes. Reina's top lieutenants were Tom Gagliano and Tommy Lucchese, close partners who would be pivotal in the upheaval to come.[14]

The New York Mafia families would soon divide into different coalitions, for and against the boss of bosses Joe Masseria. To keep track of the New York families, and their cross-country alliances, table 3–1 serves as a handy reference guide for this chapter:

Table 3–1 The Fall of the "Boss of Bosses":
Boss of Bosses, Mafia Families, and Major Participants

Giuseppe "The Clutch Hand" Morello, Boss of Bosses, ?–1910:

Morello was the "boss of bosses" until 1910 when he was convicted for counterfeiting. Sent to Atlanta Federal Penitentiary until release in 1920, then joined Masseria Family.

Salvatore "Totò" D'Aquila, Boss of Bosses, 1910–1928:

D'Aquila was the highly secretive "boss of bosses" during most of Prohibition. He was murdered by unknown assailants in Lower Manhattan in 1928.

Giuseppe "Joe the Boss" Masseria, Boss of Bosses, 1928–1931:

Masseria rose from obscurity to become boss of bosses after the death of D'Aquila. He became embroiled in a series of gang fights and was assassinated in 1931 at Coney Island restaurant by a cabal organized by his lieutenant Charles "Lucky" Luciano. The pro- and anti-Masseria coalitions were as follows:

Pro-Masseria Family Coalition:	Anti-Masseria Family Coalition:
Al Capone "Outfit" (Chicago)	**Joseph Aiello Family** (Chicago)
Chester LaMare faction (Detroit)	**Gaspare Milazzo Family** (Detroit)
	Stephen Magaddino Family (Buffalo)
Joseph Pinzolo (Bronx/Harlem): Would-be successor boss to Reina Family	**Reina Family faction** (Bronx/Harlem): Tom Gagliano and Tommy Lucchese
Alfred Mineo Family (South Brooklyn): Steve Ferrigno, lieutenant	**Joseph Profaci Family** (central Brooklyn)
Joseph Masseria Family (Manhattan): Joe Masseria, boss of bosses 1928–31 Giuseppe Morello, Masseria *consigliere* Joseph Catania **1931 cabal in Masseria Family**: Charles "Lucky" Luciano Vito Genovese Frank Livorsi Joseph Stracci	**Castellammarese clan** (central Brooklyn): Salvatore Maranzano, boss of bosses 1931 Joseph Bonanno, Maranzano lieutenant Nicola Schiro, ex-boss of Castellammarese Vito Bonventre **Castellammarese clan's hit team**: Nick Capuzzi Sebastiano "Buster" Domingo Girolamo "Bobby Doyle" Santuccio Joe Valachi

Salvatore Maranzano, Boss of Bosses, 1931:

Maranzano lead the Castellammarese clan in surprise attacks on Masseria. In 1931, five weeks after becoming "boss of bosses," he was assassinated in his Park Avenue office by a Jewish hit team organized by Charles "Lucky" Luciano, Tom Gagliano, and Tommy Lucchese. Maranzano was the last "boss of bosses." He was replaced by a power-sharing commission.

PROXY FIGHT IN CHICAGO: AL CAPONE VS. JOSEPH AIELLO

Enter Alphonse Capone. During the late 1920s, Al Capone's "Chicago Outfit" was battling Joseph Aiello's Family for bootlegging territory around the Windy City. Capone was the Brooklyn-born son of poor Neapolitan parents; Aiello was a Sicily-born "Man of Honor." Given their ethnic backgrounds and prejudices, the Sicilian *mafiosi* might be expected to back Aiello. And most did.

Joseph Aiello's strongest allies were Gaspare Milazzo in Detroit and Steve Magaddino in Buffalo, both of whom were Castellammarese. They maintained cross-country links with the Castellammarese clan of Brooklyn. They sided first with their fellow villagers, and then with fellow Sicilians. Non-Sicilians like Capone were a distant third.[15]

By contrast, as we have seen, Joe Masseria did *not* care so much about Sicilian lineage. Although accounts differ as to who approached whom first, everyone agrees on the outcome: Joe Masseria and Al Capone forged an alliance. Capone would become part of the Mafia through the Masseria Family, if he eliminated Joseph Aiello. The alliance was out in the open.[16]

FEBRUARY 1930: THE REINA FAMILY REBELS

On the evening of Wednesday, February 26, 1930, boss Gaetano Reina was walking with his blonde mistress to his parked coupe in the Bronx when assassins with a sawed-off shotgun fired ten slugs into Reina's body. As with Salvatore D'Aquila's death in 1928, it is *not* clear whether Gaetano Reina was killed by the Masseria Family. Reina was involved in the wholesale ice racket, which was awash in violence as competitors fought to control routes. Reina seemed to be expecting an attack at any minute: the police found a loaded .32 caliber revolver in Reina's pocket and a rifle with one hundred extra shells in a secret compartment in his car.[17]

Nevertheless, Masseria's subsequent actions convinced some that he ordered the hit on Reina. According to Joseph Bonanno, Masseria endorsed Joseph Pinzolo, one of his alleged sycophants, as the replacement boss for the Reina Family. Tom Gagliano and Tommy Lucchese, the top lieutenants of Gaetano Reina, began plotting their revenge. They believed that Masseria was behind Reina'a death, and they were unhappy that Pinzolo was taking over as boss. Reina's murder was "why Tom Gagliano fought with all his might against Joe the Boss," mob soldier Joe Valachi was told by the faction. The Gagliano/Lucchese faction was the first group in New York to start secretly conspiring against Joe Masseria.[18]

There are, however, reasons to doubt the Gagliano/Lucchese faction's story of why Joseph Pinzolo ascended to boss. Their faction numbered only about fifteen dissidents in the two-hundred-member Reina Family. Most seemed to have accepted Pinzolo. Gagliano and Lucchese may have simply been jealous that they were passed over for Pinzolo.[19]

MAY 1930: THE CASTELLAMMARESE CLAN REBELS

The other rebellion in New York City was among the Castellammarese clan in Brooklyn. The official "cause for war" for the Castellammarese clan was the murder of their fellow Castellammarese, Gaspare Milazzo, a boss of Detroit, Michigan. On May 31, 1930, assassins killed Gaspare Milazzo and his driver Sam Parrino in a fish market. This time, Giuseppe "Joe the Boss" Masseria's links to the assassins were close. Joe Masseria was supporting Milazzo's crosstown rival Chester LaMare, whose soldiers were identified by the police as the killers of Milazzo.[20] Milazzo's murder helped trigger a chain reaction in New York.

A REVISIONIST HISTORY OF THE
CASTELLAMMARESE WAR OF 1930–1931

Mob history really is written by the winners. The conventional history on the Castellammarese War of 1930–1931 and its leader Salvatore Maranzano has been driven by his protégé Joseph Bonanno's autobiography *A Man of Honor*. In Bonanno's romanticized account, his "hero" Salvatore Maranzano rallies the Castellammarese clan—the true defenders of the Sicilian "Tradition"—against the bastardized gangster Joe Masseria. Bonanno's compelling story of an underworld band of brothers sold many books. Is his history accurate?[21]

I plan to offer a revisionist history of the "Castellammarese War" by balancing Bonanno's version with the perspectives of others as well as with additional facts. It strips away the romanticism for a more realistic portrait of the modern Mafia.

SALVATORE MARANZANO: MAN OF HONOR
OR OPPORTUNISTIC DEMAGOGUE?

In May 1930, Maranzano was nominally just a forty-three-year-old soldier under his boss Nicola Schiro of the Castellammarese clan of Brooklyn. Back in Sicily, Maranzano had been the provincial *capo* of all the Castellammarese clans until he was forced out by the Fascist government of Benito Mussolini in the 1920s. In America, Maranzano became a successful bootlegger.[22] A pompous man, Maranzano and his supporters made sure everyone knew he had once studied to be a priest, spoke Latin, and read histories of ancient Rome.[23]

Salvatore Maranzano was a political demagogue. Back in Sicily, he had been active in electoral politics, politicking alongside his endorsed candidates. Those who saw Maranzano hold forth remember emotional speeches full of reckless charges and inflammatory rhetoric. As a mob rival, he called Joe Masseria "the poisonous snake of our family," and he said Al Capone was "staining the organization" of "the honorable society." Even Bonanno admitted Maranzano may have "overstated Masseria's avarice" and "frightened us a little in order to make us bolder."[24]

Maranzano further exploited ethnic identity, a tactic the Mafia would return to over the years. As the mob soldier Joe Valachi later testified before a Senate Committee, the Maranzano camp baldly asserted that "all the Castellammarese were sentenced to death," though the soldiers "never found out the reason." "He has condemned all of us," Maranzano told the Castellammarese, referring to Joe Masseria. "He will only devour you in time." Nicola Gentile similarly describes how Maranzano "began to inflame ... the hearts of his Castellammarese townsman inciting them to vindicate Milazzo" and then goaded "the Palermitani inciting them to vindicate Totò D'Aquila."[25]

Maranzano's rallying speeches should be taken with a mountain of salt. Nothing in Joe Masseria's past suggests he would engage in ethnic cleansing of the Castellammarese. Joe the Boss welcomed Sicilians and non-Sicilians of every region into his Family. Two of his "four we are" burglary partners —the brothers Salvatore and Giuseppe Ruffino—were in fact Castellammarese.[26] Masseria cared about greenbacks, not bloodlines.

Nonetheless, Maranzano played the ethnic-identity card effectively. Several Castellammarese and Palermitani (the fellow townsmen of D'Aquila) rallied behind Maranzano. The charges resonated: "Masseria has always been our enemy, so much that he had our boss Totò D'Aquila killed," said Vincenzo Troia.[27]

FOLLOWING THE MONEY: ECONOMIC ROOTS OF THE MAFIA REBELLION OF 1928–1931

Though less trumpeted as an "official" cause, the Reina Family and the Castellammarese clan also had strong economic motives to depose Masseria. By 1930, the Masseria Family, along with its allies, had achieved territorial dominion over most of Lower Manhattan and South Brooklyn, and also much of East Harlem. The major untapped territories were held by the Reina Family in East Harlem and the Bronx, and by the Castellammarese elsewhere in Brooklyn.

For the Reina Family faction, the replacement of Gaetano Reina with Masseria's ally Joseph Pinzolo was seen as power play in East Harlem. As exemplified by Joe Valachi's account, the anti-Masseria coalition complained that when a soldier made a lot of money, "Joe the Boss will send for him and he will tax him so much and if the guy refused, he will be a dead duck."[28]

For many in the Castellammarese clan, and others in Brooklyn, it was the Masseria Family's demands for money tributes that spurred the resentment against Joe the Boss. According to Bonanno, in the summer of 1930, Masseria coerced a $10,000 payment from Cola Schiro, the boss of the Castellammarese clan in Brooklyn. Then, on July 15, 1930, Vito Bonventre, one of the wealthiest bootleggers among the Castellammarese clan was shot down in Brooklyn. Maranzano portrayed this as a Masseria protection racket muscling in on their businesses.[29]

Even Maranzano had something of a financial angle. In the midst of the conflict, Maranzano gave his soldiers a contract to kill Joseph "Joe the Baker" Catania of the Masseria Family. His soldiers dutifully carried out the hit on Catania, though they were not told the full reasons. His soldiers later learned "that Joe Baker was hijacking [alcohol] trucks on Maranzano."[30]

Or take Joe Profaci. Profaci was not a Castellammarese. But he wanted to protect the growing profits of his olive oil company and the illegal numbers lottery in Brooklyn. Despite his wealth, Profaci was known as a cheap boss, and he did not have enough men to take on Masseria himself. The armchair general Profaci started going to strategy meetings of the Castellammarese, boasting "we are going to get rid of these [Masseria] guys, all of them."[31]

SALVATORE MARANZANO VS. JOE MASSERIA

Central to his version of the "war," Bonanno repeatedly ridicules Joe Masseria's weight and slovenliness as metaphors for a defective character. "Joe the Glutton," as Bonanno calls him, "attacked a plate of spaghetti as if he were a drooling mastiff." This somehow becomes interpreted as reflecting flaws in Joe the Boss's leadership. "Maranzano believed that Masseria was the type of man who, under intense pressure, would get crazier and crazier and fatter and fatter," asserts Bonanno.[32] This image has stuck. Most recently, in the Home Box Office (HBO) series *Boardwalk Empire*, Masseria is portrayed as a doughy, treacherous bully.

In reality, Salvatore Maranzano was less svelte than Joe Masseria. At 5 feet, 4 inches Masseria weighed 155 pounds for a body mass index of 27, while Maranzano, at 5 feet, 8 inches, weighed 218 pounds with a body mass index of 33. Or, as a doctor put it, Maranzano had a "tendency to obesity." A vain man, Maranzano took to wearing a "rubber abdominal support"—a male girdle—underneath his suits to try to smooth down his gut. And while Maranzano dressed well, Masseria was no slouch either: he was a tailor in his youth and is described as almost invariably wearing a suit and hat.[33]

Although Salvatore Maranzano spoke more eloquently than Joe Masseria, their characters were not so different. Frank Costello saw right through Maranzano. Like Masseria, Frank Costello used his native intelligence to become a wealthy bootlegger and well-coifed powerbroker in New York. Nevertheless, Costello never bought into Maranzano's image. Comparing his one-time boss Masseria to the pompous Maranzano, Costello told his friend that a "greaseball is a greaseball," by which he meant "that Maranzano, despite his polished appearance was of the same ilk as Masseria."[34]

3:50 P.M., FRIDAY, AUGUST 15, 1930, EAST 116TH STREET, ITALIAN EAST HARLEM: THE SNEAK ATTACK ON GIUSEPPE MORELLO

East Harlem was enduring a sweltering summer in 1930, with temperatures topping 100 degrees, until the heat wave broke the second week of August. That week, Giuseppe Morello went to his second-story office in a building he owned at 352 East 116th Street.

Late in the afternoon of Friday, August 15, Morello was sitting around a table in his spartan office with building contractors Joseph Perrano and Gaspar Pollaro. They were talking business. Around 3:50 p.m., there was a knock at the door, which Morello got up to answer. As Morello cracked open the door, two men pushed their way in. They fired at the sixty-three-year-old Morello, who "kept running around the office," until he succumbed to five bullet wounds. After being shot, Perrano dove out the second floor window and perished. Only Pollaro barely survived.[35]

There is no sign that the Masseria Family even knew a "war" had been declared. Giuseppe Morello was hardly expecting trouble: he went into his office unarmed and answered the door himself. He never knew his killer, Sebastiano "Buster" Domingo, a hit man imported from Chicago. Salvatore Maranzano wanted an early knockout of the veteran *consigliere* because, if Morello went into hiding, he "could exist forever on diet of hard bread, cheese and onions."[36]

The Reina Family faction in East Harlem was equally surprised by Morello's murder only blocks away. Until that evening, they had no idea there were other rebels. Gagliano and Lucchese were "sneaking" around, "not knowing there was someone else who had the same intentions." Throwing their support to the coalition, they got their vengeance when Girolamo "Bobby Doyle" Santuccio killed replacement boss Joseph Pinzolo on September 5, 1930.[37]

2:45 P.M., WEDNESDAY, NOVEMBER 5, 1930, PELHAM PARKWAY SOUTH, THE BRONX: THE LIEUTENANTS FALL

The anti-Masseria rebellion got its next big break a few months later when soldier Joe Valachi spotted Joe the Boss entering an apartment complex in the Bronx with two of his top lieutenants during the conflict, Alfred Mineo (a Brooklyn boss in his own right) and Stephen Ferrigno (Mineo's deputy). Maranzano dispatched three of his best shooters: Girolamo "Bobby Doyle" Santuccio, Nick Capuzzi, and Sebastiano "Buster" Domingo. Smuggling shotguns in guitar cases, they set up a gunner's nest in a ground-floor apartment.

On Wednesday, November 5, Masseria held a conference with a half dozen of his men at the apartment complex. Around 2:45 p.m., Ferrigno and Mineo left ahead of their boss. As they walked around the garden, shotgun blasts killed them instantly. Hearing the blasts, Joe Masseria hid inside the apartment until the police arrived. Joe the Boss had narrowly evaded gunfire again. But the rapid loss of Masseria's top two lieutenants, his *consigliere* Giuseppe Morello, and his ally Joseph Pinzolo, was destabilizing the Masseria Family.[38]

3–1: Maranzano hit man Girolamo "Bobby Doyle" Santuccio, ca. 1930. (Used by permission of the John Binder Collection)

DECEMBER 1930, BOSTON, MASSACHUSETTS: GENERAL ASSEMBLY OF THE MAFIA

The Mafia clans on the sidelines were unhappy with the bloodshed. Gangland shootings were bad for business. The Masseria Family was being decapitated. The clans called for a general assembly of Mafia representatives to take place in December 1930 in Boston.

The general assembly tried to make peace by stripping Masseria of the title of *capi di capi* and temporarily replacing him with the well-liked Gaspare Messina. The assembly then set up a commission to try to negotiate a peace between the two sides.[39]

Salvatore Maranzano would have no talk of peace with Joe Masseria still alive. Maranzano thwarted peace negotiations and made overtures to potential defectors. "Those who want to cross into my ranks are still in time to do so," said Maranzano. He sent word that if Joe the Boss were disposed of by his own men, there would be no other reprisals.[40]

THE BETRAYAL OF JOE MASSERIA

Joe Masseria's erstwhile lieutenant Charles Luciano had had enough. Luciano had not joined the Masseria Family for the vainglory of bosses. His cabal wanted to end the conflict. And the quickest way was to remove their weakened boss.

Charles Luciano, the high-stakes gambler, secretly accepted the overture from Salvatore Maranzano. They met in a private house in Brooklyn in the spring of 1931. The conversation between the men was veiled, but gravely clear:

"Do you know why you are here?" Salvatore Maranzano began.

"Yes," Luciano answered. He never would have stepped foot there had he been unsure.

"Then I don't have to tell you what has to be done," Maranzano continued.

"No," he replied.

"How much time do you need to do what you have to do?" Maranzano asked.

"A week or two," he answered. And with that, Luciano set out to betray his boss.[41]

2:00 P.M., WEDNESDAY AFTERNOON, APRIL 15, 1931, NUOVA VILLA TAMMARO RESTAURANT: THE ASSASSINATION OF JOE MASSERIA

Joe Masseria spent the winter behind guards at his penthouse atop a fifteen-story complex at 15 West 81st Street just off Central Park. Joe the Boss could not stay cooped up forever.

On Wednesday afternoon, April 15, 1931, Masseria's men persuaded him to venture out to a restaurant called the Nuova Villa Tammaro on Coney Island, Brooklyn.[42] Contrary to his image as a slob, Joe Masseria dressed dapperly: a light grey three-piece tailored suit with handkerchief, a white madras shirt, and black Oxford dress shoes. Properly attired, he went downstairs to his armored sedan and rumbled off to Coney Island.[43]

Around 1:00 p.m., Masseria's sedan arrived outside the Nuova Villa Tammaro. As Masseria walked to the restaurant, he breathed in the warm sea breeze of Coney Island.[44] Contrary to myth, Masseria did not gorge on pasta that afternoon. The purported glutton skipped lunch. Masseria sat around a table with a few men he knew, playing cards for cash and silver. The proprietor Gerardo Scarpato later claimed that he had just stepped out for a walk.[45]

For the first time in his life, Giuseppe Masseria did not see them coming. At 2:00 p.m., as Masseria was sitting in his chair, he was shot from behind. Four bullets hit his back. The fifth and fatal bullet ripped through his brain and exited his eye socket. He fell out of his chair onto the floor. Joe the Boss was dead.[46]

The gunmen walked out of the restaurant in a hurry. Whether from nerves or shock, they left behind four overcoats. The assassins got into an automobile and sped off. Police found their abandoned car about two miles away in Brooklyn. The automobile had been reported stolen; its license plates were unregistered. In the back were a pair of .38 revolvers and a .45 automatic.[47]

The question of who betrayed Joe Masseria has focused on famous *mafiosi*. Multiple insiders confirm that Charles Luciano planned Masseria's assassination. Joe Valachi later testified that he had heard that Vito Genovese, Frank "Cheech" Livorsi, Joseph "Joe Stretch" Stracci, and Ciro Terranova were among those present at the Nuova that afternoon.[48]

But there was another gangster who has since been largely forgotten. In

April 1931, John "Silk Stockings" Giustra was a thirty-two-year-old racketeer on the Brooklyn waterfront. The New York Police Department identified Giustra as their prime suspect in the shooting. In 1940, an internal NYPD note stated: "Confidential information was received by the Detective in the case that the person who shot and killed the deceased was one John Giustra," and that one of the coats left behind "was identified as the property of [Giustra]." Because Giustra himself was murdered on July 9, 1931, the NYPD closed the case.[49] In 1952, another informant on the waterfront stated: "John 'Silk Stocking' Giustre [sic] murdered Joe the Boss and thought he would take over from him," but Phil Mangano, Albert Anastasia, and others "double-crossed Silk Stocking."[50] The conflict may have been affected by yet another individual's crass ambitions.

WEDNESDAY EVENING, APRIL 15, 1931, CHARLES LUCIANO'S RESIDENCE

That evening, Charles Luciano gathered his men at his Manhattan residence. Luciano summoned Vincenzo Troia, an ally of Maranzano, to his residence for a message. "Vincenzo, tell your *compare* [godfather] Maranzano that we killed Masseria not to serve him, but for our personal reasons," Luciano warned.[51] They wanted to go back to making money.

LATE MAY 1931, CONGRESS PLAZA HOTEL, 520 MICHIGAN AVENUE, CHICAGO, ILLINOIS: GENERAL ASSEMBLY OF THE MAFIA

With Masseria's blood still on the floor of Nuova Villa, Maranzano called Al Capone in Chicago. Capone had succeeded in eliminating Joseph Aiello and had become the unquestioned crime boss of the City of Broad Shoulders. They agreed to call a general assembly of the Mafia.[52]

In late May 1931, Al Capone hosted the Mafia's general assembly at the Congress Plaza Hotel on Lake Michigan. A few hundred representatives from Cleveland, Pittsburgh, New York, and elsewhere traveled across the country to Chicago.[53] The mob was in disarray. "In the general assembly ... an indescribable confusion reigned," recalled Nicola Gentile, who attended the conclave. "Some representatives, mindful of the past dictatorial regime of Masseria . . . had proposed to elect for the job of boss of the bosses a commission composed of six," Gentile said. The idea of a power-sharing commission had a lot of support.[54]

The ambitious Salvatore Maranzano outmaneuvered them. Maranzano cynically cut a deal with the Neapolitan Al Capone, the man whom Maranzano only recently had said was "staining the organization" of the Mafia. In exchange for Capone agreeing to "affirm Maranzano's supremacy in the national scene," he would recognize Capone in Chicago after all. Next, Maranzano cajoled or intimidated the smaller clans. It worked. "Maranzano was thus elected boss of the bosses of the United States mafia," explained Gentile.[55]

JUNE 1931, FEDERAL GRAND JURY, CHICAGO, ILLINOIS

"CAPONE IS INDICTED IN INCOME TAX CASE," blared the June 6, 1931, edition of the *New York Times*. Weeks after the general assembly departed Chicago, the United States attorney for Chicago announced that Alphonse Capone was being indicted on charges of income tax evasion on $1 million of *illegal* income ($14 million in present dollars).[56]

Capone's tax indictment shook the underworld. New York mobsters hardly bothered filing income tax returns, and they certainly did not pay taxes on bootlegging and other illegal income. They would have a very difficult time explaining their assets.[57]

AUGUST 1–3, 1931, NUOVA VILLA TAMMARO, CONEY ISLAND, BROOKLYN: MEET THE NEW BOSS OF BOSSES

The Castellammarese threw a banquet in honor of Maranzano from Saturday, August 1 through Monday, August 3, 1931, under the guise of a local Italian festival. Pouring salt in the wound, they chose the same site where Joe Masseria was killed: the Nuova Villa Tammaro restaurant, freshly scrubbed of blood stains.[58]

3–2: Nuova Villa Tammaro restaurant after shooting of Joe Masseria, 1931. Salvatore Maranzano would celebrate his ascension to boss of bosses at the same site in August 1931. (Photo from the *New York Daily News* Archive, used by permission of Getty Images)

The bacchanalian weekend was an intoxicating experience for Maranzano. The clans sent fat envelopes of cash as tribute to the *capo di capi*. "In the banquet room, on the immense decorated table, with magnificent lavishness, there towered a grandiose tray on which handfuls of dollars were placed," described Gentile. The piles of money totaled $115,000 ($1.7 million in current dollars). "*Compare*, these victories have made me drunk!" admitted Maranzano. "I feel a ball of fire inside!"[59]

Like a dictator's parade, there was a palpable phoniness to the honors. The attendees were greeted by Maranzano's soldiers, who steered each attendee to the cash tray. "*Viva il nostro capo!*" shouted his soldiers. "Long live our boss!" Street guys put on airs for the refined boss. "Many, who, even being boors, cared to appear like gentlemen," Gentile recalled. His supplicants praised him a little too much, laughed a little too loudly. "I would like to go to Germany to be more secure," Maranzano mumbled nervously.[60]

EAGLE BUILDING CORPORATION, PARK AVENUE, GRAND CENTRAL BUILDING

The *capo di capi* sets up his empire. He opens an elaborate suite of Art Deco–style offices on the ninth floor of the bustling Grand Central Building at 230 Park Avenue. In the mornings, he walks through the spectacular expanse of Grand Central Station. The Eagle Building Corporation is the official name of the enterprise, though no one knows what it does exactly. He hires an English-speaking secretary. File cabinets contain the meticulous paperwork of business concerns. To be closer to work, he leases a luxurious apartment on 42nd Street in Manhattan.[61]

Beneath the surface is something else. The nominal president of Eagle Building Corporation is James Alescia, a convicted narcotics trafficker who served time at the Atlanta Federal Penitentiary. In the afternoons, the anteroom is full of gangsters waiting impatiently to see the big man. He keeps even important *mafiosi* like Steve Magaddino waiting an hour or more to see him. The *capo di capi* can do that.[62]

SAME AS THE OLD BOSS OF BOSSES

As an aficionado of ancient Rome, Maranzano should have learned from Caligula, who sought to concentrate all power in himself ("Let there be One Lord, One King," he declared). He became the first Roman emperor stabbed to death by conspirators.[63]

Maranzano proved even more power hungry than Masseria. He made a list of people he wanted dead. "Al Capone, Frank Costello, Charley Lucky, Vito Genovese, Vincent Mangano, Joe Adonis, Dutch Schultz," recounted Joe Valachi. "These are all important names at the time." They all happened to be former Masseria allies. So much for no reprisals. An FBI electronic bug picked up Steve Magaddino describing how Maranzano "wanted to shoot in the worst way" various men. "I said what are you crazy . . . there isn't any need to," recalled Magaddino. The Castellammarese, the vaunted band of brothers, started backbiting over Maranzano.[64] Perhaps even more galling, Maranzano began threatening their money, too. There were rumors that Maranzano's men were hijacking booze trucks belonging to fellow *mafiosi* and dividing the spoils. A new cabal began plotting against the *capo di capi*.[65]

Although Charles Luciano was involved again, the roles of Tom Gagliano and Tommy Lucchese of the former Reina Family have been seriously underestimated.[66] *First*, they had motive: Gagliano and Lucchese owned trucking companies in the garment district, an industry Maranzano had been eyeing. Joe Valachi recalled how Tommy Lucchese told him that the *capo di capi* "had been doing a lot of bad," and asked if "I knew if Maranzano hijacked trucks of piece goods."[67]

Second, they had means: Gagliano and Lucchese had become regulars in his Park Avenue office. Bonanno said he learned Lucchese was funneling intelligence on "Maranzano's office habits and his preoccupations with the IRS." Gentile likewise suggested there was a mole in his office.[68] *Third*, they had opportunity. Both would be present at the scene of the crime.

3:45 P.M., THURSDAY AFTERNOON, SEPTEMBER 10, 1931, OFFICE OF SALVATORE MARANZANO: KILLING THE BOSS OF BOSSES

On the afternoon of Thursday, September 10, Mr. Maranzano had his secretary, Miss Francis Samuels, keep several men waiting in the anteroom. In his office, Maranzano sat at his wide desk looking over paperwork. The metal fan buzzed next to the wall clock. Around 3:40 p.m., Tom Gagliano and Tommy Lucchese walked into the anteroom. Minutes ticked by. . . .[69]

At 3:45 p.m. four lawmen burst into the anteroom brandishing badges and guns. Mr. Maranzano had told his men that he'd received a tip that a government raid on his office was imminent. Not to worry, though. His accountants assured him his office records could withstand even the most rigorous examination by the IRS. To avoid a gun charge, Mr. Maranzano instructed his men to stop bringing firearms to the office for the near future. His bodyguard Girolamo Santuccio did not like being unarmed, but he obeyed his boss.[70]

This must have been the raid everyone was expecting. The four lawmen were dressed properly, they flashed metal badges, and they were Jews not Italians. They ordered everyone to line up against the wall of the anteroom. "Who can we talk to?" demanded an agent. Hearing the commotion, Maranzano poked his head out his office.[71]

"I am the one responsible for the office," Maranzano interjected. "You can talk to me." He was prepared for this harassment by the government. "There does not exist any contraband goods here. This office is a commercial office, in place with the law," he declared. One of the lawmen held the group in the anteroom at gunpoint, including his unarmed bodyguard Santuccio. The other agents followed Maranzano into his private office.[72]

The plan was working: they were alone with Maranzano in his inner sanctum. The real names of the lead "agents" were Sam "Red" Levine and Abe "Bo" Weinberg, and they were not IRS agents. They were professional hit men. And they were there to kill Maranzano. Given they were on the ninth floor of a busy office building, their plan was to use stilettos to quietly stab him to death. Except Maranzano figured it out. They started shouting at each other.[73]

Unarmed and outnumbered, the refined gentleman disappeared. Maranzano fought fiercely. A stiletto pierced his left elbow, causing blood to run down his muscular arm, yet he continued fighting. Noise was no longer the assassin's main concern. They reached for their guns and fired shots into Maranzano's right arm, chest, and abdomen. Riddled with bullets, Maranzano fell back into his chair. The assassins then picked up the stilettos and thrust the sharp points into him. The *coup de grâce* pierced an artery in his neck.[74]

3–3: Body of Salvatore Maranzano in his Park Avenue office, September 1931. (Used by permission of the John Binder Collection)

Red Levine ran into the anteroom and told everyone to leave. The hit men ran to the stairs, followed by Tom Gagliano, Tommy Lucchese, and the rest of the waiting men. In a bizarre coincidence, on their way out the departing hit men ran into the Irish hit man Vincent "Mad Dog" Coll, who was on his way to discuss a contract with Maranzano.[75] When Lucchese was questioned as to why he left without checking to see whether Maranzano was still alive, he said lamely, "Nobody likes to stay in a place when something happens." In truth, Lucchese had helped set the trap: his men spent the day distracting Maranzano's soldiers, keeping them from stopping by the office. Everyone had abandoned Maranzano save for two: his loyal bodyguard Girolamo Santuccio and his devoted secretary Miss Samuels, who found their boss dead in his office.[76]

THE PURGE THAT WASN'T

In the aftermath of Maranzano's murder, there were stories that his assassination was coordinated with a nationwide purge of all his loyalists. These rumors gained credence when Richard "Dixie" Davis, a disbarred mob lawyer, claimed in a 1939 *Collier's* article that hit man Bo Weinberg said there was "about ninety guineas knocked off all over the country" simultaneously in a purge that "Americanized the mobs." Less noticed was Davis's admission that he had "never been able to check up the accuracy of Bo's assertion" of a simultaneous mass murder.[77]

When historians looked for evidence of this alleged purge, they could not substantiate it. Poring over newspapers from across the country, they could find only a handful of gangland hits even conceivably connected to the Maranzano assassination.[78] Nevertheless, the "purge myth" abides. John H. Davis's *Mafia Dynasty* asserts that Luciano "ordered a purge of the old guard" in which "sixty Maranzano loyalists" were killed.[79]

The myth is too compelling; it is an archetype of the human mind. The imagery can be traced to the legendary Night of the Sicilian Vespers, when after the Easter evening prayers of March 30, 1282, Sicilians rose up and overnight massacred their French foreign rulers. Giuseppe Verdi immortalized it in his 1861 opera *I Vespri Siciliani*. Director Francis Ford Coppola and writer Mario Puzo were playing on this imagery in their 1972 masterpiece *The Godfather*. In the penultimate sequence, Michael Corleone is shown sponsoring his niece's Roman Catholic baptism as his men simultaneously assassinate his enemies in bloody hits. They are compelling images, but they are just images.[80]

"CASTELLAMMARESE WAR" OR GANG FIGHT?

This leads to a larger point about Joe Bonanno's romantic account. Painting these events as a "war" in service of a mob myth diminishes the gravity of the word *war*. The total number of casualties nationwide in the "Castellammarese War of 1930–1931" was under twenty *mafioso*.[81] To put it in perspective, recall that more than a thousand Prohibition-era bootleggers were killed in New York City between 1920 and 1930—an average of seventy-seven men a year.[82]

Although he occasionally drifts into war language, Nicola Gentile calls the conflict "The Fight between the Gangs." This is a more accurate description. In New York, outside of a small group of men around Masseria and Maranzano, most wiseguys went about their business. Giuseppe Morello and others were not even armed for much of the "war." After the police warned Masseria to stop the fighting, Masseria ordered his men to disarm. He was apparently more worried about a police crackdown.[83]

Joe Bonanno's breathless talk of Maranzano's "wartime staff" and vast supplies of "money, arms, ammunition and manpower" is just hyperbole.[84] Although Joe Valachi heard stories of war chests, he saw little money put into the fight. Valachi testified that Maranzano's four main hit men together were paid the paltry sum of "$25 a week" (about $350 in current dollars). As it was "kind of rough" to survive on his $6 split, Valachi moonlighted as a burglar to make ends meet during the "war."[85] An FBI electronic bug picked up Steve Magaddino mocking Maranzano's meager funding of the hit men. "He didn't give them anything. He only would give them sandwiches," laughed Steve Magaddino.[86]

THE "MOUSTACHE PETES"

Another myth is that the conflict was about a younger generation of "Americanized" mobsters purging the older, tradition-bound "Moustache Petes." In his book *Five Families*, journalist Selwyn Raab claims that "Luciano had become increasingly frustrated by Masseria's refusal to adopt his ideas for modernizing . . . by cooperating with other Italian and non-Italian gangs" and that he "referred disparagingly to Masseria and his ilk as 'Moustache Petes' and 'greasers.'"[87]

Labeling Joe Masseria a "Moustache Pete" renders the term meaningless: Joe the Boss enthusiastically created the first pan-Italian "Americanized" mob. There is also no sign that Masseria barred his men from working with others. The Masseria Family's members collaborated with Irish and Jewish gangsters on the docks, in the garment district, and elsewhere. Indeed, in March 1930, Masseria was arrested in a gambling resort in Miami Beach in the company of Jewish gangsters Harry Brown and Harry "Nig" Rosen.[88]

Neither did the two other *mafiosi* pointed to as "Moustache Petes" fit the stereotype of tradition-bound, ethnically isolated Sicilians. Giuseppe Morello *was* a mustachioed Sicilian, his whiskers drooping down over his gaunt face. Yet when he was boss of his Morello Family, he partnered with Irish counterfeiters Jack Gleason, Tom Smith, and Henry Thompson.[89] Even Salvatore Maranzano had in his inner circle a convicted drug trafficker in James Alescia and a Neapolitan in Joe Valachi. And it was Maranzano who ultimately validated Al Capone and his Chicago Outfit.[90]

LATE SEPTEMBER 1931:
THE CREATION OF THE COMMISSION

After Maranzano, there would never again be an all-powerful boss of bosses. Between 1928 and 1931, the Cosa Nostra saw the murders of three sitting *capo di capi*: Salvatore D'Aquila in October 1928, Joe Masseria in April 1931, and Salvatore Maranzano in September 1931. All three overreached and were violently deposed. Former *capo di capi* Giuseppe Morello was killed in August 1930 as well. The general assembly concluded that giving such a title "to just one, could swell the head of the elected person and induce him to commit unjustifiable atrocities."[91]

As we will see, new technologies and rackets were expanding opportunities for more dispersed crews of wiseguys as well. Their sophisticated operations would stretch across states and multistate regions. No dictatorial boss would be able to control everything. Although the Mafia family structure would be essential to their success, the money operations would be run by the *caporegimes* (captains) and street soldiers.

In the fall of 1931, the general assembly of the Mafia abolished the *capo di capi* title. They replaced it with a power-sharing commission. This was *not* the invention of Charles Luciano. Rather, it was the very same idea that the general assembly of the Mafia nearly adopted back in May 1931. It would serve as a forum to discuss major decisions and arbitrate disputes. As Nicola Gentile explained, "With the administration of this commission one could begin to breathe a more trustworthy air," and men could return to "the best positions from which they could gain large profits."[92]

The Commission, as it came to be called, had seven charter members. Given Gotham's importance, each of the five bosses of the New York families received a seat. These included the incumbent bosses Charles Luciano, Tom Gagliano, and Joseph Profaci, and two new bosses from Brooklyn: Vincent Mangano (who replaced a Maranzano loyalist) and Joseph Bonanno (who replaced Maranzano himself). Steve Magaddino of Buffalo got the sixth seat as an influential Castellammarese with surprising strength in upstate New York. Al Capone held the seventh seat for Chicago, which also represented by proxy the smaller western clans.[93]

Capone's seat on the Commission would be short-lived. On October 6, 1931, the trial of *United States v. Alphonse Capone* commenced in federal court in Chicago. Twelve days later, on October 18, 1931, the federal jury found him guilty of income tax evasion for failing to pay taxes on illegal revenues. Paul "The Waiter" Ricca of Chicago (who stands on the far left of the cover of this book) would take Capone's seat on the Commission. Maranzano's fear of the taxman was not so crazy after all.[94]

THE COMMISSION: FOUNDING MEMBERS, 1931

3–4: Tomasso Gagliano, boss of the Gagliano Family. (Courtesy of the National Archives and Records Administration)

3–5: Charles Luciano, boss of the Luciano Family. (Courtesy of the New York Police Department)

3–6: Vincent Mangano, boss of the Mangano Family. (Courtesy of the National Archives and Records Administration)

3–7: Joseph Bonanno, boss of the Bonanno Family. (Used by permission of the NYC Municipal Archives)

3–8: Joseph Profaci, boss of the Profaci Family. (Courtesy of the National Archives and Records Administration)

3–9: Al Capone, boss of the Chicago Outfit (© Bettman/ CORBIS)

3–10: Steve Magaddino, boss of the Buffalo Arm. (Photo by Walter Albertin, courtesy of the Library of Congress Prints and Photographs Division, New York World-Telegram and Sun Newspaper Photograph Collection)

Although Joe Bonanno and others have portrayed the "Castellammarese War of 1930–1931" as a defense of the honor of the Castellammarese clan, the facts show it to be something less romantic. Rather, the Mafia Rebellion of 1928–1931 was mostly about money and power. But the rise of the modern Mafia was more than just the result of high-level intrigue among mob bosses. Our next chapter looks at how the Mafia's soldiers gained footholds in the labor unions.

4

THE RACKETEER COMETH

How the Mob Infiltrated Labor Unions

Q. You don't call a Chinaman or an Italian a white man?
No, sir; an Italian is a Dago.
—Testimony of construction superintendent
in Congressional hearings (1890)

The thefts and pocket pickings now pale into insignificance
when compared to the achievements of the racketeers . . .
the rackets in connection with liquor, dope, food, milk, the
building trades . . . the use of gangsters in labor troubles.
—Testimony of criminologist
in Congressional hearings (1934)

In the 1950s, Giovanni "Johnny Dio" Dioguardi was a national expert on the art of labor racketeering. He had come a long way from his childhood in Little Italy.[1] When he was twenty years old in 1934, Dioguardi represented the Allied Truckmen's Mutual Association in a dispute with Local 816 of the International Brotherhood of Teamsters.[2] A labor mercenary, Dioguardi later *created* "paper locals" of the Teamsters for his ally Jimmy Hoffa. Dioguardi forged himself into a "labor consultant" by applying select mayhem at weak points in a union.[3]

But Johnny Dio had also been riding a wave of social forces for decades. He came of age as the labor movement was taking off in the 1930s, and he dealt with unions comprised of southern Italian immigrants. This chapter reveals *why* and *how* the Cosa Nostra captured so many union locals in Gotham. Demographics and the labor movement converged in the 1930s to fuel the Mafia's takeover of unions.

"ETHNIC SUCCESSION IN CRIME": AN INCOMPLETE EXPLANATION FOR ORGANIZED CRIME

In 1960, the sociologist Daniel Bell argued that organized crime was one of the "ladders of social mobility in America" for new immigrant groups.[4] Building on Bell's idea, Francis Ianni argued in his 1974 book *Black Mafia: Ethnic Succession in Organized Crime* that there was a process of "ethnic succession" in crime: as immigrant groups assimilated they were replaced by newer groups. As Ianni put it, "the Irish were succeeded in organized crime by the Jews . . . Italians came next . . . [and] they are being replaced by . . . blacks."[5]

Later writers have pointed out that the ethnic succession model is too one-dimensional. Immigrant groups were treated differently, and their respective crime syndicates emerged at different times.[6] Therefore, to understand why the Mafia became the dominant labor racketeers during the New Deal, we need to compare the Irish, Black, Jewish, and Italian gangsters against the backdrop of New York history.

THE EARLY GANGSTERS: WHY THE IRISH RACKETEERS GRADUALLY DISAPPEARED

The Irish immigrated first and assimilated earlier. The Irish Potato Famine of 1845–1852 caused hundreds of thousands of Irish to leave for New York by the Civil War. In Gotham, they endured anti-Irish and anti-Catholic bigotry, urban squalor, and poverty.[7]

By the end of the century though, the Irish were assimilating rapidly. Irish politicians were elected mayor in 1881 and 1893, and Irish voters were filling government patronage jobs.[8] By 1930, an astounding 52 percent of the City of New York's public-sector employees were Irish. As historian Jay Dolan put it, "Where once the refrain was 'No Irish need apply,' it now may as well have been 'Only Irish need apply'!"[9] Meanwhile, about 21 percent of New York's Irish were married to a non-Irish spouse, a rate three times higher than Jews and southern Italians.[10]

The Irish underworld was affected by these social forces. The assimilation of Irish immigrants reduced Irish laborers in racketeer-prone industries. "We want somebody to do the dirty work; the Irish are not doing it any longer," said a police official bluntly in 1895. "We can't get along without the Italians."[11] As Irish enclaves disappeared, so too did the Irish street gangs. When the Five Points slum was Irish, it was the home territory for Irish gangs like the Roche Guard. By the 1890s the Five Points was Italian and the Irish gangs were gone. The Hudson Dusters and the Gopher Gang were confined to the Irish West Side of Manhattan.[12]

The Irish gangsters of South Brooklyn had a sorry ending. On December 26, 1925, Richard "Pegleg" Lonergan and five men of his White Hand gang got drunk and had a bad idea. They took taxicabs over to the Adonis Social Club, an Italian mob hangout in Brooklyn. Staggering into the hall, one boasted that his brother could "lick the whole bunch single-handed." Unfortunately, Al Capone was sitting in the club, fresh from Chicago, where he had been fighting Irish bootleggers. A hail of bullets killed "Pegleg" Lonergan and two compatriots.[13]

While Prohibition temporarily boosted the Irish bootleggers, the Irish mob as a whole continued to decline. Joe Valachi started out with an Irish gang before joining the Mafia. The Irish assassin Vincent "Mad Dog" Coll ended up working for Salvatore Maranzano. Madden left for Hot Springs, Arkansas in 1935.[14] Had Irish immigration peaked forty years later, organized crime may have been quite different. We might today be discussing the Dwyer, Higgins, Lonergan, Madden, and McGrath gangs of the Irish mob.

THE RACE FACTOR: WHY AFRICAN-AMERICAN AND CHINESE RACKETEERS WERE ISOLATED

Though African-American gangsters were strong in black Harlem and San Juan Hill, there were no major black labor racketeers in New York City. This was not for lack of interest. In 1935, a former FBI agent reported that Casper Holstein, Harlem's "Bolito King" (a numbers lottery), was backing union violence in his native Virgin Islands.[15] Although Chinese tongs engaged in forms of rack-eteering in Chinatown, they were nonentities in Gotham's unions.[16] This was due in part to their smaller numbers, but it was also the result of prejudice in the underworld.

African-American and Chinese racketeers had relatively few entry points to union hierarchies. The building trades were notorious for preserving the Irish and Italian dominance of the construction industry at the expense of black workers. The International Longshoremen's Association did not have a single black union organizer on staff into the 1950s. It is inconceivable that any African-American longshoreman with criminal ties could have risen to be a union pier boss in the way that Anthony Anastasio did.[17]

Racial distrust ran through the underworld, too. As we will see, the Cor-sican drug traffickers refused to work with African Americans. The black gang-ster Frank Lucas recalls how even after he became friends with Vincent "The Chin" Gigante in prison, they "never talked business," since they "wouldn't have had anything to talk about in that sense."[18]

SOMETIME RIVALS AND FREQUENT COLLABORATORS: THE JEWISH RACKETEERS

Only the Jewish syndicates were roughly on par with the Cosa Nostra as of the 1930s. The Jewish gangsters have been portrayed as hired help for the Mafia. They were more than that. Jewish and Italian gangsters regularly met on equal footing and pulled off schemes together. Some like Meyer Lansky and Moe Dalitz worked alongside wiseguys well into the 1960s.[19]

Overall though, the Jewish crime syndicates were being surpassed by the Mafia starting roughly in the mid-1930s. Why did the Jewish labor racketeers decline?

Large-scale Jewish immigration began somewhat earlier than south Italian immigration, and Jews exited racketeer-prone industries somewhat earlier.[20] Driven out by pogroms from urbanized, artisanal communities in Eastern Europe, 64 percent of Jewish immigrants were artisans or skilled workers. By comparison, south Italian immigrants, who came largely from underdeveloped rural areas, were about 25 percent artisans and skilled workers.[21] The children of Jewish immigrants were far more likely to become business managers, sole proprietors, or professionals. Jews went to college at higher rates than any other group, especially after the Second World War. By 1950, 75 percent of second-generation Jews were white-collar workers, compared to 33 percent of second-generation Italians.[22]

Potential sources of new Jewish gangsters were disappearing as well. In the 1940s and '50s, Jews flocked to the suburbs in huge numbers, causing inner-city enclaves to recede. Brownsville, Brooklyn, was once the home base of Jewish gangsters.[23] By the time Henry Hill was growing up in Brownsville in the 1950s, he was drawn to Paul Vario's crew of the Lucchese Family.[24] The Jewish gangs also appear to be less kinship-based than the Mafia "families." Although there are dozens of books by ex-mobsters who followed relatives into the Mafia (for example, Michael Franzese's *Blood Covenant*),[25] there are virtually no equivalent memoirs by Jewish criminals who followed family into the mob. As historian Jenna Weissman Joselit puts it, organized crime "was a one-generation phenomenon" for Jews in New York.[26]

MOB ON THE ASCENT: THE ITALIAN-AMERICAN MAFIA

The Italian-American Mafia was best positioned to take advantage of the growth of labor unions in the 1930s. The reasons for this lay in patterns of immigration and labor force participation.

South Italians in the Labor Force: An "Inbetween People"

The early Sicilian immigrants, with their dark skin and unfamiliar customs, were deemed not fully "white" in the eyes of many native-born Americans. As the scholar Robert Orsi has shown, south Italians were treated like an "inbetween people," who were "neither securely white nor nonwhite."[27] When a construction superintendent was asked about Italian laborers at a Congressional hearing in 1892, he gave this revealing answer:

Q.   You don't call a Chinaman or an Italian a white man?
A.   No, sir; an Italian is a Dago.[28]

Those from the *Mezzogiorno*, the economically underdeveloped south of Italy, were largely agricultural or unskilled laborers, and came under the *padrone* system of contract labor.

As a result, Sicilians and other south Italians were relegated to the toughest, dirtiest jobs. As a 1931 study found, "The Italian has perhaps been the most generally abused of all the foreign born" and thus Italians "have done the hard and dangerous work in the community."[29] This is reflected in the labor force. Italians worked disproportionately in Gotham's most labor-intensive industries. They represented 40 percent or more of the building trades and the garment manufacturing, longshoring, and waste hauling industries (see table 4–1).

Table 4–1: The Italian-American Workforce
Italian Workers in Unionized Labor Forces in New York City, ca. 1935–1955,
~ Total Numbers and Percentage of Labor Force[30]

Building Trades	Garment Manufacturing	Longshoring	Waste Hauling
100,000 Italians (out of 231,000)	100,000 Italians (out of 250,000)	15,000 Italians (out of 24,000)	1,500 Italians (out of 2000)
43% of labor force	40% of labor force	62% of labor force	70% of labor force

South Italians were a significant portion of the seventy thousand teamsters so critical to moving goods through the city. Most of the ten thousand independent ice and coal dealers were from southern Italy. About 90 percent of the thirteen hundred licensed pushcart peddlers of fruits and vegetables were Italians. Fully one-third of the eighteen thousand members of New York's largest musicians' union were Italians who, along with African Americans and Jews, were essential to the nightclub business.[31] These were all "fragile" sectors prone to extortion or racketeering.

Why the Mafia was Poised for Labor Racketeering

Driven into the most labor-intensive jobs, Italian workers ironically came to dominate key labor forces by the 1930s (see table 4–1). The Little Italies were still thriving enclaves, skeptical of police, the home base of *mafiosi*, and the recruiting grounds for young men. At the same time, second-generation Italian Americans were increasingly accepted as "white" by society. "The Chinese who seeks to leave his Chinatown is under a severe handicap not experienced by the Italian who emerges from Little Italy," observed a sociologist in 1931.[32] During the New Deal, Italian American workers became strong constituencies, courted by labor leaders, and in control of many union locals.[33]

These forces positioned the Mafia families for labor racketeering. Racketeers preyed on industries and unions that were most accessible to them. As historian Jenna Weissman Joselit explained, early Jewish racketeers took advantage of "the kosher poultry and garment industries while the Italians followed suit by exploiting their countrymen in the fish, fruit, and vegetable markets."[34] The modern Mafia likewise thrived in industries that were heavily southern Italian.[35]

What explains this connection? There are multiple reasons:

First, union locals comprised of Italian workers demanded to be represented by Italian labor leaders. This limited rival Irish and Jewish racketeers. The Irish presidents of the ILA ceded the Brooklyn locals to Italian mobsters for this very reason. "[President] Teddy [Gleason] is still Irish. You understand? He joined forces because he got no choice," said racketeer Sonny Montella on a surveillance bug.[36] In the construction industry, while Irish leaders held on to the highest skilled building trades, there were union locals made up entirely of Italians, some of which came under the influence of *mafiosi*.[37]

Second, Italian *mafiosi* could call on neighborhood and kinship ties in Italian labor forces—"networking" in today's parlance. ILA official Emil Camarda had known Mafia boss Vincent Mangano from growing up together in Sicily. One of his successors, ILA Local 1814 official Anthony Scotto, had as an in-law Albert Anastasia. When the boxer Rocky Graziano was turning professional, connected guys in the neighborhood introduced him to Eddie Coco, a mob associate, and told the young fighter that Coco would be his new manager.[38]

Third, Italian mobsters could conversely apply social pressures to roll over dissidents. When John Montesano, the owner of a family waste-hauling business, wanted to get out of a partnership with a mobbed-up carter, the Mafia demanded he pay a gratuitous $5,000 fee. Montesano was pressured into paying by a blood relative who also happened to be a member of the mob. "What is wrong with you, kid? Every time I turn around, you are in trouble," his relative warned.[39] Similarly, it was extremely difficult to reform the Brooklyn waterfront when so many ILA thugs and convicts lived amongst the longshoremen.

Fourth, as Italian workers became business owners in these industries, it facilitated collusive behavior between business and labor. Since the waste-hauling industry was made up of Italian families who knew each other, it was easy to form cartels to exclude outsiders.[40] Likewise, as Italian construction workers became material men and suppliers, Mafia-run cartels flourished. Sammy "The Bull" Gravano, an ex-construction worker, transitioned easily into the building rackets as a rising member of the Gambino Family.[41]

THE MAFIA'S TAKEOVER OF UNION LOCALS IN THE 1930s

The Mafia families used these entry points to emerge as the top labor racketeers in industry after industry. As we saw earlier, Italian gangsters like Paolo Vacca-relli and the Anastasio brothers took over ILA locals as the workforces changed from Irish to Italian. By the 1930s, the Cosa Nostra controlled ILA locals in South Brooklyn, Staten Island, and key Manhattan piers.

New York's construction industry saw a similar evolution. During the 1920s, the Lockwood Committee investigation uncovered "tribute" payoffs to building trades czar Robert Brindell, and business cartels engineered by the building con-tractors. Out of the more than five hundred defendants who were prosecuted, *none* of the labor officials, and only a small set of building contractors, were Ital-ians. Starting in the late 1950s, scores of *mafiosi*, mob-linked labor officials, and contractors were being prosecuted or investigated for similar rackets.[42]

In Lower Manhattan's garment industry, the Mafia entered the industry after Italian workers opened their own garment shops. The Cosa Nostra was very conscious of the new opportunities this presented. "It used be that that this industry was all Jewish, but now the Italians are really getting into it," John Dio-guardi explained to other mobsters. "Guys like Joe Stretch [Joe Stracci] control big companies like Zimmet and Stracci." The Mafia focused on trucking union locals in the garment district, and on diverting production to nonunion shops.[43]

In the International Brotherhood of Teamsters, President Daniel Tobin had once dismissed Italian immigrants as "rubbish."[44] As these new immigrants became truckers, the IBT organized them. Later on, Tobin began receiving death threats from mobsters seeking to "break into our local unions." *Mafiosi* Vito Genovese and Joseph "Socks" Lanza defeated a campaign to reform IBT Local 202 by branding their opponents as Communists and making nationalist appeals to Italian teamsters. Jimmy Hoffa cut deals with Anthony "Tony Ducks" Corallo and John Dioguardi.[45] IBT official Roy Williams dealt with Italian, Jewish, and some Irish mobsters because that was "the way New York is separated out anyway."[46]

THE NEW DEAL: THE SURGE OF LABOR UNIONS IN THE 1930s

The Mafia's racketeers came to power just as the labor unions were taking off in the 1930s. Simply put, the Cosa Nostra had great timing.

After a long history of employer attacks on unions, New Deal–era legislation granted unprecedented rights and protections to labor unions.[47] Labor union membership surged. In 1908, New York City had 240,000 union members. By 1950, union membership quadrupled to a million—upwards of one-third of Gotham's workforce.[48]

Although legitimate unionists were the main beneficiaries, the Mafia took advantage of the shift toward labor as well. In the first year of operation of the government's new Regional Labor Boards (1933–34), complaints and arbitration demands against employers were filed by none other than: Building Service Employees Local 51B, represented by George Scalise, a partner of *mafioso* Anthony Carfano;[49] IBT Local 202, a mob-controlled trucking local in the fresh-food markets, which would see its union officials go to prison for racketeering;[50] and Teamsters Local 138, which was controlled by Jewish racketeer Louis "Lepke" Buchalter, who used the union and a trucking association to extort payoffs in the baking industry.[51]

Many union locals ended up sheltering racketeers from scrutiny, too. With notable exceptions, like those of David Dubinsky of the International Ladies'

Garment Workers' Union (ILGWU) and Walter Reuther of the United Automobile Workers (UAW), national unions avoided dealing with racketeers in union locals. Reform was stymied by a hands-off approach to locals, mobster intimidation, and the weakness or indifference of rank-and-file members. Meanwhile, J. Edgar Hoover's FBI was lackluster in pursuing cases of union corruption.[52]

THE MOB'S UNION LEVER

The labor union became a new lever of power for the Mafia. Not only was labor racketeering a moneymaker for the Mafia families, but it also gave them influence over businessmen and politicians in New York and the United States. "We got our money from gambling, but our real power, our real strength, came from the unions," said mobster Vincent "Fish" Cafaro. "Ultimately, it was labor racketeering that made Cosa Nostra part of the sociopolitical power structure of twentieth-century America," James Jacobs argues convincingly.[53]

Greater coordination between the Mafia syndicates, the expansion of national labor unions, and the advent of telephones and airplanes all facilitated labor racketeering across the country. "The gangsters who infiltrated a local in New York were tied into a national syndicate that included gangsters attempting to do the same thing in Chicago, Kansas City, and in numerous other locations where Teamster locals and criminal organizations existed side by side," described a report on the IBT.[54] In dealing with the International Alliance of Theatrical Stage Employees (IATSE), Chicago Outfit leader Paul Ricca told mobsters "to be free to call on Charlie Lucky [Luciano] or on Frank Costello . . . if we find any difficulties here [in New York] in our work, and if we need anything to call on them, because that is their people."[55]

Take John Dioguardi's consulting work on the ILGWU. In 1953, Dioguardi flew to California to assist mobsters in entering the garment industry in Los Angeles. He told them to target an ILGWU official. "What you've got to do is hurt this fucking guy and make him run to New York," Dubinsky advised. "Let [David] Dubinsky know you're going to have your own fucking way out here." They sent a union official to the hospital with a cracked skull, and opened a union-free shop. The kid bully from Little Italy had gone national.[56]

CASE STUDIES OF MOB POWER
OVER NEW YORK UNIONS

Equally important as taking power was keeping and using that power. The following case studies show how the Mafia controlled and exploited unions.

Case One: Squashing Union Reformers—The International Longshoremen's Association on the South Brooklyn Docks

The Mafia used fear and terror to maintain its stranglehold on the South Brooklyn waterfront. In 1939, an insurgent led a rank-and-file uprising of longshoremen. The mob's reaction taught a terrible lesson to anyone who would challenge its power.

The Mob's Waterfront in the 1930s

No outsider could crack the waterfront. Organizers for the Communist Party USA in Manhattan got nowhere on the other side of the East River. CPUSA organizers spread leaflets attacking the ILA in Brooklyn, but they gained little traction among the Catholic longshoremen.[57]

Although the prosecutor Thomas E. Dewey obtained convictions of racketeers in the restaurant and garment business, and sent Charles Luciano to prison in 1936 for a prostitution ring, he got nowhere on the waterfront. Later in life, Dewey revealed what happened. "There was a time when we thought we had it organized . . . to really make frontal assault on the waterfront," he recalled. "We finally found a policeman who would undertake to be head of the undercover investigation." The officer had second thoughts. "After a week of it, he came back and said, 'I'm sorry. I'd like to ask to be excused from this assignment,'" recounted Dewey.

The prosecutor described the web of power on the docks. "The unions were filled with ex-convicts," he noted. "They don't talk." The shippers were often complicit in schemes to ensure labor peace. "You can never tell whether what you've found is extortion or bribery," explained Dewey. Most importantly, the "political power of some people connected with the water front is very great, and they've always been close to Tammany Hall." The racket buster was stymied on the docks.[58]

The Insurgent: Peter Panto and the 1939 Campaign

Peter Panto was an unlikely insurgent. Born in America in 1911, he spent his childhood in Italy and returned to Brooklyn as a young man. Like so many poor Italians, Panto became a longshoreman on the Red Hook piers. As a member of ILA Local 929, Panto paid union dues to Anthony Giustra (brother of the slain gangster Johnny "Silk Stockings" Giustra).[59]

Panto was stirred by the indignities he suffered under his own union. Panto gave back almost half his salary through kickbacks to get work. What really bothered him was that the ILA sold eight thousand mandatory "tickets" to a Christopher Columbus Day Ball in a hall that held only five hundred. For all that, the ILA did not even hold rank-and-file meetings.[60]

In the spring of 1939, the twenty-eight-year-old Panto began organizing private meetings with fellow longshoremen. Panto had an infectious smile, he spoke both Italian and English, and he was persuasive in both. He started calling public meetings in Brooklyn. The audience grew from several hundred to over twelve hundred longshoremen by July. In Panto's speeches, he raised practical issues like: "Are you in favor of Union Hiring Halls?" or "Are you ready . . . to help organize the I.L.A. on a democratic basis?"[61] To the mob, those were dangerous ideas.

Albert the Executioner

A gangster took Panto aside one night. "*Benedetto* [blessings]," the gangster said menacingly as he sliced his finger across his neck.[62] Panto was undaunted. On Wednesday, July 12, 1939, Emil Camarda, union boss of the Brooklyn ILA locals, summoned Panto to his office. When he arrived, a bunch of goons were standing around Camarda. "Peter, some of the boys don't like the way you're calling meetings and making a rumpus," Camarda told him. "Some of them might want to harm you, but I told them you're a good fellow." Panto refused to stop.[63]

Albert Anastasia had had enough of this troublemaker. Nothing was getting through to this guy. Anastasia talked to his henchmen about "some guy Albert had a lot of trouble with down in the waterfront," who was "threatening to expose the whole thing." Albert the Executioner came up with a solution.[64]

On Friday, July 14, 1939, Panto was shaving for a night out with his fiancée. A call was placed to Panto at the store across from his boardinghouse in Red Hook. The caller persuaded him to come to a meeting. "I don't think it is entirely on the square," he told his fiancée. Nevertheless, he kissed her goodbye, put on his fedora, and walked out the door. Panto was last seen entering the automobile of an ILA official with two men, one of whom was later identified as Anthony Romero.[65]

Peter Panto looked out the window at Manhattan as the car crossed over to New Jersey. When they arrived, Panto walked into the house for the meeting. Waiting inside were James "Jimmy" Ferraco, Emanuel "Mendy" Weiss ... and Albert Anastasia. As soon as Panto walked in he realized what was happening. Panto lunged for the door. Mendy Weiss, a hulking thug, grabbed him and "mugged him." Panto bit and scratched Weiss's huge hands, desperately trying to break his grasp. We can only imagine the terror running through the young longshoreman's mind in those final moments.[66]

The men transported his dead body to the marshy meadowlands outside Lyndhurst, New Jersey. They dumped him in a shallow grave and covered him in quicklime.[67] Whenever the Mafia is romanticized as the "Honorable Society," or minimized as a supplier of victimless vice, Peter Panto's last night on earth should be remembered.

4–1: Official photograph of Peter Panto distributed by NYPD in 1939. (Courtesy of the New York Police Department)

Terrorizing the Rank-and-File Committee

After Panto disappeared, graffiti started appearing on pier facilities: "Where is Pete Panto?" It became a rallying cry. That October, Pete Mazzie, a twenty-three-year-old longshoreman, called for a public meeting of the Rank-and-File Committee. About four hundred longshoremen filled the chairs of the smoke-filled hall. A gang of thugs took seats smack in the middle of the hall.

"This is the opening of a headquarters where longshoremen can meet and talk," Mazzie declared. "The rank-and-file committee is taking up where Pete Panto left off. So any phonies present tonight will find—"

"What do you mean by phonies?" shouted a tall thug popping up from his chair.

"I'll tell you what I mean—" Mazzie tried to continue.

The thug stormed up to the speaker's table and slugged Mazzie. Another goon bashed a chair over Mazzie's head. By the time the police arrived, the hall was a wreck and Mazzie was on his way to the emergency room.[68]

4–2: Albert Anastasia, October 1936. (Courtesy of the New York Police Department)

Even as he was recovering, Mazzie was warned that he "better watch his step, and remember what happened to Pete Panto."[69] In January 1941, investigators dug up Panto's body in New Jersey. His corpse was so badly decomposed that he had to be identified by his teeth. Brooklyn District Attorney William O'Dwyer's office publicly identified the suspects as Anastasia, Ferraco, and Weiss. O'Dwyer later claimed the case fell apart on November 12, 1941, when one of the key witnesses, Abe "Kid Twist" Reles fell—or was thrown—out of the sixth-floor window of the Half Moon Hotel while under police custody. Few longshoremen believed Reles fell on his own. The violence had an effect. Panto became a martyr on the docks. But fewer and fewer longshoremen dared appear at public meetings. The uprising fell apart.[70]

Case Two: Running a Union Racket Quietly— United Seafood Workers Local 359

Although the Mafia demonstrated it was capable of extreme violence, most of the time it sought to manage its labor rackets quietly. When possible, the Cosa Nostra preferred more subtle forms of coercion, and collaboration with corrupt businessmen. This was revealed in the 1935 federal prosecution under the Sherman Antitrust Act of Joseph "Socks" Lanza of the United Seafood Workers Local 359.[71]

The Mob in the Fresh Fish Markets

Fresh fish rots quickly. This biological fact gave the fish handlers leverage beyond their rank in life. The teenage Joseph "Socks" Lanza realized this soon after he started working in the Fulton Fish Market in the 1910s. In 1923, when he was barely twenty, the precocious Lanza helped organize Local 359 of the United Seafood Workers union. Lanza's cronies founded the Fulton Market Watchmen and Patrol Association to collect a "protection fund" from retailers to prevent thefts or "labor troubles" in handling their perishable fish.[72]

The first investigations into the fish markets focused not on the Mafia, but on Jewish fish wholesalers. In July 1925, the federal government charged seventeen fish wholesalers for conspiring to violate the Sherman Antitrust Act by "creating an artificial market and dictating prices to retailers." They pled guilty and paid fines.[73] Then, in September 1926, the state attorney general charged fish companies with another conspiracy to "restrain competition, increase prices and conduct a monopoly in white fish, carp, pike and other fished used by Jewish people during the forthcoming holidays." But witnesses failed to cooperate.[74]

June 1935, United States v. Joseph Lanza, et al.,
Federal Courthouse, Manhattan

In *United States v. Joseph Lanza, et. al.*, the United States Attorney charged eighty individuals and corporations with conspiring to monopolize the fresh-water fish industry in New York City in violation of the Sherman Antitrust Act. Joseph "Socks" Lanza and his United Seafood Workers local were accused of conspiring with several crooked businessmen. The defendants included twenty-five corporations with respectable names like the Delta Fish Company, Inc., the Geiger Products Corporation, and the Lay Fish Company.[75]

The June 1935 trial did not involve any accounts of homicide or even physical assaults. Rather, the witness testimony revealed how the conspirators cleverly used a trade association and business coercion, along with the labor union and subtle threats, to obtain control of the fish markets. Lanza lurked in the background, only occasionally revealing himself.

The Trade Association and Business Coercion

The aim of the conspiracy was to control the supply of fresh fish going into New York City to thereby artificially fix prices. To accomplish this, several retail fish dealers organized into a citywide trade association. The trial testimony showed that the retail dealers combined "into what became known as the Bronx, Upper Manhattan, and Brooklyn Fish Dealers Association, with one of the defendants [Jerome] Kiselik, acting as the so-called impartial chairman."[76]

To extend their control, Kiselik and a wholesale organizer named O'Keefe set up a meeting of the fish wholesalers at the Half Moon Hotel in Coney Island, Brooklyn "to organize to remedy the market conditions in concert with retailers." Joe Lanza sat with Kiselik at a table on the dais, but he did not speak during the meeting.[77]

The businessmen defendants formed a committee to "work out a satisfactory plan for the division of profits on a percentage basis" and to "collect information as to supply, prices ... and the elimination of duplication" in the fresh-fish market of New York City. Although it sounded benign, as the court properly found, the scheme "was really one to monopolize the business" of the fish market in violation of the Sherman Antitrust Act. And it was done by businessmen.[78]

United Seafood Workers Local 359 and Subtle Threats

The fish cartel probably could not have been maintained without Joseph "Socks" Lanza and the United Seafood Workers union. As shown in detail later, cartels are intrinsically unstable, and usually require some mechanism to police the cartel. In this case, it was Joe Lanza and the United Seafood Workers union. Given that almost all the hand truckmen in the fish markets in Gotham belonged to this union, it was a powerful stick in the hands of racketeers.[79]

The Seafood Workers union was integral to policing the cartel and controlling the supply of fish. When a new retailer brought in fish he bought from outside of New York, he would be educated on the cartel's rules. Kiselik would come by to "straighten this thing out" and instruct the retailer that he "should buy fish in New York." Lanza would drop in on the conversation but say nothing. The union boss's mere presence was sufficient.[80]

For wayward retailers, Lanza engineered union problems to bring them into line. When a veteran retailer brought in fish from Philadelphia, Kiselik came by demanding to know why the retailer dared to purchase sweet-water fish in Philadelphia. The retailer replied simply that "it was cheaper." A few minutes later, fish handlers returned and took the Philadelphia fish off his truck.[81] When Booth Fisheries, one of the largest fish dealers balked at some of the association's fees, Kiselik and Lanza together paid a visit to some of Booth's intermediaries. With Lanza standing nearby, Kiselik told the intermediaries that Booth Fisheries "was not behaving in a cooperative fashion" and that he hoped "the matter might be straightened out." Booth ended up paying the agreed fees and, in exchange, was allotted 12.5 percent of the fresh-fish market in New York—a blatantly illegal allocation of the market.[82]

For Joe Lanza's "services," fish dealers funneled strange fees and payoffs to him as well. At trial, a fish retailer testified about what happened when he opened a new place of business in the market. The retailer was visited by Kiselik of the fish retailers' association. Kiselik asked the new retailer to "see his friend Joe Socks" and pay him $500 (about $8,000 in 2013 dollars). The only reason

Kiselik gave for the payment was that "Joe Socks needs the money." During an intimidating follow-up conversation with the retailer, Lanza stood silent a couple steps away. Joe Socks got his money. But he was convicted in June 1935 and sent to federal prison.[83]

Case Three: Evading a Union—Keeping Out the International Ladies' Garment Workers' Union

The Cosa Nostra's relationship to labor unions was purely opportunistic. When the Cosa Nostra could not gain control over a labor union, it often sought to end-run the union altogether. This is shown by the mob's attempts to keep out the International Ladies' Garment Workers' Union (ILGWU) from certain garment shops. It led to tragic results in 1949.

The Mafia and the Garment Industry

The garment industry's labor force was originally Jewish, and so were its gangsters. Benjamin "Dopey Benny" Fein was hired as a "labor slugger" for the United Hebrew Trades union to do battle with *shtarkes* (strongarm men) hired by employers to break strikes. In 1926, the Communist Party–controlled ILGWU brought in the gangster Arnold Rothstein to end a disastrous strike.[84] Later Jewish gangsters graduated to more sophisticated labor racketeering. In 1936, Louis Buchalter and his friend Jacob "Gurrah" Shapiro were convicted of violating the Sherman Antitrust Act by restricting competition in the fur-dressing trade.[85] Buchalter and his henchmen were later found guilty of murder for the slaying of Joseph Rosen, a candy-store owner who was cooperating in an investigation. They were electrocuted at Sing Sing in 1944.[86]

Italians who grew up in Lower Manhattan were familiar with the needles trades around them. Indeed, Joe Masseria and Charlie Luciano worked briefly in the industry before they were *mafiosi*. The Gagliano Family had held interests in piecework shops since the early 1930s.[87]

By the time the Mafia came to the forefront, the ILGWU was under the leadership of David Dubinsky, a dynamic unionist with a record of fighting both Communists and gangsters. The ILGWU became a strong union that prevented the mob from gaining control over its upper-level administration. But even Dubinsky gave up on some areas of the union, like Local 102, a trucking local hopelessly lost to gangsters.[88]

Mafiosi end-ran the ILGWU by diverting production to their own mob-owned shops. Joe Valachi described how he kept his dress shop union-free. "I never belonged in any union," Valachi recalled. "If I got in trouble, any union organizer came around, all I had to do was call up John Dio or Tommy Dio and all my troubles were straightened out."[89] By shutting out the ILWGU, these garment contractors held major competitive advantages over rival companies.

"Not to the Bothered by the Union"

Rosedell Manufacturing Company ran a nonunion garment shop on West 35th Street. In 1948, ILGWU organizer Willie Lurye was leading union picketers outside the company's building. They talked truckers out of crossing the line and slowed deliveries into the factory. Rosedell's owners cast about for someone to deal with their union problem.[90]

Rosedell's owners were put in contact with Benedict Macri. Macri had served as a front man for Albert Anastasia. His brother Vincent Macri was Anastasia's close friend and bodyguard. Rosedell's owners told Macri they wanted either "an International contract or—not to be bothered by the union." For Macri's services in dealing with the ILGWU, the owners promised Macri a 25 percent share of their business profits.[91]

Macri had no interest in getting an ILGWU contract. Macri tried to restart operations under the new "Macri-Lee Corporation," but he still could not get deliveries through his freight entrance. Next, they tried to open a secret cutting room on Tremont Avenue in central Bronx. On Friday, May 6, 1949, the ILGWU picketers got wind of it and went up to the Bronx. According to prosecutors, the pickets slashed about eighteen dresses, infuriating Macri.[92]

On Monday, May 9, 1949, Willie Lurye was back on the picket line on West 35th Street. In the late afternoon, the ILGWU organizers started to go home. Around 3:00 p.m., Lurye went into the building lobby to make a call from a telephone booth. When Lurye was in the booth, two men trapped him. He screamed in terror as they stabbed him repeatedly. Lurye, bleeding, staggered to the sidewalk. He died the next day. On May 12, 1949, an estimated one hundred thousand New Yorkers participated in or watched the funeral procession down Eighth Avenue. Lurye's grief-stricken father died the following week.[93]

An eyewitness named Sam Blumenthal told police that he saw two men attacking Lurye with a knife. Blumenthal identified them from photographs as Benedict Macri and John "Scarface" Giusto. Macri, who had gone on the lam within hours after Lurye's murder, surrendered to authorities a year later. Giusto never returned.[94]

October 1951, People against Macri,
Court of General Sessions, Manhattan

On October 11, 1951, the case of *People against Benedict Macri* commenced in a packed courtroom in Manhattan. The prosecution's initial witnesses testified as expected, establishing Macri's motives and movements that Monday. Then shockingly, the key eyewitnesses to the murder changed their stories on the stand. Sam Blumenthal developed amnesia:

> Q   Do you remember that you saw, as I have asked you, two men outside the right hand phone booth, moving their hands in the direction of inside that phone booth?
>
> . . . .
>
> A   I don't honestly know. In my imagination he did, and yet I'm not sure.
>
> . . . .
>
> Q   Did you not tell me, and swear it, on September 21st, 1951, this statement. . . . "This movement of the hands of the first and second men in the direction of the man in the booth took about a minute."
>
> . . . .
>
> A   I am in doubt of it.

Later in the trial, another prosecution eyewitness seemed to develop vision problems.[95]

With key eyewitnesses changing their stories, the jury returned a verdict of not guilty. "A lot of strange things have happened," the judge commented after the verdict. "The witness Blumenthal lost his memory; the witness Weinberg lost his vision." The judge suggested that these "strange coincidences . . . might bear some further investigation in the future."[96]

Subordination of Perjury

The district attorney's office investigated the witnesses. In March 1952, Sam Blumenthal pled guilty to perjury. Blumenthal admitted that he was approached by George "Muscles" Futterman, a business agent for a mobbed-up jewelry workers' union. Futterman gave Blumenthal $100, told him to "do what he could not to hurt Macri," and warned him that he'd be "as good as dead if you don't do what you're told." Futterman was convicted for subordination of perjury. At sentencing, the judge denounced Futterman as the front man for a "ruthless band of assassins."[97]

Although Benedict Macri escaped the law, his mob ties came back on him. In April 1954, Benedict and his brother Vincent Macri went missing after Benedict talked to authorities investigating Albert Anastasia for tax evasion. Vincent's body was found in the trunk of his brother's car. Benedict's body was never found.[98]

Case Four: Expanding a Mobbed-up Union—Teamsters Local 183 and the Waste Hauling Industry in Westchester County

We look last at how the Mafia spread rackets through mobbed-up unions. This is illustrated by the Cosa Nostra's expansion of its "property-rights" system of waste hauling to the suburbs.

The Mafia and the Waste-Hauling Industry

New York's waste-hauling industry was predominantly Italian, a legacy from when Italian immigrants were relegated to the dirtiest jobs in sanitation. As a young man, Joe Valachi worked as a garbage scow trimmer, the same workers organized by Paolo Vaccarelli. Most commercial waste haulers, or "carting companies," were small family businesses with a few trucks passed down from father to son. This was a prototypical "fragile" industry.[99]

In 1929, the City of New York started withdrawing public waste hauling for commercial businesses, viewing it as a public subsidy for private companies. This expanded the market for private waste haulers and, unintentionally, created a fat new target for racketeers.[100]

The waste-hauling cartel originated in the mid-1930s when the mob organized the carting companies using a Teamsters local and "trade associations." Mobster Joe Parisi created Teamsters Local 27 and retained Bernard Adelstein to serve as its president, even though Adelstein had no union experience and was an employer-side representative in the food industry. Meanwhile, the "Brooklyn Trade Waste Removers Association" (BTWRA) was organizing small carting companies. Soon political candidates were seeking the BTWRA's support, and officials like District Attorney William O'Dwyer were feting its president.[101]

The Cosa Nostra used Adelstein's Teamsters union and trade associations to enforce cartels over customer routes. In a perversion of the market, the carting companies "owned" their customers. They fixed routes amongst themselves and charged inflated prices to their captive customers. In March 1947, the New York Commissioner of Investigation dissolved three trade waste associations in New York City for "restricting competition by dividing territory and fixing non-competitive prices" and for "polic[ing] the industry in order to maintain their monopoly." It made little difference; the cartels quickly re-emerged with newly labeled associations.[102]

Vincent "Jimmy" Squillante ran the garbage cartel for the Mangano Family in New York City. Under the guise of the Greater New York Cartmen's Association, Squillante approached carters and promised to solve their labor problems based on his connections to Bernie Adelstein and Albert Anastasia. What Squillante was *really* offering was the customer allocation system. A carter recalled Squillante's candid explanation:

> [Squillante] brought out the point of what we call property rights. In the event a man has a customer or a stop ... and that customer moves from that stop, that man claims that empty store and his customer. No matter what customer shall move back into that store, that man has the property rights. No other cartman can go in there and solicit the stop.[103]

The Mafia's use of Bernie Adelstein's Teamsters local was integral to the scheme.

When waste haulers asked why a union was needed for family-owned businesses with "a father and 2 or 3 sons" as employees, the mobster was blunt about the union's *real* purpose. "No one would take your customers due to the fact that the union would always step in," Squillante explained.[104]

The Cosa Nostra was looking for new territories for the garbage racket. So when the City of Yonkers withdrew public waste hauling from commercial establishments in 1949, mobsters were eager to expand to the affluent suburb. They met an immovable object.[105]

Teamsters Local 456 of Westchester County

John Acropolis was an unusual labor leader. He went to Colgate University on a basketball scholarship, and he became involved with unions while driving trucks in the summer. In 1941, Acropolis was part of a reform slate of candidates who overthrew the incumbents in union elections for Teamsters Local 456 in Westchester County. His strong will earned him the nickname "Little Caesar." But Acropolis was a sincere unionist who ran a clean local.[106]

4–3: Nicholas "Cockeyed Nick" Rattenni, ca. 1930. (Used by permission of the NYC Municipal Archives)

Around 1950, mobsters Joe Parisi and Nick "Cockeyed Nick" Rattenni, and Bernie Adelstein of Teamsters Local 27, started muscling in on waste hauling in Westchester County. "They tried to talk us into giving Parisi—that is, local 27—the jurisdiction in Westchester County of all the private carting," recounted Everett Doyle of Local 456. When Acropolis refused, they took more extreme measures. Adelstein's Teamsters started threatening to put storekeepers out of business unless they switched from Rex Carting, whose workers were represented by Local 456, to a mobbed-up carting company. Rex Carting's office was torched and its trucks burned. Still, Rex Carting and Local 456 continued to hold out.[107]

2:00 a.m., August 26, 1952, Home of John Acropolis, Yonkers, New York

In the summer of 1952, Joe Parisi and Bernie Adelstein tried to strongarm Acropolis and Doyle at a labor convention in Rochester. After Adelstein outright demanded that Acropolis and Local 456 surrender its representation of Rex Carting, they got into a heated argument:

"You are not that tough. Don't think you are too tough we can't take care of you. Tougher guys than you have been taken care of," Adelstein threatened.

"It's too bad you are crippled or I would flatten you right here," Acropolis replied angrily to the peg-legged Adelstein.

Later, Parisi came up to Acropolis's hotel room. "I am through arguing with you," Parisi intoned. "There is other ways of talking care of you [sic]. We can see that it is done." Acropolis told him to get out of his room.[108]

Back home, Acropolis and his fellow union officers started receiving threats over the phone. "Don't park the car when you go home in a dark spot," they said. "Within the next week four of you are going to die."[109]

Two weeks after the Rochester labor convention, around 2 a.m. on August 26, 1952, John Acropolis was opening the door to his home after a long day. Before Acropolis could set down his car keys, someone shot him execution style twice in the back of the head.[110] The local police conducted interviews and tried to investigate various mobsters, but they made little progress.[111] The case has never been solved.

With Acropolis gone, the mob quickly completed its takeover of waste hauling in Yonkers and the surrounding communities. For the next three decades, Nick Rattenni and his mob allies controlled 90 percent of the commercial waste hauling in Westchester County, reaping millions in inflated fees.[112]

The Mafia's infiltration of labor unions in the 1930s was the turning point in its rise to power. While Prohibition was a thirteen-year binge, labor racketeering provided a steady diet of profits and power. Our next chapter looks at another new source of profits: the drug trade.

5
THE MAFIA AND THE DRUG TRADE

> My Tradition outlaws narcotics. It had always been under-
> stood that 'men of honor' don't deal in narcotics.
> —Joseph Bonanno, *A Man of Honor* (1983)

Salvatore Lucania knew an opportunity when he saw one. He lined his pockets with heroin and morphine, and set out to work the Lower East Side. It was spring 1916. America had just declared its first war on drugs. When doctors stopped writing prescriptions for heroin, addicts filled the streets, desperate for new suppliers. Lucania would later say that he knew what "them kind of addicts looked like." Approaching junkies, he "told them I had some." After a string of deals, Lucania was arrested on East 14th Street for peddling to "a dope fiend." He was convicted and spent six months in the reformatory. But prison did not reform him. In June 1923, Lucania sold heroin to an informant for federal narcotics agents. To save himself, he tipped off the agents to a trunk of narcotics at 163 Mulberry Street in Little Italy.[1]

Lucania spent the next decade scheming his way through Prohibition. He soon traded the streets for a suite at the Waldorf-Astoria, where he ran his operations as "Charles Ross." But "Charles Ross" would become better known as Mafia boss Charles "Lucky" Luciano.[2]

Luciano's drug record did not slow his rise to the top. Even when he was a boss, Luciano kept narcotics traffickers among his closest associates. This has been all but forgotten. Today, Luciano is lionized as the purported architect of the Cosa Nostra. *Time* named Luciano as one of its "100 Persons of the Century." When Luciano's drug record is discussed at all, it is usually dismissed as a youthful indiscretion, or as a sign of his disrespect for Mafia tradition.[3] It is never considered a reflection of the Mafia itself.

The first question for this chapter then is: How has the Mafia obscured its role in America's drug trade? The chapter examines the Mafia mythology on drugs. The second, bigger question is: What was its *actual* relationship to the narcotics trade? The chapter uses facts to peel back the myths.[4]

THE DRUGS SCENE FROM THE GODFATHER

It is one of the most evocative scenes from *The Godfather*. The dons from around the country are assembled around a dark table. They have come to resolve whether the Mafia will enter the drug trade. The younger dons push the aging Don Vito Corleone of New York (played by the great Marlon Brando) to give his approval. He warns them against it:

> I believe this drug business—is gonna destroy us in the years to come. I mean, it's not like gambling or liquor—even women—which is something that most people want nowadays, and is, ah, forbidden to them by the *pezzonovante* of the Church. Even the police departments that've helped us in the past with gambling and other things are gonna refuse to help us when it comes to narcotics.

The traditional Don Corleone, however, is outnumbered by his greedier colleagues. Don Zaluchi of Detroit rises to present the pro-drug rationale:

> I also don't believe in drugs. For years I paid my people extra so they wouldn't do that kind of business. Somebody comes to them and says, "I have powders; if you put up three, four thousand dollar investment—we can make fifty thousand distributing." So they can't resist.

Zaluchi proposes a compromise:

> I want to control it as a business, to keep it respectable. . . .
> *BAM! [slamming his hand on the table]*:
> I don't want it near schools—I don't want it sold to children! That's an *infamia*. In my city, we would keep the traffic in the dark people—the colored. They're animals anyway, so let them lose their souls.

Don Barzini of Brooklyn sums up their resolution, "Traffic in drugs will be permitted, but controlled." In the end, though, Don Corleone prevails by killing his greedy, racist rivals.[5]

This iconic scene from the 1972 masterpiece planted indelible images. When a young Sammy "The Bull" Gravano saw it, it reflected his ideal beliefs in the Cosa Nostra. "It was basically the way I saw the life. Where there was some honor. Like when Don Corleone, Marlon Brando, says about the drugs, sure, he owned these people, but he would lose them with that," said Gravano.[6] Mario Puzo and Francis Ford Coppola were drawing on Mafia mythology on drugs when they created this scene. The three major myths are crystalized in it.

The Myth of a Traditional Ban

The Mafia first denied having anything to do with drugs as a matter of tradition. Its members may have been bootleggers and bookies, but not dope pushers. In *The Godfather*, this myth is embodied in the character of Don Corleone, the traditional *mafioso* who stands against drugs. We can call this the *myth of a traditional ban*.

Mafiosi have long declared that they stayed out of drugs. In his bestselling autobiography *A Man of Honor*, Mafia boss Joseph Bonanno asserted, "My Tradition outlaws narcotics. It had always been understood that 'men of honor' don't deal in narcotics." Bonanno claimed that he "did not tolerate any dealings in prostitution or narcotics."[7] When Frank Costello was under investigation in 1946, he held a press conference and declared, "I detest the narcotic racket and anyone connected with it. To my mind there is no one lower than a person dealing in it. It is low and filthy-trading on human misery." Similarly, when Thomas Lucchese testified before the New York State Crime Commission in 1952, he "reserved his real indignation" for drug traffickers. "Any man who got a family should die before he goes into any of that kind of business," Lucchese insisted.[8]

The Myth of Generational Decline

As the drug convictions mounted, the families tried to blame it all on low-level, young button men. In *The Godfather*, this myth is articulated by Don Zaluchi, who laments that his soldiers were succumbing to drug money. We can call this *the myth of generational decline*.

Joe Bonanno argued that "the lure of high profits had tempted some underlings to freelance in the narcotics trade." He suggested this was due to a generational decline. "It reflected how much ground our Traditional values had lost," said Bonanno. His son, Bill Bonanno, echoed his father's sentiments, saying, "The ultimate prospect of big profits far outweighed the lingering attraction of old traditions—at least in the minds of newer leaders who were coming up through the Families."[9] Angelo Lonardo, a former underboss in Cleveland, struck similar themes in his testimony before a Senate Committee in 1988:

> It has changed since I first joined in the 1940s, and, especially, in the last few years with the growth of narcotics. Greed is causing younger members to go into narcotics without the knowledge of the Families. These younger members lack the discipline and respect that made "This Thing" as strong as it once was.

When asked about the timing of this shift, Lonardo pinned it on "the late sixties or seventies." Ironically, Lonardo himself was a convicted narcotics trafficker.[10]

The Myth of Control

Others have rationalized away the Mafia's involvement in narcotics by suggesting that at least the mob controlled the drug trade as a business. This myth is articulated by Don Zaluchi ("I want to control it as a business, to keep it respectable"), and Don Barzini ("Traffic in drugs will be permitted, but controlled"). The image of a grand conclave of the Mafia deciding the future of the drug trade suggests omnipotent power. We can call this *the myth of control*.

Writers have portrayed the entire drug trade as being controlled by a few, all-powerful *mafiosi*. In Martin Gosch and Richard Hammer's fictionalized "memoirs" of Lucky Luciano, *The Last Testament of Lucky Luciano*, Luciano purportedly makes an offer to the Federal Bureau of Narcotics (FBN) to "shut off the supply to America."[11] Joe Bonanno blamed the police's foiling of the Mafia's 1957 conference in Apalachin, New York, for stymieing a mob ban on narcotics. "If the 1957 meeting had gone according to plan there no doubt would have been a reaffirmation of our Tradition's opposition to narcotics," claimed Bonanno.[12] As we will see, politicians have contributed to this myth by blaming the entire drug trade on a single person or mob conclave.

THE HISTORICAL RECORD OF THE MAFIA AND DRUGS

Almost nothing about the Mafia mythology on drugs is true. There was no long-standing "tradition" against drug dealing. *Mafiosi* were involved in illegal narcotics almost from the beginning. Nor was the trafficking confined to younger, low-level underlings. And contrary to the myth of control, the drug trade was messy and haphazard. Ultimately, the Mafia flooded New York City and the country with narcotics. This is how they did it.

When Narcotics Were Legal, 1890–1914

When Leroy Street needed a fix, he went to the pharmacist on Avenue B who sold him heroin manufactured by Bayer of Germany. Bayer's heroin was so pure that Leroy had to dilute it with milk sugar before injecting it into his vein. "There was one drugstore that gave us Christmas presents," Street remembered. "It was really something: a brand-new, shining hypodermic needle with a little ribbon around it and a little card, 'Merry Christmas.'"[13]

New York City was an addict's paradise; drugs were cheap, easy, and everywhere. Without state or federal restrictions on heroin or cocaine, many "medicines" were little more than bottles of opiates. Coca-Cola put cocaine in its soda until 1903. And it was all legal.[14]

Narcotics were, in fact, legal throughout most of the Mafia's early existence. As a British official observed, through World War I "the supply of drugs for purposes of abuse . . . was in most countries not actually illegal."[15] The New York State legislature did not enact its first laws against cocaine and heroin trafficking until 1913–1914, and the US Congress did not do so until the Harrison Narcotics Act of 1914. Even then, the importation of heroin into the United States was not banned completely until 1924.[16] Meanwhile, Italy did not pass its first narcotics law until 1923, a weak law with a maximum penalty of six months.[17]

The Mafia could *not* have had a longstanding "tradition" against illegal narcotics trafficking because there was no such thing. When Joe Bonanno waxes on that "it had always been understood that 'men of honor' don't deal in narcotics," we have to wonder whether his memories were clouded by nostalgia or intentional misdirection. Bonanno was eighteen years old before narcotics were made illegal in his native Italy. Bayer was lawfully supplying the world with heroin. So if there was some virgin era when the Mafia eschewed drug dealing, it was practically meaningless. We should dispense with the myth of tradition.

THE DAWN OF THE DRUG PROHIBITION, 1915–1939

Drug prohibition made New York City the center of the transatlantic drug trade. Enormous amounts of narcotics flowed through the Port of New York in the 1920s and '30s. Smugglers didn't move kilos; they moved *tons*. Around Christmas 1928, a ton of narcotics was found in packing cases labeled as brushes. In April 1931, agents confiscated *three tons* of narcotics from a liner docked on the Chelsea piers. The Elias and George Eliopoulos brothers reputedly only sold narcotics in lots of a hundred kilos or more.[18]

Although traffickers of every ethnicity engaged in the drug trade, Jewish gangsters initially led the trade in New York. Arnold Rothstein was the most significant trafficker in the 1920s, though he probably never touched an ounce of heroin himself. After Rothstein was shot in the Park Central Hotel in 1928, investigators found in his safe deposit boxes the financial records of his drug smuggling. (True to myth, Rothstein's widow claimed her husband's attitude to narcotics was "one of repugnance.")[19] His deputies Irving Sobel and Yasha Katzenberg had organized new smuggling routes from Europe and Southeast Asia. The racketeer Louis "Lepke" Buchalter meanwhile had a morphine plant in the Bronx.[20]

Italian drug syndicates followed closely behind the Jewish traffickers. In the 1910s, the New York Kehillah, a Jewish community organization, hired a private investigator to report on criminal activities. When the historian Alan Block analyzed the reports on drug trafficking, he found that after Jews (31 percent), the Italians were the second largest ethnic group in the cocaine trade (8 percent), and they were the only other group that formed drug syndicates. Jews and Italians often worked in combinations in a market that was "fragmented, kaleidoscopic and sprawling."[21]

The emergence of Italian drug syndicates is confirmed by other sources as well. Prosecutions of the Brooklyn-based Camorra (mainland Italy's counterpart to the Sicilian Mafia) revealed that the Camorristas were heavily involved in cocaine dealing in the 1910s.[22] A 1917 report on drug trafficking found that "'Little Italy,' in east Harlem, is perhaps as large a market as any." Leroy Street, the addict who lived through the dawn of the drug war, confirms an early Italian presence: "The Italians were involved in the beginning," he recalled.[23]

Italian syndicates gradually surpassed Jewish gangsters as the dominant wholesalers in the 1930s. Both dealers and users witnessed this trend. "I was pushed out by the Italians about '38, '39, before the war," remembered Charlie, an independent Italian-American dealer. "Before that—the Jews had the drugs." Jack, a street dealer, saw Italian traffickers grow in influence in the '30s. "But it wasn't overnight you know . . . infiltration was gradual," said Jack. For Eddie, "Harlem was the main place. I'd buy from guys in the street. They were Italian, all Italian—the ones I knew anyhow," he remembered. African-American dealers also report a takeover by Italian syndicates in the '30s. "Who really controlled it was the bigger people on the East Side, the Sicilians . . . in the twenties the Jewish people had it," recalled Curtis, a black dealer in Harlem. As a seller named Mel recounted, "When I started dealing I had Chinese and Jewish connections; later I had Italian connections." Said Mel, "The transitions . . . all started between '35 up until '40 something, then the Italians got ahold to it."[24]

At the international smuggling level, Italian traffickers had established drug contacts throughout the Mediterranean by the 1930s. During this time, the State Department collected "Name Files of Suspected Narcotics Traffickers" on smugglers from around the world. Approximately 11 percent of the name files (65 of the 563 files) were of Italian Americans or Italian nationals.[25] They include known Mafia traffickers such as Vincenzo Di Stefano, who in 1935 was convicted for smuggling nineteen kilos of gum opium he bought in Paris aboard the steamship *Conte Grande*. Mariano Marsalisi, a fifty-something Sicily-born *mafioso* and businessman, spent much of the 1930s traveling between his residences in Istanbul, Paris, and East Harlem. Marsalisi bought trunks of narcotics all over the Mediterranean for shipment back to New York. In the mid-1930s, his partners Luigi Alabiso and Frank Caruso were convicted on smuggling charges; Marsalisi himself was convicted in 1942.[26]

The newly formed Federal Bureau of Narcotics (hereafter "FBN") began tracking the Mafia as it grew in influence in the 1930s. FBN agent Max Roder and George White conducted surveillance in Italian East Harlem and Little Italy along Mulberry Street, tracking *mafiosi* like Eugene Tramaglino and Joe Marone.[27] White and Elmer Gentry later oversaw nationwide investigations of Lucchese Family traffickers.[28] The FBN's binder of "major violators of the narcotics laws now operating in New York City" reflects this trend as well. In its February 15, 1940, binder, out of a total of 193 major violators, 84 were Italian (44 percent), and 83 (43 percent) were Jewish.[29] Along with labor racketeering, drug trafficking was the Mafia's second new source of revenues in the 1930s.

Prominent *mafiosi* began getting picked up on narcotics violations in the 1930s as well. Steve Armone, a Gambino Family captain who engaged in "large scale narcotics smuggling and wholesale distribution for many years," was convicted on narcotics charges in 1937.[30] John Ormento, the Lucchese Family's top narcotics man, was first convicted in 1937. Lucky Luciano never stopped consorting with narcotics traffickers: two of Luciano's codefendants in his 1936 prostitution-ring trial were Thomas "The Bull" Pennochio, a notorious drug trafficker on Mott Street whose wife also pled guilty to selling heroin in 1938, and Ralph Liquori, who was convicted on narcotics charges in 1938. Anthony "Tony Ducks" Corallo, the future boss of the Lucchese Family, got his name for "ducking" convictions on thirteen arrests. Nevertheless, "Tony Ducks" was finally convicted on a state narcotics charge in 1941.[31] Drug records did *not* impede their ascents in the Cosa Nostra.

Joey Rao was innovating another kind of drug smuggling at Welfare Island Penitentiary. The thirty-two-year-old head of the "Italian mob" ran the prison from his luxurious cell, where he donned silk clothes, ate lobster, and smoked cigars. He could stop fights just by walking into the ward. Rao's power derived from his fierce reputation and his "dope racket." When the Department of Corrections raided Welfare Island in January 1934, it discovered that Rao was running "a systematic traffic in narcotics within the walls." There were so many addicted inmates that they had to be segregated in the prison hospital.[32]

5–1: Steve Armone, 1942. Armone, a *caporegime* in the Mangano/Anastasia Family, was a convicted narcotics trafficker. (Used by permission of the NYC Municipal Archives)

Nicolo Gentile epitomizes the Mafia's hypocrisy on drugs. Born in Sicily in 1885, he entered the "honorable society" as a young man. Gentile became a fixer for Mafia leaders, developing contacts from Kansas City to Pittsburgh to New York. In his memoirs *Vita di Capomafia* ("Life of a Mafia Boss"), Gentile waxes eloquent about how the Mafia "claims for itself the right to defend honor, the weak, and to command respect for human justice through its affiliated members."[33]

So, naturally, Gentile became a drug trafficker. In 1937, Gentile conspired with Charles "Big Nose" La Gaipa to organize one of the largest narcotics distribution rings in America. Gentile used his connections to "organize all the drug trafficking groups and to assemble them in a syndicate, in order to have the distribution monopoly in our hands." The ring involved more than seventy smugglers and dealers who imported narcotics from Europe to New York City, and then distributed them in Southern states. Financing, underworld reputations, connections to European suppliers—these were advantages enjoyed by the Cosa Nostra. The ring was doing a multimillion dollar business when it was busted. After Gentile was indicted, he skipped bail and slipped onto a ship to Italy.[34]

THE DISRUPTION OF WAR, 1939–1945

The Second World War cut off the United States from opium sources in Southwest Asia and Southeast Asia, causing severe shortages of narcotics in New York City. Purity levels plunged. "I couldn't deal during the war. I lost my connections. Everybody did," recalled Jack.[35]

The Cosa Nostra adapted by looking south for new sources. Although Mexican poppies produced weaker opiates, they would do in a shortage. *Mafiosi* from East Harlem contacted Helmuth Hartman, a trafficker with connections to Central America. In June 1940, Frank Livorsi, Dominick "The Gap" Petrilli, and Salvatore "Tom Mix" Santoro drove to a remote Texas town to sit down with Hartman: "The boys now have enough money to buy all the narcotics you can find in Mexico. Do a good job for us," Livorsi told Hartman. They then drove to other towns along the border, striking deals with Mexican traffickers. To oversee the deals, Santoro and Petrilli regularly made road trips to Mexico in their Buick Coupe, and later even flew into Mexico City on Eastern Air Lines.[36]

Eventually, they and other *mafiosi* from East Harlem established a reliable drug route whereby curriers smuggled Mexican opium gum into the country through Arizona and California, then across the country to New York City, where chemists in clandestine laboratories processed the opium into heroin. The rings sold the heroin at the wholesale level to dealers for up to $600 an ounce.[37]

THE POSTWAR RESURGENCE IN DRUGS, 1946–1957

When the sea lanes reopened, narcotics washed over the city. Between 1946 and 1950, New York's addiction rates spiked by 36 percent. By 1957, the US Attorney was calling New York "the illicit narcotics capital of the nation."[38] The Mafia was supplying the heroin.

The Cosa Nostra's traffickers were now the dominant wholesalers due to their superior heroin. "After 1950, I switched over to the Italians in East Harlem because I got better quality stuff, and the prices were better," recalled Arthur, a dealer.[39] The mob's supply was indeed better: the heroin seized in the French Connection case was about 95 percent pure—an extraordinary level. A FBN report in 1949 found that heroin seized at its source in New York City was about 92 percent pure compared to the national average of 55 percent.[40]

Another sign of the Mafia's market power was its ability to dilute or "cut" its pure heroin while simultaneously raising prices. "When the Jews gave up, I don't know what happened. When the wops come . . . they kept raising the price," said Abe D., a Jewish dealer. "It was a beautiful thing when the Chinese and the Jews had it. But when the Italians had it—bah!—they messed it all up," said Mel. "They started diluting it to a weaker state." A longtime user concurred: "The Italians stepped on the H much more than the Jews, and they charged more money. It happened before the war," recounted Al.[41]

The Mafia's superior supply was due to its overseas connections in the underworld. Members of the Cosa Nostra enjoyed close ties to the premier smugglers of the time: the Corsican crime families. Corsica is a large island situated between France and Italy with a long tradition of banditry. From their base in the port city of Marseilles, the Corsicans had extensive connections with smugglers throughout the Mediterranean. Though French citizens, Corsicans spoke an Italian dialect and were culturally similar to Sicilians.[42] The Sicilian *cosca* and the Corsican crime families were cousins in crime, and they had built up decades of mutual trust. In 1934, the FBN found "a well-organized ring of narcotic traffickers and smugglers in Marseille, most of whom are of Corsican origin," shipping large quantities of narcotics to Italian smugglers in New York.[43]

When the war ended, *mafiosi* revived their prewar contacts with the Corsicans. Upwards of 80 percent of the heroin smuggled into the United States originated in the rich opium fields and port cities of Turkey and Lebanon, where the Corsican smugglers held sway. "The Italian domination really set in with the old French connection, when the predominance of heroin came from Turkey, Lebanon through Italy to Marseilles, following World War II," explained Ralph Salerno of the New York Police Department's intelligence unit. "Who had the bona fides to sit down with these six Corsican families? Only the Italians, and a few Jews who lingered in the field," said Salerno.[44]

Black gangsters by comparison could not establish direct connections to suppliers. The State Department files on international traffickers record *no* Africans or African Americans.[45] "I don't believe there was a black man who could bring into the United States from the outside two kilos of heroin up to 1960," said Salerno. "You could have had forty million dollars, and if you were a black man, you couldn't even get to sit down with that Corsican."[46] It was not until the 1970s that Frank Lucas, frustrated by the Mafia's dominance, became the first black trafficker to establish a connection to heroin suppliers in Southeast Asia.[47]

Mafia traffickers further benefitted from belonging to the strongest organized crime syndicates in the underworld. Large-scale, international drug trafficking was a logistical nightmare. A customs officer explained the essential role of organized crime:

> You need someone in Europe, you need couriers, you need financing people, you need somebody that knows something about traveling, how to get United States documentation, who the buyers would be in the United States. Only this can be known by someone, and not by some clown who decides all of a sudden to do it in some European capital. . . . It requires a lot of people, a lot of effort, and it is criminal, so it is organized.[48]

As FBN agent Maurice Helbrant explained, "Touch dope and you will run into other branches of organized crime. Touch organized crime and sooner or later you will run into dope."[49]

THE 107TH STREET MOB

Mafiosi sheltered their wholesaling and distribution operations in Italian East Harlem. These densely populated streets were impenetrable to outsiders. "Since everyone knew everyone else, a narcotics agent found it impossible to maintain surveillance in this neighborhood," said FBN agent Charles Siragusa. "Life on the narrow sidestreets would come to a standstill. Every eye would fix on the agent."[50]

Law enforcement dubbed the Lucchese Family's traffickers the "107th Street Mob."[51] *Mafiosi* financed, manufactured, and moved heroin through Italian East Harlem. It became an industry cluster for narcotics similar to alcohol wholesaling on the Curb Exchange during Prohibition. Although various Mafia drug traffickers operated in East Harlem, the Luccheses clearly lead the postwar resurgence in drugs. In spring 1947, Charles "Little Bullets" Albero and Joseph "Pip the Blind" Gagliano were convicted of running "an East Harlem narcotics peddling combine said to be the biggest in the East."[52] They were quickly replaced by other Lucchese traffickers.

5–2: John "Big John" Ormento (center) and Nicholas "Big Nose" Tolentino (in glasses) being booked in 1958. The New York Mafia's drug traffickers dominated heroin wholesaling in the United States starting in the mid-1930s. (Used by permission of the Associated Press)

On the surface, John Ormento looked like any other American success story. Born in East Harlem, he rose from his humble origins to live in the fashionable section of Lido Beach on Long Island. By night, Mr. Ormento frequented the

Copacabana, his 240-pound frame draped in finely tailored suits. But by day, "Big John" Ormento ran narcotics operations from East 107th Street with his smuggling partner Salvatore "Tom Mix" Santoro. The FBN accurately identified Ormento as a "top figure in the NYC underworld" who knew many "narcotic sources in Mexico, Canada and Europe."[53] By the age of forty, he had three separate convictions under the Harrison Act. Nevertheless, Ormento was a longtime *caporegime* in the Lucchese Family, and he attended the 1957 Apalachin conference of top mobsters.[54]

THE DRUG DISTRIBUTION NETWORK

The Cosa Nostra's influence was magnified by New York's pivotal spot in the wholesaling network. As drug historian Eric Schneider explains, "New York served as the central place that established the hierarchical structures of the market, with virtually the entire country as its hinterland and other cities serving as its regional or local distribution centers."[55]

Mafia traffickers in New York City financed, diluted, and wholesaled drugs nationwide. Dealers from Philadelphia, Baltimore, and Washington, DC, traveled to New York to buy drugs. In 1924, federal agents discovered that Cincinnati peddlers were getting their narcotics from New York wholesalers. New York *mafiosi* became the primary suppliers for Chicago, which in turn supplied smaller Midwestern cities. In one major case, traffickers smuggled heroin into New York, cut the heroin in clandestine laboratories, and then redistributed kilo packages to Chicago, Cleveland, Las Vegas, and Los Angeles.[56]

For the vast market of addicts in New York City, Mafia wholesalers relied on local gangsters for retail street distribution. "The black people handled the largest quantity of drugs after it left the big connections, when it came to the country," explained Curtis, a black dealer with Sicilian suppliers.[57] "The Italians were the ones who brought the dope in, but they didn't have the connects to peddle it," remembered Bumpy Johnson's widow.[58] "The lowest level the Italians would get to was when they sold a quarter kilo to a black—he's the only guy that can successfully sell it in Harlem," agrees Salerno.[59] This move away from retail street distribution and toward wholesaling insulated the Mafia. "The key figures in the Italian heroin establishment never touched heroin," confirmed David Durk, a narcotics officer.[60]

The Cosa Nostra established links to major African-American gangsters like Nat Pettigrew and Freddie Parsons to distribute heroin to dealers in black neighborhoods. The FBN discovered that George Anderson "was one of the chief links between the negro dealers in Harlem and the Italian wholesalers in the upper east side of New York City." Herbert Drumgold bought narcotics "in large quantities from Italian dealers in the Upper East Side of New York City" to resell "to dealers, who in turn sell direct to addicts."[61]

Ellsworth "Bumpy" Johnson oversaw much of the retail heroin distribution in Harlem. "Anyone living in Harlem knew the name Bumpy Johnson. He was a *boss*," recalled Frank Lucas.[62] Johnson cultivated a façade as a businessman, churchgoer, and benefactor. Behind the scenes, he collected kickbacks from dealers and financed drug operations. Convicted three times on narcotics charges, he helped inundate Harlem with drugs supplied by the Cosa Nostra.[63]

Once drugs reached the streets, the Mafia had no real control over who bought them. The postwar heroin spike devastated poor teenagers in black and Puerto Rican neighborhoods. "Every time I went uptown, somebody else was hooked, somebody else was strung out," remembered Claude Browne. "Drugs were killing just about everybody off in one way or another."[64] Low said the addicts were increasingly "Spanish boys in the eighteen, nineteen bracket. I used to see them turning into bums, being all dirty."[65] Piri Thomas grew up on 104th Street (blocks from the mob's trafficking center), and he mainlined heroin as a teenager. "It becomes your whole life once you allow it to sink its white teeth in your blood stream," Thomas said.[66]

The Mafia cultivated an image for shielding Italian neighborhoods from drug pushing. "During the 1950s on Mulberry Street, in the lower part of Manhattan, the Italian gangsters' image was 'We keep the drug pushers out of the neighborhood.' And they did," said Salerno. "But it wouldn't stop them from selling a kilo of heroin to someone, as long as they knew he wasn't going to try to trickle it back into their neighborhood."[67]

The notion that the Mafia could build moats around Italian neighborhoods proved illusory. Salvatore Mondello, who grew up in East Harlem during the 1930s and '40s, recalls:

Some of my friends tried reefers. The racketeers never distributed reefers on the street. It would have been dangerous to sell that stuff on their home turf. Their honest neighbors would have strongly disapproved. But reefers, I imagine, could be bought elsewhere. Some of my friends could have bought them on other streets in East Harlem.[68]

Though less prevalent, some inner-city Italian youths got hooked on heroin from East Harlem. Dom Abruzzi started snorting heroin "because it was so cheap—a dollar and a half apiece to split a three-dollar bag—and everybody was getting so high and seemed so happy."[69] Eddie became addicted from breathing in the dust from a Mafia cutting operation where he worked. East Harlem was slowly undermined by drugs smuggled into the country by the Mafia.[70]

IN SEARCH OF A GRAND CONSPIRACY

Politicians and writers have searched for a single, grand conspiracy to explain the entire drug trade. In the 1950s, FBN Commissioner Harry Anslinger and his deputy Charles Siragusa claimed that Luciano was secretly the "the kingpin" of all the narcotics traffic between "the United States and Italy."[71] However, when the drug historians Kathryn Meyer and Terry Parssinen reviewed the FBN's massive surveillance records on Luciano in Italy, they found no evidence that the aging Luciano controlled the transatlantic trade. In my examination of Anslinger's personal papers, I found no prized document showing Luciano pulling the strings of the drug trade from Italy.[72]

Others have seized on a meeting at the *Hotel et des Palmes* in Palermo, Sicily, in October 1957. The FBI had long known about this meeting of a dozen Sicilian and America *mafiosi*, including Joe Bonanno and Carmine Galante. FBI director Louis Freeh later speculated that the meeting was held to enlist the Sicilian Mafia in the drug trade.[73] In her 1990 book *Octopus: How the Long Reach of the Sicilian Mafia Controls the Global Narcotics Trade*, the journalist Claire Sterling saw in this meeting the organization of the entire drug trade:

Although there is no firsthand evidence of what went on at the four-day summit itself, what followed over the next thirty years has made the substance clear.

Authorities on both sides of the Atlantic are persuaded by now that the American delegation asked the Sicilians to take over the import and distribution of heroin in the United States, and the Sicilians agreed.[74]

This has been recycled endlessly, most recently by the writer Gil Reavill who cites Sterling's story even while admitting it is a "largely unsourced account."[75]

But there *was* firsthand evidence of what went on at the 1957 gathering. Tomasso Buscetta was one of the dozen *mafioso* at the *Hotel et des Palmes*. Buscetta later became a *pentito* (penitent witness) after his sons were killed, and he was the key witness in the "Pizza Connection" heroin prosecution of the 1980s. Buscetta *never* testified that the 1957 gathering was a "summit" to plan a direct Sicily-to-America heroin connection. No such connection was established for another *two decades*. Wiseguys do not have twenty-year drug plans.[76]

These writers miss the point. No single cabal could predetermine the entire drug trade. There *was* conspiracy in the drug trade. But it was not a single grand conspiracy by a few, omnipotent men. Rather, the drug trade involved many small conspiracies, composed of fluid coalitions of *mafiosi* who put together schemes as the opportunities arose.

MAFIA DRUG OPERATIONS

Joseph Orsini treated countries like his mistresses. A native Corsican, he was convicted of collaborating with the Nazis, and fled France for the United States. In January 1949, he met Salvatore "Sally Shields" Shillitani, a member of the Lucchese Family, and proposed they go into business together. Orsini brought in his Corsican drug contacts; Shillitani brought in his fellow *mafiosi*. All the partners invested money in a fund to finance their operations. The ring met in restaurants, hotel rooms, a construction company office—even on Ellis Island, as Orsini awaited deportation to Argentina for immigration violations.[77]

To get heroin to New York, the ring constantly adapted. One of the Corsicans had a connection for opium in Yugoslavia. He shipped the opium to Marseilles, where it was converted into morphine then shipped to Paris to be processed into heroin. The ring then sent Americans with automobiles on "vacations" to Paris, where the cars were loaded up with heroin in hidden caches and shipped back to the United States. The ring was hardly flawless. Investors squabbled over deliveries. The automobile scheme was shut down when too many cars were returning empty. One disastrous day, French police seized a three-hundred-kilo shipment from a boat docked in Marseilles. But because the ring's "merchandise" was so perfect, it still made profits from the kilos that made it to New York.[78]

The Orsini-Shillitani ring was fairly typical of Mafia drug rings. Table 5–1 summarizes characteristics of Mafia drug operations for which we have good information. First, the drug rings involved many different coconspirators. Second, they were financed by several *mafiosi* pooling their money. Third, the drug rings were opportunistic. Traffickers crossed Mafia family lines, bought from whatever source was available, and smuggled in the drugs by any means necessary.

Table 5–1:
Characteristics of Mafia Drug Operations from
Federal Cases in the New York Area (≤ 1963)[79]

Name of Case	Conspirators	Financing	Drug Source	Families Involved
U.S. v. Agueci (1962)	29	Multiple investors	Italy	Genovese members
U.S. v. Bentvena (1962)	13+	Unclear	Montreal, Canada	Bonanno & Lucchese members
U.S. v. Aviles (1959)	15+	Multiple investors	Cuba, Mexico, Puerto Rico	Genovese & Lucchese members
U.S. v. Reina (1957)	8+	Multiple investors	France & Italy	Genovese & Lucchese members
Valachi scheme (1952)[80]	8	Multiple investors	France	Genovese members
U.S. v. La Gaipa (1937)	70+	Unclear	Europe	Mangano members

THE FRENCH (CANADIAN) CONNECTION

When viewed against this background, the famous "French Connection" case of the early 1960s looks less the mark of something new and more like any other Mafia drug operation. The case was immortalized by William Friedkin's 1971 Academy Award–winning film *The French Connection* starring Gene Hackman. The reporter who wrote the book on which the film was based trumpeted the case as "The World's Most Crucial Narcotics Investigation."[81] It wasn't.

In reality, the scheme was a small, family affair involving Pasquale "Patsy" Fuca, his brother Joe, and his father Tony. Patsy's uncle was Angelo "Little Angie" Tuminaro, a trafficker for the Lucchese Family. With their Corsican partners, they refined Turkish opium into heroin in Marseilles. They concealed the heroin in the undercarriage of a 1960 Buick Invicta owned by a Parisian television host, who shipped his car to Montreal, Canada. After smuggling the packages across the border, they stashed the ninety-seven pounds of heroin in cellars around New York.[82]

The case might have been called the *French*-Canadian *Connection* to reflect the Mafia's latest adaptation to the drug war. The Canadian Mafia long had its own drug trade. Canadian boss Rocco Perri's associates were into narcotics trafficking as early as the 1920s.[83] When customs enforcement increased on the New York waterfront in the late 1950s and the 1960s, the wiseguys looked north for new drug routes. "When the heat was being put on New York [traffickers would] swing through French Canada because of all the [Montreal] air traffic," explained Ralph Salerno.[84] This gave rise to mob traffickers like Frank and Joseph Controni of Montreal, and Albert and Vito Agueci of Toronto, who smuggled drugs through Canada to New York City.[85]

NARCOTICS CONVICTIONS OF *MAFIOSI*, 1916–1963

The Mafia's entrenchment in the narcotics trade is also reflected in conviction rates. Table 5–3 below shows *mafiosi* from the New York metropolitan area convicted on drug charges. To address the myth of generational decline, the table is limited to *mafiosi* who were both born by 1920 *and* convicted by 1963. This places them in the same generation as the leading purveyors of this myth, Joe Bonanno (born 1905) and Angelo Lonardo (born 1911). The pre-1963 time limitation counters the perception that Mafia trafficking only began with the French Connection case, or as Lonardo put it "the late sixties or seventies."

As the table shows, more than 150 *mafiosi* in the New York area alone were convicted on narcotics violations by 1963. Given that Joe Valachi testified there were about two thousand active and twenty-five hundred inactive members in the New York area, this meant that one in thirty-three *mafiosi* were *convicted* traffickers. This is astounding given how weak narcotics enforcement was at the time. As late as 1950, the NYPD's narcotics squad had 18 officers; in 1965, the FBN had only 433 employees nationwide. Many mob traffickers evaded the law. Valachi estimated that about "75 tops, maybe 100" in the 450-man Genovese Family were into narcotics—*about one in six.*[86]

MAFIA LEADERS INVOLVED IN DRUGS

Contrary to myth, drug trafficking was *not* confined to low-level mobsters. Table 5–2 below shows that all five families had high-ranking leaders with early narcotics convictions:

Table 5–2: Known Leaders of the New York Families with Narcotics Convictions (≤ 1963)		
Individual (earliest narcotics conviction)	**Top Position Obtained**	**Family**
Charles "Lucky" Luciano (1916)	Boss	Genovese
Dominick "Quiet Dom" Cirillo (1953)	Boss	Genovese
Anthony "Fat Tony" Salerno (1958)	Boss	Genovese
Vito Genovese (1959)	Boss	Genovese
Vincent "The Chin" Gigante (1959)	Boss	Genovese
Natale "Diamond Joe" Evola (1959)	Boss	Bonanno
Carmine "Lilo" Galante (1962)	Boss	Bonanno
Anthony "Tony Ducks" Corallo (1941)	Boss	Lucchese

Salvatore "Tom Mix" Santoro (1952)	Underboss	Lucchese
Stephen Armone (1935)	Caporegime	Gambino
Joseph "Joe Piney" Armone (≤1963)	Caporegime	Gambino
Joseph "Jo Jo" Manfredi (1952)	Caporegime	Gambino
Rocco Mazzie (1959)	Caporegime	Gambino
John "Big John" Ormento (1937)	Caporegime	Lucchese
Nicholas "Jiggs" Forlano (1935)	Caporegime	Magliocco

The bosses profited from narcotics behind the scenes, too. Nicolo Gentile's boss Vincent Mangano approved of Gentile's drug trafficking scheme in exchange for a split of the profits.[87] Joe Valachi recalls a highly revealing conversation he once had with his boss, Vito Genovese:

> He said to me, "Did you ever deal in junk?"
> I said, "Yes."
> He said, "You know you ain't supposed to fool with it."
> Vito looked at me and said, "Well, don't do it again."
> "Okay," I said.
> Of course, I don't pay any attention to this. This is how Vito was.[88]

This veiled conversation shows how easily a mob boss could look the other way.

Joe Bonanno's pontifications on drugs are undermined by some damning facts as well. Bonanno portrays his "hero" Salvatore Maranzano as the quintessential "Man of Honor." Yet as we saw earlier, Maranzano had a convicted drug trafficker in James Alescia as a partner at his Park Avenue office. Bonanno offers no explanation for Maranzano and Alescia.[89]

"I did not tolerate any dealings in prostitution or narcotics," Bonanno claimed when he was boss. But in 1959, Carmine "Lilo" Galante, a *caporegime* in the Bonanno Family, was arrested and later convicted for smuggling heroin through the Montreal airport and into New York City.[90] Not only was Galante left untouched, but he later became acting boss of the Bonanno Family.[91] Joe Bonanno conveniently omits any mention of Galante in his autobiography *Man of Honor*. Bill Bonanno tries to shore up his father's omission in Bill's own 1991 autobiography *Bound by Honor*. Bill admits that Galante was a trafficker, but claims his father had no forewarning:

My father was heartbroken by this, although unwilling to do anything about it. There was a standing death sentence for anyone who openly defied an iron-clad rule of the Family—such as the one against dealing drugs.

"Leave him alone; doesn't matter now," my father told me and those in the administration of the Family.

Bill Bonanno claims that he "would have struck out in retaliation" against Galante. However, in a 1979 *New York Times* article, Bill Bonanno is quoted as saying that Carmine Galante "was like an uncle," and that Bill was a "godfather to one of [Galante's] children."[92]

Then there is Natale "Joe Diamond" Evola. Natale Evola was an usher at Joe Bonanno's wedding, and the Bonannos lionize Evola as one of the "boys of the first day." In 1959, however, Evola was convicted for a narcotics conspiracy. Nevertheless, Evola became boss of the Bonanno Family in the 1970s, and the Bonannos say nothing of his drug record.[93] The facts, it seems, would have gotten in the way of a good myth.

POLICE CORRUPTION

Don Corleone was wrong about the police refusing to help, too. The FBN, in fact, was borne out of a corruption scandal in its predecessor agency, the old Narcotics Bureau. In 1930, a grand jury in New York charged narcotics agents with rampant misconduct and falsification of cases under its commissioner Levi Nutt. But what brought Nutt down were the revelations that his son-in-law took a loan from Arnold Rothstein, the biggest narcotics trafficker in the country, and that Nutt's own son represented Rothstein in a tax-evasion proceeding.[94]

The FBN's New York office became a den of corruption. When rookie agent Jack Kelly joined the New York office in the early 1950s, he was warned to "try to find someone honest or at least honest when they are working with you." FBN agent Tom Tripodi saw agents routinely take money in raids; they called it "'making a bobo' (a bonus)." Corrupt agents rationalized this by saying they were just taking "Mob money. Drug money."[95]

The FBN was a paragon of virtue compared to the narcotics units of the NYPD. "I won't say that every New York City police officer was dishonest, but finding one who wasn't was an exception," said Kelly.[96] In 1951, a Brooklyn grand jury found that "from top to bottom of the plainclothes division," the police had formed "criminal combines" with narcotics peddlers. The Knapp Commission later singled out corruption in the narcotics units as the most serious problem facing the NYPD.[97]

Corruption insulated traffickers on multiple levels. "The New York Police Department charged me two thousand dollars a month in order to operate between 110th Street and 125th Street," said Arthur. "I couldn't get busted in there. I was on the pad." The Cosa Nostra neutralized high-level investigations, too. If narcotics agents uncovered a *mafioso* during an investigation, the target would disappear, and the agents would be sent off on a wild goose chase by a senior officer on the take. When Frank Serpico joined the plainclothes division, he was told he could arrest blacks and Puerto Rican dealers, but "the Italians, of course, are different. They're on top, they run the show, and they're very reliable, and they can do whatever they want." In 1969, nearly the *entire* seventy-six member elite Special Investigation Unit (SIU) of the NYPD was transferred out on corruption charges.[98]

The low point was the mob's theft of the heroin seized in the French Connection case. The NYPD had stored the ninety-seven pounds of heroin they had seized in the case in the NYPD's Property Clerk's Office. Then eighty-one pounds of it, with a street value of $10 million, disappeared. The mastermind was Vincent "Vinnie Papa" Papa of the Lucchese Family. After the debacle, NYPD commissioner Patrick Murphy concluded that "the single most dangerous feature of organized crime syndicates was their ability to corrupt or co-opt local law enforcement."[99]

MAFIA EDICTS AGAINST DRUGS

There is one grain of truth in the mythology. Some Mafia leaders *did* issue bans on drugs. According to Joe Valachi, in 1948, Frank Costello, boss of the Luciano Family "ordered its membership to stay out of dope." The next edict was issued in 1957 when "all families were notified—no narcotics." This ban was largely ignored, too.[100] Wiretaps of the DeCavalcante Family in New Jersey record their amazement at all the drug dealing: "Half these guys are handling junk. Now there's a [Mafia] law out that they can't touch it."[101]

Still others tried issuing "no-drugs" orders in their families. Mob boss Paul Castellano barred narcotics under penalty of death, yet Castellano's own *consigliere* had a son who dealt. Lucchese Family *caporegime* Paul Vario outlawed dealing in his crew after his boss Carmine Tramunti was convicted on drug charges. It did not matter. Vario could not stop his own crew from dealing.[102] The ineffectiveness of these bans shows that "the godfathers" were not omnipotent.

There were human factors at work, too. Hypocrisy was part of the mobster life. Vito Genovese's veiled conversation with Joe Valachi shows how the bosses looked the other way. Bill Bonanno likewise suggests willful ignorance. He admits that "the Family's Administration ... received envelopes of cash from time to time in exchange for keeping quiet. No one asked questions about where this money came from or how it was earned."[103]

Some *mafiosi* were in denial, too. In the 1930s, public opinion turned strongly against drug sellers as middle-class users devolved into street addicts. No one was lower than the "dope fiend" except the "junk dealer." Even hardened *mafiosi* had trouble admitting they were into narcotics. Although Joe Valachi readily recounted murders he committed, he sheepishly downplayed his drug dealing, claiming he only sold "small amounts to get back on my feet." In fact, the FBN had been tracking Valachi's drug trafficking since the 1940s, and it obtained multiple convictions of him. Meanwhile, Nicolo Gentile tried to blame his involvement with narcotics trafficking on woman problems and business debts.[104]

It seems even wiseguys could feel shame. Just not enough to stop taking their cut.

Table 5–3:
Mafiosi in the New York Area with Narcotics Convictions, 1914–1963
(born ≤ 1920 with conviction ≤ 1963)[105]

No.	Individual	Year of Birth	Year of Conviction	Approx. Age	Source on Conviction	Source on Mafia Affiliation
1.	Angelo Abbrescia	1900	1953	53	BOP FOIA	FBN
2.	Luigi Alabiso	1883	1935	52	FBN	FBN

3.	James Alescia	1900	1923	23	*New York Times*	*New York Times*
4.	Philip Albanese	1907	1946	47	BOP FOIA	FBN; Hearings
5.	John Albasi	1910	1955	45	BOP FOIA	FBN
6.	Charles Albero	1902	1942	40	BOP FOIA	FBN; Hearings
7.	Dominick Allocco	1913	1948	35	BOP FOIA	FBN
8.	Michael Altimari	1913	1945	32	BOP FOIA	FBN; Hearings
9.	Salvatore Ameli	1916	1955	39	FBN	FBN
10.	Frank Amendola	1899	1939	40	BOP FOIA; FBN	FBN
11.	Germaio Anaclerio	1917	1937	30	BOP FOIA	FBN; Hearings
12.	Anthony Annicchiarico	1920	1956	36	BOP FOIA	FBN
13.	John Ardito	1919	1947	28	BOP FOIA	FBN; Hearings
14.	Joseph Armone	1917	≤1963	Not clear	Hearings	Hearings
15.	Stephen Armone	1899	1935	36	BOP FOIA	Hearings
16.	Alfonso Attardi	1900	1938	38	BOP FOIA	FBN
17.	Mario Avola	1912	1955	43	BOP FOIA	FBN
18.	Arnold Barbato	1911	1942	31	BOP FOIA	FBN
19.	Savatore Barbato	1913	1947	34	BOP FOIA	FBN
20.	Charles Barcellona	1915	1962	47	BOP FOIA	FBN; Hearings
21.	Sebastiano Bellanca	1904	1939	35	Hearings	FBN; Hearings
22.	Joseph Bove	1909	1958	49	FBN	FBN
23.	Angelo Buia	1910	1939	29	BOP FOIA	Hearings
24.	Matildo Buia	1908	1938	30	BOP FOIA	FBN
25.	Philip Buzzeo	1917	1957	40	BOP FOIA	FBN
26.	Frank Callace	1901	1943	42	Hearings	Hearings
27.	Charles Campisi	1912	1956	44	FBN; Hearings	Hearings
28.	Thomas Campisi	1911	≤1963	Not clear	Hearings	Hearings
29.	Gaetano Capalbo	1914	≤1945	Not clear	FBN	FBN
30.	Anthony Carminati	1912	1943	31	BOP FOIA	Hearings
31.	Frank Caruso	1911	1946	35	BOP FOIA	Hearings
32.	James Casablanca	1913	≤1963	Not clear	Hearings	Hearings
33.	Joseph Casablanca	1911	≤1945	Not clear	FBN	FBN
34.	Vincent Casablanca	1913	1941	28	BOP FOIA	Hearings
35.	Peter Casella	1907	1958	51	FBN	Hearings
36.	Steve Casertano	1903	≤1963	Not clear	Hearings	Hearings
37.	James Cusamono	1903	1940	37	FBN	FBN
38.	Samuel Cavalieri	1911	1943	32	Hearings	Hearings
39.	Arthur Celi	1917	1947	30	BOP FOIA	FBN

40.	Ralph Ciccone	1910	1959	49	FBN	FBN
41.	Anthony Ciccone	1918	1941	23	BOP FOIA	Hearings
42.	Bendetto Cinquegrana	1913	1956	43	BOP FOIA	FBN; Hearings
43.	Benedetto Coniglio	1916	1947	31	BOP FOIA	FBN
44.	Thomas Contaldo	1913	1938	25	BOP FOIA	FBN
45.	Anthony Corallo	1913	1941	28	FBI FOIA	FBI FOIA
46.	Frank Corona	1909	1956	47	BOP FOIA	FBN
47.	Vincent Corrao	1909	≤1963	Not clear	Hearings	Hearings
48.	Michael Corsaro	1911	≤1941	Not clear	FBN	FBN
49.	Anthony Crisci	1911	1957	46	BOP FOIA	FBN
50.	Alfred Criscuolo	1911	≤1963	Not clear	Valachi	Hearings
51.	Edward D'Argenio	1900	1954	54	BOP FOIA	Hearings
52.	James De George	1913	1954	39	BOP FOIA	FBN
53.	William DeMartino	1910	≤1945	Not clear	FBN	FBN
54.	Theodore DeMartino	1912	1939	27	BOP FOIA	Hearings
55.	Joseph Dentico	1898	1952	54	BOP FOIA	FBN
56.	Joseph D'Ercole	1911	1941	30	BOP FOIA	FBN; Hearings
57.	Joseph DiPalermo	1907	1959	52	BOP FOIA	FBN; Hearings
58.	Louis Dioguardo	1912	1940	28	FBN	FBN
59.	Anthony DiPasqua	1912	1942	30	FBN	Hearings
60.	Vincent Di Pietro	1910	1939	29	BOP FOIA	FBN
61.	Vincent Di Stefano	1905	1935	30	BOP FOIA; FBN	FBN
62.	Anthony Donato	1914	1954	40	FBN	FBN
63.	Frank Donato	1910	1953	43	FBN	FBN
64.	Alfred Embarrato	1909	1935	26	BOP FOIA	FBN
65.	Natale Evola	1907	1959	52	BOP FOIA	Hearings
66.	Rosario Farulla	1882	1957	75	FBN	FBN
67.	Nicholas Forlano	1915	1935	20	Hearings	Hearings
68.	Cosmo Franco	1906	1944	38	BOP FOIA	FBN
69.	Joseph Gagliano	1904	1947	43	Hearings	Hearings
70.	Charles Gagliodotto	1908	1950	42	Hearings	FBN; Hearings
71.	Agatino Garufi	1905	1939	34	BOP FOIA	FBN
72.	Carmine Galante	1910	1962	52	Hearings	Hearings
73.	Joseph Gennaro	1910	1937	27	BOP FOIA	FBN
74.	Vito Genovese	1897	1959	62	BOP FOIA	Hearings

75.	Eugenio Giannini	1906	1946	40	BOP FOIA	FBN; Hearings
76.	Salvatore Giglio	1906	1941	35	BOP FOIA	FBN
77.	Anthony Granza	1915	1940	25	BOP FOIA	FBN; Hearings
78.	Alfred Guido	1911	1940	29	BOP FOIA	FBN
79.	Florio Isabella	1911	≤1963	Not clear	Hearings	Hearings
80.	Charles La Cascia	1916	1955	39	BOP FOIA	FBN
81.	Daniel Lessa	1915	1947	32	BOP FOIA	FBN
82.	Benjamin Licchi	1913	1956	43	FBN	FBN; Hearings
83.	Joseph Licchi	1919	1956	37	FBN	FBN; Hearings
84.	John Linardi	1908	1929	21	BOP FOIA	FBN
85.	Ralph Liquori	1910	1938	28	*New York Times*	*New York Times*
86.	Anthony Lisi	1911	1940	29	BOP FOIA	FBN
87.	Frank Livorsi	1903	1942	39	BOP FOIA	FBN; Hearings
88.	Peter LoCascio	1916	1949	33	FBN	FBN; Hearings
89.	Angelo Loiacano	1913	1962	49	FBN	FBN; Hearings
90.	Paul Lombardino	1912	1951	39	FBN	FBN; Hearings
91.	Philip Lombardo	1908	≤1963	Not clear	Hearings	FBN; Hearings
92.	Joseph LoPiccolo	1918	1958	40	Hearings	FBN; Hearings
93.	Charles Luciano	1897	1916	18	NYMA	Hearings
94.	Salvatore Maimone	1913	1959	46	FBN	FBN; Hearings
95.	John Malizia	1912	1957	45	FBN	FBN
96.	Francesco Mancino	1906	1962	56	FBN	FBN
97.	Salvatore Maneri	1912	1963	51	FBN	FBN
98.	Richard Manfredonia	1908	1945	37	BOP FOIA	FBN
99.	Joseph Marone	1904	1946	42	BOP FOIA	FBN; Hearings
100.	Mariano Marsalisi	1879	1942	63	FBN	FBN; Hearings
101.	Nicholas Martello	1907	1938	21	BOP FOIA	FBN; Hearings
102.	James Massi	1908	1958	50	BOP FOIA	FBN; Hearings
103.	Vincent Mauro	1916	1963	47	Hearings	Hearings
104.	Rocco Mazzie	1916	1959	43	Hearings	FBN
105.	Lester Miraglia	1916	1957	41	BOP FOIA	FBN
106.	Pasquale Moccio	1918	1956	38	Hearings	Hearings
107.	Samuel Montemurro	1917	1952	35	BOP FOIA	FBN
108.	Sebastiano Nani	1906	1954	48	BOP FOIA	Hearings
109.	George Nobile	1910	1958	48	FBN	FBN; Hearings
110.	Lorenzo Orlando	1901	1958	57	BOP FOIA	FBN

111.	John Ormento	1912	1937	25	BOP FOIA	FBN; Hearings
112.	Theodore Orzo	1904	1953	49	BOP FOIA	FBN
113.	Vincent Panebianco	1920	1937	17	BOP FOIA	FBN
114.	Orlando Paoli	1912	1954	42	FBN	FBN
115.	Vincent Papa	1917	1959	42	FBI FOIA	FBI FOIA
116.	Andinno Pappadia	1914	1959	45	FBN	FBN
117.	Anthony Peloso	1907	1946	39	BOP FOIA	FBN
118.	Thomas Pennochio	1890	1926	36	NYMA	NYMA
119.	Armando Perillo	1902	1948	46	FBN	FBN
120.	Joseph Perretti	1907	1939	32	FBN	FBN
121.	Peter Perretti	1895	1939	44	FBN	FBN
122.	Dominick Petrilli	1900	1942	41	Hearings	Hearings
123.	James Picarelli	1906	≤1963	Not clear	Hearings	FBN; Hearings
124.	Salvatore Pieri	1911	1954	43	BOP FOIA	FBN; Hearings
125.	Rosario Pisciotta	1920	1951	31	BOP FOIA	FBN
126.	Carmine Polizzano	1920	1959	39	*New York Times*	*New York Times*
127.	Frank Presinzano	1902	1942	40	BOP FOIA	FBN; Hearings
128.	Stephen Puco	1918	1950	32	BOP FOIA	FBN; Hearings
129.	Joseph Ragone	1918	1954	36	BOP FOIA	FBN; Hearings
130.	Giacomo Reina	1909	1959	50	BOP FOIA	FBN; Hearings
131.	John Riccardulli	1912	1941	29	BOP FOIA	FBN; Hearings
132.	Rosario Rinaldi	1917	1955	38	BOP FOIA	FBN; Hearings
133.	Arnold Romano	1914	≤1953	Not clear	FBN	FBN
134.	Nunzio Romano	1909	1954	45	BOP FOIA	FBN
135.	Hugo Rossi	1901	1953	52	BOP FOIA	FBN; Hearings
136.	Leonard Salemi	1912	≤1940	Not clear	FBN	FBN
137.	Angelo Salerno	1902	1962	60	FBN	FBN; Hearings
138.	Anthony Salerno	1911	1958	45	BOP FOIA	FBN
139.	Salvatore Salli	1909	1950	41	BOP FOIA	FBN
140.	Carmelo Sansone	1912	1956	44	BOP FOIA	FBN; Hearings
141.	Aniello Santagata	1888	1956	68	Hearings	FBN; Hearings
142.	Salvatore Santoro	1915	1952	37	BOP FOIA	FBN; Hearings
143.	Giovanni Schillaci	1902	≤1947	Not clear	FBN; Hearings	Hearings
144.	Salvatore Shillitani	1908	1951	44	BOP FOIA	Hearings
145.	Joseph Schipani	1912	1938	26	FBN	FBN
146.	John Stopelli	1907	1951	44	FBN	FBN
147.	Joseph Stallone	1907	≤1953	Not clear	FBN	FBN
148.	John Tamberlani	1892	1940	48	FBN	FBN

149.	Peter Tambone	1920	1956	36	BOP FOIA	FBN
150.	Anthony Tacoma	1906	1953	47	FBN	FBN
151.	Enrico Tantillo	1916	≤1945	Not clear	FBN	Hearings
152.	James Tessalone	1899	1944	45	FBN	FBN
153.	Joseph Tocco	1902	1944	42	BOP FOIA	FBN
154.	Nicholas Tolentino	1909	1947	38	BOP FOIA	FBN; Hearings
155.	Eugene Tramaglino	1915	1951	36	FBN	FBN; Hearings
156.	Angelo Tuminaro	1910	1962	52	FBN	FBN; Hearings
157.	Joseph Valachi	1903	1959	56	BOP FOIA	Hearings
158.	Joseph Vento	1913	1952	39	BOP FOIA	FBN
159.	Salvatore Vitale	1903	1936	33	FBN	FBN; Hearings

6

THE MOB NIGHTLIFE

Anything can happen now that we've slid over this bridge. . .
anything at all.
　　　　　　　—F. Scott Fitzgerald, *The Great Gatsby* (1925)

Don't ask me why, but people seem to want to come to
a mob place. Maybe it's the excitement of mingling with
mobsters.
　　　　　　　—Vincent "Fat Vinnie" Teresa,
　　　　　　　My Life in the Mafia (1973)

Thirty-year-old Frank Sinatra walked off stage after 2:00 a.m. to the whistles of adoring patrons under the papier-mâché palm trees of the Copacabana in midtown Manhattan. Sinatra had flown in from Hollywood, where he'd been filming *It Happened in Brooklyn,* to make a surprise appearance beside comedian Phil Silvers (who later played Sergeant Bilko on *The Phil Silvers Show*). In the audience were Broadway singer Ethel Merman, Pulitzer Prize–winning playwright Sidney Kingsley, actress Paula Stone, and restaurateur Toots Shor. Gliding among them were the "Copa Girls," the nineteen-year-old ingénues whose long legs and demure smiles became club trademarks under the talented management of Monte Prosser.[1]

Presiding over the Copa behind the scenes was its hidden owner, Frank Costello. Mr. Costello was the bootlegger turned businessman, the street gangster who became a political fixer—and the secret acting boss of the Mafia's Luciano Family. Or as his nickname said, he was the "Prime Minister of the Underworld."[2]

Nighthawks who stepped out on the town for jazz on 54th Street, or drinks at a nightclub in the Village, or a prizefight at Madison Square Garden were at some point enjoying a mob-run production. Gangsters had an outsized influence over Manhattan's nightlife. They kept the doors open and the booze flowing. Mobsters, or glamorized versions of them, became part of the nightly allure. This chapter is a tour through the mob nightlife.

THE LINGERING HANGOVER OF PROHIBITION

The Mafia's influence over Manhattan's nightlife was due to the lingering aftereffects of Prohibition. The mix was one part cultural and one part legal.

Repeal ended the ban on alcohol, but *not* gangsters in the liquor business. Between 1920 and 1933, speakeasies were the only place where drink and music could be enjoyed together. The Jewish and Italian gangsters who ran them *loved* the nightly entertainment business. So when Prohibition ended, many former bootleggers and speakeasy operators slid over to newly legal bars and nightclubs.[3] "Nightclubs are big business for mob guys. They pick them because they like to cabaret, themselves," recalled Vincent "Fat Vinnie" Teresa. "It's also a place to go where you'll find women, loads of women, and you get a chance to be in the limelight."[4]

Although section one of the Twenty-First Amendment famously provided that Prohibition "is hereby repealed," lawmakers wary of returning to the wide-open saloon *also* inserted section two, which gave the states virtually unlimited power to regulate booze.[5] In 1934, New York's State Liquor Authority (NYSLA), began issuing a dizzying array of regulations over bars and nightclubs. The NYSLA could revoke a liquor license—a death sentence for nightspots—for anything from "improperly marked taps" to "undesirables permitted to congregate."[6] What's more, such violations could be reported by any beat cop on the street.

This bred venality in the nightclub business. As the Knapp Commission on police corruption found: "Selling liquor by the drink is governed by a complex system of state and local laws, infractions of which can lead to criminal penalties, as well as suspension or loss of license." As a result, liquor "licensees are highly vulnerable to police shakedowns."[7] Mobsters were often the ones keeping the cops at bay.

JAZZ CLUBS ON 52ND STREET

For New Yorkers wanting to hear the new music coming out of New Orleans during Prohibition, speakeasies were the place to go. Gangsters became an inseparable part of the jazz scene. At the Cotton Club in Harlem, Duke Ellington and Cab Calloway created the music of the Harlem Renaissance. Its owner was the bootlegger Owney "The Killer" Madden, and its patrons included *mafiosi* like Joe Valachi. This was not unusual. As a New York jazzman said, "no popular speakeasy seemed devoid of hoodlum associations, backing or control, regardless of whether a top performer's name like Club Durant or Club Richman appeared on it." In Chicago, Al Capone, a jazz enthusiast, controlled the top clubs. "To our amazement Capone would come over to the bandstand every few minutes or so and give each member of the band a twenty-dollar bill and then return to his table beaming and smoking fat cigars," recalled Teddy Wilson.[8]

Many bootleggers and speakeasy operators shifted over to legitimate clubs after Repeal. The bootlegger and jazz enthusiast Joe Helblock opened Onyx on West 52nd Street, a platform for Charlie "Bird" Parker and Dizzy Gillespie as they were inventing modern bebop. Sherman Billingsley, an ex-convict who worked for the Detroit mob, first opened The Stork Club as a speakeasy with underworld partners, including for a time Frank Costello. The Stork Club on East 53rd Street became a fashionable nightspot where celebrities like Lucille Ball and Damon Runyon mixed with wiseguys like Sonny Franzese.[9]

Although mob clubs offered essential venues, they were tough, treacherous places for musicians. "Around New York and Chicago 'The Boys' pretty much told you where you were going to work. The union didn't say nothin'," said jazz bassist Pops Foster. "The working conditions were horrible, really," recounted pianist George Shearing. When jazzman Mezz Mezzrow was going through heroin withdrawal, his nightmares were of the mobsters: "Legs Diamond and Babyface Coll and Dutch Schultz and Scarface and Louis the Wop, along with a gang of other mugs I couldn't quite recognize but still their murderous leers were sort of familiar, had been chasing me all over the Milky Way," dreamed Mezzrow. Louis Armstrong spent his early career dodging mobsters until he hired Joe Glaser (a man who once worked for Capone) to be his manager. Glaser "saved me from the gangsters," said Satchmo.[10]

6-1: Times Square, 1933. Even after repeal of Prohibition in 1933, the mob had an outsized influence on Manhattan's nightlife. (Photo by Samuel H. Gottscho, courtesy of the Library of Congress Prints and Photographs Division, Gottscho-Schleisner Collection)

THE COPACABANA, 10 EAST 60TH STREET

The Copacabana at 10 East 60th Street was the center of the mob nightlife in Manhattan. On any night, there was "someone from each family in there," confirmed a *mafioso*. Anthony "Tony Pro" Provenzano and Anthony "Fat Tony" Salerno kept a regular table with boxing mobsters Frankie Carbo and Frank Palermo. In they'd strut in silk suits, ridiculing waiters, then making up for it with big tips. When they wanted to talk business, wiseguys paid the wait captain to keep nearby tables unoccupied.[11]

Mobsters were part of the Copa's electric atmosphere. Hollywood actors, judges, and New York Yankees would literally bump into *mafiosi* like Joseph "Joe Stretch" Stracci or Frank "Frankie Brown" Bongiorno. They became part of the allure of the Manhattan nightlife. "A well-known gangster was respected as much as any movie star or politician," said actor George Raft. To most night owls, who never saw the barrel end of their guns, they were no more threatening than underworld characters from *The Great Gatsby*.[12]

Frank Sinatra had great times with the boys at the Copa. He had been looking up to them since his childhood in Hoboken, New Jersey, where young Francis grew up a skinny, lonely only child in the same neighborhood as Angelo "Gyp" DeCarlo, a *caporegime* in the Mafia. On his way up the nightclub circuit, Sinatra became pals with Willie Moretti, a vicious enforcer for Frank Costello.[13]

Sinatra's mob connections were first exposed in February 1947 when a newspaper revealed that he had given a special performance in Havana, Cuba, for a gathering of Lucky Luciano with other mobsters. Then, in August 1951, bandleader Tommy Dorsey told the *American Mercury* that when Sinatra was trying to get out of his band contract, Dorsey was intimidated into signing a release of Sinatra after being visited by three toughs who said "sign or else." Notwithstanding the bad publicity, Sinatra continued to socialize and do business with *mafiosi*. In 1962, Sinatra invested $50,000 in the Berkshire Downs horse track, which witnesses testified was secretly owned by the Patriarca Family. In 1963, the Nevada Gaming Control Board pulled his gaming license for hosting Sam Giancana at Sinatra's Cal-Neva Lodge.[14]

6–2: Singer Frank Sinatra talking with boxer Rocky Graziano at the Copa, 1946. (© Bettmann/CORBIS)

While denying his mob connections publicly, behind closed doors the Chairman of the Board was something of a want-to-be mobster who socialized with *mafiosi* throughout his adult life. "Sinatra's always talking about the mob guys he knows. Who gives a damn, especially if you're a mob guy yourself?" said Vinnie Teresa. He was drawn to the life. "Frank Sinatra loved gangsters, or at least the world they lived in," observed George Jacobs, his longtime valet. But he was no gangster himself. "Dad was interested in the wise guys because they were so *different* from him," explained his daughter. The skinny kid from Hoboken with the tough-guy persona was imitating life.[15]

PROFESSIONAL BOXING

Professional boxing was always a controversial sport on the edge of the law. Congress actually outlawed the interstate transportation of fight films between 1912 and 1939. The New York legislature did not fully legalize decision prizefights until 1920, believing they promoted gambling. Gamblers hovered around boxing gyms to get tip-offs—or worse, a deal to fix a fight—from boxers. The gambling stakes grew after the advent of nationally televised boxing matches. Mobsters lived in the same rough world as pugilists and were naturally drawn to them, too.[16]

The New York State Athletic Commission (NYSAC) was the nominal regulator of the sport. It had dismal beginnings. In 1925, promoter Tex Rickard was forced to hand over 25 percent of the gross receipts of the fight between Jack Dempsey and Luis Firpo to William J. McCormack, licensing commissioner of the NYSAC, "for his permission to let the fight go on."[17] Mostly, the NYSAC was just ineffectual. It was difficult to prove a gangster's hidden interest in a fighter. Even when the NYSAC issued a suspension, promoters crossed state lines to find another sanctioning body.[18]

"The Combination"

The Cosa Nostra moved into prizefighting in the 1930s principally behind Paolo "Frankie" Carbo and his partner Frank "Blinky" Palermo. Carbo was born on the Lower East Side in 1904 to respectable parents who found themselves with an incorrigible child and sent him away to a Catholic protectory. The nuns could not stop young Carbo's thirst for the criminal life: the police would arrest him twenty different times for charges ranging from juvenile delinquency to murder. In 1924, when he was twenty years old, Carbo killed a taxicab driver in the Bronx. He went on the lam for four years before pleading guilty to manslaughter in 1928.[19]

6–3: Frankie Carbo, ca. 1928. Carbo was a *de facto* boxing commissioner due to his influence over managers and fighters. (Used by permission of the John Binder Collection)

After getting out of Sing Sing, Carbo was looking for new enterprises, and he was drawn to the fight game. In the early 1930s, he started hanging around the famed Stillman's Gym on 55th Street and 8th Avenue in midtown Manhattan.[20] The *mafioso* was enthusiastic and knowledgeable about boxing, charming everyone from lowly pug fighters to top promoters. "I like boxing.

I don't know other business," he told confidants. Still, Carbo was foremost a solider in the Lucchese Family. His business consisted of taking hidden interests in boxers, bookmaking bets on fights, and then fixing those fights.[21]

Carbo's partner was Frank "Blinky" Palermo of Philadelphia. They were a feared pair. "Blinky" was a bug-eyed, gravel-voiced, strutting rooster of a man with ties to Philly's Jewish gangsters. Carbo was the shadowy power broker they called "Mr. Gray." Both loved boxing and making money off boxing. They and their associates came to be known as "The Combination," the underworld's commissioners of boxing.[22]

They captured professional boxing using tactics not unlike those the Mafia used elsewhere: they targeted fragile producers (individual boxers), gained control over key geographic spaces (Madison Square Garden), and used coercive industry associations to keep everyone in line (the Boxing Managers Guild and the International Boxing Club).

Fragile Fighters

The boxer, for all his athletic strength, had a glass jaw in the mob system. Most came from working class backgrounds, with little education and few prospects outside the ring. And they could not get *into* the ring unless they fought by the mob's rules. "You want to know why they control boxing? It's poor, hungry people," said former welterweight champion Don Jordan of the mob's influence. "In each state there's another syndicate person waiting to see you."[23]

Fighters could only get professional matches through mobbed-up managers. When the young Rocco Barbella (the future "Rocky Graziano") started showing promise, neighborhood gangsters sent him his first professional manager, Eddie Coco. "You better do what Eddie says. He's an important guy and he's going to get you some matches," they told him. Coco changed Barbella's name, arranged his first pro matches, and told him when to "carry" an overmatched opponent. "No fighter can get anywhere without us," mob guys warned a young Jake LaMotta. "Carbo had the middleweight division sewed up," recalled the fighter Marty Pomerantz. "They made sure there was a huge amount of betting. 'Don't knock this guy out. Knock that guy out. Maybe you don't have to win this.' All of that went on."[24]

Prizefighters who refused to carry a weaker opponent, or take dives, could be shut out from future matches. "The implication is that if you don't do certain things, you're not going to get certain fights," explained Danny Kapilow, a boxer in the 1940s. "You were almost blackballed at that time." It is sometimes forgotten that Jake La Motta took his infamous dive against Billy Fox (managed by Palermo) to get a title shot for the middleweight crown.[25]

Boxers knew even worse things could happen. "With Steve [Belloise], there came a time in the '40s that he started to talk around the gym about the fighters' organizing," recounted Kapilow. "Somebody quickly put a piece in his ear. That was the end of that. They're not going to talk about it." As former heavyweight champion Joe Louis testified in retirement, "Fighters have been taken advantage of by the underworld. A lot of managers, even a lot of promoters, get backing from outside world, outside people, who are gangsters and hoodlums." Louis, who ended up broke himself, could have been speaking from personal experience.[26]

Madison Square Garden, Eighth Avenue and 50th Street

For boxers, the apex was a fight at the old Madison Square Garden, in operation from 1925 through 1968. The cavernous arena in Hell's Kitchen could seat eighteen thousand spectators, all seemingly atop the ring. The Garden was described as "the center, the pivot of boxing" in America.[27]

Carbo gained access to the Garden through the legendary promoter Michael "Uncle Mike" Jacobs of the Twentieth Century Sporting Club. In the 1930s, Jacobs skillfully promoted a young Joe Louis, the first African-American heavyweight champion to gain a nationwide following. He parlayed the Brown Bomber's popularity into an exclusive lease of the Garden.[28]

The problem with success was that Jacobs suddenly needed lots of boxers to fill matches at the Garden. Carbo had scores of fighters in his pocket. Soon, the Lucchese Family soldier would be dictating fight cards on the nation's premier boxing stage.[29]

The Boxing Managers Guild

Carbo and Palermo maintained power through their influence over the managers. When most managers made less than $1,000 a year (less than $8,000 a year in present dollars), Carbo was known for doling out cash to struggling managers for food or rent. Managers became so ingratiated that when they found their newest fighter, "Mr. Gray" came calling for favors. Carbo and Palermo's influence extended to every corner of the fight game. Outside New York and Philadelphia, they had collusive arrangements with managers in the Midwest boxing centers of Chicago, Detroit, Toledo, and Youngstown, Ohio.[30]

Their power was enhanced by the Boxing Managers Guild. This shadowy front operated on subtle extortion and hidden interests. Out-of-state boxing managers were forced to "cut in" the guild before they could even hope to get a fight in New York. Television contracts for fights were decided behind closed doors by the guild, which favored fighters in which Carbo and Palermo held interests. An investigation later found that the guild "engaged in monopolistic practices" and "abrogated to itself the conduct and regulation of boxing in New York."[31]

When economic coercion was insufficient, Carbo and Palermo drew on past talents. After the boxing promoter Ray Arcel staged Saturday fights without Carbo's permission, he was assaulted with a steel pipe in front of Boston Garden. Subsequently, four bombs ripped through the Boston house of Arcel's business associate Sam Silverman. "The threat of the same for anyone else even thinking about not cooperating with Carbo & Co. was enough to bring the entire sport into line," recalled trainer Angelo Dundee.[32]

December 1946, Stillman's Gymnasium on Eighth Avenue

The stench of sweat permeated the dressing room at Stillman's Gymnasium, where up-and-coming boxers trained. "How you feel Rocky? Like to make a good deal on this fight?" offered the gambler. The boxer Rocky Graziano was in training for his match against "Cowboy" Reuben Shank at Madison Square Garden on December 27, 1946. The gambler reappeared a few days later. "Don't forget that that deal is still on. You'll make a hundred grand," he said to Graziano.[33]

After the District Attorney's office went public with the bribe offer, Graziano tried to backpedal from his original account, claiming he thought the offer was "a joke." Still, the entire situation reeked. Graziano's manager was Eddie Coco, a *caporegime* in the Lucchese Family (who in 1953 killed a car wash owner over a bill). The knockout artist Graziano was a 4-to-1 favorite over the journeyman Shank, but a gambling syndicate was reportedly placing huge bets on Shank. Suddenly, on Christmas Eve, two days before the match, Graziano pulled out of the fight claiming a back ailment.[34]

The District Attorney's office believed Graziano knew gangsters had already bet heavily on Shank, and he was worried about crossing them if he did not take a dive. The New York State Athletic Commission (NYSAC) temporarily revoked Graziano's license for failing to report the bribe offer. The 1946 bribe debacle portended an era of scandal in boxing that ultimately brought down Carbo and Palermo.[35]

The Downfall of the International Boxing Club

The most audacious monopoly in boxing was initiated not by gangsters, but by prestigious businessmen. Truman K. Gibson Jr. was a prominent Chicago lawyer and civil rights leader who had helped heavyweight champion Joe Louis with his tax problems. In 1949, Gibson approached James Norris and Arthur Wirtz, who controlled the Chicago Stadium, the Detroit Olympia Arena, and the St. Louis Arena, and proposed that they create a dominant boxing promotion company: the International Boxing Club (IBC). They first struck a deal with the aging Joe Louis: in exchange for shares in the IBC, Louis would secure exclusive fight contracts for the IBC with the four leading contenders and then give up his heavyweight title. In the euphemisms of monopoly, it was proposed that they all "work together now and keep the events for our building and not create a competitive situation that would be harmful to all."[36]

The only problem was that they had left Carbo out of the scheme. Gibson explains what happened next. "In New York the first fight that we tried to stage, the Graziano-La Motta fight, suddenly was called off because Graziano developed an illness and we had a picket line around Madison Square Garden," Gibson recounted. They knew instantly who was behind it. "[T]he organization of managers . . . the Carbo friendship with managers over the years," cited Gibson. Cosa Nostra was threatening the IBC's ability to fill its fight cards. "I was having a great deal of guild trouble," James Norris concurred. So they decided "to live with" the underworld. They put Carbo's very pretty, if very unqualified, girlfriend Viola Masters on their payroll and funneled "goodwill" payments to him through business fronts.[37]

As the 1950s went on, and rumors of fixed fights threatened to destroy the sport, government officials were pressured to go after Carbo, Palermo, and their business associates. First, in July 1958, the Manhattan District Attorney's Office brought misdemeanor charges against Carbo for his unlicensed management of fighters. In the middle of trial, he pled guilty.[38]

To break up the IBC, the Justice Department brought a federal civil action against the IBC for violating the Sherman Antitrust Act. In January 1959, the United States Supreme Court affirmed the trial court's judgment, holding that the IBC was a monopoly. The trial court had found that the IBC had used its power to promote 93 percent of all the championship fights in all divisions.[39]

Then, in September 1959, the United States Attorney for Los Angeles brought federal criminal charges against Carbo and Palermo, Truman K. Gibson Jr., and *mafiosi* Louis Dragna and mob associate Joe Sica for using extortion "to obtain a monopoly in professional boxing." Promoter Jackie Leonard testified that Carbo and Palermo were dictating his fight cards in Los Angeles and trying to muscle in on the earnings of welterweight champion Don Jordan. When Leonard resisted, Joe Sica told him "the same thing could happen to me that happened to Ray Arcel." Shortly after, Leonard was assaulted outside his garage. The jury convicted the defendants, and the judge sentenced Carbo and Palermo to twenty-five years in prison.[40]

Their glorious nights at the Copa were done.

OUTLAWING GAY LIFE IN THE 1930s

Perhaps the most surprising aspect of the mob nightlife was the Mafia's ownership of gay bars and nightclubs. The Mafia specialized in illegal markets, which is what gay bars became in Gotham. The historian George Chauncey has shown that gay life was remarkably visible from the 1890s until it was forced underground in the 1930s. New York State's liquor laws barred "disorderly" premises, which the NYSLA interpreted as serving drinks to gays and lesbians, and the City of New York barred the employment of homosexuals. The NYSLA and NYPD closed hundreds of gay bars in the 1930s and '40s. Using this threat, vice police shook down bars "which catered heavily to . . . homosexuals soliciting partners," according to the Knapp Commission on police corruption.[41]

Wiseguys muscled in on the vulnerable owners of gay establishments with protection rackets and skimming operations. "Even if you came in [and] tried to open a gay bar, you would be contacted by the Family, and be informed it was a closed shop," explained a bartender. Cosa Nostra then had the cash and clout to keep open gay bars in which it held hidden interests.[42]

Though it seems unthinkable today, there were also cultural reasons for the Mafia's association with gay bars. Chauncey has documented the presence of many *finocchio* ("fairies") among working-class, southern Italian men in the early 1900s; Italian bachelors would get serviced by *finocchio* without thinking themselves gay. During Prohibition, gangsters ran the speakeasies with "coarse" entertainment like Dutch Schultz's Club Abbey on West 54th Street, featuring Jean Malin's "pansy act" show.[43]

Even in its formative decades, the Cosa Nostra had some members who engaged in forms of same-sex acts or transgender dressing. According to FBI informants, David Petillo "in his early teens was reputed to be a 'fairy,'" and "dressed as a woman" to disguise himself while executing hits. (Petillo was convicted with Charles Luciano for compulsory prostitution in 1936). Similarly, Charles Gagliodotto reportedly wore dresses and carried his gun in a purse so often he was known in the Genovese Family as the "fag hit-man." Later, the wiseguy operator of the Stonewall Inn, whose father was a prominent *mafioso*, had male lovers. Mobster Joseph "Crazy Joey" Gallo talked about how "normal, natural and unremarkable" homosexuality was in prison. Gallo held interests in gay bars including the Purple Onion and Washington Square.[44]

Gay Nightclubs in the 1930s and '40s

Vito Genovese's crews in Greenwich Village held the most interests in gay establishments in Manhattan going back to the 1930s. Genovese associate Steve Franse ran the Howdy Club at 47 West 3rd Street in Greenwich Village, the first nightclub catering to lesbians after they were outlawed by the NYSLA. It featured Blackie Dennis, a male impersonator, who dressed in tuxedoes and wore slicked-back short hair. "She was the best looking and most popular singer in the whole Village," remembered a club regular. The club even did promotional photographs with women dressed in football gear. During the Second World War, sailors docked in New York went to the Howdy Club, some meeting other homosexuals in public for the first time.[45]

6–4: Promotional photograph for the Howdy Club, ca. 1935. Steve Franse ran the Howdy Club under Vito Genovese's Mafia crew in Greenwich Village. (Used by permission of the Lesbian Herstory Archives)

In 1943, the mob opened Tony Pastor's Downtown, which billed itself as "One of New York's Most Colorful Nite-Clubs." Lesbians at the bar would send over drinks to attractive girls, and there were Sunday cocktail dances for women.

The manager of Tony Pastor's Downtown was Joseph Cataldo. Behind the scenes, Joseph "Joe the Wop" Cataldo was a longtime *mafioso* under the Genoveses.[46]

Even the Cosa Nostra's power had its limits when the public's enmity toward "degenerates" required a crackdown. In 1944, the NYSLA suspended the license of the Howdy Club for presenting shows by Leon La Verdi, who "exhibited feminine characteristics which would appeal to any male homosexual." Steve Franse argued that "La Verdi had been doing the same act for about 10 years without complaint." It did not work, and the Howdy Club closed permanently. That same year, Joe Cataldo was found guilty of "permitting Lesbians to loiter on the premises," resulting in the suspension of Tony Pastor's license. However, Tony Pastor's managed to reopen and remain in business until 1967, when the NYSLA revoked its liquor license for permitting "homosexuals, degenerates and undesirables to be on the license premises."[47]

The 181 Club, 181 2nd Avenue

"The most famous fag joint in town," screamed tabloid journalists pressuring officials to shutter its doors.[48] Patrons and employees of the 181 Club saw their place differently. "It was like the homosexual Copacabana," said Bertie, a tuxedoed waiter. As she described it,

> it was a lovely club. Wedgwood walls, white and blue. It had a nice stage. They had the cream of the crop, as far as female impersonators. They weren't just drag queens. These were guys that had talent behind their costumes. The costumes were lavish and wonderful. They had borzoi . . . with rhinestone collars.[49]

"All the butches worked at this club as waiters and 'Chorus Boys,'" a regular recalled. Buddy Kent performed there as Fred Astaire, with black tails, a top hat, and a cane. "It was showbiz, and very, very glamorous," Kent recounted proudly. The audiences were a mix of gawking straight couples, closeted gays and lesbians, "and racketeers."[50]

The Mafia kept open the doors of the 181 Club. Vito Genovese was once its hidden owner, and its manager was Steve Franse. Even during the height of the crackdown on gay life in New York, the 181 Club survived and prospered from 1945 to 1953. "The cops were paid off," explained Buddy Kent.[51]

Mob-Owned Gay Bars in the 1950s

Franse ran the 181 Club from 1945 until 1953, when he moved it to 82 East 4th Street and renamed it Club 82. It became the most popular drag spot in the 1950s. Greta Garbo and Judy Garland were among the celebrities who attended shows at Club 82. Terry Noel, a female impersonator, did three shows a night, six nights a week, not getting off until 4:00 a.m. Noel said "the club owners had a certain influence over the vice cops, if you get my drift, and we were in less danger from them than the owners when it came to leaving in drag."[52]

On June 19, 1953, Steve Franse left Club 82 at 4:30 a.m. to meet up with Pat Pagano and Fiore Siano. They wanted to see Joe Valachi's new restaurant in the Bronx. Valachi gave them a tour of his place, ending up in the kitchen. "That's when it happens," Valachi describes:

> Pat grabs [Franse] from behind—he has got him in an armlock—and the other guy, Fiore, raps him in the mouth and belly. . . . I'm standing guard by the kitchen door when Pat lets go and Steve drops to the floor. He is on his back, and he is out. They wrap this chain around his neck. He starts to move once, so Pat puts his foot on his neck to keep him there. It only took a few minutes.

Vito Genovese ordered the murder of Franse. Vito's wife Anna Genovese had sued Vito for maintenance and, to the shock of everyone, tried to identify his underworld assets. Anna was involved in nightclubs with Franse, and Vito blamed him for not keeping a lid on her.[53]

After Franse, Genovese *caporegime* Anthony "Tony Bender" Strollo took over the Genovese nightclubs in the Village. After Strollo disappeared in 1962, Tommy Eboli took over the family's bars and nightclubs in the Village. Later in the '60s, Matthew "Matty the Horse" Ianniello, another Genovese *caporegime*, took interests in gay bars and pornographic bookstores in Times Square.[54]

Other *mafiosi* controlled gay bars elsewhere in New York. Edward "Eddie Toy" DeCurtis of the Gambino Family held interests in gay establishments on Long Island. In the 1960s, DeCurtis was convicted of allowing "lewd, indecent and disorderly homosexual activities" at his Magic Touch restaurant on Long Island. Anthony "Fat Tony" Rabito of the Bonanno Family "controlled a bunch of fag bars" in New York. And Salvatore "Solly Burns" Granello reportedly held hidden interests in gay bars on the East Side of Manhattan.[55]

Mafia Management of Gay Bars

With little competition, Mafia-run bars could charge high prices for lousy amenities. Most were hidden away on side streets, their windows painted dark, and they peddled watered-down, bootleg liquor supplied by mafiosi. "We would . . . take [brand label] bottles, and pour whatever swill we could get into it," recounted Chuck Shaheen, a bartender at mob-run gay bars. Even at the glamorous 181 Club, the overpriced drinks were dismal. "The drinks were all watered, God knew what they were," remembered a patron.[56]

The toxic arrangement with the police wrought indignities. To appease hostile neighbors, the police staged raids periodically. White lights would blink on when a raid was happening. Humiliated patrons stood in the harsh light of a dank basement before being hauled off in a paddy wagon. "If they took you in, it was usually for 'disturbing the peace' or 'impersonating' somebody of the opposite sex," said Buddy Kent shaking her head.[57]

Starting in the 1950s, the Mattachine Society, the first gay-rights organization in New York, began criticizing the vice police and the Mafia itself. "The Mafia has been in the business for years," charged Mattachine leader Richard Leitsch in 1967, "primarily because the legal setup has been such as to discourage legitimate business from operating [gay] bars." Frustration with the mob system of bars culminated in a revolt that now symbolizes the gay rights movement.[58]

The Stonewall Inn, 53 Christopher Street

If the 181 Club was the gay Copacabana, then the Stonewall Inn was the dive bar. The Stonewall had no running water behind the bar, so its bartenders just dipped used glasses in a basin of dirty water, refilled the glasses, and served other customers. The toilets routinely overflowed, leaving the bathroom soaked. Like the 181 Club though, the Stonewall was operated by members and associates of the Genovese Family. Chuck Shaheen, who opened the Stonewall with its mob owners, said that Matthew "Matty the Horse" Ianniello was "the real boss, the real big boss." Its bouncer Ed "The Skull" Murphy confirmed that Cosa Nostra made $1200 monthly payoffs to the NYPD's sixth precinct in exchange for letting the Stonewall operate without a liquor license, and tipping off its managers to planned raids.[59]

On June 28, 1969, that arrangement was disrupted by a raid executed by an honest vice cop. The historian David Carter has shown that Seymour Pine, the newly appointed commander of the local vice squad, was really after its mob owners for other crimes. "We weren't concerned about gays. We were concerned about the Mafia," Pine maintained. This is supported by contemporaneous news accounts: "Police also believe the club was operated by Mafia connected owners," reported the *New York Daily News*.[60]

This time, the drag queens fought back. "You already got the payoff, here's some more!" screamed Ray "Sylvia Lee" Rivera throwing pennies at the police. "Why do we have to pay the Mafia all this kind of money to drink in a lousy fuckin' bar?" protested Rivera. "It wasn't my fault that the bars where I could meet other gay people were run by organized crime," thought Morty Manford, a Columbia student who was at the Stonewall that night. By that Sunday, June 29, protestors handed out leaflets attacking "the Mafia monopoly."[61]

During the riots, someone wrote this graffiti on the Stonewall Inn's boarded-up windows:

GAY
PROHIBITION
CORUPT$ COP$
FEED$ MAFIA

And that informal haiku says it all.

6–5: Graffiti on Stonewall Inn, 1969. The outlawing of homosexuality meant that the Mafia controlled many of the gay and lesbian bars in New York City. (Photo by Fred W. McDarrah, used by permission of Getty Images)

PART 3

THE MOBBED-UP METROPOLIS

The 1950s

7

THE LIVES OF WISEGUYS

I never was a crumb, and if I have to be a crumb I'd rather
be dead.
                                        —Charles Luciano (1936)

And what did I get out of it? Nothing but misery.
                                        —Joseph Valachi (1963)

Philip "Philly Katz" Albanese was part of the wave of street soldiers who
reshaped organized crime on the waterfront. Born to immigrant parents on
the Lower East Side, Philip went bad as a young man and, in 1935, was sent
to prison for robbery. When he got out, Albanese did strongarm work for the
Luciano Family and became a public loader of fruit on the Hudson River piers
when they were still majority Irish. He also started moving narcotics on the
waterfront.[1]

Albanese enjoyed his new prosperity by moving his family to the upper-
middle-class neighborhood of Riverdale in the north Bronx. In 1946, he was
convicted on a narcotics conspiracy, but the drug sentences were weak then, and
he spent only nine months in jail. In the early 1950s, Albanese moved his family
again, this time to suburban Valley Stream, Long Island.[2]

Then the Internal Revenue Service went after him. Federal prosecutors
showed that Albanese "operated behind a paper wall of false and fictitious
records to disguise his own financial interests" in a loading company. In 1954,
Albanese was convicted of tax evasion for failing to pay $6,700 in taxes on his
loader income between 1946 and 1950 (over $55,000 in 2013 dollars). At sen-
tencing, prosecutors called him "one of the criminal rats which infest our water-

front today." Enraged by the remark, Albanese leapt up out of his chair and yelled, "My business was oranges and grapefruits which come in on freighters!"[3]

We now have rich sources on the lives of wiseguys like Phil Albanese. In 1963, Senator John McClellan conducted groundbreaking hearings on the Cosa Nostra (hereafter "the McClellan Committee hearings"), which collect a wealth of untapped data on mob soldiers and their criminal activities. In addition, there are now dozens of mob memoirs, trial transcripts, and transcripts of *mafiosi* wiretaps. Although these sources have to be used with care, they can provide great insights on everyday life in the mob.[4] Using the tools of social history, we can better understand the lives of wiseguys.

THE LIVES THEY CHOSE

Most young men who joined the Mafia did *not* do so because they lacked other choices but because they wanted to be wiseguys. For all the talk of the Honored Society defending the Sicilian peasantry, twentieth-century New York City was not *Il Mezzogiorno* (impoverished Southern Italy). Although Sicilian immigrants faced rampant bigotry and tough working conditions, Italian Americans soon had unprecedented opportunities. Gotham had nearly a million manufacturing jobs for blue-collar workers, and the economy was fairly booming after the Great Depression. By 1950, New York's unemployment rate was under 7 percent and most children (86 percent) ages fourteen to seventeen were attending school. To join the Mafia was to rebel *against* the immigrant Italian work ethic.[5]

Wiseguys themselves almost never claim that they needed to join the Cosa Nostra to escape grinding poverty. Rather, most simply wanted an easier life. "I was never a crumb, and if I have to be a crumb I'd rather be dead," said Charles Luciano. He described a "crumb" as the ordinary man "who works and saves and lays his money aside."[6] As ex-*mafioso* Rocco Morelli explained, "I was always looking for a hustle, a get-rich-quick scheme—whatever it took to make a buck so I wouldn't have to work hard like my dad."[7] The Cosa Nostra subverted the work ethic. "You can lie, steal, cheat, kill, and it's all legitimate," marveled Benjamin "Lefty Guns" Ruggiero, who grew up in lower-middle-class Knickerbocker Village.[8] The mobster lifestyle fascinated young men. "All we knew was that they were better off than everybody else and people treated them as if they were important," Willie Fopiano recalled of Boston's North End mobsters. "They seemed to move in some exciting, secret world that was invisible to anyone who wasn't one of them."[9]

The Cosa Nostra was peddling an idea to young men drawn to its promises of honor and loyalty. "So many fine words! So many fine principles!" Antonio Calderone remembered of his initiation ceremony into the Mafia. "I really felt that I belonged to a brotherhood that had honor and respect," recalled Sammy "The Bull" Gravano, the son of middle-class parents from Bensonhurst, Brooklyn. Of course, the Cosa Nostra did not live up to advertising. As Calderone discovered: "So many times over the ensuing years did I find myself confronted by a lack of respect for these rules—by deceit, betrayal, murder committed precisely to exploit the good faith of those who believed in them." Likewise, Gravano became disillusioned. "I got to learn that the whole thing was bullshit," Gravano said. "I mean, we broke every rule in the book."[10]

GOING TO THE OFFICE

Mafia soldiers went to their version of the office. The mobster's office was usually hidden behind a front, literally and figuratively. Federal narcotics agent Charles Siragusa recalls the "many political clubs that were hangouts for the gangster elite" in the 1930s. The front of the Abraham Lincoln Independent Political Club in Williamsburg, Brooklyn, had an espresso machine and card tables, where men played pinochle and talked football. In the back of the club, behind a door marked "Private," was the office where mob boss Joe Bonanno conducted the real business.[11]

Others preferred the anonymity of shabby storefronts. Cantalupo Realty looked like any another real-estate office in Brooklyn. However, as the front man Joseph Cantalupo recalled, each day *mafiosi* "were buzzed in daily through the small gate at the office waiting room, past what was my desk, down a short corridor to the private office on the left where [Joe] Colombo sat directing the traffic of his crime family." New England boss Ray Patriarca's office was at the rear of a vending machine business. "The place was far from classy, more poor than rich, but when people spoke of 'the Office' this is what they meant," said Joe "The Animal" Barboza.[12]

The wiseguy's day had its own kind of rhythm. "Everybody socialized while Nicky conducted business in another room," said mob soldier Andrew DiNota, describing Gambino Family *caporegime* Nicholas Corozzo's social club. Goodfellas would sit around gossiping and trading information about potential scores, like which new gambling card games to shake down or new truck shipments to hijack. Then, at night, the crew "would hit various nightclubs or restaurants popular with the wiseguys and sit around planning new scores or reminiscing about old ones," said Joseph Pistone, the undercover FBI agent who infiltrated the Bonanno Family.[13]

STREET WORK

So, what exactly did wiseguys do for "work"? In 1963, the McClellan Committee hearings identified hundreds of Mafia soldiers and their activities. Based on data collected by the McClellan Committee, table 7–1 shows the top activities of the New York Mafia's soldiers in the 1950s and early 1960s:

Table 7–1: The Work of Wiseguys Top Activities of the Soldiers of the New York Families, ca. 1950–1963[14] (n=162)		
	Categories of Activities	Percentage of Soldiers
1.	**Gambling**: Bookmaking for sports betting or illegal numbers lotteries.	61%
2.	**Strongarm**: Assault and battery, extortion, or murder.	49%
3.	**Narcotics**: Illegal drug trafficking or drug conspiracies.	31%
4.	**Loansharking**: Loans above maximum interest rates and illegal collection methods.	20%
5.	**Criminal Receiver**: Possessing or selling goods stolen by thievery or hijacking.	13%

6.	**Labor Racketeering**: Bribery of union officials, embezzlement of union funds, extortion of employers, Hobbs Act or antitrust violations.	13%
7.	**Alcohol Tax**: Evasion of alcohol taxes or bootlegging or moonshining operations.	11%
8.	**Vending**: Coin-operated cigarette, jukebox, or pinball machines.	8%
9.	**Counterfeiting**: Forgeries of money, checks, or government stamps.	3%

We have previously explored the cornerstone activities of gambling (chapter 2), labor racketeering (chapter 4), and narcotics trafficking (chapter 5). Now let us look briefly at some of the wiseguy's other major activities.

Strongarm: Assault and Battery, Extortion, and Murder

The Cosa Nostra had earned its reputation for violence. Nearly half of New York's soldiers had been involved in "strongarm" crimes like assault and battery, usually to enforce other rackets. Extortion—obtaining property through fear of violence—was a common crime of wiseguys, too. The Mafia's power rested, ultimately, on its capacity for violence.

Many of the Mafia's top leaders started out as strongarm men, including Luciano Family boss Frank Costello (convicted of illegal gun possession in 1915), Lucchese Family boss Carmine Tramunti (convicted of felony assault in 1931), and Gambino Family boss Paul Castellano (convicted of robbery in 1934).[15] Mob leaders were always on the lookout for potential new soldiers, too. Andrew DiDonato gained attention of mobsters after he started extorting money from other criminals despite being only 5 feet, 9 inches and 160 pounds. "They knew if they fucked around with me, I'd get 'em with my fists, or a bat, or a tire iron," said DiDonato of his shakedown targets. A Gambino Family crew soon recruited him into the mob.[16]

And sometimes the mob's soldiers murdered people. Contrary to myth, not every *mafioso* was a murderer (see below). But the Mafia's enforcers racked up a grisly human toll. Joe Valachi publicly detailed his roles in executing six different people.[17] Gambino Family underboss Salvatore "Sammy The Bull" Gravano confessed to being involved in some way in eighteen homicides.[18] Some were utterly remorseless: Carmine "Lilo" Galante was clinically diagnosed as a "psychopath" by prison psychiatrists in Sing Sing.[19]

Wiseguys tried to rationalize away various murders. "We do not kill innocent people," insisted Vincent "Fish" Cafaro. He then ticked off what he saw as justifiable reasons for committing homicides, like being "a rat" or "your family got abused by someone." The mob's soldiers purported to distinguish themselves from professional contract killers. "I don't believe in killing for money," asserted Joseph "Hoboken Joe" Stassi. "There was always another reason, cheating or talking to the law, disobeying orders. They had a reason, even if the reason wasn't always right."[20]

The *mafioso* lived knowing that he, too, could be eliminated by those around him. "Whenever a surprise meeting was called . . . there was always a sense, a fear, that this was it for you," recalled Anthony "Tony Nap" Napoli.[21] As FBI agent Joe Pistone explained, "Wiseguys wake up every day, aware that this may be the day that they get killed, at any moment, for lots of different reasons."[22] Although the Commission promised to protect wiseguys from arbitrary killings, there were no guarantees if you crossed the wrong man. "Goodfellows don't sue goodfellows," said a *mafioso* on a surveillance bug. "Goodfellows kill goodfellows."[23] This realization helped fuel the fast times and high living of wiseguys.

Loansharking

Wiseguys went into loansharking because it was relatively simple, drew little attention from law enforcement, and was more profitable than bookmaking. Mob loansharks lent money above the maximum legal interest rates to bookmakers, gamblers, and overextended businessmen—people who could not get credit through banks. Of course, the terms and interest were steep: repayments at 2 to 5 percent or more *per week* (annual percentage rates of over 150 percent per year). "If a guy borrowed $10,000 and the loan shark charged him two points, he would have to pay $200 a week in interest—which was known as the vig or the juice—every week, and he still owed," explained Philadelphia mobster Philip Leonetti.[24]

Despite—or because of—their reputation for knee-capping deadbeats, the mob's collectors only had to resort to violence sparingly for ordinary debtors. They wanted repeat customers, and they mostly relied on implicit threats. Showing up at night on the debtor's doorstep was usually intimidating enough to ensure repayment. "There's only two people I had to hit to collect. Physically, hit, I mean. Only two people. I think that says something about the reputation I had," Sammy Gravano said of his loansharking.[25] Mobster John Dalessio actually took his daughter on debt-collection trips around Staten Island. "Once a week, we'd cruise the Island in the Caddy and make stops at people's houses so my father could collect debts owed from various gambling operations," recalled his daughter. "He'd emerge seconds later carrying an envelope or paper bag."[26] The Mafia's trademark for violence had its advantages.

Criminal Receiver: Fencing Stolen Goods, Thievery, and Hijacking

Criminal receivers sold ("fenced") stolen goods ("swag"). Receiving was often related to thefts and hijackings. Manhattan was full of high-end consumer goods that wiseguys loved to steal. Joe Valachi got his start as a burglar who stole silk and jewelry from Manhattan stores then sold the swag to professional fences.[27] "The Mafia is not primarily an organization of murderers. First and foremost, the Mafia is made up of thieves," said FBI agent Joe Pistone.[28]

The Cosa Nostra specialized in hijacking targeted trucks on the highways around New York City. For a split of the profits, they would get inside tips of a lucrative shipment. Sometimes, the driver himself was involved. "Pricey stuff gets shipped everywhere. Truck drivers out for a quick buck will turn to us," said Louis Ferrante. "Some ask me to tie them up and leave them somewhere to make it look good."[29] Like on the waterfront, shippers put up with occasional thefts because the New York market was too large to abandon. The Mafia developed fencing operations, too. "Most of the hijack loads, whether it's cigarettes, liquor, furs, appliances, or food, are shipped by the mob to discount stores they own or have connections with," Vinnie Teresa explained. "In a matter of hours it's distributed."[30]

Alcohol Tax: Bootlegging, Moonshining, and Tax Evasion

Perhaps most surprising was the wiseguys' continued role in illegal alcohol sales *after* the repeal of Prohibition in 1931. This was another example of how over-regulation fostered organized crime. Through the 1950s, the federal excise tax on whiskey was extremely high at $10.50 a gallon. (If the excise tax had kept up with inflation, it would be $90 a gallon in 2013 dollars instead of its current rate of $13.50). State and local fees and regulations further drove up the price of booze. Bootlegged, tax-free liquor offered significant cost savings for New York's bars and nightclubs, in which mobsters often held hidden interests.[31]

7–1: Joseph DiPalermo, John Longo, Nicholas Palmotto, and Carmine Galante, arrested for alcohol tax violations in 1947. (Used by permission of the John Binder Collection)

After repeal, Carlo Gambino and his brothers became the leaders of "a notorious, daring group of bootleggers" that operated secret, unlicensed alcohol distilleries around Brooklyn, New York, and Newark, New Jersey. The Gambinos supplied huge quantities of untaxed booze to Manhattan bars and nightclubs. Mob-run gay bars were infamous for their bootleg liquors.[32]

The Mafia's bootleggers were significant enough to be targeted by federal law enforcement well into the 1950s. As we will see, the most important mob bust in history involved Treasury Department agents of the Alcohol and Tobacco Tax Division, who were investigating mob moonshiners around Apalachin, New York, in 1957.

Vending Machines

The Mafia's most peculiar business was coin-operated vending machines. Yet it makes sense in light of the mob's practices. Organized crime first got into vending machines as an offshoot of gambling slot machines. Wiseguys then created noncompetitive "routes" for their machines by coercing bars, restaurants, and stores into using *only* the mob's "union"-sanctioned machines. Joseph "Crazy Joe" Gallo, a.k.a. the "jukebox king," got his nicknames for assaulting bar owners who replaced his machines.[33] The racket was easy to monitor: Gallo's machines were either in the bar or they weren't. This currency-only business was also conducive to income tax evasion.[34]

Senator John McClellan's committee hearings of 1957–1959 documented pervasive racketeering in the vending-machine business in New York City. Charles Lichtman, a vending-machine jobber, became enmeshed in bizarre schemes by mobsters. After Lichtman sold a new game machine to a bar owner in 1930, his mechanic was kidnapped by Dutch Schultz's gang until he removed the machine. Later on, after Lichtman became a union leader in the business, he was paid by the Associated Amusement Machine Operators of New York to "protect the locations of the various [AAMONY] operators" by picketing businesses that put in new machines by outside vendors. The mob finally shut out Lichtman from the industry. "You have no racket connections, you are nobody, so you are out," Joe Valachi told him bluntly.[35]

THE MOB'S MONEY

There has been much speculation about the Mafia's money. In 1967, the President's Commission on Law Enforcement estimated that organized crime made gambling profits "as high as one-third of gross revenue—or $6 to $7 billion each year." The commission warned that it "cannot judge the accuracy of these figures" of gambling profits.[36] Nevertheless, writers have seized on these unreliable figures to give distorted pictures of the mobster life. One criminologist claimed that "any given member of Cosa Nostra is more likely to be a millionaire than not."[37] Another book on the Mafia quotes a cop as stating, "Even a simple soldier these days can wind up a millionaire."[38] Mob insiders, however, have consistently refuted the notion that ordinary soldiers routinely became millionaires.[39]

At the other end of the spectrum, a new history book on the Mafia portrays the soldiers as indigents, and mob bosses like Vito Genovese and John Gotti as having "a middle-class lifestyle—but nothing more."[40] The book erroneously suggests that *mafiosi* had little wealth because their gambling operations made only small profits.[41]

Both side of this debate suffer from an incomplete analysis. The narrow focus on gambling presents a skewed picture of the Cosa Nostra's diverse sources of income. Furthermore, both sides fail to account for the spending habits of wiseguys. Members of the New York families could make substantial cash incomes. However, they typically consumed it in ways which did not foster long-term wealth.

Diversified Income: The Wiseguys' Rackets

Mobsters had to deal with interruptions in their incomes. Rackets could dry up for long stretches of time, causing low-level wiseguys to struggle financially. Stints in prison were an occupational hazard, too. When the police busted down the door of Joseph "Joe Dogs" Iannuzi, he was worried less about the charges than the disruption to his illegal income. "I was now unemployed," said Iannuzi.[42]

The New York families therefore diversified into a wide variety of criminal enterprises, racketeering activities, and quasi-legitimate businesses.[43] Although bookmaking was a common activity, as we saw in chapter 2, the wiseguys utilized it for basic "work" income and to raise capital for more profitable activities. Few wiseguys limited themselves *solely* to gambling. As shown in table 7–1, less than 10 percent of the New York soldiers identified by the 1963 McClellan Committee hearings were engaged only in gambling. Thus, it is inaccurate to project small profits from low-level bookmaking as representative of all the Mafia's income streams.

Many wiseguys were engaged in more profitable activities. Roughly 40 percent of the Mafia soldiers identified by the 1963 McClellan Committee hearings were engaged in narcotics trafficking, labor racketeering, or both (see tables 7–1 and 7–3). High-level narcotics trafficking at the smuggling and wholesale level often generates extraordinary profits and income.[44] This was especially true during the 1930s through 1960s when the New York Mafia had cartel power over America's wholesale heroin markets.[45]

Labor racketeering generated diverse and lucrative sources of income as well. "We got our money from gambling, but our real power, our real strength came from the unions," testified Vincent "Fish" Cafaro.[46] The mob's power over unions translated into various revenue streams, including receiving bloated union salaries and no-show jobs, embezzling union treasuries and pension funds, taking bribes from employers for "strike insurance racket" and "labor peace," using unions to set up employer cartels and collect employers' association dues, and leveraging power over unions to gain competitive advantages for mob-owned businesses.[47] Lucchese Family associate Henry Hill remembered how *caporegime* Paulie Vario used his power over a bricklayers' union to create no-show union construction jobs. "We didn't even show up regular enough to pick up our own paychecks. We had guys we knew who were really working on the job bring our money," recalled Hill.[48]

Suburban Mobsters

Another indication of the *mafiosi's* economic mobility was the flight to the suburbs after the Second World War. By the 1950s, many wiseguys had achieved roughly middle-class lives in suburban communities around the New York metropolitan area.

Like other prospering New Yorkers, successful wiseguys began moving out of inner city neighborhoods to the suburbs. As we have seen, the Mafia's traditional strongholds were Italian East Harlem, Lower Manhattan, South Brooklyn, and, to a lesser extent, South/Central Bronx. Although mobsters would continue to go into "work" in these neighborhoods, many changed their personal residences to the outer boroughs and suburban communities. "So, in the 1930s and 1940s the racketeers were our neighbors on One Hundred and Seventh Street," remembers Salvatore Mondello, a resident of East Harlem. "The wealthiest men on my street, they left first for better neighborhoods and newer horizons."[49] The statistics in table 7–2 bear out Mondello's observation.[50]

Table 7–2: The Move to the Suburbs Personal Residences of Soldiers of the New York Families, ca. 1950–1963[51] (n=162)	
Outer Boroughs and Suburbs ~ 52%	
Suburban New Jersey (excluding Newark, Camden, and Jersey City)	11%
Queens	10%
Westchester, Dutchess, or Rockland Counties (surrounding counties of NYC)	9%
Long Island	7%
North Bronx	6%
East Bronx/Pelham Bay	5%
Staten Island	4%
Traditional Mob Strongholds ~ 43%	
Brooklyn	22%
Lower Manhattan	12%
East Harlem	5%
South/Central Bronx	4%
Other Neighborhoods ~ 5%	
Manhattan–Other	3%
Metro New Jersey (Newark, Camden, and Jersey City)	2%

More than half of the soldiers identified by the 1963 McClellan Committee hearings were residing in the outer boroughs and suburbs. Mobsters sprung up in upscale communities like Rego Park, Queens, and Lido Beach, Long Island as largely assimilated suburbanites. By 1963, 80 percent of the New York Mafia's soldiers had been born in the United States.[52]

Take Joe Valachi, whose experience was a microcosm of the wiseguy life. The son of working-class immigrants, Valachi grew up in a cold-water tenement in East Harlem. At age nineteen, Valachi was sentenced to Sing Sing, where he made his first real contacts with *mafiosi*. After being initiated into the Cosa Nostra in 1930, he did strongarm work for underboss Vito Genovese, engaged in heroin trafficking, worked as a bookie and loanshark, and used his loansharking business to obtain interests in a union-free shop in the garment district and vending machines in bars. He later purchased the Lido Restaurant in the Bronx and bought a house for his family in Westchester County in order "to be in a nice neighborhood."[53] In 1959, his fortunes reversed when he was convicted of narcotics trafficking and condemned to a long sentence in federal prison. Unable to earn on the streets, Valachi lost the restaurant, the house in the suburbs, and ultimately his wife.[54]

Or consider John "Sonny" Franzese. The seventeenth child of Neapolitan immigrants, Franzese grew up in Brooklyn when the families were recruiting new men in the 1930s. The young thug was brought into the Mafia by Sebastian "Buster" Aloi of the Profaci Family. He was drafted into the United States Army during the war, but he was discharged in 1944 for his "pronounced homicidal tendencies." He rose quickly with the Profaci Family as a brutal enforcer, loanshark, and extortionist who collected skims from Brooklyn bars and restaurants. He met his beautiful wife while she was working as a coat-check girl at the Stork Club. In the late 1940s, he opened the Orchid Room tavern in the burgeoning neighborhood of Jackson Heights, Queens. In 1960, he moved his family into a spacious suburban home on Long Island he bought for $39,000 (about $300,000 in 2013 dollars).[55]

While they were never millionaires, both *mafiosi* enjoyed middle-class suburban lives for decades. The fact that uneducated street thugs like Valachi and Franzese could obtain middle-class status is a perverse tribute to the capacity to make money under the Mafia.

The Wealthy Ones

A smaller minority of *mafiosi* made it big. Joe Valachi estimated his Genovese Family had "about 40 to 50 wealthy ones."[56] Although the net worth of a gangster is always elusive, based on evidence from tax evasion prosecutions, FBI wiretaps, and other reliable sources, there are documented cases of *caporegimes* and bosses who became rich on rackets:

- Luciano Family *caporegime* Michael "Trigger Mike" Coppola became rich from bootlegging, the numbers lottery, and labor racketeering. Coppola's wife once saw him count out $219,000 in cash on their dining room table. He explained to her that it was his regular share of the Harlem numbers. He bought a house near the ocean in Miami Beach, and he flew around the country to mob hotspots like Las Vegas. Coppola would later plead guilty to evading $385,000 in income taxes between 1956 and 1959 (about $3 million in unpaid taxes in 2013 dollars) on millions more in income.[57]

- Another Luciano *caporegime* named Ruggiero "Richie the Boot" Boiardo lived like a king in New Jersey. He first made his money as a bootlegger and speakeasy operator around Newark. As a young man, he bought audacious jewelry like a two-hundred-fifty-stone diamond belt buckle worth $5,000 in 1931 ($75,000 in 2013 dollars). Boiardo later used his profits from illegal booze and the numbers lottery to build Vittorio Castle, a lavish banquet hall with grape vineyards in the middle of Newark that attracted celebrities from New York City. He later built a "castle-like" miniature mansion worth over $75,000 in 1954 (over $650,000 in 2013 dollars) in the wealthy township of Livingston, New Jersey.[58]

- Genovese Family boss Anthony "Fat Tony" Salerno feasted on a variety of rackets. He held interests in the East Harlem numbers lottery and loansharking operations, engaged in labor racketeering with the International Brotherhood of Teamsters, and ran many construction industry rackets. In the 1950s, Salerno split his time between his horse ranch in Dutchess County, his apartment in tony Gramercy Park South, and his house on the exclusive Venetian Islands in Miami. In 1978, Salerno pled guilty to criminal charges of gambling and tax evasion for failing to pay $76,578 in income taxes ($273,000 in unpaid taxes in 2013 dollars) on over a million dollars in income.[59]

- Lucchese Family boss Anthony "Tony Ducks" Corallo started out life as a humble tile setter in East Harlem, then spent the rest of his life looting labor unions and industries in New York. As a venal labor racketeer, he took to flashing fat wads of cash, and moved his family into the wealthy neighborhood of Malba, Queens. In 1968, Corallo was convicted along with others of paying a $40,000 bribe for the award of an $840,000 city parks contract (a $268,000 bribe for a $5.6 million contract in 2013 dollars). The FBI placed an electronic bug in Corallo's black Jaguar. One day, Corallo's driver spotted FBI agents trailing them. His driver suggested they were following them because they thought Corallo controlled the toxic-waste-disposal business. "They're right," responded Corallo, unaware he was on tape.[60]

- Gambino Family boss Paul Castellano wanted to appear to be another successful businessman in his fifteen-thousand-square-foot mansion on Todt Hill in Staten Island. When FBI agents wiretapped his estate, however, they discovered that his "legitimate" businesses were bolstered by racketeering. His son's Scara-Mix Concrete Company enforced a concrete cartel on Staten Island. His meat companies and union ties gave him monopolistic power in the wholesale meat markets. Meanwhile, his "industry association" controlled no-show jobs in the garment district. Castellano's power and income derived largely from the Gambino Family's control of key union locals. "Our job is to run the unions," Castellano was picked up saying on a bug.[61]

The Ghost of Al Capone: Avoiding Fixed Assets

When the Treasury Department convicted Al Capone on tax evasion charges for failing to report income from *illegal* sources, it had a lasting impact on the Mafia. According to a report by Chicago bankers in the 1930s, mobsters began putting money into legitimate businesses so they could "withstand an investigation and show that they were earning sufficient income to enjoy the expensive living they were enjoying." The New York Mafia was permanently affected by the Capone prosecution, too. "After Capone went down, word spread around the Mob: give Uncle Sam his vig," said Louis Ferrante. "I wasn't going the way of Capone," vowed Lucchese Family associate Henry Hill. "That was the hardest part; hiding the money, not making a hit."[62]

The threat of an Internal Revenue Service (IRS) investigation caused *mafioso* to hide cash or avoid too many fixed assets that marked wealth. Big savings accounts and large homes had to be justified with "legitimate income" from businesses. New England boss Gennaro "Jerry" Angiulo beat the IRS by gradually funneling money from his illegal gambling operations into his golf course, a bowling alley, hotels and motels. Henry Hill laundered money through a shirt company and "paid cash for everything [so] there were no records or credit card receipts." As FBI agent Joe Pistone said, "The IRS doesn't have a chance against wiseguys" because they paid for everything with thick rolls of "Lincolns and Hamiltons."[63]

These extralegal measures did not encourage optimal savings and wealth creation. Jimmy Fratianno had to take hidden interests in casinos, with no paperwork, and stash away stacks of cash. *Mafiosi* could not simply use their cash to purchase major assets like homes. "You have to either borrow money or something if you want to buy a house. [The IRS] would say where did you get the money," explained Fratianno.[64] This frustrated normal investments. "They can't invest it without going through fucking fronts . . . what good is it?" complained Fratianno. "Even when they die, their heirs's got to hide the money."[65] The wife of a Gambino Family soldier lamented how she and her husband had to limit their legal assets. "Later on, when the money started coming in, everything we ever bought in the way of property—houses, office buildings, and so on and so forth—had someone else's name on the papers, not ours," said Lynda Milto.[66] Put another way, the Lucchese Family never had a pension and savings plan. Most wiseguys would not have contributed to it anyway.

In 1954, the Justice Department prosecuted Frank Costello for federal income tax evasion under a different theory. Rather than trying to establish all of Costello's illegal income, the government went through the arduous process of proving that the mob boss's spending far exceeded his declared income and assets. At trial, prosecutors painstakingly called 144 witnesses and introduced

368 exhibits to prove that Costello and his wife spent nearly $60,000 in 1948 ($580,000 in 2013 dollars) and more than $90,000 in 1949 ($872,000 in 2013 dollars).[67]

Although this prosecution strategy was difficult to replicate, it provided an early window on the mob lifestyle. Costello's rampant consumption was not unusual. Wiseguys spent money at astonishing rates.

Spending Money Like Water

Wiseguys spent their money on a high-consumption lifestyle. When Vincent "Fish" Cafaro was asked what he did with the millions of dollars he made, he described a spendthrift life:

Senator Nunn:	Did you save any of it? ...
Mr. Cafaro:	Nope.
Senator Nunn:	What happened to it?
Mr. Cafaro:	You want to tell them, Eleanore [his wife]? I spent it, Senator. Just gave it away. ... As I was making it, I was spending it: women, bartenders, waiters, hotels. Just spending money.
Senator Nunn:	Spending, $400,000, $500,000, $600,000, $700,000 a year?
Mr. Cafaro:	Sure.
Senator Nunn:	A million dollars a year in some years?
Mr. Cafaro:	If I had it to spend, I'd spend $3 million.[68]

Wiseguys spent their money on all kinds of lavish consumption, starting with the mob nightlife. "Most of them like to be in the limelight. They like to get all dressed up and go to a fancy place with a broad on their arm and show off," explained Vincent "Fat Vinnie" Teresa. Sammy "The Bull" Gravano recounted his big-spending nights on the town picking up tabs, leaving huge tips, and ordering champagne and prime steaks. "It was let's go to the Copa ... and I'm broke again and its macaroni and ricotta at home," said Gravano.[69]

Wiseguys tended to spend freely in their personal relationships, too. Anthony "Gaspipe" Casso recounted "spending money like there was no tomorrow" with his young wife. They went on frequent vacations to Saint Thomas, Bermuda, and Las Vegas, routinely dined at the best restaurants in Manhattan, and always saw the latest Broadway shows.[70] Quite often, wiseguys were spending money on mistresses, too. "Everybody who had a girlfriend took her out on Friday night ... wives went out on Saturday night," recounted the wife of Henry Hill.[71] The other woman could be costly. "Some wiseguys will set their girlfriends up with an apartment and stipend," said Joe Pistone.[72]

Mobsters loved precious jewelry, stylish clothes, and new automobiles, too. As a young bootlegger, Charles "Lucky" Luciano took to wearing real gold jewelry.[73] The attendees of the 1957 meeting of the Mafia at Apalachin drove luxury Lincolns and Cadillacs. Gangsters wanted to signal their success in the neighborhood. "Ninety percent of mob guys come from poverty," Vincent Teresa explained in 1973. "Now they made it. They got money, five-hundred-buck silk suits, hundred-buck shoes, ten-grand cars ... [t]hey want everyone to know they've made it."[74]

Ironically, many wiseguys ended up blowing their own money on gambling. "Whether we bet on horses or sports or dice or cards, gambling was like breathing for Mob guys—we couldn't live without it," said Sal Polisi. "That's not to say everybody was good at it. Most Mob guys were chronic losers, and a lot of those who weren't were mediocre at best."[75] John Gotti was a compulsive gambler who reportedly lost $90,000 on college bowl games over a single weekend.[76]

Spending on the mob lifestyle often came at the expense of long-term savings or housing. "We'd cash the checks [from no-show jobs], and by Monday we'd blown the money partying or buying clothes or gambling," recalled Henry Hill. "I said I didn't have to save it because I would always make it. And I wasn't alone," explained Hill, who still managed to buy a house on Long Island for his wife. Other mob spouses were less lucky. "Tommy DeSimone always drove around in a brand-new car and wore expensive clothes, and he and Angela lived in a two-room tenement slum," said Hill's wife, Karen.[77] Mobsters simply spent their money on different things than responsible citizens. Indeed, the reason that reporters were surprised that John Gotti lived in a modest house in Howard Beach was that he routinely emerged from chauffeured cars in custom-made suits at some of Manhattan's finest clubs and restaurants.[78]

Still, the mob lifestyle was fun to them. "I like gamblin'; I like women," said Charles Luciano when he was asked how he spent his millions. "Those are the two things that make money go fast. It came and it went."[79] Lucky Luciano's attitude toward money was not unusual. "The money rolled in. Sometimes it went out faster than I could steal it, but I liked the life," Vinnie Teresa explains.[80] Gambling was simply a form of regular entertainment for them. "We were at the track, shooting craps in Vegas, playing cards, and betting on anything that moved. Not a thrill like it in the world," Henry Hill recalled fondly.[81] This kind of economic consumption hardly fostered wealth. But goodfellas valued it more than retirement savings. After all, a Mafia soldier never knew how long he had.

MYTHS ABOUT THE WISEGUY LIFE

Now that we've seen what the life was, we should clear up what it was not. Let us dispense with some of the major myths about being a wiseguy.

Myth Number One: "Made My Bones"

The first myth is that no one could become a "made man" until he first murdered someone for the Mafia. Mario Puzo popularized the idea in the 1969 novel *The Godfather* by having Sonny Corleone say: "I 'made my bones' when I was nineteen, the last time the Family had a war."[82] The phrase referred to transforming a living human into a stack of bones.[83]

This idea was revived by the 1997 film *Donnie Brasco*, based loosely on FBI agent Joseph Pistone's infiltration of the Bonanno Family. In the climactic (fictionalized) scene, the FBI pulls Brasco off the hit that will let him become a "made man" only seconds before the target is about to be shot.[84] But in his book, Joe Pistone described a highly malleable "rule" that was routinely disregarded. Pistone recalls how *caporegimes* "sometimes lied by omission on that issue to get a guy made," saying that "close friends or relatives" were proposed for membership despite no hits, and that some prospects just paid off their *caporegime* to get made.[85]

The bloodbath from such a homicidal rule makes it incredible, too. There were approximately five thousand "made men" in Gotham by the 1950s. Given that some mob hitters killed several people, for each *mafioso* to "make his bones," the homicides would exceed five thousand victims. Yet there were under six thousand total homicides from *all* sources in New York City during the 1930s.

Even if these alleged mob corpses were spread over the 1940s and '50s, the mayhem from that many gangland hits would have been intolerable. "It would have been impossible for every made guy to have killed for such exalted status," concludes writer Carl Sifakis.[86]

Myth Number Two: "The Mafia's Code of *Omertà*"

Another myth is that, until recently, *mafiosi* strictly adhered to *omertà* (the code of silence). Joe Valachi is mistakenly called "the first Mob turncoat to break the Mafia's code of *omertà*."[87] But Valachi did not testify until 1963. Long before Valachi, *mafiosi* were singing to the G-men:

- In the 1890s, Charles "Millionaire Charlie" Matranga testified in court against rival *mafiosi* in New Orleans. After the Matrangas were shot up, Charlie cooperated with the police in bringing charges against Joe Provenzano. In 1890, Matranga testified that Provenzano had threatened "bloodshed all along the wharf" if he did not get a piece of the waterfront.[88]
- Francesco Siino was the boss of a 670-member *cosche* in southwestern Sicily. During a bloody fight with rivals, he became an informant for a *questore* (government official). "I know that the cause of persecution of so many sons of good mothers is none other than that infamous cop-lover Francesco Siino," yelled a *mafioso* as he was being arrested.[89]
- In the 1910s, the Morello Family, the "First Family" of New York, was crippled by informants. Facing prison time for counterfeiting, Salvatore Clemente, a close confidant of the Terranova brothers, became a paid informant for the United States Secret Service. For years, Clemente fed the Secret Service a steady stream of intelligence on the Morello Family.[90]
- In 1921, New York City detective Michael Fiaschetti persuaded Bartolo Fontano to confess to a murder he participated in with a gang of *mafiosi* called "the Good Killers." Fontana revealed an interstate network of mobsters, including future boss Stefano Magaddino.[91]
- As the drug war heated up, *mafiosi* began trading information to avoid charges. As we saw earlier, in 1923, none other than Charles Luciano cooperated with federal agents to stay out of prison.

- Then there is Nicola Gentile, who became a fugitive on drug charges in 1939. In his memoirs, Gentile boasts of exercising "superhuman control over myself" to resist interrogation. The State Department's files tell a different story: it was *Gentile* who was pestering the government for a deal. On March 29, 1940, a cable said Gentile had "given valuable information ... and it is believed that his testimony would be valuable in pending cases."[92]

- Detroit *mafioso* Chester LaMare, meanwhile, had been informing for the United States Secret Service in its counterfeiting investigations.[93]

- In 1937, Dr. Melchiorre Allegra revealed the inner workings of the Sicilian Mafia. Dr. Allegra was a physician in Sicily who became a member of the Pagliarelli Family. After he was arrested in 1937, Allegra agreed to give testimony about the Sicilian Mafia. Long before Valachi, Dr. Allegra testified about the structure, practices, and rituals of his *cosche*.[94]

- In 1945, Peter "Petey Spats" LaTempa was to be the key witness corroborating Ernest "The Hawk" Rupolo's confession implicating Vito Genovese in the 1934 murder of Ferdinand Boccia. LaTempa committed suicide while in protective custody.[95]

- In the early 1950s, Lucchese Family soldier Eugene Giannini was informing for the Federal Bureau of Narcotics. Giannini revealed secrets such as how "the mob is broken down in geographic organizations," that Tommy Lucchese's "primary sphere of activity was in the garment center," and that Lucchese had "group leaders" like Joseph Rosato under him. On September 20, 1952, a hit team sent by Joe Valachi shot Giannini twice in the head before symbolically dumping his body on East 107th Street.[96]

- Around the same time, Dominick "The Gap" Petrilli, ironically, was informing on Gene Giannini. "The Gap is back. He got picked up in Italy for something and made a deal with the junk agents," warned Anthony "Tony Bender" Strollo, a lieutenant of Genovese. On December 9, 1953, three assassins murdered Petrilli at a bar in the Bronx.[97]

- In July 1958, Cristoforo Rubino became another informer to fall before testifying against Mafia drug traffickers. A week before he was to testify before a grand jury investigating Vito Genovese and other traffickers, Rubino was shot dead on a Brooklyn sidewalk.[98]

- In May 1962, Profaci Family dissident Larry Gallo disclosed to the FBI the existence of "The Commission," one of the most explosive secrets of the Cosa Nostra. Gallo revealed that "JOSEPH PROFACI, THOMAS LUCHESE [*sic*], CARLO GAMBINO, and VITO GENOVESE were due a high degree of respect and were members of the leadership group called 'The Commission.'"[99]

We know there were other early informers whose names remain hidden behind black marker in redacted FBI files. The Freedom of Information Act (FOIA) bars the disclosure of deceased informants, even if they passed away fifty years ago. But the truth has a way of rising to the surface. Former FBI agent Anthony Villano said he knew of a dozen "member sources," including "a couple names that would shock both the public and the LCN."[100] In coming years, we may be surprised by which Men of Honor betrayed each other to the feds.

Myth Number Three: "There's No Retiring from This"

The last major myth is that wiseguys could never leave the life. "Just when I thought I was out, they pull me back in," Michael Corleone laments in *The Godfather Part III*. "You took an oath. There's no retiring from this," Tony Soprano tells a soldier who wants out in *The Sopranos*.[101]

Except that many wiseguys *did* retire. As of the 1950s, Joe Valachi testified that while there were two thousand active members in New York City, there were also "about 2,500 or 3,000" men who were "*inactive* members."[102] So, who were these thousands of erstwhile *mafiosi* who had left the life? They fall roughly into two categories: (1) businessmen, and (2) old men.

Some *mafiosi* found more profitable work outside crime. Take William Medico of Pittston, Pennsylvania. Medico grew up in the same Sicilian neighborhood as mob boss Russell Bufalino. He joined Bufalino's northeastern Pennsylvania family, and he was arrested several times in this youth. Then, something unusual happened: he became a successful businessman. He built Medico Industries, Inc., into one of the biggest heavy-equipment companies in Pennsylvania, even fulfilling defense contracts for the United States Army.

While Bill Medico continued to associate with the Bufalino Family, he was preoccupied with his legitimate business. In November 1957, Medico let his cronies borrow a company car to drive to the Mafia meeting in Apalachin, but he did not bother attending himself. After Apalachin, Medico agreed to be interviewed about his business by FBI agents, who found nothing illegal. Unlike Paul Castellano's business interests, the government identified no racketeering activities associated with Medico Industries or the heavy-equipment industry in general. Bill Medico was never again charged with a crime. The wiseguy had more or less gone legit.[103]

Many more simply aged out of the life. When Salvatore Falcone reached his seventies he retired to Miami, Florida, like thousands of other elderly snow birds. Informants said that "due to advanced age and ill health, he has been replaced by his brother JOSEPH FALCONE of Utica, New York." The FBI noticed that after Joseph "Staten Island Joe" Riccobono entered his seventies, he "sort of retired" to the status of "an elderly statesman." Meanwhile, the aging *mafioso* Minetto Olivere left the Milwaukee Family for California, where he "retired and manages the local American-Italian Club in San Diego."[104]

Even a turncoat could leave if he was no longer a threat. At the end of his memoirs *Vita di Capomafia* ("Life of a Mafia Boss"), Nicola Gentile renounced "my active life as a member of the honorable society," saying he was leaving as "a lonely and embittered old man."[105] Although the Mafia considered killing him, they let him die in poverty in rural Sicily. "The rules of the Cosa Nostra aren't always carried to the extreme," explained Antonio Calderone.[106]

Such were the lives of wiseguys.

Table 7–3: New York's Soldiers
Backgrounds of Soldiers of the New York Families
Identified in 1963 McClellan Committee Hearings[107]
(n=162)

	Name	DOB	Place of Birth	Residence (ca. 1950–63)	Activities
			Bonanno Family		
1.	Michael Consolo	1903	Sicily	Queens	Alcohol; robbery; strongarm
2.	Nicholas Marangello	1913	NYC	Lower East Side	Gambling
3.	Frank Mari	1926	NYC	Lower East Side	Gambling; loanshark
4.	John Petrone	1896	NYC	Bronx (east)	Counterfeit
5.	Angelo Presinzano	1908	NYC	Brooklyn	Strongarm
6.	Frank Presinzano	1902	NYC	Little Italy, Man.	Gambling; narc
7.	Philip Rastelli	1918	NYC	Brooklyn	Strongarm
8.	Anthony Riela	1896	Sicily	West Orange, NJ	Gambling; strongarm
9.	Michael Sabella	1911	NYC	Long Island	Gambling; loanshark
10.	Joseph Spadaro	1906	NYC	Queens	Labor racket; strongarm
			Gambino Family		
11.	Andrew Alberti	1920	NYC	Bronx (central)	Gambling; loanshark
12.	Germaio Anaclerio	1917	NYC	East Harlem	Gambling; narc
13.	Joseph Armone	1917	NYC	Brooklyn	Gambling; labor racket; narc
14.	Eduardo Aronica	1890	Sicily	Queens	Alcohol; receiver
15.	Peter Baratta	1902	NYC	Bronx (east)	Strongarm
16.	Charles Barcellona	1915	Sicily	East Harlem	Narc
17.	Ernesto Barese	1920	Naples, IT	Ft. Lee, NJ	Receiver
18.	Sebastiano Bellanca	1904	Sicily	Ft. Lee, NJ	Narc
19.	Anthony Carminati	1912	NJ	Bronx (central)	Narc
20.	James Casablanca	1913	NYC	Bronx (east)	Narc
21.	Matthew Cuomo	1905	NYC	Bronx (central)	Alcohol; gambling; receiver; strongarm

22.	Alex Dallesio	1913	NYC	Staten Island	Gambling; loanshark; vending
23.	John Dallesio	1911	NYC	Staten Island	Gambling; loanshark; vending
24.	Mike Dallesio	1912	NYC	Staten Island	Gambling; loanshark; vending
25.	Nicholas DiBene	1905	NYC	Bronx (north)	Strongarm
26.	Alex De Brizzi	1892	NYC	Staten Island	Gambling; labor racket; loanshark; vending
27.	Charles De Lutro	1916	Not known	Little Italy, Man.	Gambling; loanshark; strongarm
28.	Michael Galgano	1913	US	Bronx (east)	Narc; gambling; strongarm
29.	Frank Gagliardi	1907	US	Brooklyn	Loanshark; receiver
30.	Charles Gagliodotto	1908	NYC	Lower East Side	Gambling; narc; strongarm
31.	Pasquale Genese	1911	NYC	Bronx (east)	Gambling; strongarm
32.	Anthony Granza	1915	Upstate NY	Bronx (north)	Gambling; narc
33.	Giuseppe LoPiccolo	1918	Chicago	Upper East Side	Gambling; labor racket; loanshark; vending
34.	Frank Luciano	1900	Salerno, IT	Queens	Counterfeit; gambling; receiver; strongarm
35.	Joseph Manfredi	1926	NYC	Lodi, NJ	Narc; strongarm
36.	James Massi	1908	NYC	Bronx (north)	Gambling; narc
37.	Frank Moccardi	1917	NYC	Westchester	Gambling
38.	Michael Pecoraro	1901	NYC	Upper West Side	Alcohol; receiver
39.	Lawrence Pistone	1927	Not known	Brooklyn	Gambling; loanshark; strongarm
40.	Hugo Rossi	1901	Sicily	E. Village, Man.	Narc
41.	Giacomo Scalici	1902	Sicily	Bronx (north)	Alcohol
42.	Salvatore Scalici	1886	Sicily	Burlington, NJ	Alcohol
43.	Mike Scandifia	1920	NYC	Hillsdale, NJ	Gambling; loanshark; receiver; strongarm
44.	Giacomo Scarpulla	1899	Sicily	Bronx (east)	Alcohol; strongarm
45.	James Stassi	1913	NJ	Union, NJ	Gambling
46.	Joseph Stassi	1907	NJ	Union, NJ	Gambling

47.	Arthur Tortorella	1913	NYC	Brooklyn	Loanshark; receiver; strongarm
48.	Peter J. Tortorella	1915	NYC	Brooklyn	Gambling; strongarm
Genovese Family					
49.	Settimo Accardi	1902	Sicily	Bloomfield, NJ	Loanshark; strongarm
50.	Philip Albanese	1907	NYC	Long Island	Gambling; loanshark; narc
51.	Charles Albero	1902	NYC	Bronx (north)	Gambling; narc; strongarm
52.	Joseph Agone	1913	NYC	Lower East Side	Gambling; labor racket; strongarm
53.	John Ardito	1919	NYC	Queens	Gambling; narc
54.	Joseph Barra	1928	NY	Westchester	Strongarm
55.	Albert Barrasso	1908	NJ	Bloomfield, NJ	Strongarm
56.	Joseph Bernava	1899	NYC	Midtown Man.	Gambling; strongarm
57.	Anthony Boiardo	1914	NJ	Essex Fells, NJ	Gambling; strongarm
58.	Paul Bonadio	1903	NYC	Fort Lee, NJ	Labor racket
59.	Lorenzo Brescia	1905	Bari, IT	Long Island	Gambling; strongarm
60.	Thomas Campisi	1911	NJ	Newark, NJ	Alcohol; receiver; strongarm
61.	Antonio Caponigro	1912	Chicago	Short Hills, NJ	Alcohol; receiver; strongarm
62.	Anthony Carillo	1902	Naples, IT	Queens	Gambling; loanshark
63.	Frank Caruso	1911	NYC	Brooklyn	Narc; strongarm
64.	Salvatore Celambrino	1903	US	Staten Island	Gambling; labor racket; receiver
65.	Lawrence Centore	1907	NYC	Bronx (north)	Gambling; vending
66.	Mike Clemente	1908	NYC	Brooklyn	Labor racket; strongarm
67.	Earl Coralluzzo	1915	WV	Westchester	Receiver
68.	Alfred Criscuolo	1911	NYC	New Milford, NJ	Gambling; narc
69.	Alfred Cupola	1902	NYC	Queens	Gambling
70.	Pete De Feo	1902	NYC	W. Village, Man.	Gambling; strongarm
71.	Anthony DeMartino	1910	NYC	Bronx (south)	Gambling; vending
72.	Benjamin DeMartino	1913	NYC	Long Island	Gambling; loanshark; strongarm

73.	Theodore DeMartino	1912	NYC	Bronx (east)	Gambling; narc; strongarm; vending
74.	Cosmo DiPietro	1930	NYC	Lower East Side	Loanshark; narc; strongarm
75.	Anthony Ferro	1918	NYC	Bronx (east)	Gambling; loanshark
76.	Frank Galluccio	1898	Naples, IT	Brooklyn	Receiver; strongarm
77.	Mario Gigante	1923	NYC	Westchester	Gambling; strongarm
78.	Vincent Gigante	1928	NYC	W. Village, Man.	Gambling; narc; strongarm
79.	August Laietta	1906	US	Queens	Gambling; loanshark
80.	Joseph Lapi	1910	NYC	Queens	Gambling; receiver
81.	Ernest Lazzara	1914	NJ	Franklin, NJ	Gambling
82.	Frank Livorsi	1903	Chicago	Long Island	Alcohol; narc; strongarm
83.	Andrew Lombardino	1905	NJ	Florham Park, NJ	Gambling; strongarm
84.	Paul Lombardino	1912	Sicily	Newark, NJ	Gambling; narc; strongarm
85.	Philip Lombardo	1908	NYC	Bronx (east)	Narc; receiver; strongarm
86.	Sebastian Ofrica	1916	NYC	Brooklyn	Gambling; strongarm
87.	Michael Maione	1911	NYC	Westchester	Strongarm; counterfeit; alcohol
88.	Anthony Marchitto	1911	NJ	Jersey City, NJ	Gambling; labor racket; receiver
89.	Gaetano Martino	1900	Sicily	Brooklyn	Labor racket
90.	Alfonso Marzano	1890	Naples, IT	Little Italy, Man.	Counterfeit
91.	Vincent Mauro	1916	NYC	Bronx (north)	Gambling; narc; strongarm
92.	Louis Milo	1916	NYC	Bronx (south)	Gambling
93.	Sabato Milo	1923	NYC	Long Island	Gambling; loanshark
94.	Thomas Milo, Sr.	1902	NYC	Westchester	Alcohol; gambling
95.	Barney Miranda	1916	Naples, IT	Brooklyn	Gambling
96.	Pasquale Moccio	1918	NYC	Westchester	Gambling; labor racket; loanshark; narc
97.	George Nobile	1910	NYC	Little Italy, Man.	Gambling; narc
98.	Louis Pacella	1921	NYC	East Harlem	Gambling
99.	Joseph Pagano	1928	NYC	East Harlem	Gambling; narc

100.	Pasquale Pagano	1921	NYC	Bronx (north)	Labor racket; narc; strongarm
101.	Carmine Persico	1933	NYC	Brooklyn	Gambling; receiver; strongarm
102.	David Petillo	1908	NYC	Midtown Man.	Narc; strongarm
103.	James Picarelli	1906	NYC	Brooklyn	Gambling; narc; vending
104.	Rudolph Prisco	1909	NYC	Rockland Cnty.	Gambling
105.	Joseph Rao	1901	NYC	East Harlem	Gambling; strongarm
106.	Nicholas Rattenni	1907	NYC	Westchester	Gambling; labor racket; strongarm
107.	Charles Tourine, Sr.	1906	NJ	Midtown Man.	Alcohol; gambling; strongarm
108.	Angelo Salerno	1902	NYC	Bronx (south)	Narc; vending
109.	Anthony Salerno	1911	NYC	Dutchess County	Gambling; vending
110.	Ferdinand Salerno	1924	NYC	Bronx (north)	Gambling; vending
111.	Batisto Salvo	1906	NYC	Westchester	Gambling
112.	John Savino	1924	NYC	Long Island	Gambling; loanshark
113.	Giovanni Schillaci	1902	Sicily	Westchester	Narc
114.	Fiore Siano	1927	NYC	East Harlem	Narc; strongarm; vending
115.	George Smurra	1910	NYC	Brooklyn	Gambling; strongarm
116.	John Stopelli	1907	NYC	Brooklyn	Labor racket; narc; strongarm
117.	Joseph Stracci	1906	NYC	Englewood, NJ	Gambling; labor racket; strongarm
118.	Frank Tieri	1904	Naples, IT	Brooklyn	Gambling; loanshark
119.	Joseph Tortorici	1909	NYC	Brooklyn	Alcohol; labor racket; strongarm
120.	Joseph Valachi	1903	NYC	Westchester	Gambling; labor racket; narc; strongarm
Lucchese Family					
121.	Frank Arra	1908	NYC	Queens	Gambling
122.	Joseph Bendenelli	1910	NYC	Long Island	Gambling; strongarm
123.	Nicholas Bonina	1928	NYC	Queens	Narc; strongarm
124.	Frank Callace	1901	IT	Bronx (south)	Gambling; narc
125.	Frankie Carbo	1904	NYC	Camden, NJ	Gambling; strongarm

126.	Sam Cavalieri	1910	NYC	Queens	Gambling; narc; strongarm
127.	Edward D'Argenio	1900	Naples, IT	Brooklyn	Gambling; narc
128.	Thomas Dioguardi	1916	NYC	Long Island	Labor racket; loanshark
129.	John Dioguardi	1914	NYC	Long Island	Alcohol; labor racket; strongarm
130.	Charles DiPalermo	1925	NYC	Lower East Side	Alcohol; counterfeit; narc
131.	Vincent Corrao	1909	NYC	Brooklyn	Narc
132.	Joseph DiPalermo	1907	NYC	Little Italy, Man.	Alcohol; narc; receiver; strongarm
133.	Salvatore Granello	1924	NYC	Lower East Side	Gambling; loanshark
134.	Anthony Lisi	1911	Sicily	Lower East Side	Narc; strongarm
135.	Salvatore Lo Proto	1926	NJ	Lodi, NJ	Gambling; strongarm
136.	Salvatore Maneri	1912	Sicily	Staten Island	Narc; receiver
137.	Neil Migliore	1933	NYC	Queens	Gambling; loanshark; strongarm
138.	Vic Panica	1924	NYC	Queens	Gambling; strongarm
139.	Andinno Pappadia	1914	NYC	Long Island	Gambling; labor racket; strongarm
140.	Vincent Potenza	1927	NYC	Little Italy, Man.	Receiver
141.	Charlie Rao	1889	Sicily	Westchester	Loanshark
142.	Salvatore Shillitani	1908	NYC	East Harlem	Gambling; narc; strongarm
143.	Nicholas Tolentino	1909	NYC	East Harlem	Narc
144.	Angelo Tuminaro	1910	NYC	Brooklyn	Narc
145.	Joseph Vento	1913	NYC	Queens	Alcohol; narc
146.	Anthony Vadala	1899	Sicily	Queens	Gambling
147.	James Vintaloro	1911	NYC	Bronx (north)	Gambling; labor racket
			Profaci Family		
148.	Tony Abbattemarco	1922	NYC	Brooklyn	Gambling; loanshark
149.	Frank Abbattemarco	1899	NYC	Brooklyn	Gambling; loanshark
150.	Cassandros Bonasera	1897	Sicily	Brooklyn	Gambling; loanshark
151.	Al D'Ambrosio	1925	NYC	Brooklyn	Receiver; strongarm

152.	Salvatore D'Ambrosio	1925	NYC	Brooklyn	Strongarm
153.	Bartolo Ferrigno	1904	Sicily	Brooklyn	Counterfeit; strongarm
154.	Cosmo Frasca	1907	NYC	Brooklyn	Gambling; strongarm
155.	Albert Gallo	1930	NYC	Brooklyn	Gambling; strongarm
156.	Joseph Gallo	1929	NYC	Brooklyn	Gambling; strongarm; vending
157.	Lawrence Gallo	1927	NYC	Brooklyn	Gambling; strongarm
158.	Joseph Magnasco	1925	NYC	Brooklyn	Receiver; strongarm
159.	Sebastiano Nani	1906	Sicily	Brooklyn	Labor racket; narc; strongarm
160.	Frank Profaci	1907	Sicily	Brooklyn	Gambling; loanshark
161.	Cristoforo Rubino	1919	Sicily	Queens	Strongarm
162.	Joseph Schipani	1912	NYC	Brooklyn	Gambling; loanshark; narc

MOUTHPIECES FOR THE MOB

Crooked Cops, Mob Lawyers, and Director Hoover

> I kept thinking of the mess I was in, and I couldn't help
> longing for the days when I was just a kid mouthpiece,
> making lots of money as a shyster in the magistrate's court.
> —Mob lawyer J. Richard "Dixie" Davis (1939)

> I have in mind that I was originally advised by Rosen that
> the Mafia or anything like it in character never existed in this
> country. I have been plagued ever since for having denied its
> existence.
> —FBI Director J. Edgar Hoover (1970)

On the evening of Saturday, December 7, 1929, the Tepecanoe Democratic
Club was throwing a dinner in honor of Magistrate Judge Albert H. Vitale
at the Roman Gardens restaurant in the Bronx. Al Vitale had been a party hack
before being appointed to the city magistrates' court, which gave him jurisdiction over criminal proceedings. The fifty guests included not only an NYPD
detective, criminal defense lawyers, and bail bondsmen, but also *mafiosi* Daniel
Iamascia, Joseph "Joe the Baker" Catania, and his brother James Catania. It was
just another evening among cronies in the Tammany Hall legal machine.[1]

Except on that night, *other* gangsters decided to crash the party. At 1:30
a.m., seven gunmen marched into the dining room and relieved the fifty guests
of $5,000 in cash and jewelry.[2] When news of the robbery—and Judge Vitale's
sordid guests—hit the papers, the media frenzy forced a bar association inquiry

into his links to gangsters. Vitale acknowledged being acquainted with Ciro "The Artichoke King" Terranova, whom he "regarded as a successful business man." He also admitted receiving a $19,000 "loan" from none other than Arnold Rothstein (over $250,000 in 2013 dollars). In all, Vitale made $165,000 during his four years on the bench (over $2.3 million in 2013 dollars), which he attributed to "fortunate investments."[3]

Following a trial on judicial misconduct charges, on March 13, 1930, the State Appellate Division removed Vitale from the bench. Yet Vitale thrived in his career as a private lawyer. During a federal trial in 1931, a witness testified that a gangster had bragged, "Vitale is my friend and can reach any judge in New York, even though he is not on the bench."[4]

The Mafia families maintained their power by neutralizing law enforcement in New York. They started with payoffs to crooked cops and judges. When that did not work, mobsters turned to criminal defense lawyers, the so-called mouthpieces for the mob. The Cosa Nostra also flourished because the Federal Bureau of Investigation was on the sidelines during the mob's ascent. A recently discovered handwritten note by J. Edgar Hoover, along with accounts by FBI agents, may finally explain Hoover's position on the Mafia.

CROOKED COPS

As we have seen, the Mafia's first line of defense was corrupt cops. Not every cop was dishonest. But before the Mafia even existed, from the 1890s Lexow Committee hearings to the 1972 Knapp Commission report on police corruption, there was a tradition of bribe taking and extortion by the NYPD.[5] The Cosa Nostra attained quasi-immunity from local police. "Wiseguys like Paulie [Vario] have been paying off the cops for so many years they have probably sent more cops' kids to college than anyone else," explained Lucchese family associate Henry Hill.[6] When narcotics detective Robert Leuci tried to investigate Al "Sonny Red" Indelicato's crew, Leuci's sergeant came by with an ex-federal narcotics agents to warn: "These [Indelicatos] are good people, they've done the right thing before. . . . You better think about what you're doing."[7]

Wiseguys were so entrenched in Gotham that even honest police were largely resigned to them. "During his police career, my father had known his share of mobsters. With his Bronx squad commanded pals, he often went to Joe Cago's [Joe Valachi's] Lido restaurant," recalled the son of an honest Irish cop. Absent a murder charge, or case requiring inside information, "even honest cops, for the most part, looked the other way."[8] When NYPD detective Frank Serpico tried to break up a numbers shop, a Genovese Family *caporegime* intervened: "What kind of guy are you? There're other honest cops, but at least they honor the contracts," said the goodfella.[9]

CORRUPTION IN THE COURTHOUSES

Even good cases against mobsters could die behind the scenes. In Chicago and Atlantic City, Al Capone and Enoch "Nucky" Johnson built ties to Republican political machines. In New York, the mob's links to labor unions and the Tammany Hall Democratic machine had a strong, if subtle influence on judges and the District Attorney's Office. *Mafiosi* Vince Mangano and Joe Bonanno had "political clubs" for a reason. "To be behind bars means one thing in his underworld society: You're in because you're stupid and you don't have any influence," recounted James Horan, an investigator for prosecutors Thomas E. Dewey and Frank Hogan.[10] "In those days we were practically immune from prosecution," confirms Henry Hill. "See, the local politicians needed the rank and file of our unions ... [and] we hardly had to worry about the courts, since Paulie [Vario] made judges."[11]

The Kings County (Brooklyn) courthouse in South Brooklyn was especially compromised by organized crime. In the 1940s, state special prosecutor John Harlan Amen obtained the removal of a Brooklyn magistrate judge for bribery, and the forced resignation of the District Attorney William Geoghan. (Geoghan's replacement William Dwyer himself fell under suspicion for failing to convict Albert Anastasia).[12] The Brooklyn courthouse's corruption continued through the 1960s. "Deals were made, cases sold—that courthouse was a marketplace, not a hall of justice," said undercover detective Robert Leuci. "A defendant with money had a better than fifty-fifty chance of buying his way out of any kind of case."[13] Leuci built corruption cases for the United States attorney, including a bribery conviction of Edmund Rosner, a prominent defense attorney caught on tape paying cash for secret court documents.[14]

Even New York's old coroner's office, which employed the medical examiners who investigated causes of death, had corruption problems. "The coroner's office was an important one for a political machine to control. It was a place where a case could be fixed or disposed of early, before public outcry could build up," explained coroner George LeBrun. A corrupt coroner could botch a case for others to exploit. "Even when a prosecutor went ahead and obtained an indictment, a skillful defense lawyer could make good use of the coroner's verdict in raising a question of reasonable doubt in the minds of a trial jury," said LeBrun.[15]

The New York State Joint Legislative Committee on Crime conducted a study of felony arrests of organized crime figures between 1960 and 1970 in the courts around New York City. The study found that 44 percent of indictments against mobsters were dismissed before trial compared to only 11 percent of all indictments. Furthermore, of 536 organized crime figures arrested on felony charges, just 37 were sent to prison—less than 7 percent.[16] The rap sheets of *mafiosi* typically have many charges, but relatively few convictions and little prison time. Before 1959, Anthony "Tony Ducks" Corallo was charged with felonies eleven different times, but he was convicted only once and spent a total of six months in prison. Alex Di Brizzi was arrested twenty-three times on charges ranging from bookmaking to felony assault, but he got away with fines and suspended sentences through 1958. We will never know how many of these cases were fixed.[17]

"MOUTHPIECES FOR THE MOB": CRIMINAL DEFENSE ATTORNEYS

When all else failed, and a major felony was set for trial, *mafiosi* turned to criminal defense attorneys to talk them out of trouble. The New York bar had had criminal defense specialists since the notorious firm of Howe & Hummel was put on retainer by Frederika "Mother" Mandelbaum, Gotham's biggest fence.[18] Starting during Prohibition, gangsters relied more and more on criminal defense lawyers or "mouthpieces," as the goodfellas called them. These "mouthpieces for the mob" became essential to the New York Mafia.[19]

The Mob Temptation for Lawyers

Mobsters were unlike most clients. They often led intriguing lives on the edge of infamy. Defense lawyers knew the complications—and temptations—of representing gangsters.

Samuel S. Leibowitz was one of the finest criminal defense lawyers (and later federal judges) of the twentieth century. During Prohibition, he obtained acquittals of Al Capone and Vincent "Mad Dog" Coll among other gangsters. Although Leibowitz made no apologies for providing a zealous defense, he knew the hazards of representing gangsters. "The doctor uses all the skill and scientific knowledge at his command, yet takes every precaution not to become infected by the germs of his patient," described Leibowitz. He expanded on his colorful analogy:

> Figuratively speaking, I made it my business to don a "white gown" to avoid exposure to antisocial germs. The regrettable fact is that a few specialists in this field neglected to distinguish between their professional obligations and their social life and made the mistake of not wearing a "white gown" any of the time. At the end of the legal day's work they hobnobbed on intimate terms with their virulent clients and thus brought disgrace on themselves and dishonor on a noble profession.[20]

When Washington lawyer Edward Bennett Williams took on Frank Costello as a client, he was fascinated when Costello took him to the Copacabana and introduced him to celebrities and bookmakers. However, Williams learned to keep his mob clients at arm's length. "You need me. I don't need you," he told them.[21] Florida defense attorney Frank Ragano regretted getting too close to clients like *mafiosi* Carlos Marcello and Santo Trafficante. "My gravest error as a lawyer was merging a professional life with a personal life," said Ragano. "I gradually began to think like them and to rationalize their aberrant behavior."[22]

Mob Lawyers

Other lawyers crossed over the line from professional advocate to partners in crime. J. Richard "Dixie" Davis left a white-shoe law firm in Manhattan for the excitement of representing Harlem numbers runners, whose defenses were paid for by high-level gangsters. Davis was by all accounts an excellent defense attorney. "Davis was a very bright, imaginative, twisted-minded, young man," said Thomas E. Dewey, who faced him in court. By thirty, Davis had turned himself into a leading defense lawyer and married a Broadway showgirl.[23]

Then Davis crossed the line between defending his clients in court and helping them run the Harlem numbers lottery. Davis began hanging out with his top client Dutch Schultz, a trigger-happy gangster with links to the Mafia. Late one night, in a cheap hotel room, Davis witnessed Dutch Schultz put a gun into the mouth of one of his underlings . . . and fire. "I was scared. It is very unhealthy to be an eyewitness to a murder when a man like Schultz is the killer," said Davis. "I kept thinking the mess I was in, and I couldn't help longing for the days when I was just a kid mouthpiece, making lots of money as a shyster in the magistrate's court."[24]

Dewey brought an indictment against Davis to pressure him to testify not only against the gangsters but also against Tammany Hall district leader James "Jimmy" Hines. Hines had been providing protection to the Harlem numbers lottery by telling judges he got appointed to dismiss charges against Schultz's men. "Davis was nothing but an expendable and replaceable young lawyer. They could have found another one of those, but Hines was at the top," explained Dewey.[25] Davis's testimony ultimately helped convict Hines. Though he avoided a long sentence, J. Richard "Dixie" Davis was disbarred in 1937, his legal career over at thirty-two.[26]

Other attorneys dashed across the line to criminality. Frank DeSimone was literally a mob lawyer. He graduated from the University of Southern California School of Law in 1932, passed the bar, and practiced law in Los Angeles for the next twenty years. In that time, DeSimone quietly rose to become boss of the Los Angeles Mafia family. DeSimone developed contacts with the Lucchese Family of New York, and was called "the lawyer" by informants.[27]

Criminal defense attorney Robert Cooley became enmeshed in the world of the Chicago Outfit in the 1970s and '80s. Mobsters called Cooley "the mechanic" for his ability to fix cases. "For the first eleven years of my legal career, almost every day I gave out bribes—and not just to judges," admitted Robert Cooley. He started socializing with mobsters, too. "Four times, I shared a last meal with a gangster before he went off to his death. Each one was calm and unsuspecting," Cooley recounted. Sickened by the violence, Cooley became an informant for the government and testified as a witness against dozens of mobsters.[28]

Defense Lawyer Tactics: Playing the Identity Card

Most criminal defense attorneys did their work within the bounds of the law and were unrepentant about providing a zealous defense. Asked how he could represent accused mobsters, Bobby Simone cites the defense lawyer's creed: "The simple answer—the presumption of innocence owed every criminal defendant and the proposition that no one is guilty until and unless a jury, or in some cases a judge, says so after a fair trial."[29] Others argued that they were defending constitutional rights. "Strike Force attorneys and FBI agents acted like they were doing God's work, and therefore didn't have to play by the rules," argued Las Vegas mob lawyer (and now mayor) Oscar Goodman. "That's not what the Constitution says, nor is it what the Bill of Rights is about."[30]

The defense lawyer's tactics were not always pretty. A favorite tactic of some was playing the ethnic-identity card. Italian immigrants had often been grotesquely attacked as criminals by the press and politicians. The largest mass lynching in American history took place in 1890 in New Orleans when eleven Italians were hung by a mob after their acquittals and mistrials on charges of assassinating police chief David Hennessy. Modern defense lawyers, however, tried to portray hardened, wealthy *mafiosi* as nothing more than innocent ethnic martyrs. After a meeting of the Mafia was discovered in Apalachin, New York, in November 1957, attorneys for the mob attendees played the ethnic card aggressively.[31] During the trial of the Apalachin attendees, the defense made this a central theme. "All these men are Italian. Is that why they are here in this courtroom?" asserted a defense lawyer at trial. "What's on trial here? The Sons of Italy?" another lawyer asked rhetorically.[32]

Mob front groups used similar tactics. In 1960, a member of an "Italian-American service organization," identified as "William Bonanno, a wholesale food distributor from Tucson, Ariz.," condemned the "stereotyping of Italian-Americans as gangsters," which he said was "causing financial, social and moral damage to the whole Italian-American community." Bonanno, the "food distributor," was in fact a gangster who later peddled memoirs romanticizing his life in the Mafia.[33]

Criminal defense lawyers and mob front groups put the Department of Justice on the defensive with accusations of anti-Italian bias. "In the 1960s and 1970s, after we publicly entered the battle, the FBI was constantly attacked as being anti-Italian because of our efforts to break La Cosa Nostra," said FBI agent Dennis Griffin. "Defense attorneys attacked me personally with this charge when I was on the witness stand testifying against Mob leaders."[34] Mafia boss Joseph Colombo formed the "Italian-American Civil Rights League" to protest outside the Manhattan office of the FBI. "Mafia, what's the Mafia?" said Colombo. "There is not a Mafia." Cowed by the protests, Attorney General John Mitchell barred the Department of Justice from using the words "Mafia" and "Cosa Nostra."[35] Not everyone bought it though. State senator John Marchi denounced the Civil Rights League, saying, "Italian-Americans have been had."[36]

Defending the Constitution

Other times, the mob's lawyers were defending important constitutional protections. After the media turned Frank Costello into a high-profile target, the police ran nonspecific, twenty-four-hour wiretaps not only on his home telephone, but on all pay phones in restaurants he frequented. Police then transcribed the conversations on the phones, whether Costello was a participant or not. Costello's attorney, Edward Bennett Williams, who read hundreds of these transcripts, explained the Fourth Amendment problems with this. "Husband-and-wife calls were monitored. The tender words of sweethearts were heard by a third ear. In short, hundreds of wholly innocent, law-abiding and unsuspecting citizens were deprived of their right to communicate privately," recounted Williams. As Costello's attorney, Williams spent years challenging this and other due process issues, culminating in two appearances at the Supreme Court.[37]

Perhaps the most interesting legal quandary was the 1959 case against the Apalachin attendees. Dozens of high-level mobsters were caught in upstate New York at what we now know was a crucial meeting of the Cosa Nostra. The *mafiosi* were not there just for a barbeque. But prosecutors could not get any of the wiseguys to flip and testify about the criminal aims of the meeting. Nonetheless, a federal jury convicted them on an attenuated theory of conspiracy. The Court of Appeals reversed on the ground that the government had not met its burden of proof beyond a reasonable doubt. The Court was troubled by the theory of the case. As one of the judges pointed out, "The indictment did not allege what the November 14, 1957 gathering at Apalachin was about, and the government stated at the beginning of the trial could it could present no evidence of its purpose."[38]

Most defense lawyers for the mob were simply asserting guarantees of the United States Constitution, which provides more robust protections and due process rights for the accused than any other written constitution. Mobsters certainly recognized its importance. After he was deported to Italy, Charles Luciano complained about how Italian police once held him for eight days without a formal charge. "It couldn't happen in the good old days in New York. My lawyer woulda had me out on bail inside forty-eight hours. These people don't know what the word bail means," said Luciano.[39]

RECORD ON THE MAFIA: LOCAL FAILURE vs. STATE AND FEDERAL SUCCESS

Perhaps the clearest sign of the paralysis of local law enforcement is comparing its weak record to that of state and federal law enforcement. With few exceptions, the most significant and effective crackdowns on early *mafiosi* were carried out by federal or state officials.

The Morello Family was decimated by the United States Secret Service, not by the NYPD. Al Capone was brought down by the United States Treasury Department's tax unit, not by the Chicago police. The Federal Bureau of Narcotics obtained far more convictions of New York Mafia drug traffickers than the local narcotics unit. The 1957 Apalachin meeting was uncovered by the New York State Police and the Treasury Department's Alcohol and Tobacco Tax Unit.

Even "local" officials who attacked the mob had first built up a political base in federal or state appointments. Before Thomas E. Dewey was elected Manhattan district attorney in 1937, he was the assistant United States attorney who obtained convictions of Waxey Gordon, and a state special prosecutor who convicted racketeers. Likewise, before Rudolph Giuliani became mayor, he oversaw federal prosecutions of the Mafia as the United States attorney for the Southern District of New York.[40] This comparison is all the more impressive considering that the premier federal investigative agency was on the sidelines.

DIRECTOR HOOVER'S FBI, 1924–1957: HOOVER'S REFUSAL TO ACKNOWLEDGE THE MAFIA

The Mafia families were fortunate that the Federal Bureau of Investigation was *not* actually investigating them. For his first thirty-three years as FBI director, between 1924 and 1957, J. Edgar Hoover took few sustained actions against the Mafia. Indeed, Hoover refused to publicly acknowledge its existence.

Conspiracy theories have sprung up claiming Hoover was compromised by organized crime. In his bestseller *Official and Confidential: The Secret Life of J. Edgar Hoover*, Anthony Summers offered lurid stories of J. Edgar Hoover dressed in drag at Washington parties. He claimed that Meyer Lansky blackmailed the director with a photo of him in a dress.[41] Summers's primary "witness" was Susan Rosenstiel, who had a conviction for attempted perjury, and who for years had been trying to sell her story for money.[42] The story is absurd. Hoover would have been ousted had he been going to Washington parties in drag in the 1950s. Mobsters of that era dismiss the story. "Are you nuts?" said Vincent Alo, a partner of Lansky. "There was never no such picture. If there was, I'd have known about it, being so close to Meyer."[43]

The truth about Hoover's reluctance is more complex, but ultimately more fascinating. A recently released FBI document of Hoover himself sheds new light on his beliefs. To understand the document, and Hoover's position on the mob, we need to understand the man and his times.[44]

Hoover's Overarching Purpose: Rooting out Spies and Subversives

Jay Edgar Hoover's top priority, his *raison d'être*, had always been rooting out spies and "subversives" from America. As a young special assistant to Attorney General A. Mitchell Palmer, Hoover enthusiastically planned raids on anarchists during World War I.[45] When Hoover was appointed director of the Bureau of Investigation in 1924, he professionalized the scandal-ridden agency by reforming hiring and standardizing its procedures. He also expanded intelligence gathering on "subversives" like Socialist writer Theodore Dreiser. In 1929, Bureau agents even ransacked the New York office of the American Civil Liberties Union.[46]

Hoover was not always chasing ghosts though. During World War II, the FBI captured Nazi spies and saboteurs, and it began tracking secret agents of the Soviet Union. In 1943, the FBI recorded a Soviet diplomat paying a leader of the Communist Party USA (CPUSA) to develop intelligence on the Manhattan Project to build the atomic bomb. In 1947, the National Security Agency disclosed to FBI officials that under its "VENONA project," NSA cryptologists had decoded messages indicating that Soviet espionage had penetrated the United States government.[47]

During the Cold War, Hoover turned the FBI into more of an internal security ministry than a law enforcement agency. He poured resources into counterintelligence indiscriminately, and he dangerously blurred the line between actual enemies of the state and political dissidents. These remained the FBI's top targets through the 1950s, even after the CPUSA had been decimated.[48] Hoover had FBI agents assembling dossiers on teachers. "The bureau was sending raw and confidential file material on the suspected Communist activities of teachers to local school boards throughout the country," said Attorney General Herbert Brownell, who stopped the practice.[49]

Hoover's tunnel vision came at a cost to other FBI functions. Even after anticommunists like Robert F. Kennedy and Senator John McClellan had expanded their attention to organized crime and racketeering in the 1950s, Hoover continued to obsess about the remnants of the CPUSA. As late as 1959, the FBI's New York field office had only 10 agents assigned to organized crime compared to over 140 agents pursuing a dwindling population of Communists.[50] As a result, the FBI lacked adequate intelligence on the Mafia.

The Rise of the Mafia and the Kefauver Committee

By contrast, Hoover resisted investigating the "hoodlums," as he called them. Given that the Constitution left most police powers to states and cities, the FBI's role regarding crime was unclear. Hoover declared his opposition to a "national police force" early on, and he lambasted corrupt cities where "the local officer finds the handcuffs on himself instead of on the criminal, because of political influence."[51] His position initially had much support among commentators and Congressmen.[52] The Senate was controlled by state-rights politicians or segregationists like Strom Thurmond who disliked federal officers interfering in "local" matters.[53]

But Hoover was a federalist when it suited him. He exploited high-profile crime issues to increase funding for the FBI. In 1933–34, Hoover seized on the public clamor over Midwest bank robbers John Dillinger and Pretty Boy Floyd to lobby Congress to pass federal laws covering traditionally local crimes like bank robbery, kidnapping, automobile theft, and transportation of stolen property across state lines. According to one civil rights lawyer, "[Hoover] would say one day, 'We are not a police agency.' The next day for a bank robbery, kidnapping or auto theft, he would be a police agency. When it came to the Mafia or narcotics, 'We're not a police agency.'"[54] While Hoover was trumpeting questionable statistics about automobiles recoveries by the FBI, the bulk of new agents were assigned to gathering intelligence on subversives.[55]

As organized crime grew in strength, however, local officials began requesting assistance from the Department of Justice and the FBI.[56] In March 1949, the head of the Crime Commission of Greater Miami (a second home to many New York *mafiosi*) warned that "the influence of the national crime syndicate is so great that where the group has rooted itself, law abiding citizens and officials are silenced either through wholesale corruption or through threats and intimidation."[57] In 1949, an organization of mayors wrote to the new attorney general Howard McGrath, stating, "The matter is too great to be handled by local officials alone, since the organized crime element operates on a national scale across State boundaries."[58] McGrath held a crime conference but did little else. McGrath and Hoover were reluctant to get the FBI involved in what they thought was purely "local" vice crime. However, McGrath and Hoover were largely ignorant of the Mafia families, their cross-country networking, and their substantial effects on interstate commerce.[59]

Then, in April 1950, Kansas City mobsters Charles Binaggio and Charles "Mad Dog" Gargotta were found murdered in a Democratic Party club. (Binaggio was boss of the Kansas City Mafia with links to the governor). The *Kansas City Star* identified Binaggio as a "local representative of the national crime syndicate." The *Star* called on "J. Howard McGrath and J. Edgar Hoover, head of the Federal Bureau of Investigation . . . to investigate and 'break' this syndicate."[60]

These calls fell on deaf ears. On April 17, 1950, Attorney General McGrath testified before a Senate subcommittee that the Justice Department had "no evidence" of "any great national (crime) syndicate of any size." In response, Senator Homer Capeheart called the statements "surprising." He said that "either there is or there isn't a nationwide syndicate," and that "the Attorney General should know about it."[61] McGrath, who'd only been in office eight months, was clearly relying on Hoover's FBI.

So instead, Senator Estes Kefauver seized the issue to secure limited (in retrospect inadequate) funding for Congressional hearings on organized crime in 1950–51. With a small staff of twelve investigators, and no real assistance from the FBI, Kefauver tried to prove the existence of the Mafia in hearings around the country. The Kefauver Committee hearings were a television sensation, with over six hundred witnesses, including such gangsters (and secret *mafiosi*) as Frank Costello, Carlos Marcello, Willie Moretti, and Paul Ricca.[62]

But the committee staff was overwhelmed, and they could not get an informant to testify publicly about the Mafia. "The committee found it difficult to obtain reliable data concerning the extent of Mafia operation, the nature of the Mafia organization, and the way it presently operates," admitted the committee.[63] "The committee has diligently, but unsuccessfully, pursued the trail of the Mafia," wrote the *New York Times*.[64] Nonetheless, as politicians are wont to do, Kefauver exaggerated his findings. For example, he claimed that "the Mafia today actually is a secret international government-within-a-government. It has an international head in Italy—believed by United States authorities to be Charles (Lucky) Luciano." Although Luciano had been a New York boss, by 1951 he was idling in exile, and he certainly was not the "international head" of a "secret international government-within-a-government."[65]

To Hoover, the parade of hoodlums was a distraction from the Communists. It shows in his testimony before the Kefauver Committee on March 26, 1951. That same morning, a federal jury in Manhattan was hearing evidence in the trial of Julius and Ethel Rosenberg for conspiracy to commit espionage, which Hoover would dub the "Crime of the Century."[66] In his testimony, Director Hoover never acknowledges the Mafia's existence. While witnesses from the Federal Bureau of Narcotics and the Justice Department repeatedly reference "the Mafia," Hoover conspicuously avoids the word, instead dismissively referring to "hoodlums."[67] Hoover lectured the senators, saying that local authorities were responsible for hoodlums, while the FBI was responsible for "internal security" against "Communists and subversive forces."[68] In fact, Hoover cited his top priority (national security) in the process of turning down new FBI jurisdiction to go after organized crime:

> Senator Wiley: Do you think it would help some in this country if your jurisdiction were extended?
>
> Mr. Hoover: I do not. I am very much opposed to any expansion of the Federal Bureau of Investigation. I think it is too big today. We have had to take on additional duties and responsibilities . . . *because of the national security.*[69]

Due in part to his own intransigence, Hoover got his way, and Congress passed no new federal laws for the FBI. The Mafia emerged unscathed, again.

Hoover's Disbelief in the Mafia

This brings us to the heart of the matter. Most theories about Hoover's inaction assume that he "must have known" about the Mafia's existence, but that he dissembled because he did not want to pursue it. A recently released FBI document and firsthand accounts by FBI agents point to another reason. Simply put, Hoover genuinely did *not* believe in the existence of the Mafia.

The Federal Bureau of Investigation had virtually no intelligence on the Mafia families, the largest crime syndicates in the United States, through the late 1950s. FBI Boston field agent Neil Welch remembers his fellow field agents circulating the Federal Bureau of Narcotics's lists of *mafiosi* because the FBI kept no such information.[70] As FBI Chicago field agent William Roemer observed, "Mr. Hoover had no knowledge of organized crime in the United States because except for a 'special' such as CAPGA (code name for 'reactivation of the Capone gang') in Chicago, which lasted just a few months in 1946, the Bureau had never investigated organized crime."[71] This deprived Hoover of even basic intelligence on the Cosa Nostra. There is no evidence that Hoover knew about the Commission or understood its interstate connections. There is no evidence that Hoover knew of the existence or structure of the five Mafia families of New York. In fact, between 1924 and 1957, the director of the FBI never publicly uttered the word "Mafia" or "La Cosa Nostra."

The FBI's intelligence failure was exposed by its flat-footed response to news that dozens of *mafiosi* were caught meeting at Apalachin, New York, on November 14, 1957 (see chapter 10). When a Senate committee asked the FBI for intelligence on the attendees, the FBI had little to provide. "The FBI didn't know anything, really, about these people who were the major gangsters in the United States," recounted Robert Kennedy, counsel to the Senate committee. "I sent the same request to the Bureau of Narcotics, and they had something on every one of them."[72] In the weeks after Apalachin, FBI officials were still denying the existence of the Mafia. On November 21, 1957, a reporter quoted an "unimpeachable source" within the FBI pooh-poohing the idea of a Mafia, saying "nothing of any substance has ever been shown in this respect, nothing has even come close to doing so." Remarkably, the source acknowledged that "the FBI never has investigated the Mafia."[73] As late as January 8, 1958, an internal FBI report stated: "No indication that alleged 'Mafia' is an actual and existent organization in NY area, but is convenient term used to describe tough Italian hoodlum mobs."[74]

FBI officials under Hoover have since come forward to talk about the director's blind spot regarding the Mafia. "'They're just a bunch of hoodlums,' Hoover would say. He didn't want to tackle organized crime," confirms William Sullivan, former third-in-command of the FBI.[75] Or as former assistant FBI director Cartha "Deke" DeLoach explained:

> His profound contempt for the criminal mind, combined with his enormous faith in the agency he had created, persuaded him that no such complex national criminal organization could exist without him knowing about it. He didn't know it; ergo it did not exist.[76]

FBI official Oliver "Buck" Revell recalled an extraordinary conversation that he'd had with Director Hoover on February 8, 1971. Hoover was welcoming Revell to his role heading up a new FBI assault on the Cosa Nostra. After some pleasantries, Hoover became reflective on his disbelief in the Mafia's existence. "We didn't have any evidence," Hoover insisted. "Not until they held that hoodlum conference up in Apalachin, New York, back in '57."[77]

These accounts can now be corroborated by the written words of Hoover himself. On December 30, 1970, Hoover sent an interoffice memorandum to his deputies asking them to read Ed Reid's 1969 book on the mob, *The Grim Reapers*.[78] Hoover handwrote a revealing note at the bottom. The document reads:

December 30, 1970
Copies of the GRIM REAPERS have been sent to Mr. Gale and Mr. Rosen, with the message that Mr. Hoover wishes them to read it.
hwg [Secretary Gandy].
I have in mind that I was originally advised by Rosen that the Mafia or anything like it in character never existed in this country. I have been plagued ever since for having denied its existence. H[79]

The "Rosen" to which the director referred in his note was Alex Rosen, assistant director of the General Investigative Division for thirty years under Hoover.[80] Although Hoover may have been blaming Rosen unfairly, the note gives us a rare glimpse into Hoover's thinking on the Mafia. At some point, Hoover believed that "the Mafia or anything like it in character never existed in this country," and he therefore "denied its existence." He regretted his stance, feeling "plagued ever since" for his longstanding position.

Still, how could Hoover have doubted the existence of the Mafia for so long? The Federal Bureau of *Investigation* should have investigated stories corroborating the existence of the Mafia far more seriously. "It's inexcusable for them to say they couldn't have been using that [intelligence] function to at least be aware of what the hell is going on," said William Hundley, a top lawyer in the Justice Department.[81] Nor is it satisfactory to blame Senator Kefauver's flawed hearings, as some have suggested, for the FBI director's refusal to acknowledge the Mafia. It is preposterous to expect Senate staff to prove a crime syndicate to the Federal Bureau of Investigation. Had Hoover used some of the FBI's intelligence function to investigate the Mafia, it might have supplied the Kefauver Committee with the sources it needed. At a minimum, Hoover could have given more informative responses. Take the fine answer of a Bureau of Narcotics agent in 1957 to a Kefauver-inspired question about an international "head of the Mafia":

Senator Ives: I am curious to know where the head of the Mafia is today. What country? Sicily, still?

Mr. Pera: Well, a study of their organization, as it exists, would indicate to us that it is a loose organization, that there is no autocracy in it, that it is composed of a group of individuals who discuss with each other what is mutually beneficial to them and come to agreement on lines of action that is mutually acceptable to them.[82]

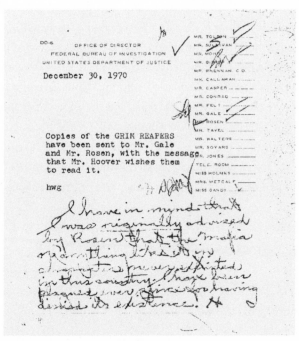

8–1: Handwritten note of J. Edgar Hoover, 1971. (Courtesy of the Federal Bureau of Investigation)

Or take J. Edgar Hoover's own later description in January 1962: "No single individual or coalition of racketeers dominates organized crime across the nation. There are, however, loose connections among controlling groups in various areas through family ties, mutual interest, and financial investment."[83] Or in September 1963, when Hoover explained that the Cosa Nostra was "a strong arm of organized crime in America" but that there was other organized crime, too.[84]

In fairness to Hoover, doubting the Cosa Nostra's existence was not a lunatic position in the 1950s. Before the Apalachin meeting and mob soldier Joe Valachi's public testimony of 1963, before the later flood of Mafia prosecutions (and even after), many people doubted the existence of the Mafia. "Regardless of what anyone else may say on the subject, there is no Sicilian Mafia, or simply 'Mafia' in the United States," declared the historian Giovanni Schiavo on November 16, 1957, days after the Apalachin meeting.[85] When FBI witness Joe Valachi testified before a Senate committee in 1963, he was attacked and belittled not only by fellow *mafiosi*, but by criminologists as well. In a 1969 essay titled "God and the Mafia," the criminologist Gordon Hawkins mocked Valachi's testimony, claiming that evidence of the Mafia is "on examination to consist of little more than a series of dogmatic assertions."[86] But Valachi was a legitimate *mafioso* whose testimony was mostly right, and the esteemed criminologist was mostly wrong. Indeed, Valachi's testimony had already been thoroughly corroborated by multiple sources by 1969.[87] Simply put, Mafia skeptics could not (or would not) accept that there were secret alliances of "families" dedicated to lives of crime and bound by common rituals and practices that operated in the United States.

But enough about Hoover. Let us look at the events in the Mafia that changed his mind: the events of 1957, the mob's terrible year.

THE ASSASSINATIONS OF 1957

The Volcano.

—Joe Bonanno on New York in the 1950s,
A Man of Honor (1983)

They had been hunting Frank Costello at night. On the evening of Tuesday, April 30, 1957, Costello, the boss of the Luciano Family, was out on the town with his pals Anthony "Little Augie Pisano" Carfano and Frank Erickson. That same night, a police detective was conducting surveillance at the Waldorf Astoria Hotel in an unrelated matter when he recognized Costello walking into the hotel bar.

The detective then spotted something else: two other men were surreptitiously trailing Costello's party. The lawman decided to keep an eye on them. When Costello left the Waldorf Astoria to stroll around midtown Manhattan, the two suspicious men were following him again from a distance. The police detective did not have enough to go on though, so he filed the observation away in his memory. Within days, the detective would learn the full implications of what he had seen.[1]

In the spring of 1957, the New York Mafia was fat, prosperous, and growing. The Mafia families controlled key union officials and held influence over businessmen in major industries. They were the top crime syndicates in Gotham, and they were the dominant heroin traffickers in America.

By Thanksgiving 1957, the Cosa Nostra would be in disarray. Internal conflicts would erupt into the public at a level unseen since 1931. Two Mafia bosses would be violently deposed, an underboss murdered while grocery shopping, and the wiseguys exposed to new scrutiny. Nineteen fifty-seven was to be the mob's *annus horribilis*.

Drawing on previously unpublished sources, this chapter re-creates the Mafia assassinations of 1957 and explores the underlying causes of the conflict. The unraveling of the mob leadership in the fifties revealed flaws present since the origins of the modern Mafia.

THE HUNTING OF A MOB BOSS: FRANK COSTELLO AND VITO GENOVESE

The men hunting Frank Costello were sent by his own underboss, Vito Genovese. He was a treacherous man to have as an underboss. He had little hesitation about arranging the deaths of *mafiosi* he had known for decades. Genovese soldier Joe Valachi testified before Congress that he executed hits on Steve Franse and Eugene Giannini on the direct orders of Vito Genovese. Genovese tried justifying his role in the 1951 murder of Willie Moretti, the longtime underboss of the Luciano Family, who the Commission thought was talking too openly about the Mafia. "It was supposedly a mercy killing because he was sick," Valachi recounted. "Genovese told me 'The Lord have mercy on his soul, he's losing his mind.'"[2]

Vito Genovese could make deals with anyone—and then promptly double-cross them. Take Genovese's machinations with Fascist Italy during the Second World War. Genovese plied Fascist officials with enormous cash tributes amounting to $250,000. He even received a personal decoration from the dictator Benito Mussolini. After the Axis powers fell, Genovese weaseled his way into the confidences of the United States Army occupation authorities. He promptly betrayed their trust by becoming a black marketeer of diverted American gasoline supplies.[3]

Because of Genovese's ruthlessness, stories arose whenever people died around him. For example, rumors swirled when Genovese married Anna Vernotico on March 30, 1932, only two weeks after her first husband Gerard Vernotico was found murdered. "Associates believed Vito had her husband strangled to death so that he could marry her," writes Selwyn Raab in his book *Five Families*. Left out of the story is that a New York court had already granted

Anna's petition for a divorce in January 1932, which was due to become a final judgment ninety days later in April 1932. Genovese would have been risking a murder charge to save a few weeks. In fact, Genovese was not a suspect in the case. Rather, the police believed that Gerard Vernotico, a gangster with a lengthy record, was killed by other racketeers.[4]

Genovese has also been blamed for the death of Pete LaTempa, a witness in the homicide case against Genovese for the 1934 murder of Ferdinand Boccia. LaTempa died from a drug overdose while in protective custody on January 15, 1945. "The city medical examiner reported that the pills LaTempa swallowed were not the prescribed drugs and contained enough poison to 'kill eight horses,'" asserts Raab. This is not accurate. The toxicology report found prescription barbiturates in his system. Investigators discovered that LaTempa had received a prescription (from a doctor with the district attorney's office) for Seconal—a barbiturate. Moreover, LaTempa had previously attempted suicide by hanging on December 6, 1944. Based on this evidence, the district attorney ruled LaTempa's death a suicide. In short, Vito Genovese's record is sordid enough without repeating demonstrably inaccurate stories.[5]

Vito Genovese moved on Costello in the spring of 1957 after sensing the boss's vulnerability. The sixty-six-year-old Frank Costello had grown tired of the mob's street operations. Costello once boasted of knowing "the better people and nothing but the better. I know some of the biggest utility men, some of the biggest businessmen in the country."[6] The "better people" apparently did not include the *caporegimes* in his mob syndicate, with whom Costello had weak relations.[7]

The mob boss was having personal problems as well. He had suffered through recurring bouts with throat cancer, which turned his voice gravely. In the late 1940s (long before *The Sopranos* invented a mob boss in therapy), Frank Costello was seeing a psychiatrist in Manhattan.[8] His disastrous testimony before the Kefauver Committee in March 1951, televised to a national audience, made him a target of law enforcement. In 1954, Costello was convicted of federal income tax evasion. His lawyers would spend years trying to overturn his conviction while he was out on bail.[9]

9–1: Frank Costello, testifying before the Kefauver Committee, 1951. (Photo by Al Aumuller, courtesy of the Library of Congress Prints and Photographs Division, New York World-Telegram and Sun Newspaper Photograph Collection)

11:00 p.m., Thursday, May 2, 1957, 115 Central Park West, Manhattan: The Attempt on Frank Costello

On the evening of Thursday, May 2, 1957, Frank and his wife Loretta went to see friends at the elegant L'Aiglon Restaurant. The dinner party included Mr. and Mrs. Al Miniaci, president of Paramount Vending, with whom Costello did business; Mr. and Mrs. Generose Pope, the publisher of *Il Progresso*, the Italian-language newspaper of which Costello was a longtime backer; and William Kennedy, owner of a modeling agency. After dinner, the group strolled down East 55th Street to the Monsignore Restaurant, where they met up with Frank Bonfiglio, a Brooklyn businessman who Costello had known for decades.[10]

Despite his good spirits, Costello's legal problems were weighing on him. He placed a call at about 10:45 p.m. to a Philadelphia lawyer. Frank returned to the table to apologize for having to leave early; he would be taking an 11:00 p.m. telephone call at home from his Washington attorney. His wife Loretta wanted to stay. So Costello left with Mr. Kennedy in a taxicab bound for the Upper West Side.[11]

At about 10:55 p.m., the taxicab arrives at Costello's upscale co-op apartment complex overlooking Central Park. The boss gets out of the cab and walks into the building's lobby. Then, a black Cadillac pulls up behind the parked cab. A hulking thug gets out of the Cadillac and rushes into the lobby.[12]

"This is for you Frank!" he shouts. Costello reacts, turning toward the shout. In a split second, a freakish bullet grazes the skin beneath Costello's right ear, furrows under the hair of his scalp, and exits, smashing into the marble wall of the foyer. Feeling a sting and the blood pouring down his neck, Costello staggers to the leather couch in the lobby. "Somebody tried to get me," Frank cries. The doorman and William Kennedy then took him to Roosevelt Hospital.[13]

Don Vito Rallies the *Caporegimes*

The gunman's macho shout may have saved Costello's life. The doctors who treated his wound at the hospital concluded that Costello had turned his head at the very last moment. So instead of the bullet shattering his skull, Costello walked away with a flesh wound.[14]

According to underworld sources, the gunman who botched the assassination was twenty-nine-year-old Vincent "The Chin" Gigante, a husky former boxer who had become a mob soldier for Genovese. "The Chin wasted a whole month practicing," mocked Joe Valachi, a fellow hit man for Genovese.[15] The NYPD believed that Thomas Eboli, a *caporegime* close to Genovese, was driving the getaway car. Tommy Eboli's company put up $76,000 ($500,000 in 2013 dollars) as collateral for Gigante's bail.[16]

Rather than trying to deny he was behind it, Vito Genovese proceeded to stage a *coup d'état* in the Luciano Family. The rank and file had little affection for their absentee boss. For all of Costello's ease around New York's power brokers, Genovese better understood that the real power in the mob was in its street crews. So while Costello was out hobnobbing with celebrities and politicians, Genovese was building loyalty among the *caporegimes*.

Genovese tested that loyalty in the days following the botched attempt. "Vito called a meeting of all his lieutenants to condone his attempt on Costello's life," describes an FBI report. "All of the lieutenants showed up at the meeting except Augie Pisano."[17] It was an impressive show of strength. "After the Costello shooting, his Family rallied around Genovese," confirms Joe Bonanno. Genovese then made his move: "Don Vito" proclaimed himself boss of the Luciano Family and named Gerardo "Gerry" Catena as his underboss.[18]

9–2: Vito Genovese, ca. 1934. (Courtesy of the New York Police Department)

Genovese and his soldiers braced for retaliation. The man they feared the most was Albert "The Executioner" Anastasia, who was furious about the attempt on his longtime ally Costello. Anastasia polled the Commission to see if it would remain neutral if he went after Genovese. The Commission's members warned Anastasia that they would oppose him if he turned it into a wider conflict. They persuaded him to stand down.[19]

The Trial of Vincent Gigante

Frank Costello had had enough of the mob life. He was already preoccupied with his own legal and health problems. Waging a prolonged fight against Genovese was unpalatable. He decided to retire as boss.[20]

Although police detectives believed that Costello had seen the gunman's face, he was completely unhelpful to their investigation. Costello insisted that he never had "an enemy in the world." In response, a detective quipped, "Whoever this guy was, he had a very strange way of showing his friendship."[21]

The following year, in May 1958, Vincent "The Chin" Gigante went on trial for the attempted murder of Frank Costello. Gigante's criminal defense attorney Maurice Edelbaum exploited Costello's unwillingness to identify the shooter:

> "Do you know any reason why this man should seek your life?" Edelbaum asked.
> "None whatsoever," replied Costello.
>
> . . . .
>
> "Tell us the truth," Edelbaum demanded in theatrical fashion. "Who shot you?"
>
> "I'll ask you who shot me," Costello replied with a sly smile. "I don't know. I saw no one at all."

The victim had rendered himself useless as a witness.[22] That left the building doorman as the sole eyewitness to identify Gigante. Unfortunately, the star witness was completely blind in one eye and impaired in the other. Edelman destroyed the doorman's testimony on cross-examination.[23]

Shortly before midnight, the jury returned its verdict: not guilty. Loud applause broke out in the gallery; the defendant's wife Olympia and four children burst into tears.[24] When the cheering stopped, Gigante was released by the court. The Chin walked over to Frank Costello, who was sitting in the back of the gallery. "Thanks, Frank," said Gigante.[25]

The Luciano Family was not the only one of the original five families wracked with strife during the 1950s. Even more severe problems were stirring in the old Mangano Family.

MOB PATRICIDE: VINCENT MANGANO AND ALBERT ANASTASIA

By 1951, Albert Anastasia had been the underboss to the Mangano Family for twenty years. The young Umberto Anastasio had come up under the tutelage of Vincent and Philip Mangano. Albert the Executioner was their enforcer on the waterfront, and he was underboss to their mob family. Albert once said that Vince Mangano was "like a father to him."[26]

After decades as their underboss though, resentments had arisen. Anastasia's ambitions were frustrated by the long tenure of the Mangano brothers. He was having a difficult time masking his contempt for Vince Mangano. "He always keeps surprises in store," Anastasia sarcastically told a guest of his boss. For his part, Mangano was distrustful of Anastasia's close alliance with Frank Costello. "Mangano and Anastasia were at a stage where they feared one another," recalled mob boss Joe Bonanno.[27]

Vincent Mangano went missing in early spring 1951. Then, on April 19, 1951, the bullet-riddled corpse of his brother Philip Mangano turned up in a marsh in Brooklyn. The police sought to question Anastasia and his associates about the gangland-style hit. But nobody was talking to the police. The homicide of Phil Mangano was never solved. Vince Mangano's body was never even found.[28]

The Commission wanted to know what happened to Vince Mangano. He was after all one of the original charter members. The Commission summoned Anastasia to a meeting. "He neither denied nor admitted rumors that he was behind Vincent's disappearance," recalled Joe Bonanno, a Commission member. "However, he said he had proof that Mangano had been plotting to kill him" and that "if someone was out to kill him, then he had the right to protect himself." His ally Frank Costello, as boss of the Luciano Family, backed up Anastasia's version of events before the Commission. Their message was clear enough. The Commission was not about to challenge them.[29]

Vince Mangano had never been pure in these matters anyway. In April 1931, Mangano betrayed his boss Joe Masseria by joining Salvatore Maranzano. Then, after Maranzano's assassination in September 1931, Mangano became boss of the Brooklyn waterfront by pushing aside Frank "Cheech" Scalise.[30] It was not exactly a pristine rise to power.

The flaw was present in the Mafia since the very beginning. The Mafia families were well-structured to allow their members to make money. The Commission provided a forum to arbitrate ordinary disputes and preserve general standards for the Cosa Nostra. But the Mafia, like other crime syndicates, really had no peaceful means to resolve severe conflicts among its top leaders. They could not call the police or bring a civil action in court. Rather, they took matters into their own hands. Take the case of Anastasia's underboss Frank Scalise.

THE UP-AND-DOWN LIFE OF FRANK "CHEECH" SCALISE

After a lifetime in the mob, Frank "Cheech" Scalise had reason to be cynical.

He had once been a boss. Back in 1930, Scalise was one of the first to answer Salvatore Maranzano's calls for a revolt against Joe Masseria. As reward, Maranzano offered Scalise the opportunity to become a boss on "the condition that he would eliminate [Vincent] Mangano at the first opportunity." Scalise took the deal to become boss.[31]

Then, Scalise delayed the hit. Growing impatient, Maranzano demanded to know why Mangano was still alive. Scalise tried to explain that he was unable to develop "any pretext to kill [Mangano] in order to justify his action with his countrymen." The boss of bosses was extremely unhappy with Scalise.[32]

Fearing that Maranzano would send killers after *him*, Scalise spilled the beans about the murder scheme to Mangano's allies. This further fueled the conspiracy against Maranzano. As we saw, Charles Luciano's hit men killed Salvatore Maranzano in his Park Avenue office on September 10, 1931. Although Scalise probably saved his own life by revealing the scheme, he was not going to be a boss anymore. "Scalise's star fell. Scalise had been too close a supporter of Maranzano," explained Bonanno. Scalise was demoted from boss and replaced by Vince Mangano. Scalise had gone from boss to has-been in a few months.[33]

Frank Scalise as Underboss: Franchising the Mob

It took twenty years for Scalise to claw his way back. Ironically, he returned over the dead body of Vince Mangano. Albert Anastasia made Scalise his new underboss in 1951. The mob's rackets were booming at the time. Crooks all over New York wanted in on the Cosa Nostra.

By 1956, Scalise decided it was his turn to cash in on his position as underboss. "Frank Scalise was accused, which was true, of commercializing this Cosa Nostra," Joe Valachi explained. Scalise used his authority as underboss to sell memberships in the Mafia for cash payments. "It was rumored amongst us boys that he received about 40,000" dollars from each payee to become a soldier, recounted Valachi. Selling mob memberships was resented by the existing wiseguys. "We were all stunned when the word got out," said Valachi. "In the old days a man had to prove himself to get it."[34]

Scalise's actions offended not only their pride, but also their power and money. Albert Anastasia reportedly felt threatened by all the new men that Scalise was turning into soldiers. All these newly minted soldiers were beholden to Scalise. They might someday be used in a revolt against Anastasia.[35] In addition, Scalise's rapid sale of mob memberships probably reduced the value of *existing* mob memberships. Although the soldiers would never put it in raw economic terms, as we saw earlier, much like a guild system or a franchise, "made men" could make more money by excluding others from the rackets.[36] Lots of wiseguys wanted Scalise to be stopped.

Monday Afternoon, June 17, 1957, Produce Store, Arthur Avenue, The Bronx: Punishing Frank Scalise

Frank Scalise was always drawn to the Belmont/Arthur Avenue neighborhood, the Little Italy of the central Bronx. Unlike the Cosa Nostra, the residents there lived up to their Italian customs. Frank's brother Jack Scalise still ran a candy store in the neighborhood. Even after Frank moved out to City Island, on the water, he drove to the Italian shops along Arthur Avenue.[37]

On Monday afternoon, June 17, 1957, Frank Scalise was grocery shopping at a produce store on Arthur Avenue. He bought some fresh peaches and lettuce for ninety cents. As Scalise was stuffing the change back into his pocket, a pair of men brushed past the grocery proprietor. Before anyone knew what was happening, the gunmen took aim at Scalise and fired shots into his cheek, the side of his neck, and his larynx. He fell down dead atop his scattered change. The gunmen ran to a black sedan out front. A couple weeks later, Frank Scalise's other brother Joseph went missing and was presumed dead.[38]

Unlike after the attempt on Costello, Albert Anastasia did not bother going to the Commission to avenge the shooting of his underboss Scalise. After all, Anastasia had personally approved it. Carlo Gambino, a low-profile *caporegime* originally from Palermo, Sicily, was promptly named as his underboss. Despite the elimination of the despised Scalise, tensions were still growing in the Anastasia Family.[39]

THE LIFE OF A MOB BOSS: ANASTASIA'S DUAL FAMILIES

The NYPD's files on Albert Anastasia are stored at the New York Municipal Archives in Manhattan. Barely touched fifty years later, the files paint a rich portrait of Anastasia's life in the mid-1950s. What comes across in the files is how Anastasia compartmentalized his life. There was the Anastasia family of the New Jersey suburbs. Then there was the Anastasia Family of the New York underworld. Though he tried to keep his dual lives separate, they were never that far apart.

After the Second World War, Anastasia moved his wife and children to suburban Fort Lee, New Jersey. Anastasia bought a spacious Spanish-style house for $75,000 (about $650,000 in 2013 dollars) on the bluffs overlooking the Hudson River. It was surrounded by a steel perimeter fence and guarded by a pair of Doberman Pinschers. Fort Lee was a well-heeled New Jersey suburb with something of a mob enclave. Around the block was his mobster friend Joe Adonis. Anastasia soldiers Ernesto Barese, Paul Bonadio, and Sebastiano Bellanca had also moved to the neighborhood.[40]

9–3: House of Albert Anastasia on the bluffs overlooking the Hudson River in Fort Lee, New Jersey, 1957. (Photo from the *New York Daily News* Archive, used by permission of Getty Images)

Given Anastasia's obscene violence, it is often forgotten that he had a home life. He carried pictures of his wife and children in his wallet, and he phoned them whenever he was coming home late. On May 12, 1957, only ten days after the attempt on Costello, Anastasia went ahead with a christening ceremony of his new baby girl at the Essex House Hotel off Central Park, just a few blocks from the site of the Costello shooting. Albert had his brother Father Salvatore Anastasio perform the christening before hundreds of guests. That fall, his son Albert Anastasio Jr. entered his first year of law school at New York Law School.[41]

When asked about his work, Albert Sr., as well as members of his family, would point to his garment factory. "He is in the dress business in Pa.," his son would say. Anastasia indeed owned a garment factory 130 miles away in Hazelton, Pennsylvania. It was a nonunion factory in the heart of coal country in the Wyoming Valley, a region rife with mob influence. The International Ladies' Garment Workers' Union struggled to organize the workers in the face of a depressed economy and intimidation by *mafiosi* like Russell Bufalino and Tommy Lucchese. Anastasia let his underlings run his factory and keep out the union organizers.[42]

Anastasia spent most of his days across the Hudson River in New York City. What he did in the city was often a mystery to his family. As his son later said, his father "was not the type of man that was asked about his personal business."[43]

ANASTASIA'S GAMBLING PROBLEM

In 1957, Anastasia was spending a lot of his time in New York wagering on sports. Anastasia had a gambling problem.

"Albert was losing heavy at the track, he was there every day, and he was abusing people worse than ever on account of that," Joe Valachi recalled.[44] Police investigators later discovered that Anastasia had fallen four months behind on the mortgage payments on his house in 1957. This despite the fact Anastasia was carrying around ample cash from his income from his garment factory and underworld sources.[45]

Anastasia's gambling was enabled by his sidekick Anthony "Cappy" Coppola. They met when Coppola was making a delivery for his family's business and hit it off immediately. Although the press dubbed Anthony Coppola his "bodyguard," that is an overstatement. Coppola was Anastasia's driver and errand boy, personal bookie, and goodtime pal. Mostly, Albert and Cappy bet on the ponies during the day and spent nights out in Manhattan. "Cappie is a clown and a bookie," described an ex-boxer who knew them from the race-track.[46] Another *mafiosi* deep into gambling recalled how Anastasia and Cappy were always asking for his opinions on sports bets. Whenever the telegraphed results of sporting events came in, they would be promptly relayed to Cappy's hotel room. "Invariably, [Albert] was in the room," the *mafiosi* remembered.[47]

ANASTASIA'S ENCROACHMENTS

Anastasia's steep gambling losses may have had bigger consequences for the mob. Although Anastasia had always been an avaricious boss, he began acting more aggressively in his dealings with the other New York families.

According to multiple sources, Albert Anastasia began encroaching on the interests of others in 1956 and 1957. For example, Anastasia tried speaking to Vito Genovese and even Frank Costello about some internal matters in their mob syndicate. "We will take care of our family, you take care of yours," he was told brusquely.[48]

Anastasia was eyeing the casino business in Cuba, too. This was the territory of Tampa Bay boss Santo Trafficante and his gaming partner Joe Silesi. One night over dinner with Joe Silesi in New York, Anastasia brought up Trafficante's bid for gambling concessions at the new Havana Hilton in Cuba. "I understand you'[ve] got a chance to get the Hilton casino," asked Anastasia, who wanted a piece of the action. This surprised Silesi. Although he knew others were interested in the Havana Hilton, Silesi never guessed that the New York boss was among them. Anastasia later brought this up directly with Trafficante. "I hear you've got an application in for the Hilton," Anastasia pried. "It looks like a big thing."[49]

Meanwhile, the soldiers were still unhappy that Anastasia had let Scalise bring in so many new members into their ranks. There were rumors that Anastasia had taken a cut of Scalise's fee for new members. Anastasia was increasingly abusive to some of his own men, too. "Albert Anastasia was doing so much wrong and it was up to his family to act," said Joe Valachi, recalling the view of the wiseguys.[50]

News of Anastasia's overreaching spread through the Mafia. In New England, members of the Patriarca Family began worrying that their old ally Anastasia might turn on them. Vinnie Teresa of Boston recalls that they "were afraid he wanted to take over the whole mob, become the boss of bosses." An FBI informant close to the mob in Cuba said that "the very size of his organization posed a control threat to the Mafia itself," which feared "an eventual bitter struggle for power" if Anastasia's family kept expanding. Another source based in Los Angeles said the Commission felt Anastasia "was too power-hungry and would be picking off the 'Bosses' one by one."[51]

If this sounds vaguely familiar, recall how the plots began against Joe Masseria and Salvatore Maranzano. The rebellion of 1928–1931 started as reactions against the boss of bosses abusing his power and interfering with other Mafia families.[52] In 1956–57, Anastasia was starting to act like a boss of bosses. Toppling overly powerful bosses seems to have been a natural response of the wiseguys.

A WEEK IN THE LIFE OF A MOB BOSS: MONDAY, OCTOBER 21–THURSDAY, OCTOBER 24, 1957

Anastasia regularly kept suites at the luxurious Warwick Hotel and the San Carlos Hotel in Manhattan for himself and his pals and business associates. So when Tampa Bay boss Santo Trafficante flew into town the week of October 21, 1957, Anastasia reserved a suite at the Warwick. Although we do not know if they reached any agreements, Anastasia and Trafficante used the rooms to hash over the casino business in Cuba.[53]

On Thursday, October 24, Coppola spent the afternoon gambling in a room at the Warwick with Anastasia and Anthony "Little Augie Pisano" Carfano. They poured over horse scratch sheets, placed bets, smoked cigarettes, and waited for news of the winners. It was a rainy Thursday night in New York. Anastasia and Carfano wanted to eat out at a restaurant anyway. Coppola begged off, saying he was tired. After finishing dinner, Anastasia took Coppola's car and drove himself home that night to Fort Lee, New Jersey.[54]

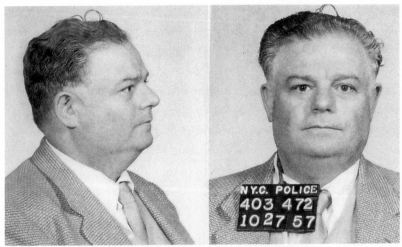

9–4: Anthony "Cappy" Coppola was Anastasia's bookie and goodtime pal in 1957. (Used by permission of the NYC Municipal Archives)

FRIDAY MORNING, OCTOBER 25, 1957, FORT LEE, NEW JERSEY, AND MIDTOWN MANHATTAN

Albert Anastasia woke up in his own bed on Friday morning, October 25, 1957. He saw off his son Albert Jr., the law student, on his way out the door at 7:30 a.m. The mob boss got dressed in a brown suit, white shirt, and tie. He was going to meet up with his *caporegime* Vincent Squillante, and get a haircut at Arthur Grasso's barbershop at the Park Sheraton.[55]

At about that same time, Santo Trafficante was checking out hurriedly from the Warwick Hotel. He had an early morning flight. Trafficante would be in Florida by the afternoon.[56]

Before he left his house in Fort Lee, Anastasia made a phone call to Coppola in his room at the San Carlos Hotel, instructing him to place some bets. "He wanted to place some doubles," Coppola recalled. Cappy was supposed to meet up with Albert about 11:30 a.m., on the way to place bets at the race track. Anastasia stuffed $1,900 in cash into his pockets (about $15,000 in 2013 dollars), got into Coppola's borrowed car, and drove himself to Manhattan.[57]

At 9:28 a.m., Anastasia pulled into a rental garage on West 54th Street. It was a brisk fall morning in Manhattan. Anastasia met up with Vincent Squillante, and they walked over to the Park Sheraton Hotel on the corner of West 56th Street and 7th Avenue.[58]

On the ground floor of the Park Sheraton that same morning was boxing manager Andrew Alberti and his fighter Johnny Busso, who had a room at the hotel. At about 9:15 a.m., they went downstairs to the hotel restaurant for breakfast and mingled in the lobby. Alberti was not supposed to be managing boxers. The New York Athletic Commission had officially banned him from boxing because of his ties with mobsters. Andy Alberti was especially close to Steve Armone and Joseph Biondo of the Anastasia Family.[59]

10:15 A.M., OCTOBER 25, 1957, BARBERSHOP OF THE PARK SHERATON HOTEL, MANHATTAN

Albert Anastasia's favorite place for a haircut was Arthur Grasso's barbershop at the Park Sheraton. The proprietor ran an old-style barbershop with mirrored walls, chrome-and-baby-blue barber chairs, shoe shines, and skilled Italian barbers. Anastasia went there twice a month for a trim.[60]

At 10:15 a.m., Anastasia and Squillante walked into the barbershop and hung up their jackets. "Haircut," Anastasia nodded. The barber escorted Anastasia over to barber chair number four with a corner window. Squillante eased into another chair for a shave.[61]

The proprietor Arthur Grasso came over to greet Mr. Anastasia. As the barber spread the cloth over Anastasia's white shirt, and the shoeshine polished his brown shoes, Grasso pulled up a stool to catch up with his friend. At about 10:20 a.m., Grasso got up from his stool to check the soap machine. Anastasia let his head hang limply forward so that the barber could clip behind his neck. He was completely relaxed. . . . [62]

Two men in hats and aviator glasses slipped across the threshold of the barbershop, black gun barrels poking out from their coats. The lead gunman walked briskly up to the rear right side of Anastasia's chair and fired away— BANG BANG BANG! "They went off fast; sounded like firecrackers," recalled Grasso. Anastasia bolted out of his chair in pain, breaking the chair's foot

9–5: Police photo of Anastasia Family associate Andrew Alberti, 1957. (Used by permission of the NYC Municipal Archives)

rest as he lunged toward the mirrors. Rushing up to the left side of the chair, the second gunman emptied his revolver at the wobbling mob boss—BANG BANG BANG BANG! But it was the lead gunman who fired the fatal round: a .38-caliber bullet struck the back of Anastasia's head and lodged in the left side of his brain. Anastasia collapsed between his barber chair and the next chair to the right.[63]

The assassins made their escape. They tried exiting through the side door, but the door was locked. The lead gunman turned around and backtracked through the main doors. "Nobody move," warned the second gunman to the barbers crouching down in fear.[64] The lead gunman dumped his .38-caliber Colt revolver in the glass vestibule of the hotel before exiting onto the sidewalk of West 55th Street. They scurried down the steps of the nearby subway station and escaped on a departing train. A city worker later found the second gunman's .32-caliber Smith & Wesson revolver in a waste box in the station.[65]

Back at the barbershop, the employees were in shock. The proprietor Arthur Grasso had literally crawled out of the shop to a ticket office next door. The only person with the presence of mind to try to help Anastasia was a physician who happened to be getting a haircut. Anastasia's upper torso was twisted over, his white shirt splattered in blood, and his face pressed onto the cold floor. The doctor checked for a pulse. Anastasia was gone.[66]

THE NYPD INVESTIGATION

Police responded to the scene within minutes. Flocks of newspaper reporters descended on the barbershop to cover the daytime murder of a mobster. Anthony "Tough Tony" Anastasio was notified about his brother while at his office at the International Longshoremen's Association in Brooklyn. He sped over to Manhattan. After seeing his brother on the floor, Tony left the barbershop weeping in despair.[67]

Although the police tried to get clear descriptions of the gunmen, some of the eyewitnesses may have been intimidated by this gangland shooting. The NYPD later conducted polygraph examinations of the barbershop employees. The polygraph examiner found "deception" in the answers of three barbers regarding whether they could positively identify the shooters. The examiner concluded that the barber who was shaving Squillante in chair number four had lied about being unable to identify the shooters because he was in "fear for self & family," and did not "care who knows he is lying."[68] The police never found evidence that any of them were involved. They were simply too scared to talk.

9–6: Body of Albert Anastasia in hotel barbershop, October 25, 1957. (Photo by George Silk, used by permission of Time Life Pictures/Getty Images)

Meanwhile, Anastasia's *caporegime* Vincent Squillante was nowhere to be found. During the shooting, Squillante had run out of the barbershop with lather dripping off his face. He subsequently refused to cooperate with the NYPD's investigation. According to the NYPD report of his 1958 interrogation, Squillante flatly "refused to answer any questions on the grounds that he might incriminate himself."[69]

The police nevertheless put together descriptions of the shooters from the barbershop employees willing to talk. At 4:44 p.m. that afternoon, the NYPD sent out a Teletype message: "HOMICIDE OF ALBERT ANASTASIA, OCT 25, 1957." The lead gunman was described as a white male around forty years old, 5'8" and 180 pounds, with "sallow complexion." He was dressed in a grey suit and fedora hat. The second gunman was described as a white male about thirty years old, 5'5" and 150 pounds, with "light complexion" and a "thin black pencil mustache." He was dressed in a brown suit and hat, and had on dark green aviator glasses. Both suspects spoke American English with no foreign accent.[70]

THE MOBSTERS BEHIND THE PLOT

There is virtual unanimity in the underworld about who was behind the plot to kill Anastasia. "I believe that Vito Genovese worked hand in hand with [Carlo] Gambino and [Gambino deputy] Joe [Biondo]," said Joe Valachi in his 1963 testimony before Congress. Genovese went so far as to warn Valachi to "stay away from Albert's men."[71] Vincent "Fat Vinnie" Teresa stated that Vito Genovese was the "mastermind of the conspiracy," and Carlo Gambino was the "inside man" in the plot.[72] New York boss Joe Bonanno said that "the indications were that it was men within [Anastasia's] own Family."[73]

Vito Genovese and Carlo Gambino had strong motives to kill Anastasia. As long as Anastasia was alive, Genovese had to worry that the volatile Albert would come after him. Eliminating Anastasia would also end any of Frank Costello's lingering notions about returning as boss. For the quietly ambitious Gambino, as the underboss of the Anastasia Family, he would be the logical successor to become the next boss once Albert was gone.[74]

For a long time, the NYPD focused on Santo Trafficante as a suspect in the plot.[75] Trafficante was, after all, meeting with Anastasia in the days leading up to his murder. The Florida boss may have had second thoughts about letting Anastasia get a foothold in Havana. In November 1959, two years after the shooting, the NYPD was requesting that the Tampa Bay police put surveillance on Trafficante. But without the FBI's involvement, the NYPD was never able to question Trafficante in Florida or Cuba. So the investigation of him fizzled.[76]

THE SUSPECTED SHOOTERS

In contrast to the plotters, the identities of the shooters are still the subject of debate. This section lays out the evidence for the top suspects.

Profaci Family soldier Joseph "Crazy Joe" Gallo *told* people that he and his brother's crew were the shooters. In a 1963 article for the *Saturday Evening Post*, a gambler named Sidney Slater said that Joey Gallo had once boasted to him in a bar, "You can just call the five of us the barbershop quintet."[77] In his 1976 tell-all book, Peter "The Greek" Diapoulos, an associate of the Gallo crew, claimed that Vito Genovese and Joseph Profaci "gave that piece of work to our crew, designating Larry and Joey Gallo and Joe Jelly [Joseph Gioielli]."[78]

There are strong reasons to doubt that the Gallo brothers were the actual shooters. The Gallo crew was part of the Profaci Family. The Gallos had no connections to either Vito Genovese or Carlo Gambino. Moreover, the man they called "Crazy Joe" Gallo was known as an unreliable braggart. In his 1963 article, Sidney Slater acknowledged: "It's even possible Joey was boasting, having his kind of fun."[79] The Gallo brothers were not the type of men that the Profaci Family would lend out to another mob family to execute a high-level assassination. There are more compelling suspects.

In 2001, veteran mob journalist Jerry Capeci first reported that the Anastasia assassination was carried out by a crew selected by Gambino *caporegime* Joseph Biondo.[80] According to Capeci's report, the crew leader was Stephen Armone. He reported that the "primary shooter" was Stephen "Stevie Coogan" Grammauta, a then-forty-year-old heroin trafficker, and that the "second shooter" was Arnold "Witty" Wittenberg, a then-fifty-three-year-old Jewish drug dealer. Capeci cited unidentified "knowledgeable sources on both sides of the law" as the basis for his report. Given Capeci's proven track record and deep sources in the mob and law enforcement, his report must be taken seriously.[81]

Documentary evidence has since been discovered that corroborates the story that Steve Grammauta was the lead gunman, and that he was acting under the direction of Joseph Biondo. The documents are stored separately in the FBI records in the National Archives at College Park, Maryland, and in the NYPD's files on the Anastasia case in the New York Municipal Archives. There is no indication that the FBI and the NYPD shared these documents at the time.

In an FBI report dated January 3, 1963, a confidential Mafia informant told the FBI that Joseph Biondo and Andrew Alberti helped organize the crew, and that the contract was given to "Steve Grammatula [*sic*]" whose "nickname is Steve Coogan." The informant explained that since "Anastasia frequented the barbershop at the Park Sheraton Hotel," the crew arranged so that "the guns were in the hotel room of Johnny Busso /PH/, a fighter." (The informant did *not* assert that Busso knew of the assassination plot, and there is no evidence that Busso was in any way involved). The informant stated that "Grammatula [*sic*] went to the hotel, got the guns, shot Anastasia, and caught [the] subway and went home."[82] The informant's account is all the more credible because Grammauta was never publicly identified as a suspect, and Alberti's and Busso's presence that morning at the Park Sheraton Hotel was not reported by the newspapers. The informant was therefore not simply repeating what he had read in the papers.[83]

The NYPD's internal files on the Anastasia investigation confirm that Andrew Alberti and Johnny Busso had a room at the Park Sheraton hotel, and they were in the lobby that morning. According to the NYPD's report on its interrogation of Busso, the boxer recalled how "on the morning of October 25, 1957, he received a phone call in his room from Andrew Alberti," who then "came up to his room." They went down for breakfast in the hotel restaurant at "about 9 or 9:15 AM." Busso said that he "spoke with numerous persons in the lobby of the hotel that morning in question, but does not remember Alberti introducing him to [Anastasia]."[84] For his part, Andy Alberti admitted that he ran into Anastasia that morning in the Park Sheraton lobby, and that they had a conversation during which Anastasia "spoke . . . about Busso's coming fight at the Garden." Although Alberti claimed he had no information on the murder, he also told the police that "he would not give any information, even if he possessed it, pertaining to this or any other crime." The police knew they were dealing with a mobster: the report on Alberti notes that his associates "include Joseph and Stephen Armone."[85] In November 1964, Alberti would be killed by a shotgun blast in what the police believed was a gangland murder.[86]

Steve Grammauta's background and appearance made him a logical suspect as the lead gunman. Grammauta was a low-profile *mafioso* with close ties to the Armone brothers of the future Gambino Family. He would be convicted with Joseph Armone (the brother of Stephen Armone) for running a heroin ring that they operated between 1956 and 1960. Furthermore, Grammauta fits the description of the first gunman, a "white male around forty-years-old" (Grammauta was forty in October 1957) with a "sallow complexion" (the man nicknamed "Stevie Coogan" had pale skin).[87]

Based on these sources, we can broadly outline the assassination plot. By the fall of 1957, the grievances against Albert Anastasia have reached a boiling point. Carlo Gambino's trusted lieutenant Joseph Biondo secretly assembles a team to eliminate the boss. Biondo selects his close associate Steve Armone to lead a crew of gunmen. They know that Anastasia gets his hair cut twice a month at the barbershop on the ground floor of the Park Sheraton hotel. So they stash revolvers in the room of one of Andy Alberti's fighters, who stay at the hotel before fights. They confirm that the boss is getting his regular trim on the morning of Friday, October 25, 1957. Steve Grammauta and the second gunman get the revolvers from the hotel room, put on their hats and aviator glasses, and head downstairs. At about 10:20 a.m., they slip across the threshold of the barbershop. . . .[88]

THE AFTERMATH

"ANASTASIA SLAIN IN A HOTEL HERE," read the *New York Times*.[89] The murder of Albert Anastasia shook up the underworld. There had not been a public assassination of a New York Mafia boss since the murder of Salvatore Maranzano in September 1931. (Vince Mangano's killing in 1951 was carried out in secret).[90]

Carlo Gambino and his lieutenants moved swiftly to claim the mantle of leadership. As Joe Bonanno discovered, after Anastasia was killed, the plot's "second phase involved the quick recognition of Carlo Gambino as Anastasia's successor."[91] With the backing of Vito Genovese and Tommy Lucchese, Gambino became the boss of the new Gambino Family. Gambino named Joe Biondo as his underboss as reward for his ruthless service.[92]

The murder and replacement of Anastasia took place without major opposition. By October 1957, few wiseguys had any desire to avenge Anastasia.[93] The ferocity of "The Executioner" shocked even other mobsters, who wondered when they might be his next victim. The murders of Vincent and Philip Mangano, the dumping of Peter Panto in a lime pit, the unpredictable outbursts of rage—it was too much even for his closest associates. "I ate from the same table as Albert and came from the same womb, but I know he killed many men and he deserved to die," said his brother Anthony Anastasio to FBI agents in a confidential conversation.[94]

With all the upheaval in New York, the Commission called a national meeting in 1957. The main purposes of the meeting would be to affirm Vito Genovese's accession as boss of the new Genovese Family and to introduce "Gambino to the important men in our world."[95] Don Vito wanted to hold the meeting in Chicago. But Stefano Magaddino of Buffalo persuaded the Commission to hold it at his friend Joseph Barbara's fifty-eight-acre estate in upstate New York. Barbara's place was located outside the factory town of Endicott in a village called Apalachin.[96]

10

APALACHIN

There's the state troopers.
—Mrs. Josephine Barbara (1957)

We didn't have any evidence of a national syndicate. Not until they held that hoodlum conference up in Apalachin, New York, back in '57.
—FBI Director J. Edgar Hoover (1971)

1944, ROUTE 17, OUTSIDE ENDICOTT, NEW YORK

The thief just wanted some company gas. With American soldiers fighting the *Wehrmacht* and Imperial Japan, the home front was rationing petroleum. But somehow Joseph Barbara Sr., a businessman who owned a bottling plant in Endicott, New York, always had extra gasoline. So an employee took a company truck with two containers of gas to Route 17 outside Endicott, where he stashed them in some bushes.[1]

Just then, state trooper Edgar D. Croswell was driving by on patrol. Born in Woodstock, New York, Croswell graduated from business college in the teeth of the Great Depression and took jobs with local police and as a detective in Sears, Roebuck's mail-order division. When he was twenty-eight years old, in August 1941, Croswell accepted an assignment with the New York State Police and spent the war patrolling southern New York out of Troop C's substation in Vestal, New York. It was a good fit. Six feet tall and angular, with piercing grey eyes, Croswell was something of a loner and a workaholic; he once said,

"My hobby is police work." A soft-spoken man who disliked guns, he believed in relentless investigations.[2]

Trooper Croswell was *not* a trifling man. So when the man coming out of the bushes gave only vague answers to his questions, Croswell searched the bushes and found the gas. Nearby was a truck registered to Mission Beverage Company. Back at the police substation, the thief confessed to stealing the gas. Croswell called the company's owner, a Mr. Joseph Barbara.

Trooper Croswell's first encounter with Joe Barbara was very strange. When Barbara arrived at the substation, Croswell noticed the businessman had a revolver on his belt. Barbara was brusque and dismissive, too. "As soon as I explained the situation to him he wanted no part of it. He didn't want the man arrested or anything done," recalled Croswell. "Back in 1944 or 1945, 10 gallons of gasoline was pretty precious. It just aroused my suspicion who he was."[3]

Croswell did some digging on Barbara. The Pennsylvania police had thick files on him. Barbara lived a gangster's version of the American dream. Barbara arrived at Ellis Island in 1921 when he was fifteen years old, and like many Sicilian immigrants, he found work in the Endicott-Johnson Shoe factories in the "Triple Cities" of Binghamton, Endicott, and Johnson City. Barbara, however, had no desire to end his days as a broken-down cobbler. In 1928, he joined up with Sicilian *mafiosi* in the lawless coal country of northeastern Pennsylvania, where he became a bootlegger, and was arrested as a prime suspect in three brutal murders, including one by strangulation. In 1933, Barbara returned to Endicott with his illegal earnings. He promptly started a bottling company, married a pretty local girl, and took on all the appearances of a legitimate businessman.[4]

With no charges to press, Croswell dropped the gas matter. But he would remember Barbara.

1949, TELEPHONE WIRETAP ON
JOSEPH BARBARA'S HOUSE, APALACHIN, NEW YORK

Croswell's views on Joe Barbara hardened after their first encounter. In 1946, Barbara pled guilty to violating federal regulations in hoarding 300,000 pounds of sugar. This rationing offense meant something else to Croswell: Barbara, the former bootlegger, had 150 tons of sugar to produce moonshine liquor. There was also the company he kept. "Every investigation of any importance that we conducted in that area concerning vice or gambling seemed to center around Joseph Barbara and the people who associated with him," Croswell recounted. The ostensible business executive surrounded himself with men like: Anthony "Guv" Guarnieri, who had served time for gun and gambling crimes; Patsy Turrigiano, a bootlegger and moonshiner; and Emanuel Zicari, a convicted counterfeiter. Behind the respectable façade, Barbara the businessman still had another foot in the underworld.[5]

Croswell began investigating Barbara with a doggedness bordering on obsession. Around 1949, he obtained a court order to wiretap Barbara's telephone. This was the first of several wiretaps that the New York State Police and the Broome County district attorney ran on Barbara's home intermittently between 1949 and 1956. Croswell would go the DA's office to read transcripts of Barbara's latest phone conversations. It was discovered that Barbara was calling major racketeers from around the country, such as Russell Bufalino of Pennsylvania. But the *mafiosi* kept their conversations short and nonincriminating: "That matter we talk about, we fix," and "Okay, I meeta you at where we say."[6]

Next, through undisclosed means, Croswell and a local reporter acquired Barbara's bank records. Large sums of money unconnected to any business transaction were being transferred one way into Barbara's account from men in Pennsylvania.[7] Still, no proof of a crime.

So Croswell took a fateful measure: twice weekly, he began personally spying on Barbara's estate. "As a steady routine I took to driving by his house and jotting down the license numbers of the visiting cars and cross-checking their owners," said Croswell. Barbara would turn on the floodlights and look blinkered-eyed out his window at the statie. Croswell admitted that such actions were part of "a little campaign of harassment we carried on against Barbara for years."[8]

THURSDAY, OCTOBER 18, 1956, ROUTE 17, OUTSIDE OF WINDSOR, NEW YORK

The Southern Tier region of New York was enjoying a glorious Indian summer the third week of October 1956, with temperatures reaching the seventies and fall colors at their peak, but the white Oldsmobile flashing by on Route 17 was not taking a leisurely drive.[9]

State Trooper Fred Leibe chased the speeding car for five miles before forcing it to the side of the highway outside Windsor, New York. The angry driver got out and walked to the back of the car. He was a short, paunchy man with beady eyes, who did *not* match the physical description on his driver's license. When Leibe asked the speeder the date of birth on "his" license, he got it wrong. Leibe arrested him. He told the three riders in the white Oldsmobile to follow his squad car back to the substation, but they ducked away on a highway exit.[10]

Croswell, now a sergeant, and Trooper Leibe unraveled the driver's identity. The speeder admitted to Leibe that his real name was Carmine "Lilo" Galante, and that the license belonged to Joseph DiPalermo, who the police found out was a narcotics trafficker. Most troubling, they discovered that Galante had served a long sentence in Sing Sing for shooting a policeman who surprised him during an armed robbery in New York City. Croswell found out that Galante had checked into a suite at the stately Arlington Hotel on Wednesday, October 17, 1956, along with the gangsters Joseph Bonanno, John Bonventre, Frank Garofalo, and Louis Volpe. What's more, they charged their bills to . . . Joe Barbara's bottling company.[11]

SATURDAY, OCTOBER 27, 1956, BINGHAMTON, NEW YORK

After Galante was indicted, odd things started to happen. On Saturday, October 27, 1956, Captain Chris Gleitsmann and a junior sergeant in the police department of West New York, New Jersey, drove three hours in a police car to see Croswell and his partner Vincent Vasisko at a Binghamton substation. Captain Gleitsmann offered to pay Galante's fine and "consideration" for the officers if they would release Galante. A prepared Croswell showed the police captain Galante's hideous criminal record, and told him they weren't going to intercede. "Now that it is all over, what did they send you up here with?" Croswell asked. Gleitsmann held up one finger. "Do you mean a thousand dollars?" said Croswell. "Yes," he replied.[12]

A few days later, a state assemblyman called the local district attorney to check if he could "do something" for Galante.[13] Next, Galante's lawyer tried bribing the judge. "Brother Galante wanted to do something useful for the youths to compensate for his poor boyhood himself," the judge recounted. Galante's lawyer offered to give $500 to any boy's charity of the judge's choosing, *if* he imposed no jail time. The judge threatened to punch the lawyer, and he sentenced Galante to thirty days.[14]

The instincts of the state police were right. Lilo Galante was in Binghamton in October 1956 to attend the national meeting of the Commission. After checking into their rooms at the Arlington Hotel, the Bonanno Family representatives attended meetings at Joe Barbara's estate in nearby Apalachin. On his way out, Galante traversed the dirt roads of Apalachin until reaching Route 17, where he opened the throttle and sped east to Brooklyn.[15]

OCTOBER 1957, ESTATE OF JOSEPH BARBARA, APALACHIN, NEW YORK

"Gang Lord Anastasia Is Murdered," read the *Binghamton Press* on October 25, 1957.[16] The beautiful, raven-haired Mrs. Josephine Vivona Barbara was worried. Her husband had been in New York City on the same day Anastasia was shot. Now fifty-two years old, Joe Barbara had had a major heart attack in January 1957, which nearly killed him. "Have you read or heard about the Anastasia murder?" she asked her husband. "Yes," he replied in English. Seeing the housekeeper, Joe switched over to Italian, and then they went to the bedroom to finish the conversation in private.[17]

As we saw earlier, the assassinations of 1957 led to a national meeting of the Cosa Nostra. Stefano Magaddino persuaded Cosa Nostra leaders to hold the meeting at his friend Joe Barbara's fifty-eight-acre estate in Apalachin. In 1947,

Barbara had built his English-manor-style stone house on a hill at 625 McFall Road, a secluded, dead-end road. The meeting was set for Thursday, November, 14, 1957.[18]

Barbara busily prepared for the meeting. On November 5, he placed a big order with Armour and Company in Binghamton: 207 pounds of prime-cut steak, 20 pounds of veal chops, and 15 pounds of deli meats.[19] "All the people who mattered from the whole country had been invited," recalled Bonanno. "Everyone was talking about the Big Barbeque at Apalachin."[20]

WEDNESDAY, NOVEMBER 13, 1957, PARKWAY MOTEL, VESTAL, NEW YORK

On the afternoon of Wednesday, November 13, the twenty-one-year-old Joseph Barbara Jr., who had dropped out of college to help out his father, was sitting in his office at the Canada Dry bottling plant in Endicott. The phone rang. It was Joe, Sr.: some friends of ours needed rooms. Like a good son, Joe Jr. drove to nearby Vestal to make reservations at the Parkway Motel.[21]

In a bit of cosmic timing, Sergeant Edgar Croswell was also due at the Parkway Motel that afternoon. Someone had written a bad check to the proprietors, who called the New York State Police. Ed Croswell had been promoted to the Bureau of Criminal Investigation (BCI) of the state police, an elite plainclothes unit in charge of investigating felony crimes. He was now also a divorced bachelor living at the Vestal police barracks, where he kept "pretty much to himself" and stayed busy with the investigative work he liked so much. He rounded up Trooper Vasisko and, both in plain clothes, they headed over to the motel to investigate the bad check. Around 3:30 p.m., while standing at the front desk with the proprietor Mrs. Helen Schroeder, Croswell recognized Joe Barbara's son driving up to the motel parking lot.[22]

Croswell decided to eavesdrop on the kid. "We have checked on his father's activities for many years and it is just interesting sometimes what you can hear if you step out of sight when someone is around," Croswell explained. The lawmen ducked behind the wall dividing the front desk from the living room of the proprietor, who acted as if all was normal.[23]

Joey Barbara walked in and made reservations for three rooms for Wednesday, November 13, and Thursday, November 14, to be charged to his father's plant. When the proprietor asked the young man to register the guests' names, he said he did not know their names, as the rooms were for "a Canada Dry convention."[24]

Croswell and Vasisko decided to check on Joe Sr.'s activities. The staties first went by the plant; they saw nothing unusual. Around 7:00 p.m., they drove by the Barbara estate and saw sleek automobiles in the front parking lot. They ran the plates on their Teletype machine back at the substation: a 1957 pink Lincoln belonging to James La Duca of Buffalo, a 1957 black Cadillac registered to Alfred Angelicola of New Jersey, and a 1956 blue Pontiac belonging to Patsy Turrigiano, a Barbara associate whom Croswell once arrested for operating an illegal still. Given the presence of the moonshiner, Croswell called Kenneth Brown and Arthur Ruston of the Treasury Department's Alcohol and Tobacco Tax Unit's office in Binghamton, with whom he had been working in monitoring Barbara's men.[25]

Around 9:00 p.m., a 1957 blue Cadillac registered to Buckeye Cigarette Service Co. of Cleveland, Ohio, pulled up to the Parkway Motel. When Mrs. Schroeder asked the occupants to register their names, they declined, assuring her that "Mr. Barbara would take care of it." The men were, in fact, John Scalish, boss of the Cleveland Family, and his *consigliere* John DeMarco, a convicted extortionist. The pair belonged at the meeting. Scalish and DeMarco were always making new partnerships in the Midwest and beyond. The Cleveland Family was among the first to develop interests in the new casinos in Las Vegas, providing protection for a share of the skim.[26] The Clevelanders retired to their rooms.

They had no idea they were being watched.

THURSDAY MORNING, NOVEMBER 14, 1957, THE ASSEMBLY

The big day arrived. On Thursday morning, November 14, 1957, Joseph Barbara Sr. rose early, dressed in a crisp white shirt and dark business suit, and walked down to the kitchen, where Mrs. Barbara was cooking breakfast for some attendees who'd stayed in guest bedrooms. At 8:00 a.m., Joe Barbara enjoyed breakfast with his houseguests, chattering away in Italian. Although the weather was dreary and overcast, spirits were high among the old friends.[27]

Beginning at 9:00 a.m., dozens of muscular, late-model American automobiles rumbled onto Barbara's property, and wiseguys started piling out of the cars. "Good morning, how do you do? Glad to see you," said Barbara as he welcomed the men with hearty handshakes. "How are you feeling?" the guests asked their host. "How is the family?"[28]

They came from all over America. With the leadership turmoil in their ranks, the New York families sent high-level delegations, totaling eighteen men or about a quarter of the attendees. Reflecting its position as host, upstate New York had the most attendees, with twenty-two men. Meanwhile, roughly thirty out-of-state mobsters had come from across America and even from Cuba. They came from Boston, Havana, Kansas City, and Los Angeles. Barbara and his men acted like airport shuttles, picking up those flying in on Mohawk Airlines at the Tri-Cities Airport.[29]

The goodfellas enjoyed themselves. In Barbara's garishly huge living room (it had seven davenport sofas), fifteen mobsters played pinochle, their cash piling up on the card tables. Smaller groups gathered in Barbara's office, in guest bedrooms, and in the summer house. John Montana of Buffalo did not arrive until close to noon; he told Barbara his "car had broke down" and was "sorry for being late." Manny Zicari was in charge of cooking steak sandwiches at the outdoor barbeque behind the front garage. The *mafiosi* helped themselves to cold cuts, fruit, and cake at the outdoor buffet. They were having a great time.[30]

THURSDAY AFTERNOON, NOVEMBER 14, 1957, THE DRAGNET

In the early afternoon, Mrs. Barbara retreated to the breakfast nook with her housekeeper Marguerite Russell. Around 12:40 p.m., she saw a strange car in the front parking lot. Vasisko was at the wheel while Croswell and Treasury agents Brown and Ruston took down license plate numbers. "There's the state troopers," exclaimed Mrs. Barbara as she stared out the window.[31]

The dozen or so *mafiosi* standing at the outdoor barbeque behind the garage had already spotted the strange car driving up and down McFall Road. They migrated to the parking lot to watch the lawmen. Decked out in silk suits, gold watches, and pointy dress shoes, the assembled men "looked like a meeting of George Rafts," described Croswell.[32]

Overwhelmed, Trooper Vasisko backed the car out of the driveway and drove down McFall Road to regroup about half a mile from Barbara's house. Croswell radioed for reinforcements: "I requested Sergeant Kennedy to get us all the uniformed men that he could down there in a hurry." The troopers set up a roadblock by parking their car at the base of the dead-end McFall Road. Shortly after setting up the roadblock, one of Barbara's men Ignatius Cannone drove past them on his way to Barbara's house.[33]

At 1:15 p.m., the *mafiosi* in Barbara's house sent down Bartolo Guccia, a Barbara associate who ran a local fish business, to trawl for more information. The troopers recognized Guccia's truck and let him pass. The fishmonger drove past them a little way, then suddenly spun around and went back up the hill to Barbara's house. Minutes ticked by tensely. . . .

THE McFALL ROADBLOCK

Inside the house, Vito Genovese was stewing. This was supposed to be his coronation as boss. Vito had always wanted the meeting held in Chicago. Now, Barbara's man was saying the police had blocked the road. Don Vito was *not* about to go traipsing through the woods. To hell with that, Vito was leaving the way he came. The drivers went outside to start their engines.[34]

At 1:20 p.m., Barbara's local man Emanuel Zicari drove down the road in the first automobile with an unfamiliar passenger. Uncertain what to do, Croswell initially let Zicari pass the roadblock, but then he abruptly changed his mind. "We hadn't completely formulated our plan as to what we were going to do, and I also knew Zicari," Croswell later testified, explaining the chaotic situation. He decided to radio Sergeant Kennedy to pick up Zicari's car on the highway and identify his passenger. It was Dominick Alaimo, a union representative (and secret *caporegime* in the Bufalino Family) from Pittston, Pennsylvania.[35]

At 1:25 p.m., the next car to roll down the hill was a power-packed, black 1957 Chrysler Imperial. At the wheel was Northeast Pennsylvania boss Russell Bufalino. New York boss Vito Genovese was in the front passenger seat. Piled in the back were the members of the Philadelphia delegation, including boss Joe Ida, his underboss Dominick Oliveto, and Genovese's underboss Gerry Catena. The state police instantly recognized Bufalino, a notorious racketeer. They frisked all the men, finding no weapons. When Croswell asked Bufalino what he was doing at the house, Bufalino responded with what became a familiar refrain: "Barbara had been sick, so he came up here and brought some friends and had gone up to visit." Don Vito told them only his height, then asked the troopers whether he had to answer any of their questions. "No, you don't have to answer them," a trooper replied. "Well, I would rather not," Genovese said defiantly.[36]

The next two cars were driven by Barbara men, Nat Cannone and Patsy Turrigiano. Since they were locals like Zicari, they were allowed to pass the road-block and report voluntarily to the Vestal substation.[37]

By then reinforcements from Troop C had arrived. Croswell immediately sent them off to patrol for the runners. Twenty state police troopers set up a dragnet around Apalachin. Meanwhile, Croswell focused on the McFall road-block. Throughout that afternoon and evening, cars carrying mobsters sporadically came down the hill.[38]

- New York boss Carlo Gambino was riding in a 1956 Lincoln chauffeured by his *caporegime* Paul Castellano, himself a future boss of the family.[39] Riding in the car with them was Armand Rava, a bitter holdover from the Anastasia regime (Gambino would have Rava killed a few weeks after Apalachin). Following them was Gambino's *consigliere*, Joseph "Staten Island Joe" Riccobono. Although this was supposed to be Carlo Gambino's coming out party, this is not what he had in mind. The low-profile Gambino, who had always eschewed the public spotlight, would soon be introduced to all of America under banner headlines.[40]
- It must have felt like *déjà vu* for New York boss Joseph Profaci and his underboss/brother-in-law/chauffeur Joseph Magliocco. In December 1928, Profaci and Magliocco had been arrested together with twenty-one other *mafiosi* at the Statler Hotel in Cleveland. Prior to Apalachin,

the '28 Cleveland conclave had been the largest Mafia meeting to be disrupted by police. Almost thirty years later, Profaci and Magliocco were being hauled off to another stationhouse for questioning about another meeting. Their *caporegime* Salvatore Tornabe was also caught at the roadblock.[41]

- The Lucchese Family of New York was represented at Apalachin by three high-ranking lieutenants. *Consigliere* Vincent Rao departed alone in his 1956 Cadillac Coupe. *Caporegime* John "Big John" Ormento of East Harlem—the most significant narcotics trafficker in the country—was caught at the roadblock as well in his black '57 Chevy convertible. *Caporegime* Joseph "Joe Palisades" Rosato, a racketeer in the garment district, was also netted at McFall Road.[42]

- Before the DeCavalcante Family took over, northern New Jersey was treated as a satellite of the New York families, and its attendees reflected this relationship. Anthony Riela, a member of the Bonanno Family in Essex County, New Jersey, provided rooms at his cheap airport motel for out-of-town delegates with flights in Newark. Meanwhile, the elder statesmen of the Apalachin meeting was sixty-nine-year-old, Sicilian-born Charles Salvatore Chiri of Bergen County, New Jersey.[43]

- The Patriarca Family of New England sent Frank Cucchiara, its *consigliere* from Boston. His boss Raymond Patriarca had good relations with the New York families, which agreed to give the Patriarca Family dominion from Boston to the Connecticut River. Cucchiara indeed was escorted by Natale Evola of the Bonanno Family of New York.[44]

- From the South came Dallas boss Joseph Civello. Born in Louisiana, the tall, lanky Civello became a liquor-store owner and drug trafficker in Texas. He served six years in Fort Leavenworth for his role in a massive narcotics ring. After his release in 1944, he gradually rose through the ranks to become boss of the Dallas Family in 1956.[45]

- Most delegates from upstate New York had driven their own automobiles to Apalachin, and so tried leaving by car on McFall Road. From Auburn, New York, the Monachino brothers, Patsy and Sam, had close ties to the Profaci Family. The Monachinos drove down in their 1957 Oldsmobile with Anthony "Guv" Guarnieri and Patsy Sciortino.[46] Meanwhile, the much younger Valenti brothers, Constenze (age thirty-three) and Frank (age forty-six), of Rochester, New York, departed in a sleek, blue-and-white 1957 Chrysler Saratoga convertible. Poor Joey Barbara left in the least stylish vehicle, a company station wagon.[47]

- Joseph Falcone was driving his older brother Salvatore Falcone, head of the Magaddino Family's interests in Utica. They brought their notorious enforcer Rosario Mancuso, a 235-pound thug who had a conviction for assault with intent to murder for a brutal beating he inflicted.[48] The Falcones had an estimated 80 to 100 made men, and vice was so pervasive that Utica was nicknamed "Sin City of the East."[49] Croswell was later assigned to a probe of corruption in Utica. Using wiretaps, Croswell discovered that Deputy Police Chief Vincent Fiore was tipping off brothels and gambling houses to police raids, and he even supplied private protection to Albert Anastasia in Utica. Fiore was forced to resign and subsequently convicted.[50]

THE CHASE BEGINS

With troopers at the McFall roadblock rounding up friends of theirs, some attendees decided to take their chances on foot. About 1:45 p.m., Treasury Agent Brown saw about eight or ten men "in close single order file walking from the back of the Barbara residence" toward the woods. About 2:00 p.m., Treasury Agent Ruston saw another "three or four men running across that open area" behind Barbara's house. The escape had begun.

Croswell directed Treasury Agent Brown and Trooper T. G. Sackel to go after them. To encircle the runners, they drove a police car southeast to McFadden Road, the next dirt road over on the other side of the trees. The lawmen got out of the car to hunt for the hoodlums.[51]

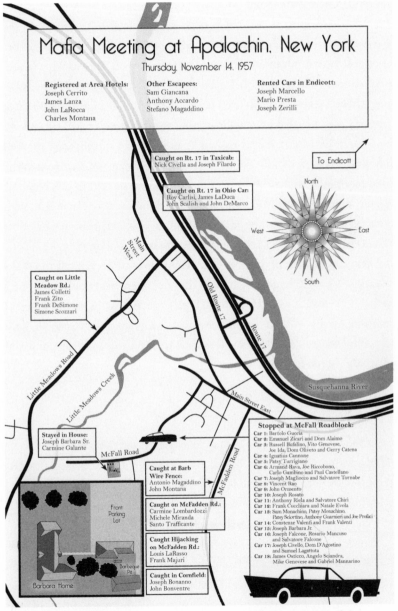

Mafia Meeting at Apalachin, New York
Thursday, November 14, 1957

Registered at Area Hotels:
Joseph Cerrito
James Lanza
John LaRocca
Charles Montana

Other Escapees:
Sam Giancana
Anthony Accardo
Stefano Magaddino

Rented Cars in Endicott:
Joseph Marcello
Mario Presta
Joseph Zerilli

Caught on Rt. 17 in Taxicab:
Nick Civella and Joseph Filardo

To Endicott

Caught on Rt. 17 in Ohio Car:
Roy Carlisi, James LaDuca
John Scalish and John DeMarco

North

West   East

South

Caught on Little Meadow Rd.:
James Colletti
Frank Zito
Frank DeSimone
Simone Scozzari

Main Street West

Old Route 17

Route 17

Little Meadows Road

Little Meadows Creek

Susquehanna River

Main Street East

Stayed in House:
Joseph Barbara Sr.
Carmine Galante

McFall Road

Stopped at McFall Roadblock:
Car 1: Bartolo Guccia
Car 2: Emanuel Zicari and Dom Alaimo
Car 3: Russell Bufalino, Vito Genovese,
       Joe Ida, Dom Oliveto and Gerry Catena
Car 4: Ignatius Cannone
Car 5: Patsy Turrigiano
Car 6: Armand Rava, Joe Riccobono,
       Carlo Gambino and Paul Castellano
Car 7: Joseph Magliocco and Salvatore Tornabe
Car 8: Vincent Rao
Car 9: John Ormento
Car 10: Joseph Rosato
Car 11: Anthony Riela and Salvatore Chiri
Car 12: Frank Cucchiara and Natale Evola
Car 13: Sam Monachino, Patsy Monachino,
        Patsy Sciortino, Anthony Guarnieri and Joe Profaci
Car 14: Constenze Valenti and Frank Valenti
Car 15: Joseph Barbara Jr.
Car 16: Joseph Falcone, Rosario Mancuso
        and Salvatore Falcone
Car 17: Joseph Civello, Dom D'Agostino
        and Samuel Lagattuta
Car 18: James Osticco, Angelo Sciandra,
        Mike Genovese and Gabriel Mannarino

Caught at Barb Wire Fence:
Antonio Magaddino
John Montana

Caught on McFadden Rd.:
Carmine Lombardozzi
Michele Miranda
Santo Trafficante

Caught Hijacking on McFadden Rd.:
Louis LaRasso
Frank Majuri

Caught in Cornfield:
Joseph Bonanno
John Bonventre

McFadden Road

Front Parking Lot

Barbeque Pit

Barbara Home

10–1: Joseph Barbara Sr.'s estate in Apalachin, NY, 1957. The majority of the attendees of the Mafia meeting were caught at the McFall roadblock. Other attendees were caught trying to escape through the surrounding trees and dirt roads. (Map by Ted Pertzborn)

Buffalo's Man of the Year

The first runner they caught was John Montana of Buffalo, New York. Brown and Sackel found Montana hopelessly tangled on a barbed-wire fence, his expensive coat enmeshed in the jagged metal. Worse still, Montana knew he was about to face a very public fall from grace. The Honorable John C. Montana was a former City of Buffalo councilman, successful businessman, and civic benefactor. In 1956, Montana was named Buffalo's "Man of the Year" by the Erie Club, an association of police officers. Behind his sterling image, Montana held a virtual monopoly on taxicabs in Buffalo, and he was second-in-command of the Magaddino Family of Buffalo, known as "the Arm" for its influence throughout western New York. Standing nearby Montana, in fact, was an out-of-breath Antonio Magaddino, his suit pants covered in burrs and mud.[52]

Sitting in the back of the police car, Montana tried desperately to salvage his reputation. He told Sergeant Croswell that he "knew many prominent people" and that if Croswell "would let him go back to get his car, he might be able to do something for me." When that did not work, Montana tried to explain his presence: on his way to Pennsylvania, he had car troubles and coincidentally stopped by Barbara's home for some repairs.[53]

Man of Honor in the Cornfield

One of the New York City bosses ran like a rabbit into a cornfield. After apprehending Montana, Treasury Agent Brown and Trooper Sackel next found Joseph Bonanno and his uncle John Bonventre in the cornfield adjoining Barbara's property. At the substation, Trooper Vasisko questioned Bonanno, who at that time admitted he was at the house "visiting" his friend Joe Barbara.[54]

To save face, Joe Bonanno later concocted a story that he was *not* at Barbara's home and was "wrongly implicated in the whole mess." In his 1983 autobiography *A Man of Honor*, Bonanno claimed that while in Italy, he gave his driver's license to his brother-in-law to renew it, who gave it to *another* friend Gaspar DiGregorio. DiGregorio then just happened to be picked up by the police while on a hunting trip with John Bonventre in the vicinity of Apalachin. Bonanno called it a "messy haphazard juxtaposition of people and events—a human comedy."[55]

He was lying. What Bonanno did not realize was that the New York State Police also identified him through his social security card: "Identified through Social Security as Joseph Bonanno. ... Had cards in his possession—Social Security Card 080-14-[XXXX]." He further "gave permanent address as 1847 East Elm Street, Tucson, Arizona"—Bonanno's new home out west.[56] Moreover, the police found that *no* rifles or shotguns were in the men's possession, a major hole in Bonanno's hunting trip story, given how hard the troopers were looking for guns.[57]

Runners in the Woods along McFadden Road

Another set of runners made it to the woods east of Barbara's property, where they hid among the trees and cockleburs. To make matters worse, it started drizzling at 2:30 p.m.

One has to feel a little bad for Tampa Bay boss Santo Trafficante. Earlier that week, Trafficante was basking in the tropical sun as manager of the Sans Souci Casino in Havana. This was just supposed to be a day trip, some business to take care of before his forty-third birthday on November 15. Albert Anastasia had been eyeing gambling in Cuba, so Trafficante came to lay down his marker. The gambling mogul flew in on the late-morning flight to Binghamton. He had barely arrived at Barbara's house before police were on the scene. In the woods, he met up with Carmine Lombardozzi and Michele Miranda, both *caporegimes* from New York.[58]

At 3:30 p.m., Trafficante, Lombardozzi, and Miranda ventured onto McFadden Road, another road on the eastern side of the trees. A patrol car spotted the trio of wiseguys. Two troopers got out of the car and "ran towards these subjects, who started back into the woods." The police fired four warning shots into the air before the mobsters finally stopped.[59]

Real Estate Investors from Jersey

A pair of hapless mobsters from the DeCavalcante Family of New Jersey could have been performing a comedy routine. During the panic, Francesco "Fat Frank" Majuri and Louis "Fat Lou" LaRasso took off huffing and puffing on foot. At about 2:15 p.m., they waved down Glenn Craig, a local resident driving by on Little Meadows Road. They told Craig they were looking for land; as luck would have it, Craig was looking to sell his land. After going through the ruse of negotiations, Majuri and LaRasso told Craig that they'd "get back within a week or so and they would try to get money from some union bank . . . in New Jersey." They then offered him $10 for a ride to Binghamton. They did not get far. When a state trooper stopped Craig's car on McFadden Road, the corpulent, nattily dressed out-of-towners were obvious suspects.[60]

The New Jerseyians gave perhaps the most laughable explanation for their presence in Apalachin. Majuri flatly denied knowing Barbara. He said that they were just looking "to purchase real estate" to build a summer cottage. According to their story, in the wee hours of November 14, 1957, Majuri and LaRasso spontaneously decided to jump on the 7:00 a.m. Pennsylvania Railroad train to Binghamton. They claimed they could not locate their real estate broker, so they took a taxicab to Apalachin and wandered around until it started drizzling.[61]

Mobsters from out West

As if by instinct, taking off in the opposite direction from the eastbound runners were a half-dozen *mafiosi* from western cities. From the City of Angels came mob boss Frank DeSimone and his underboss Simone Scozzari. DeSimone was actually a licensed attorney of the California bar when he assumed leadership of the Los Angles Family in 1956. During the panic, they went west across McFall Road into a stand of pine trees on the other side. They made it to Little Meadows Road, where they were apprehended by a patrol car. At the Vestal substation, the police searched Scozzari and found $600 in cash and a check for $8,445 to his order ($74,000 in 2013 dollars). Not bad, considering he told the state police he was unemployed.[62]

Far less glamorous were a pair of bosses from small western families, James "Black Jim" Colletti of Pueblo, Colorado, and Frank Zito of Springfield, Illinois. They had remarkably similar lives. Both grew up in Sicily in the 1890s, came to America in the 1910s, and migrated west to work as miners: Colletti in the metals mines of Colorado; Zito in the coal mines of Illinois.[63] Each forged himself into the crime boss of his mid-sized city: Colletti in Pueblo, population 63,000; and Zito in Springfield, population 81,000. They each collected revenues from gambling and vice in their cities. They also had some legitimate businesses: Colletti owned the Colorado Cheese Company; Zito held interests in taverns.[64]

They even flew into Binghamton together that morning, and they were wandering the woods together by that afternoon. The police patrolling Little Meadows Road found an exhausted Zito sitting on the stoop of a house. His friend Colletti was standing nearby.[65]

The Kansas City Taxicab Caper

Kansas City boss Nick Civella and his *caporegime* Joseph Filardo had traveled by train to Binghamton, leaving them without transportation during the raid. This was somewhat ironic given Civella's influence over the International Brotherhood of Teamsters. By 1957, Civella was dipping into the Teamsters' pension fund to finance mob ventures.[66] During the round up, the Missouri men crossed McFall Road into the wilderness. They hiked for over a mile, and eventually found Apalachin Elementary School. There they asked to place a call for a taxicab. The sight of rough men in rumpled coats summoning a cab to an elementary school on a Thursday afternoon caused school staffers to call the police.[67]

The state police sent out an all-points bulletin: stop a blue city cab with two male passengers believed traveling west to the Erie Railroad Station in Owego. Civella and Filardo really had no idea where they were going. Troopers reached the railroad station but found no sign of them; perhaps they missed a train. The troopers back at the Vestal substation could hardly believe their eyes when a blue city cab fitting the bulletin's description drove right past the substation. The police stopped the cab and questioned the taxicab's passengers. Civella claimed he was just a "salesman" and that he did not know any Joe Barbara.[68]

Hunt for the Ohio Cadillac

The Clevelanders, whose late reservations at the Parkway Motel triggered the ensuing events, very nearly escaped. During the raid, John Scalish and John DeMarco hiked through the woods and somehow made it back to the motel, where they had left their blue Cadillac that morning. They decided to get the hell out of Dodge. With their muddy shoes and trousers covered in burrs, Scalish and DeMarco got into their car and headed east on Route 17. Riding in the back seat were James La Duca and Roy Carlisi of Buffalo, who also had rooms at the Parkway Motel.

Meanwhile, Croswell remembered that the Ohio Cadillac was still at the Parkway Motel. He was not going to give the Cleveland mobsters a car to slip through the net. The state police dispatched troopers from the Vestal substation to search for the blue Cadillac with Ohio plates HM-373. It was a close call. The car had already left the Parkway Motel. Squad cars whizzed down Route 17 in a hunt for the Ohio Cadillac. The Clevelanders made it past Endicott and reached the outskirts of Binghamton, where, at 4:40 p.m., they were pulled over by a trooper.[69]

THE ESCAPEES

Some mobsters eluded the dragnet that day. A handful of runners escaped on foot. Others stayed put in Barbara's house and waited out the police.

The Hertz rental office in Endicott had unusual customers the evening of November 14, 1957. At 6:00 p.m., in walked Joseph Zerilli, boss of the Detroit mob, to rent a car for a one-way drive to Brooklyn. Around 8:00 p.m., in walked "Paul Scarcelli" and another man "in his early thirties." Paul Scarcelli was the alias used by Mario Presta, Frank Costello's top wiseguy in New Orleans. Presta's traveling partner was Joseph Marcello, the younger brother of New Orleans boss Carlos Marcello. Presta and Marcello were runners from Barbara's house: the rental agent said they were "well dressed but in wet, bedraggled clothing."[70]

Carmine "Lilo" Galante got the last laugh on the state police. The narcotics trafficker had learned from his speeding incident. Rather than fleeing the scene, he laid low—literally. When the Barbaras' housekeeper returned on Saturday, November 16, the spare bedroom downstairs was closed. "Don't go in," Mrs. Barbara told her. The next morning, the housekeeper saw two men eat breakfast and leave with Emanuel Zicari. She identified one of the guests from a photograph: it was Galante.[71]

After insisting the meeting be held in Apalachin, it would have been insulting for Buffalo boss Stefano Magaddino not to show up with his legion of men. Sure enough, the staties searched Barbara's barn and found a 1957 Lincoln coupe containing personalized luggage with the initials "S.M." and worn garments and papers marked "Steve Magaddino."[72]

Meanwhile, the Pennsylvania police discovered that San Francisco underboss James Lanza and San Jose boss Joseph Cerrito stayed at the Hotel Casey in Scranton, Pennsylvania, on November 13 as guests of Russell Bufalino. Meanwhile, Pittsburgh boss John LaRocca registered at the Arlington Hotel on November 13 with his underboss Michael Genovese.[73]

The big men from Chicago, the second city of the mob, seem to have been present, too. Confidential FBI memoranda report that Sam Giancana and Tony Accardo "were in attendance at the Apalachin meeting [and] both escaped the police raid."[74] FBI agent William Roemer, who ran a wiretap on the Chicago Outfit, confirms their attendance as well. Giancana's daughter has also revealed that her father said he escaped at Apalachin by running into the woods. Given Chicago's seat on the Commission, it would have been surprising had they not attended.[75]

On Friday afternoon, November 15, 1957, the police spotted twenty-four-year-old Lucchese Family soldier Neil Migliore's 1957 Lincoln at Barbara's house, and his car was later involved in an automobile accident in Binghamton at 8:00 p.m. that same evening. The State Commission had a confidential informant who reported that Migliore only "came to Binghamton to drive other participants of the Apalachin meeting of New York City" and it was "not believed that he attended the meeting."[76]

So, who was Migliore picking up? The State Commission had another informant who placed New York boss Thomas Lucchese in the area,[77] and the state police found a business card of his *caporegime* Carmine Tramunti near Barbara's estate.[78] Both would have been welcome at the meeting. But there is no wiretap, eyewitness testimony, hotel reservation, or other physical evidence to prove Lucchese's or Tramunti's attendance, so they remain suspected attendees.

In sum, there is proof for seventy-two men in attendance at the Apalachin meeting, as shown in table 10–1. There has been speculation about others,[79] but no solid evidence.[80] Though some *mafiosi* may have avoided all detection whatsoever, there were likely fewer than a dozen. None of the eyewitnesses at the commission hearings or at the subsequent federal trial testified to seeing "100+ mobsters in attendance," as suggested by writers.[81] Rather, the best eyewitness testimony was by Marguerite Russell, the Barbara's former housekeeper, who was one of the few nonmobsters in the house. She testified that "between 60 and 70" men were in attendance, with "possibly more."[82] For his part, Croswell said, "I don't think more than three or four could possibly have gotten away."[83] The State Commission and the FBI conducted aggressive nationwide investigations of other possible escapees, using confidential informants, field agents, and wiretaps. It is unlikely that dozens more mobsters avoided detection altogether.

THURSDAY NIGHT, NOVEMBER 14, 1957, THE INTERROGATIONS

As night fell, the last automobiles trickled down McFall Road. Around 8:15 p.m., the Pennsylvania mobsters still in the house gave up their wait. Pittsburgh underboss Mike Genovese, his *caporegime* Gabriel Mannarino, and Pittston *mafiosi* James Osticco and Angelo Sciandra drove fatefully to the roadblock.[84]

Back at the Vestal substation, the state police were overrun with mobsters. "The place was a madhouse. The uniformed men were running back and telling me such and such a car," recounted Croswell. "The place was just in turmoil." In the BCI office, the Teletype machine was clicking away with transmittals of prison records revealing the sordid backgrounds of the detained men. The *mafiosi* had the run of the rest of the substation, from the recreation room to the two bedrooms to the other offices.[85]

Over the next several hours, the police searched and questioned all the men. They found no guns, but lots of money: several men were carrying $2,000 to $3,000 in rolls of bills (about $16,000 to $24,000 in current dollars). The Mafia clearly ran a cash business. Trooper Vasisko took the lead in interrogating the attendees. The questioning got nowhere though. Most kept repeating the refrain: they "came up to visit a sick friend, Joseph Barbara."[86]

Sergeant Croswell called his superiors in the state police to discuss whether they could hold the men on any criminal charges. Gun violations? They found no firearms. Disorderly conduct? The men were calm. Conspiracy? Potentially, but they had no evidence of what was being planned. Besides, with their cash, the men would easily make bail. So they were released.[87]

FRIDAY, NOVEMBER 15, 1957

After finishing the interrogations at 1:00 a.m., Croswell stayed up the rest of the night fielding calls pouring in from reporters. The news went national overnight. "POLICE NAB 67 MAFIA CHIEFS IN BACKWOODS," blared the front page of the *Chicago Tribune.* "Cops Seize 67 Big-Shot Racketeers," echoed the *San Francisco Chronicle.* The *New York Times* headline read, "65 Hoodlums Seized in a Raid and Run out of Upstate Village." The *Daily News* meanwhile declared, "SIEZE 62 MAFIA CHIEFTANS IN UPSTATE RAID."[88]

Within days, officials were announcing investigations of Apalachin. In Albany, Governor Averell Harriman ordered State Investigations Commissioner Arthur Reuter to "look into the activities and associations" of the attendees. Meanwhile, a state legislative watchdog committee began serving subpoenas to probe the "criminal intent" of the gathering. Grand juries were underway, too. Down in Washington, DC, the McClellan Committee investigating labor racketeering had recently heard testimony from the Federal Bureau of Narcotics (FBN) about the Mafia. "I've seen the list of these fellows—and some of them, we are interested in," said Robert F. Kennedy, chief counsel to the McClellan Committee.[89]

FBI Director Hoover made no public statements.

APALACHIN MYTHS AND MISPERCEPTIONS

Like everything about the Mafia, myths and misperceptions have cropped up around the Apalachin meeting. The popular image of Apalachin is that it was deep in the hinterlands, a ridiculous place to hold a meeting of the mob. In its December 1957 issue, *Life* magazine mocked the venue, writing, "You wouldn't think that would be noticed in a town the size of Apalachin (pop. 277), especially since one of the Caddies was an old 1956."[90] The 1999 film *Analyze This*

(Warner Brothers) starring Robert De Niro, plays up the setting to comic effect: wiseguys are portrayed threatening cows and hijacking a farmer's tractor to escape.

Apalachin was, in fact, in the heart of a manufacturing region full of *mafiosi*. Joe Barbara's home was only eight miles from his bottling plant in Endicott, a factory town of fifteen thousand, and it was only fifteen miles outside Binghamton, a booming industrial city of eighty-five thousand. The Cosa Nostra had a strong presence in the area. "The Mafia was considered a local fraternal organization. There were perhaps fifty families in Endicott thought to be 'connected,'" remembered Ron Luciano, who grew up in Endicott. "When Sicilian immigrants flooded into America, the town of Endicott attracted many Castellammarese," adds Joe Bonanno.[91]

Another set of conflicting myths paints the state troopers *either* as innocent rubes who fell upon a meeting of the mob *or* as devious cops bent on extracting bribes from it. "The Hick Cops Bust up Joe's Nice Barbecue," chuckled *Life*.[92] Taking a different tact, Joe Bonanno tried to smear the state troopers as corrupt. Bonanno claimed they were "getting greedy and were making exorbitant demands on Barbara in exchange for their cooperation."[93] None of these myths is true.

As should be evident, Sergeant Croswell was no country bumpkin. Rather, Croswell was an intrepid, savvy, and resourceful investigator; he was a detective's detective. Conversely, Joe Bonanno's corruption smear is just that—a smear. This book has documented many cops in league with the mob. But this label does not apply to Sergeant Croswell and Troop C of the New York State Police. Reporters who covered Croswell invariably describe him as "incorruptible," a "dedicated police officer," and "honest, alert and conscientious."[94] Further, Bonanno fails to explain how his *caporegime* Carmine Galante could have spent ninety days in jail there in 1956 if Troop C could be bought. Croswell and Vasisko had *rejected* a bribe attempt.

Although Croswell was an honest cop, some of his freelance tactics were controversial even at the time. An appellate judge dubbed him "a modern Inspector Javert" after reviewing his thirteen-year personal campaign against Barbara.[95] The state police's detention of the men was of questionable legality in 1957, and it would almost certainly be ruled unconstitutional today. Under the Fourth Amendment, the state police had no reasonable suspicion or probable cause of criminal activity to detain, search, and question the men for hours at the Vestal substation. All that the state police knew was that individuals with criminal records had parked their cars at a private residence.[96] "Actually, we had no legal basis for doing what we did do," Croswell later candidly admitted. "If we stuck directly to the letter of the law, we couldn't have found out what we did," he acknowledged.[97]

Lastly, a major conspiracy theory was ignited by Jewish gangster Joseph "Doc" Stacher when he told the authors of a 1979 biography of Meyer Lansky that Apalachin was a set-up of Vito Genovese. "Meyer and I were invited but he sent word that as it was November he did not want to make the journey north from Miami," asserted Stacher. He suggests that Lansky tipped off the police to the meeting. "Nobody to this day knows that it was Meyer who arranged for Genovese's humiliation," claimed Stacher.[98]

This story has all the makings of a tall tale. It rests entirely on Stacher, who was known as a "boastful" man prone to self-aggrandizement. Lansky never corroborated the story, and it has not come up in any wiretap. The story is implausible on its face, too. Apalachin was strictly a meeting of the Cosa Nostra with no Jewish or Irish gangsters, which was not unusual for high-level Mafia meetings. Moreover, it would have been wildly out of character for Lansky to alienate the entire Commission to satisfy a grudge. "When it came to the mechanics of group relations, Meyer also had the ability, rare at any age, to mediate and settle difference through intelligence and reason," described a better biography of Lansky.[99]

THE AGENDA

Speculation has raged about the purposes of Apalachin. Statements by informants have leaked out that, when combined with other facts, reveal the agenda of the meeting.

At the top of the agenda was resolving the leadership successions following the assassinations of 1957. The Apalachin attendees were high-ranking *mafiosi* who had survived the assassinations of the early 1930s. They had little desire for another bloody conflict. Joe Valachi said the meeting was "to talk about . . . justifying the shooting Albert Anastasia." Other informants have confirmed that dealing with the 1957 killings was the crucial issue.[100]

Casino gambling in Cuba was a pressing matter, too. Anastasia had been seeking to encroach on Santo Trafficante's casino interests in Havana. FBI informants reported that Apalachin included "consideration of an agreement about the Havana gambling situation and other gambling in Florida." Trafficante went to stave off future encroachments. It was all for naught. In thirteen months, the Cuban revolution would reach Havana.[101]

For other attendees, Apalachin was another opportunity to discuss more traditional issues of territory and cooperation. Former Teamsters president Roy Williams testified of a conversation he had with Nick Civella after the mobster was caught at Apalachin. "Civella told me that, among other things, territory and cooperation was discussed," Williams recounted. "Civella said he had Kansas City as his territory. He had working relations with other areas. He had friends in Chicago, he had friends in Cleveland, and he had friends in New Orleans."[102]

Others claim narcotics was on the agenda. After fibbing about his presence, Joe Bonanno tried to spin its purpose: "Another item on the Apalachin agenda was supposed to be the narcotics issue," said Bonanno. "If the 1957 meeting had gone according to plan there no doubt would have been a reaffirmation of our Tradition's opposition to narcotics."[103] Journalist Selwyn Raab asserts an "emergency item on the agenda was setting policy on coping with the stricter new federal law—the Boggs-Daniel Act—and dealing with the Sicilian heroin importers."[104] The author Gil Reavill goes further, writing that New York bosses (without Commission member Tommy Lucchese even present) *did* reach an agreement that morning in Apalachin. Supposedly, they agreed that "the American Mafia gets out of the wholesale heroin smuggling business" by spinning off importing and smuggling to "the Corsicans," while "retail street distribution, that's another matter."[105]

The notion that the Apalachin summit's focus was to be on drugs is dubious. The Mafia had been heavily involved in narcotics trafficking since the 1930s. Three attendees—John Ormento, Frank Cucchiara, and Joseph Civello—were already convicted narcotics offenders. Moreover, the Boggs-Daniel Act was enacted to fanfare in July 1956, three months *before* the October 1956 meeting of the Commission.[106] It is difficult to understand why *mafiosi* would travel from all over the country, again, for an "emergency item" that had been in the news prior to the 1956 meeting. Meanwhile, Reavill's questionable account fails to appreciate long-term historical trends: as we saw earlier, the American Mafia had relied on Corsican drug smugglers since the 1930s, and it had been moving away from risky "retail street distribution" and toward wholesaling for decades.[107]

OMERTÀ HOLDS

In 1958, the State Commission of Investigation in New York and the McClellan Committee in Washington, DC, subpoenaed attendees to testify about the meeting. After pleading the Fifth Amendment, and much legal wrangling, some did testify.

It was a farce. New York boss Joseph Profaci claimed he just stopped by Barbara's while selling olive oil for his Fratelli Berio Distributing Company. Profaci told Barbara to "have faith in God." Meanwhile, Joseph Magliocco testified that he was just chauffeuring Profaci and did not know they were going to Barbara's: "The first time I heard it, it was this time we take the road to get up into the hill by Barbara," insisted Magliocco.[108] In his testimony before the McClellan Committee in Washington, John Montana stuck to his story that he had just coincidentally stopped by Barbara's house for car repairs. "Mr. Montana, you did not realize until the following day that you had five other friends that were present at that meeting?" Robert Kennedy asked incredulously. "I did not," Montana insisted.[109] Meanwhile, Lucchese *consigliere* Vincent Rao said he went for free food. "There's nothing to discuss," Rao shrugged. "I went and had a steak and it was an expensive steak."[110]

In 1959, the Justice Department prosecuted the Apalachin attendees on an attenuated charge of conspiracy. Conceding that they lacked any evidence about the criminal aims of the meeting, federal prosecutors grasped for a theory: they alleged that during the forty minutes after Mrs. Barbara saw the state police (12:40 p.m. to 1:20 p.m.), the attendees entered into a conspiracy to commit perjury and obstruct justice, should they later be called to testify publicly. The jury convicted twenty of the attendees on this theory, but the Court of Appeals reversed all of their convictions.[111]

The *mafiosi* caught at Apalachin ultimately escaped the law by maintaining *omertà*. Although the wall of silence had been breached in the past, none of the Apalachin attendees turned state's evidence. Had even a single defendant turned state's evidence and testified about the meeting's criminal purposes, the convictions almost certainly would have been upheld. The leadership of the American Mafia would have been imprisoned in one fell swoop. But the attendees knew the state police had nothing on any of them, so none of them flipped. *Omertà*, the conspiracy of silence, ironically, had beaten a conspiracy case.

FALLOUT WITHIN THE MAFIA

Notwithstanding its legal victory, the Cosa Nostra suffered lasting consequences from Apalachin. On a personal level, Joe Barbara never recovered from the scrutiny. On June 15, 1959, he died of another heart attack at the age of fifty-three. His daughter attacked reporters covering his funeral: "You call us murderers, but you're the biggest murderers of us all," she screamed.[112]

Apalachin publicly exposed and embarrassed the leadership of the Mafia. A wiretap picked up a conversation on Apalachin between Steve Magaddino and Sam Giancana:

> Giancana: I hope you're satisfied. Sixty-three of our top guys made by the
>   cops.
> Magaddino: I gotta admit you were right, Sam. It never would've happened
>   in your place.
> Giancana: You're [f-----] right it wouldn't. This is the safest territory in
>   the world for a big meet. . . . We got three towns just outside of
>   Chicago with the police chiefs in our pocket. We got this ter-
>   ritory locked up tight.[113]

Joe Bonanno saw it as an unmitigated disaster. "It was horrendous: all those men caught in the same place, a ton of publicity, a public-relations coup for law enforcement, a field day for journalists," lamented Bonanno.[114] Apalachin further undermined the authority of the bosses. "The soldiers felt that if the soldiers made that kind of a meet and everyone got arrested they all would die if they made a mistake like the bosses," complained Valachi.[115]

For the mob, 1957 marked a divide: Before Apalachin and After Apalachin. As Lucchese Family associate Henry Hill explained, the year 1956 was "a glorious time" because it was "just before Apalachin, before the wiseguys began having all the trouble."[116] Their troubles started when a stubborn man changed his mind.

THE SEAT OF GOVERNMENT, WASHINGTON, DC, NOVEMBER 1957

Though some like to imagine that FBI Director Hoover had a miserable day that Friday, November 15, 1957, this is more *schaudenfreude* than fact. Neither the *Washington Star* nor the *Washington Post* carried the news from Apalachin, and Attorney General Rogers was tied up in a cabinet meeting. The director kept his appointment with a bureau photographer, took his regular call from Clyde Tolson, and spoke with an Illinois congressman, the governor of Arizona, and a federal judge.[117] But this was the calm before the storm.

By Monday, November 18, 1957, it was apparent that Apalachin would be a reckoning. Over the weekend, the United States Attorney for New York distanced himself from Hoover by going on record stating that the Apalachin meeting was "further proof of the existence of a criminal syndicate organized across state lines."[118] That Monday morning, the first call into Hoover was from Attorney General Rogers. Meanwhile, the McClellan Committee was banging doors for intelligence on the attendees. "The FBI didn't know anything, really, about these people who were the major gangsters in the United States," recounted Robert Kennedy. "I sent the same request to the Bureau of Narcotics, and they had something on every one of them."[119]

DIRECTOR HOOVER BECOMES A BELIEVER

It took the colossal embarrassment of Apalachin to shake up Hoover. "Apalachin hit the FBI like a bomb," recalled William Sullivan. Hoover went into a tirade, first blaming assistant FBI director Al Belmont, then the field agents in upstate New York. On November 27, 1957, twelve days after Apalachin, Hoover ordered all field offices to gather intelligence on the ten biggest "hoodlums" in their region under the Top Hoodlum Program.[120]

Hoover further assigned William Sullivan, head of the FBI's Research and Analysis Section, to write a comprehensive report on organized crime. Sullivan appointed one of his best men, Charles Peck, to lead the project. Since the FBI had so little intelligence on the Mafia, Peck's team relied on news articles, the Kefauver Committee hearings, and other enforcement agencies.[121]

Completed in July 1958, Peck's 280-page report contradicted Hoover's longstanding position. "There have been again insistent allegations of the existence of the Mafia in the United States. There have been also denials," the report opened diplomatically. After setting forth all the evidence, the report stated forcefully: "The truth of the matter is, the available evidence makes it impossible to deny logically the existence of a criminal organization, known as the Mafia, which for generations has plagued the law-abiding citizens of Sicily, Italy, and the United States."[122]

With trepidation, Sullivan submitted the report to the director. Hoover responded quickly with a handwritten note: "The point has been missed. It is not now necessary to read the two volume monograph to know that the Mafia does exist in the United States." Sullivan felt relieved. "The battle had been won. Hoover finally gave in," said Sullivan.[123] Behind the scenes, the FBI's field agents went into action. "A furious Hoover declared war on the mob," remembered William Roemer, a field agent who installed a wiretap dubbed "Little Al" in the headquarters of the Chicago Outfit.[124]

Robert Kennedy's appointment as United States attorney general ratcheted up the pressure on the FBI. "Through well placed informants we must infiltrate organized crime groups to the same degree that we have been able to penetrate the Communist Party and other subversive organizations," Hoover instructed the FBI's field offices on March 1, 1961. FBI field agents developed high-level moles within the Mafia through the FBI's new Top Echelon Criminal Informant Program. Field agents planted dozens more electronic surveillance (ELSUR) bugs into the bars, social clubs, and backroom offices of *mafiosi*. Then, in 1963, the FBI flipped Genovese Family soldier Joe Valachi and persuaded him to testify publicly about the Mafia. Suddenly, the Cosa Nostra's innermost secrets were being revealed on national television.[125]

The lives of the wiseguys would never be the same again.

Table 10–1:
Attendees of the November 14, 1957, Mafia Meeting in Apalachin, New York[126]

No.	Region/Family	Name	Position	Sources on Attendance
		New York City (18 attendees)		
1.	NYC/Bonanno Family	Joseph Bonanno	Boss	Caught in cornfield
2.	NYC/Bonanno Family	John Bonventre	Underboss	Caught in cornfield
3.	NYC/Bonanno Family	Natale Evola	*Capo.*	Stopped at McFall roadblock
4.	NYC/Bonanno Family	Carmine Galante	*Capo.*	Identified by housekeeper
5.	NYC/Gambino Family	Carlo Gambino	Boss	Stopped at McFall roadblock
6.	NYC/Gambino Family	Paul Castellano	*Capo.*	Stopped at McFall roadblock
7.	NYC/Gambino Family	Carmine Lombardozzi	*Capo.*	Caught on McFadden Rd.
8.	NYC/Gambino Family	Armand Rava	*Capo.*	Stopped at McFall roadblock
9.	NYC/Gambino Family	Joseph Riccobono	*Consigliere*	Stopped at McFall roadblock
10.	NYC/Genovese Family	Vito Genovese	Boss	Stopped at McFall roadblock
11.	NYC/Genovese Family	Gerardo Catena	Underboss	Stopped at McFall roadblock

12.	NYC/Genovese Family	Michele Miranda	*Consigliere*	Caught on McFadden Rd.
13.	NYC/Lucchese Family	Vincent Rao	*Consigliere*	Stopped at McFall roadblock
14.	NYC/Lucchese Family	John Ormento	*Capo.*	Stopped at McFall roadblock
15.	NYC/Lucchese Family	Joseph Rosato	*Capo.*	Stopped at McFall roadblock
16.	NYC/Profaci Family	Joseph Profaci	Boss	Stopped at McFall roadblock
17.	NYC/Profaci Family	Joseph Magliocco	Underboss	Stopped at McFall roadblock
18.	NYC/Profaci Family	Salvatore Tornabe	*Capo.*	Stopped at McFall roadblock
Upstate New York (23 attendees)				
19.	Auburn, NY	Patsy Monachino	Soldier	Stopped at McFall roadblock
20.	Auburn, NY	Sam Monachino	Soldier	Stopped at McFall roadblock
21.	Auburn, NY	Patsy Sciortino	Soldier	Stopped at McFall roadblock
22.	Endicott, NY	Joseph Barbara Sr.	Boss[127]	Stayed in home
23.	Endicott, NY	Joseph Barbara Jr.	Not known	Stopped at McFall roadblock
24.	Endicott, NY	Ignatius Cannone	Soldier	Stopped at McFall roadblock
25.	Endicott, NY	Anthony Guarnieri	*Capo.*	Stopped at McFall roadblock
26.	Endicott, NY	Bartolo Guccia	Soldier	Stopped at McFall roadblock
27.	Endicott, NY	Patsy Turrigiano	Soldier	Stopped at McFall roadblock
28.	Endicott, NY	Emanuel Zicari	Soldier	Stopped at McFall roadblock

29.	Buffalo, NY	Stefano Magaddino	Boss	Luggage/papers at Barbara's
30.	Buffalo, NY	Roy Carlisi	*Capo.*	Caught on Rt. 17 in Ohio car
31.	Buffalo, NY	Dom D'Agostino	*Capo.*	Stopped at McFall roadblock
32.	Buffalo, NY	James La Duca	*Capo.*	Caught on Rt. 17 in Ohio car
33.	Buffalo, NY	Samuel Lagattuta	*Capo.*	Stopped at McFall roadblock
34.	Buffalo, NY	Anthony Magaddino	*Capo.*	Caught on McFadden Rd.
35.	Buffalo, NY	John C. Montana	Underboss	Caught on McFadden Rd.
36.	Buffalo, NY	Charles Montana	Not known	Registered Parkway Motel
37.	Rochester, NY	Constenze Valenti	Not known	Stopped at McFall roadblock
38.	Rochester, NY	Frank Valenti	Not known	Stopped at McFall roadblock
39.	Utica, NY	Salvatore Falcone	Not known	Stopped at McFall roadblock
40.	Utica, NY	Joseph Falcone	Not known	Stopped at McFall roadblock.
41.	Utica, NY	Rosario Mancuso	Soldier	Stopped at McFall roadblock
Northeastern States—Other (14 attendees)				
42.	Boston, MA	Frank Cucchiara	*Consigliere*	Stopped at McFall roadblock
43.	Northern New Jersey	Salvatore Chiri	*Capo.*	Stopped at McFall roadblock
44.	Northern New Jersey	Anthony Riela	*Capo.*	Stopped at McFall roadblock
45.	Northern New Jersey	Frank Majuri	Underboss	Caught on McFadden Rd.

46.	Northern New Jersey	Louis LaRasso	*Capo.*	Caught on McFadden Rd.
47.	Philadelphia, PA	Joseph Ida	Boss	Stopped at McFall roadblock
48.	Philadelphia, PA	Dominick Oliveto	Underboss	Stopped at McFall roadblock
49.	Northeast PA	Dominick Alaimo	*Capo.*	Stopped at McFall roadblock
50.	Northeast PA	Russell Bufalino	Boss	Stopped at McFall roadblock
51.	Northeast PA	Gabriel Mannarino	*Capo.*	Stopped at McFall roadblock
52.	Northeast PA	James Osticco	Underboss	Stopped at McFall roadblock
53.	Northeast PA	Angelo Sciandra	*Capo.*	Stopped at McFall roadblock
54.	Pittsburgh, PA	John LaRocca	Boss	Registered Arlington Hotel
55.	Pittsburgh, PA	Michael Genovese	Underboss	Stopped at McFall roadblock
Midwestern States (8 attendees)				
56.	Springfield, IL	Frank Zito	Boss	Caught on Little Meadow Rd.
57.	Chicago, IL	Sam Giancana	Boss	FBI wiretaps; told daughter.\
58.	Chicago, IL	Anthony Accardo	*Consigliere*	FBI wiretaps
59.	Detroit, MI	Joseph Zerilli	Boss	Rented car in Endicott
60.	Cleveland, OH	John Scalish	Boss	Caught on Rt. 17 in Ohio car
61.	Cleveland, OH	John DeMarco	*Consigliere*	Caught on Rt. 17 in Ohio car
62.	Kansas City, MO	Nick Civella	Boss	Caught on Rt. 17 in taxicab

63.	Kansas City, MO	Joseph Filardo	*Consigliere*	Caught on Rt. 17 in taxicab
Western States (5 attendees)				
64.	Los Angeles, CA	Frank DeSimone	Boss	Caught on Little Meadow Rd.
65.	Los Angeles, CA	Simone Scozzari	Underboss	Caught on Little Meadow Rd.
66.	San Jose, CA	Joseph Cerrito	Boss	Registered at Scranton hotel
67.	San Francisco, CA	James Lanza	Underboss	Registered at Scranton hotel
68.	Pueblo, CO	James Colletti	Boss	Caught on Little Meadow Rd.
Southern States (4 attendees)				
69.	Dallas, TX	Joseph Civello	Boss	Stopped at McFall roadblock
70.	New Orleans, LA	Joseph Marcello	Underboss	Rented car in Endicott
71.	New Orleans, LA	Mario Presta	Not known	Rented car in Endicott
72.	Tampa, FL, and Cuba	Santo Trafficante	Boss	Caught on McFadden Rd.

CONCLUSION
NEW YORK'S MAFIA

Nostalgia is . . . a rust of memory.
—Robert Nisbet (1982)

When they were struggling to survive in the 1910s, Joe Masseria, Charles Luciano, and Giuseppe Morello could scarcely have imagined that their lives would someday become a canvas for American popular culture. The Mafia has been the backdrop used to explore themes of family and immigration (*The Godfather*), America's coming of age (*Boardwalk Empire*), and suburban angst and mortality (*The Sopranos*). It is used to sell rap music (*Yo Gotti*), "reality television" (*Mob Wives*), video games (*Mafia II*), and even a mobster "lifestyle" magazine (*Mob Candy*).

This rests on a thick layer of nostalgia. Perhaps the greatest myth about the Mafia is that its members were a special band of brothers, that they were "Men of Honor" who forged a loyal fraternity of goodfellows. Mobsters like Joe and his son Bill Bonanno have peddled such stories for decades. When people learn you are writing a book on the Mafia, you often hear some variation of the following: "I happen to think that the Mafia did some good," or "at least they had a code," or "they were honorable when they first started out."

This book is skeptical that there was ever a golden era of gangsters. The Mafia that emerges from the primary sources is an opportunistic crime syndicate that rose up within the historical context of New York City. The wiseguys broke every one of their "rules," trafficked drugs almost from the beginning, became government informers, betrayed each other, lied, and cheated. In other words, they were not much different than the younger *mafiosi* who followed.

To be sure, the Mafia families were extraordinary crime syndicates. The Cosa

Nostra was unquestionably the strongest criminal organization in New York. The Mafia families were in control of major union locals in Gotham and were linked to national unions like the Teamsters; they were the dominant narcotics wholesalers throughout the eastern half of the United States; they effectively managed professional boxing, reaped the Harlem numbers lottery, neutralized the local police, and were feared and respected by other criminals.

But the truth is that the Mafia was very much propelled by the forces of New York history. Simply put, the Italian-American gangsters had terrific luck. They were on the verge of extinction in the 1910s, only to see their fortunes reversed by the passage of Prohibition. They were then poised demographically to take over New York's unions just as the labor movement was surging in the 1930s. Gotham was an embarrassment of riches for sophisticated racketeers. They could extract payoffs from the huge waterfront, skim profits from bustling industries, cater to the Manhattan nightlife, and feed the appetites of thousands of heroin addicts.

It is time to put the Mafia back into the history of New York City. The *mafiosi* did not emerge out of thin air and take over by sheer force of will. This was very much New York's Mafia.

NOTES

INTRODUCTION: *THE GODFATHER* vs. NEW YORK HISTORY

1. For the history of the Morellos, see Mike Dash, *The First Family: Terror, Extortion, Revenge, Murder, and the Birth of the American Mafia* (New York: Random House, 2009), pp. ix–x, 222–24, 305–306.

2. *Hearings before the Permanent Subcommittee on Investigations of the Committee on Gov. Operations: Organized Crime and the Illicit Traffic in Narcotics*, Senate, 88th Cong., 1st Sess., 270–73 (1963) (testimony of Joseph Valachi).

3. *New York Times*, March 20, 1971, July 22, 1975; *Time*, September 29, 1986; Joseph Bonanno with Sergio Lalli, *A Man of Honor: The Autobiography of Joseph Bonanno* (New York: Simon & Schuster, 1983).

4. New York University Law Professor James B. Jacobs first showed me that serious research could be done on the Mafia. In the summer of 1997, I worked as his research assistant while he worked on his book *Gotham Unbound: How New York City Was Liberated from the Grip of Organized Crime* (New York: New York University Press, 1999), which focused on initiatives in the 1980s and '90s by the Justice Department and the Giuliani administration to purge the Mafia from six industries. We also coauthored an article on an anti-Mafia agency called the Trade Waste Commission. James B. Jacobs and Alex Hortis, "New York City as Organized Crime Fighter," *New York Law School Law Review*, 42, nos. 3–4 (1998): 1069–92, reprinted in *Organized Crime: Critical Concepts in Criminology*, vol. 4, ed. Frederico Varese (London: Routledge, 2010), pp. 179–200.

5. I am inspired by such authors as Mike Dash and Jerry Capeci, who combine exhaustive research with compelling narrative history. Mike Dash, *First Family*, pp. x–xi; Jerry Capeci and Tom Robbins, *Mob Boss: The Life of Little Al D'Arco, the Man Who Brought Down the Mafia* (New York: Thomas Dunne Books, 2013).

CHAPTER 1: A CITY BUILT FOR THE MOB

1. For example, Anthony M. DeStefano, *King of the Godfathers: Joseph Massino and the Fall of the Bonanno Crime Family* (New York: Pinnacle, 2007). Even Selwyn Raab's fine journalistic account *Five Families: The Rise, Decline, and Resurgence of America's Most Powerful Mafia Empires* (New York: St. Martin's Griffin, 2005) focuses on Mafia leaders from the 1960s onward.

2. Thomas E. Rush, *The Port of New York* (New York: Doubleday, 1920), pp. 11–12; New York State Crime Commission, *Study of the Port of New York* (Albany, NY: n.p., 1953), p. 17; James T. Fisher, *On the Irish Waterfront: The Crusader, the Movie, and the Soul of the Port of New York* (Ithaca, NY: Cornell University Press, 2009), p. 1.

3. Rush, *Port of New York*, p. 124; Edwin G. Burrows and Mike Wallace, *Gotham: A History of New York City to 1898* (New York: Oxford University Press, 2000), pp. 665–66, 741–44, 1116–25.

4. Port of New York Authority, *Outlook for Waterborne Commerce through the Port of New York* (New York: n.p., 1948), pp. 53–55, 74.

5. *Report of the Engineer-in-Chief, on the Improvement of Water Front* (New York: n.p., April 26, 1871), p. 3; Michael Woodiwiss, *Organized Crime and American Power: A History* (Toronto: University of Toronto Press, 2001), p. 159.

6. *Report of the Joint Legislative Committee to Investigate the Affairs of the City of New York on the Dept. of Docks* (Albany, NY: n.p., January 31, 1922), p. 11.

7. New York Department of Docks, *Report of the Dept. of Docks, 1872 & 1873* (New York: n.p., 1874), pp. 15–16.

8. *Report of the Executive Committee to the New York City Council of Political Reform on the Operations of the Dept. of Docks* (New York: n.p., 1875), pp. 11–12.

9. *Report and Proceedings of the Senate Committee Appointed to Investigate the Police Dept. of the City of New York* (Albany, NY: n.p., 1895), p. 42.

10. Letter to F. H. La Guardia from Commissioner of Docks, April 27, 1934, in Box 121, in Subject Files, Papers of Mayor Fiorello La Guardia (hereafter "La Guardia Papers") in New York City Municipal Archives, New York, NY (hereafter "NYMA"); Letter from John McKenzie to the Board of Commissioners, May 24, 1934, in Box 121 of La Guardia Papers (NYMA). Unless indicated otherwise, dollar figures have been adjusted to current value using the inflation calculator at: http://www.bls.gov/data/inflation_calculator.htm (accessed May 19, 2013).

11. *Waterfront Investigation: Hearings before a Subcommittee of the Committee on Interstate and Foreign Commerce*, Senate, 83d Cong., 1st Sess., 72–73, 462 (1953); Daniel Bell, *The End of Ideology* (New York: Collier Books, 1961), pp. 175–209.

12. Letter from Am. Hawaiian Steamship Co. to Pacific Consolidators, March 2, 1934, in Box 121 in La Guardia Papers (NYMA).

13. *Waterfront Investigation: New York, Interim Report of the Committee on Interstate and Foreign Commerce*, Senate, 83d Cong., 1st Sess., 6–9 (1953).

14. Oral history with Sam Madell, quoted in Jeff Kisseloff, ed., *You Must Remember This: An Oral History of Manhattan from the 1890s to World War II* (New York: Schocken Books, 1989), p. 522; *Special Report of the Waterfront Commission of New York Harbor* (New York: 1970), pp. 4–5, 8.

15. *Public Hearings (No. 5) Conducted by the New York State Crime Commission Pursuant to the Governor's Executive Orders* (New York: n.p., 1953) (testimony of Joseph Ryan), pp. 3607–10; Charles P. Larrowe, *Shape-up and Hiring Hall; a Comparison of Hiring Methods and Labor Relations on the New York and Seattle Water Fronts* (London: Cambridge University Press, 1955), p. 43; Mayor's Committee on Unemployment, *Report on Dock Employment in New York City and Recommendations for its Regularization* (New York: n.p., 1916), p. 27.

16. *Waterfront Investigation*, 489–90 (1953); *Public Hearings (No. 5)*, pp. 3611–45, 3704 (1953).

17. Mayor's Committee on Unemployment, *Report on Dock Employment in New York City and Recommendations for its Regularization* (New York: n.p., 1916), p. 10; Elizabeth Ogg, *Longshoremen and Their Homes* (New York: Greenwich House, 1939), pp. 28–29; Charles B. Barnes, *The Longshoremen* (New York: Russell Sage Foundation, 1915), pp. 4–8.

18. Oral history with Frank Barbaro, quoted in Myrna Frommer and Harvey Frommer, *It Happened in Brooklyn: An Oral History of Growing Up in the Borough in the 1940s, '50s, and '60s* (New York: Harcourt Brace, 1993), pp. 228–29; Deirdre Marie Capone, *Uncle Al Capone: The Untold Story from Inside His Family* (New York: Recap, 2011), p. 28.

19. My thanks to Rick Warner for citations clarifying Paul Kelly's gang affiliations. *New York Herald*, March 29, 1908; Herbert Asbury, *The Gangs of New York: An Informal History of the Underworld* (New York: Alfred A. Knopf, 1927), p. 273; *New York Sun*, September 15, 1910; *New York Times*, May 13 and October 22, 1919, March 14, 1920, and April 5, 1936; Richard J. Butler, *Dock Walloper: The Story of "Big Dick" Butler* (New York: G. P. Putnam's Sons, 1933), pp. 200, 221; Joseph Ryan, "Highlights of My Labor Career" (unpublished manuscript), quoted in Maud Russell, *Men Along the Shore* (New York: Brussel and Brussel, 1966), pp. 112–19; David Critchley, *The Origin of Organized Crime in America: The New York City Mafia, 1891–1931* (London: Routledge, 2008), pp. 19–20.

20. *Public Hearings (No. 5)*, pp. 3608–62 (1953) (testimony of Joseph Ryan); *Waterfront Investigation: New York–New Jersey: Report of Committee on Interstate and Foreign Commerce*, Senate, 83d Cong., 1st Sess. (1953).

21. *Public Hearings (No. 5)*, pp. 1593–94 (1953) (testimony of Constantino Scannavino); *Public Hearings (No. 5)*, pp. 1508–29 (1953) (testimony of Vincent Mannino).

22. Joseph Bonanno with Sergio Lalli, *A Man of Honor: The Autobiography of Joseph Bonanno* (New York: Simon & Schuster, 1983), p. 169; *Public Hearings (No. 5)*, pp. 1527–28 (1953) (testimony of Mannino); *New York Times*, September 18, 1930, October 3, 1941, October 7, 1941, December 19, 1952, and March 2, 1963.

23. FBI Report, The Criminal Commission, December 19, 1962, in Records of the Federal Bureau of Investigation, Record Group 65, National Archives and Records Administration at College Park, MD (hereafter "NARA College Park"). Thanks to the Mary Ferrell website for making this and other FBI files on the Mafia available online at http://www.maryferrell.org. FBI Report, Activities of Top Hoodlums in the New York Field Division, September 14, 1959, in FBI Freedom of Information Act ("FOIA") File on Top Hoodlum Program (copy in possession of author); *Public Hearings (No. 5)*, pp. 3152–63 (1953); *New York Times*, December 14, 1952, October 26, 1957.

24. Bonanno, *Man of Honor*, pp. 156, 170–71; *Public Hearings (No. 5)*, pp. 1690–98 (testimony of Umberto Anastasio); *New York Times*, April 29, 1923, October 26, 1957; Gen. Investigative Intelligence File, Albert Anastasia, February 25, 1954, in FBI FOIA File on Albert Anastasia (copy in possession of author).

25. *New York Times*, December 24, 1919, August 10, 1924, October 11, 1968; James B. Jacobs, Coleen Friel, and Robert Radick, *Gotham Unbound: How New York City Was Liberated from the Grip of Organized Crime* (New York: New York University Press, 1999), pp. 33–41.

26. *Public Hearings (No. 5)*, pp. 2091–2112 (1953) (testimony of Michael Clemente); FBI Memorandum, La Cosa Nostra, New York Waterfront, January 21, 1964, in RG 65 (NARA College Park); *New York Times*, January 22, 1953.

27. United States Census Bureau, *1920 Federal Population Census*, Dist. 920, Alessandro Di Brizzi, New York, NY.

28. *Public Hearings (No. 5)*, pp. 1910–39 (1953) (testimony of Alex Di Brizzi); *Waterfront Investigation*, pp. 438–39 (1953) (testimony of Joseph Ryan); FBI New York Office Report, Activities of Top Hoodlums in the United States, October 15, 1959, in RG 65 (NARA College Park).

29. New York Department of Planning, "Total and Foreign-Born Population New York City, 1890–2000," http://www.nyc.gov/html/dcp/pdf/census/1790–2000nyc-total.foreign birth.pdf (accessed May 19, 2013).

30. *Report of the New York City Commission on Congestion of Population* (New York: n.p., 1911), p. 85.

31. Oral history with Joseph Verdiccio, quoted in *Oral History of Manhattan*, p. 343.

32. Arthur Train, *Courts, Criminals, and the Camorra* (New York: Charles Scribner's, 1912), p. 241.

33. Joseph Valachi, "The Real Thing: The Exposé and Inside Doings of Cosa Nostra," p. 6 (unpublished autobiography), in Boxes 1 & 2, Joseph Valachi Personal Papers, in John F. Kennedy Presidential Library and Museum, Boston, MA (hereafter "JFK Library").

34. Bonanno, *Man of Honor*, p. 79.

35. John Manca and Vincent Cosgrove, *Tin For Sale: My Career in Organized Crime and the NYPD* (New York: William Morrow, 1991), pp. 34–36.

36. Arcangelo Dimico, Alessia Isopi, and Ola Olsson, "Origins of the Sicilian Mafia: The Market for Lemons" (working paper, University of Gothenburg, Gothenburg, Sweden, May 2012), http://gupea.ub.gu.se/ bitstream/2077/29193/1/gupea_2077_29193_1.pdf (accessed May 19, 2013); Paolo Buonanno et al., "On the Historical and Geographic Origins of the Sicilian Mafia" (working paper, University of Bergamo, Bergamo, Italy, February 2012), http://papers.ssrn.com/sol3/papers.cfm?abstract_id=2009808 (accessed May 19, 2013); Salvatore Lupo, *History of the Sicilian Mafia*, trans. Antony Shugaar (New York: Columbia University Press, 2011), p. 216; John Dickie, *Cosa Nostra: A History of the Sicilian Mafia* (New York: Palgrave Macmillan, 2005), pp. 38–39, 201–202.

37. I am indebted to Joshua B. Freeman's *Working Class New York: Life and Labor since World War II* (New York: New Press, 2000), pp. 2–22, and to Howard Kimeldorf's *Reds or Rackets: The Making of Radical and Conservative Unions on the Waterfront* (Berkeley: University of California Press, 1988), pp. 67–70, for highlighting the importance of small manufacturers and shippers in New York.

38. These statistics are calculated from data in United State Department of Commerce, *Census of Manufacturers, 1954, Vol. III, Area Statistics, Industry Statistics for Geographic Divisions, States, Standard Metropolitan Areas, Counties and Cities* (Washington, DC: GPO, 1955), in the charts at 104–4, 131–5, 131–30, 134–3, and 137–3.

39. Jacob Riis, *How the Other Half Lives: Studies among the Tenements of New York* (New York: Scribner, 1890), p. 69; Governor's Advisory Commission, Cloak, Suit, and Skirt Industry, *New York City: Report of an Investigation* (Albany, NY: n.p., 1925), pp. 1–2.

40. *Commission on Congestion of Population*, p. 149.

41. Oral history with Abe Feinglass on June 9, 1981, in Wisconsin Historical Society, Madison, WI; Dr. Michael Porter, *The Competitive Advantage of Nations* (New York: Free Press, 1990).

42. Burrows and Wallace, *Gotham*, pp. 437, 723–24; New York State Department of Labor, *Report of the Industrial Commissioner to the Hotel and Restaurant Wage Board* (Albany, NY: n.p., 1935), pp. 18–20.

43. United States Department of Agriculture, *The Wholesale Fruit and Vegetable Markets of New York City* (Washington, DC: GPO, 1940), pp. 6–7.

44. *Report of the Executive Committee to the New York City Council of Political Reform on the Operations of the Dept. of Docks* (New York: n.p., 1875), p. 13; *Commission on Congestion of Population*, p. 11.

45. Police Department of the City of New York, *Our Grave Traffic Problem; Suggestions for Relief* (1924), p. 6; *Report to the Honorable James J. Walker, Mayor, on Highway Traffic Conditions and Proposed Traffic Relief Measures for the City of New York* (New York: n.p., 1929), p. 24.

46. Police Department of the City of New York, *Our Grave Traffic Problem*, p. 7.

47. *Investigation of Improper Activities in the Labor or Management Field. Hearings before the Select Committee on Improper Activities in the Labor or Management Field*, Senate, 85th Cong., 2d. Sess., 6751–52 (1958) (testimony of John Montesano).

48. Oral history of Frank DiTrapani, quoted in *An Oral History of Manhattan*, p. 125.

49. Max Block, *Max the Butcher: An Autobiography of Violence and Intrigue* (Secaucus, NJ: Lyle Stuart, 1982), pp. 88–94, 106.

50. *Schechter Poultry Corp. v. United States*, 295 U.S. 495 (1935); Andrew W. Cohen, "The Era of Big Gonif Was Over," reposted by Eric Rauchway, *The Edge of the American West* (blog), May 27, 2008, http://chronicle.com/blognetwork/edgeofthewest/2008/05/27/the-era-of-big-gonif-was-over/ (accessed May 19, 2013).

51. Stephen H. Norwood, *Strike-Breaking and Intimidation: Mercenaries and Masculinity in Twentieth-Century America* (Chapel Hill: University of North Carolina Press, 2001), pp. 171–93.

52. Bonanno, *Man of Honor*, p. 79.

53. *New York Times*, August 10, 1933; Robert F. Himmelberg, *The Origins of the National Recovery Administration: Business, Government, and the Trade Association Issue, 1921–1933* (New York: Fordham University Press, 1993), pp. 1–4.

54. Benjamin Schlesinger, "Stabilizing an Industry," quoted in *Out of the Sweatshop: The Struggle for Industrial Democracy*, ed. Leon Stein (New York: Quadrangle, 1977), p. 219; International Ladies' Garment Workers' Union, *Industry Planning through Collective Bargaining* (New York: n.p., 1941), p. 10.

55. Bonanno, *Man of Honor*, pp. 152–53.

56. Grand Jury Association of New York County, *Criminal Receivers in the United States* (1928); *Investigation of So-Called "Rackets." Hearings before a Subcommittee on the Committee on Commerce*, Senate, 73d Cong., 2d. Sess., 16–17 (1934); Samuel Marx, *Broadway Gangsters and Their Rackets* (Girard, KS: H. J. Publishers, 1929), p. 13; Timothy J. Gilfoyle, *A Pickpocket's Tale: The Underworld of Nineteenth-Century New York* (New York: W. W. Norton, 2006), pp. 60–61, 318–20.

57. Jenna Weissman Joselit, *Our Gang: Jewish Crime and the New York Jewish Community, 1900–1940* (Bloomington: Indiana University Press, 1983), pp. 36–39; Fire Department of the City of New York, *Incendiarism in Greater New York* (December 1912), pp. 14–16.

58. Thomas M. Pitkin and Francesco Cordasco, *Black Hand: A Chapter in Ethnic Crime* (Totowa, NJ: Rowman and Littlefield, 1977); Joselit, *Our Gang*, pp. 39–40.

59. Oral history of Peter Rofrano, quoted in *An Oral History of Manhattan*, p. 364.

60. Jeffrey Scott McIllwain, *Organizing Crime in Chinatown: Race and Racketeering in New York City, 1890–1910* (London: McFarland, 2004), pp. 130–34.

61. Crime Commission of New York State, *Report to the Commission of the Sub-Commission on Police* (Albany, NY: n.p., 1927), p. 23; NYPD, *Annual Report for the Year 1930* (New York: n.p., 1931), p. 8.

62. Special Committee Appointed to Investigate the Police Department of the City of New York, *Investigation of the Police Dept. of the City of New York, Proceedings from March 9 to June 5, 1894* (Albany, NY: n.p., 1895), pp. 25, 42.

63. Commission to Investigate Allegations of Police Corruption and the City's Anti-Corruption Procedures, *Commission Report* (New York: 1972), p. 125.

64. *The Transit Problems of New York City* (New York: n.p., 1919), p. 20; Robert A. Caro, *The Power Broker: Robert Moses and the Fall of New York* (New York: Vintage, 1975), pp. 71–86.

65. Raymond D. Horton, *Municipal Labor Relations in New York City* (New York: Praeger, 1973), p. 17.

66. *Report of the Joint Legislative Committee to Investigate the Affairs of the City of New York on the Dept. of Docks* (New York: n.p., 1922), p. 5; State of New York, *Report and Summary of the Evidence of the Joint Legislative Committee to Investigate the Affairs of the City of New York* (Albany, NY: n.p., 1922), p. 74; New York City Commissioner of Accounts, *Investigating City Government in the La Guardia Administration* (New York: n.p., 1937), p. 36.

67. The first use of the term *fragile* to describe an industry susceptible to racketeering was in Ronald Goldstock et. al., *Corruption and Racketeering in the New York*

City Construction Industry: The Final Report of the New York State Organized Crime Task Force (New York: New York University Press, 1990), of which Dr. James B. Jacobs was the principal draftsman. As the *Final Report* explained, "The power of so many people in the construction process to impose delay costs on a construction project is what we mean by 'fragility.'" See page 59.

68. *Report of the Executive Committee to the New York City Council of Political Reform on the Operations of the Dept. of Docks* (New York: n.p., 1875), p. 11; New York City Commissioner of Accounts, *The Pushcart Problem in New York City* (New York: n.p., 1917), pp. 3–4.

69. Valachi, "The Real Thing," p. 6-1 (JFK Library).

70. *New York Times*, October 15, 1935, October 24, 1935, October 31, 1936, March 3, 1937; Thomas E. Dewey, *Twenty against the Underworld* (Garden City, NY: Doubleday, 1974), pp. 278–86.

71. Nicholas Pileggi, *Wiseguy: Life in a Mafia Family* (New York: Simon & Schuster, 1987), pp. 48–49.

72. State of New York, *Report of the Joint Legislative Committee on Taxicab Operation and Fares* (1936), p. 13; James V. Maresca, *My Flag Is Down: The Diary of a New York Taxi Driver* (New York: E. P. Dutton, 1948), p. 146.

73. *New York Times*, October 31, 1959.

74. Letter from M. J. Cashall to D. J. Tobin, March 29, 1934, in Box 20, Records of the Int'l Brotherhood of Teamsters, 1904–52 (WHS); David Witwer, *Corruption and Reform in the Teamsters Union* (Chicago: University of Illinois Press, 2003), pp. 114, 264 n. 38.

75. New York State Food Investigating Commission, *Report of the Committee on Terminals and Transportation* (New York: n.p., 1913), p. 29.

76. State of New York, *Report of the Attorney General in the Matter of the Milk Investigation* (Albany, NY: n.p., 1910), p. 12; *New York Times*, February 6, 1930, March 29, 1930, September 6, 1930, and March 3, 1940.

77. Block, *Max the Butcher*, pp. 79, 94–95.

78. *Investigation of Improper Activities*, pp. 11517–46 (1958); *New York Times*, June 25, 1996.

79. United States Department of Agriculture, *Wholesale Fruit and Vegetable Markets*, p. 6; Charles E. Artman, *Food Costs and City Consumers* (New York: n.p., 1926), p. 15.

80. Dash, *First Family*, pp. 150, 245–62.

81. Report on Rackets, October 29, 1937, in Box 134 of La Guardia Papers (NYMA); *New York Times*, May 14, 1937.

CHAPTER 2: PROHIBITION AND THE
RISE OF THE SICILIANS

1. This conversation is verbatim from the testimonies of police detectives Giuseppe Caravetta and Emil Panevino in *People against Pietro Lagatutta and Giuseppe Masseria,* Case No. 1714 (N.Y. Ct. Spec. Sess. 1913), Microfilm 1714, Trial Transcripts of the County of New York, 1883–1927, John Jay College of Criminal Justice, New York, NY (hereafter "JJC"). Thanks to David Critchley for pointing me toward these microfilms.

2. Ibid.

3. Ibid.; testimony of Giuseppe Masseria and Pietro Lagatutta in *People against Lagatutta and Masseria* (JJC).

4. Richard Warner and Mike Tona discovered the birth certificate of Giuseppe Masseria, January 17, 1886, Utliziale dello Stato Civile del commune di Menfi, IT, cited in Richard N. Warner, "On the Trail of Giuseppe 'Joe the Boss' Masseria," *Informer: The History of American Crime and Law Enforcement* (February 2011): 56–58; *New York Times,* April 16, 1931.

5. Unless stated otherwise, in this book all dollar figures are cited in their original amounts and then converted to 2013 dollars using http://www.bls.gov/data/inflation_calculator.htm.

6. Testimony of John Simpson and William Kinsler in *People against Lagatutta and Masseria* (JJC).

7. Testimony of Masseria in *People against Lagatutta and Masseria* (JCC).

8. Ibid.

9. Ibid.

10. Thomas Hunt, "Year-by-Year: Charlie Lucky's Life," *Informer: History of American Crime and Law Enforcement* (April 2012): 35–61; United States Census Bureau, *1920 Federal Population Census,* Salvatore Lucania, Enumeration District No. 1, New York, NY.

11. Report of Dr. Harry Freedran, Charles Luciano [undated], 1936, in Box 13, Thomas E. Dewey Papers, Department of Rare Books, Special Collections and Preservation, University of Rochester, Rochester, NY ("UR").

12. Report of Dr. L. E. Kinholz, Charles Luciano, June 30, 1936, in Box 13, Dewey Papers (UR); United States Census Bureau, *1920 Federal Population Census,* Salvatore Lucania, District No. 1, New York, NY.

13. Report of Dr. Freedran (UR); *New York Times,* June 19, 1936.

14. *New York Times,* June 19, 1936.

15. Report of Dr. Kinholz, in Box 13, Dewey Papers (UR). Luciano may have enjoyed drugs too much. "He is a drug addict," stated his first prison psychiatrist in 1936, who recommended that due "to his drug addiction he should be transferred to Dannemora Prison" in Dannemora, New York. This prison had a mental health hospital. Ralph Blumenthal, *Miracle at Sing Sing: How One Man Transformed the Lives of America's Most Dangerous Prisoners* (New York: St. Martin's Press, 2004), p. 166. Sometime after his transfer to Dannemora, Luciano denied drug use to another psychiatrist, who found no addiction at this later time. Report of Dr. Freedran (UR).

16. Report of Dr. Kinholz and Dr. Freedran, both in Box 13, Dewey Papers (UR).

17. Report of Dr. Freedran in Box 13, Dewey Papers (UR); Luciano quoted in Leonard Lyons, "The Man Who Was Lucky," *Esquire* (April 1953): 66–67, 127–31; FBI Memorandum, Re: Charles Luciana, August 28, 1935, in FBI Freedom of Information Act File (hereafter "FOIA") of Charles Luciano (copy in possession of author).

18. United States Census Bureau, *1920 Federal Population Census*, Salvatore Lucania, District No. 1, New York, NY.

19. Mike Dash, *The First Family: Terror, Extortion, and the Birth of the American Mafia* (New York: Simon and Schuster, 2009), pp. 147, 150.

20. Ibid., pp. 234–36.

21. David Critchley, *The Origin of Organized Crime in America: The New York City Mafia, 1891–1931* (New York: Routledge, 2009), pp. 121, 155.

22. United States Secret Service, Daily Reports for New York District Office, January 27, 1912, April 27, 1915, May 29, 1915, each in Records of the United States Secret Service, Record Group 87, in National Archives and Records Administration, College Park, MD (hereafter "NARA College Park").

23. *New York Times*, January 16, 1920; Michael A. Lerner, *Dry Manhattan: Prohibition in New York City* (Cambridge, MA: Harvard University Press, 2007), pp. 40, 64.

24. National Commission on Law Observance and Enforcement, *Enforcement of the Prohibition Laws: Official Records*, Senate, 71st Cong., 3d Sess. (Washington, DC: GPO, 1931), 203, 716.

25. Lerner, *Dry Manhattan*, p. 95.

26. National Commission, *Enforcement of the Prohibition Laws*, p. 723.

27. Tom Geraghty, quoted in Jeff Kisseloff, ed., *You Must Remember This: An Oral History of Manhattan from the 1890s to World War II* (New York: Schocken Books, 1989), p. 584.

28. Caroline F. Ware, *Greenwich Village, 1920–1930: A Comment on American Civilization in the Post-War Years* (New York: Houghton Mifflin, 1935), p. 56; Critchley, *Organized Crime*, p. 143.

29. Roger Touhy with Ray Brennan, *The Stolen Years* (Cleveland: Pennington Press, 1959), pp. 63, 65.

30. *Brooklyn Standard Union*, July 22, 1931; *New York Post*, February 29, 1932.

31. Mark H. Haller, "Bootleggers and American Gambling 1920–1950," in Commission on the Review of the National Policy Toward Gambling, *Gambling in America: Appendix* (Washington, DC: GPO, 1976), pp. 109–11.

32. Joseph Bonanno with Sergio Lalli, *A Man of Honor: The Autobiography of Joseph Bonanno* (New York: Simon and Schuster, 1983), pp. 65, 75.

33. Nick Gentile, *Vita di Capomafia* (Rome: Editori Riuniti, 1963), pp. 80, 87.

34. Lerner, *Dry Manhattan*, p. 146.

35. Malcolm F. Willoughby, *Rum War at Sea* (Washington, DC: GPO, 1964), pp. 32–33.

36. George Wolf with Joseph DiMona, *Frank Costello: Prime Minister of the Underworld* (London: Staughton, 1975), pp. 12–15, 22, 50–51.

37. Ibid.; *Costello vs. United States*, 365 U.S. 265 (1961); *Investigation of Organized Crime in Interstate Commerce, Hearings before the Special Committee to Investigate Organized Crime in Interstate Commerce, Part 7*, Senate, 81st Cong., 2d Sess. (1951), 895, 900 (hereafter "Kefauver Committee Hearings").

38. *Daily Star*, October 28, 1926; *Brooklyn Standard Union*, November 19, 1926; *New York Times*, January 27, 1926, January 21–22, 1927, January 31, 1927; Wolf, *Costello*, p. 51.

39. Kefauver Committee Hearings, 889–904 (testimony of Frank Costello).

40. *Costello vs. United States*, 365 U.S. 265 (1961).

41. *New York Times*, August 3, 1924, June 11, 1925, June 30, 1925; *New York Evening Post*, April 16, 1925.

42. Bonanno, *Man of Honor*, p. 76; Critchley, *Origin of Organized Crime*, p. 138.

43. John Morahan, quoted in Jeff Kisseloff, ed., *You Must Remember This: An Oral History of Manhattan from the 1890s to World War II* (Baltimore: John's Hopkins University Press, 1989), p. 585.

44. Ware, *Greenwich Village*, pp. 56–57; Lewis Valentine, *Night Stick: The Autobiography of Lewis J. Valentine* (New York: Dial Press, 1947), pp. 54–55.

45. Humbert S. Nelli, *The Business of Crime: Italians and Syndicate Crime in the United States* (New York: Oxford University Press, 1976), p. 172.

46. Masseria may have made key contacts while in Sing Sing. For eighteen months, between March 1914 and September 1916, Masseria's time in Sing Sing overlapped with that of Thomas "The Bull" Pennochio, a close ally of Charles "Lucky" Luciano. During Prohibition, Luciano and Pennochio would become key lieutenants of Mas-

seria. Compare Giuseppe Masseria, Inmate Admission, Sing Sing Correctional Facility Records, New York State Archives, Albany, NY (hereafter "NYSA") with Thomas Pennochio Prison File in Notorious Offenders Files, Records of the Federal Bureau of Prison, RG 129, National Archives and Records Administration, College Park, MD (hereafter "NARA College Park"); Thomas Hunt and Michael Tona, "Cleveland Convention Was to Be Masseria Coronation," *Informer: History of American Crime & Law Enforcement* (January 2010): 13–36 n. 83.

47. Critchley, *Origin of Organized Crime*, p. 155; Lerner, *Dry Manhattan*, pp. 261–263.

48. *New York Evening Telegram*, May 9, 1922; *New York Times*, May 9, 1922.

49. *New York Herald-Tribune*, May 9, 1922; *New York Evening Telegram*, May 9, 1922, August 11, 1922; *New York Times*, May 9, 1922; *People against Joseph Masseria* (1922), in New York County District Attorney Records, New York Municipal Archives, New York, NY (hereafter "NYMA").

50. *New York Call*, August 9, 1922; *New York Times*, August 9, 1922.

51. *New York Times*, April 16, 1931.

52. Wolf, *Frank Costello*, p. 69; Dash, *First Family*, pp. 271–72.

53. FBI Memorandum, General Investigative Intelligence File, October 15, 1956, in Records of the Federal Bureau of Investigation, RG 65, (NARA College Park); *New York Times*, July 24, 1929.

54. Bonanno, *Man of Honor*, p. 84; *New York Times*, April 16, 1931.

55. Kisseloff, *You Must Remember This*, p. 597.

56. Ben Wattenberg and Richard M. Scammon, *The Real Majority: An Extraordinary Examination of the American Electorate* (New York: Coward-McCann, 1970), p. 45.

57. Ira Rosenwaike, *Population History of New York City* (Syracuse, NY: Syracuse University Press, 1972), pp. 93–95.

58. Table 2–1 is based on Rosenwaike, *Population History*, pp. 77, 141, 202–204, and Federation of Jewish Philanthropies, *The Estimated Jewish Population of the New York Area, 1900–1975* (New York: n.p., 1959), p. 15. The numbers in table 3–1 are rounded down to the nearest thousand and percentage point.

59. Federal Writers' Project, "Italian Colonies in New York City, 1936," in WPA Federal Writers' Project (NYC Unit) Collection, 1936–1943 (NYMA); Tyler Anbinder, *Five Points: The 19th-Century New York City Neighborhood that Invented Tap Dance, Stole Elections, and Became the World's Most Notorious Slum* (New York: Plume, 2002), p. 375.

60. Jerry Della Femina, quoted in Myrna Katz Frommer and Harvey Frommer, ed.,

It Happened in Manhattan: An Oral History of Life in the City during the Mid-Twentieth Century (New York: Berkley Books, 2001), p. 47.

61. Gus Petruzzelli, *Memories of Growing up in Little Italy, NY* (Bloomington, IN: Xlibris, 2010), p. 11.

62. Julius Drachsler, *Intermarriage in New York City: A Statistical Study of the Amalgamation of European Peoples* (New York: n.p., 1921), pp. 43–45.

63. There were about five thousand *mafiosi* out of approximately 1,029,000 Italian Americans. *Hearings before the Permanent Subcommittee on Investigations of the Committee on Government Operations: Organized Crime and the Illicit Traffic in Narcotics,* Senate, 88th Cong., 1st Sess. (1963), 270–71 (testimony of Joseph Valachi); Rosenwaike, *Population History,* p. 205. This constitutes 0.48 percent of the total population.

64. Robert A. Orsi, *The Madonna of 115th Street: Faith and Community in Italian Harlem* (New Haven, CT: Yale University Press, 1985), pp. 103–104.

65. Clara Ferrara, quoted in *An Oral History of Manhattan,* p. 367.

66. George P. LeBrun, *It's Time to Tell* (New York: William Morrow, 1962), pp. 130–31.

67. Salvatore Mondello, *A Sicilian in East Harlem* (Youngstown, NY: Cambria Press, 2005), p. 54.

68. Pete Pascale, quoted in *An Oral History of Manhattan,* p. 365.

69. James B. Jacobs with Christopher Panarella and Jay Worthington, *Busting the Mob: United States v. Cosa Nostra* (New York: New York University Press, 1994), p. 20.

70. *Organized Crime: 25 Years after Valachi: Hearings before the Permanent Subcommittee on Investigations of the Committee on Government Affairs,* Senate, 100th Cong., 2d Sess. (1988), 236 (testimony of Vincent Cafaro).

71. Tony Napoli with Charles Messina, *My Father, My Don: A Son's Journey from Organized Crime to Sobriety* (Silver Spring, MD: Beckham Publications, 2002), p. 47.

72. *Organized Crime: 25 Years after Valachi,* 201 (testimony of Joseph Pistone).

73. Philip Carlo, *Gaspipe: Confessions of a Mafia Boss* (New York: William Morrow, 2008), pp. 5–7.

74. Vincent Teresa, *My Life in the Mafia* (New York: Doubleday, 1973), pp. 21, 23.

75. For background on the *cosche* of Sicily, see James Fentress, *Rebels and Mafiosi, Death in a Sicilian Landscape* (New York: Cornell University Press, 2000), pp. 172–74.

76. Donald R. Cressey, *Theft of a Nation* (New York: Harper and Row, 1969).

77. This section uses historical evidence to expand on the insights of criminologist Howard Abadinsky, the first academic to suggest that crime syndicates were like franchises. Howard Abadinsky, *Organized Crime,* 10th ed. (Belmont, CA: Wadsworth, 2013), pp. 7–8.

78. Roger D. Blair and Francine LaFontaine, *The Economics of Franchising* (New York: Cambridge University Press, 2005), p. 4.

79. This section expands on the insights of Italian scholar Diego Gambetta, who has written about the role of "criminal trademarks." Diego Gambetta, *Codes of the Underworld: How Criminals Communicate* (Princeton, NJ: Princeton University Press, 2011), pp. 195–229.

80. Henry Hill, quoted in Nicholas Pileggi, *Wiseguy: Life in a Mafia Family* (New York: Simon and Schuster, 1985), pp. 57–58.

81. Peter Maas, *Serpico* (New York: Viking Press, 1973), p. 156.

82. Hill, quoted in Pileggi, *Wiseguy*, pp. 56–57.

83. Michael Franzese, *I'll Make You an Offer You Can't Refuse* (New York: Thomas Nelson, 2009), p. 67; Peter Reuter, *Disorganized Crime: The Economics of the Visible Hand* (Cambridge, MA: Massachusetts Institute of Technology Press, 1983), pp. 151–72.

84. Diego Gambetta, *The Sicilian Mafia: The Business of Private Protection* (Cambridge: Harvard University Press, 1996), p. 45.

85. Joseph Pistone, *The Way of the Wiseguy* (Philadelphia: Running Press, 2004), p. 81.

86. Gambetta, *Sicilian Mafia*, pp. 45–46.

87. FBI Report, La Cosa Nostra, October 20, 1967, in RG 65 (NARA College Park).

88. John Roselli, quoted in Ovid Demaris, *The Last Mafioso* (New York: Times Books, 1981), p. 19.

89. *United States v. James Coonan, et. al.*, 938 F.2d 1533 (2d Cir. 1991).

90. Anthony Serritella, *Book Joint for Sale: Memoirs of a Bookie* (Bloomington, IN: AuthorHouse, 2011), p. 70.

91. *Organized Crime: 25 Years after Valachi*, 239–40, 301 (testimony of Joseph Valachi); Joseph D. Pistone, *Donnie Brasco* (New York: Signet, 1997), pp. 78–79.

92. Blair and Lafontaine, *Economics of Franchising*, p. 224.

93. James Fentress, *Rebels and Mafiosi: Death in a Sicilian Landscape* (New York: Cornell University Press, 2000), p. 177, n. 59.

94. *Organized Crime: 25 Years after Valachi*, 260 (testimony of Vincent Cafaro).

95. FBI Memorandum, Top Echelon Criminal Informant Program, March 20, 1962, in FBI FOIA File on Gregory Scarpa Sr. (copy in possession of author).

96. *Organized Crime: 25 Years after Valachi*, 236 (testimony of Vincent Cafaro); Jimmy Fratianno, cited in Demaris, *Last Mafioso*, p. 4.

97. Peter Maas, *The Valachi Papers* (New York: Putnam, 1968), p. 201.

98. *Organized Crime: 25 Years after Valachi*, 236–38 (testimony of Vincent Cafaro).

99. Gentile, *Vita de Capomafia*, p. 86.

100. Bonanno, *Man of Honor*, p. 159.

101. See generally Alvin Toffler, *The Third Wave* (New York: Bantam, 1991).

102. Timothy J. Gilfoyle, *A Pickpocket's Tale: The Underworld of Nineteenth-Century New York* (New York: W. W. Norton, 2007), p. 186.

103. Gentile, *Vita de Capomafia*, p. 65.

104. Mike Dash, *The First Family: Terror, Extortion, Revenge, Murder, and the Birth of the American Mafia* (New York: Ballantine Books, 2010), pp. 34, 97, 142, 183, 251.

105. Claude S. Fischer, *America Calling: A Social History of the Telephone to 1940* (Los Angeles: University of California Press, 1994), pp. 48–49, 62.

106. 48 U.S.C. §§ 1103–4 (1934); *Nardone v. United States*, 302 U.S. 379 (1937); Jacobs, *Busting the Mob*, p. 8.

107. President's Commission on Organized Crime, *Organized Crime and Money Laundering: Record of Hearing II, March 14, 1984, New York, New York* (Washington, DC: GPO, 1985), 59 (testimony of Jimmy Fratianno); Demaris, *Last Mafioso*, p. 376.

108. Investigative case file on Frank Costello in Box 52 in Kefauver Committee files; *Binghamton Press*, June 14, 1959; Jacobs, *Busting the Mob*, pp. 132, 158–59; Richard A. Posner, *Not a Suicide Pact: The Constitution in a Time of National Emergency* (New York: Oxford University Press, 2006), pp. 95–96.

109. James J. Flink, *The Automobile Age* (Cambridge, MA: Massachusetts Institute of Technology Press, 1988), pp. 130–31.

110. Maas, *Valachi Papers*, p. 44.

111. United States Treasury Department, *Traffic in Opium and other Dangerous Drug for the Year Ended December 31, 1937* (Washington, DC: GPO, 1938), pp. 60–61.

112. Mark H. Haller, "Bootleggers and American Gambling 1920–1950," in Commission on the Review of the National Policy Toward Gambling, *Gambling in America: Appendix* (Washington, DC: GPO, 1976), p. 116.

113. Dennis Griffin, *The Battle for Las Vegas: The Law vs. The Mob* (Las Vegas: Huntington Press, 2006), pp. 4–7.

114. Shane White, Stephen Garton, Stephen Robertson, and Graham White, *Playing the Numbers: Gambling in Harlem between the Wars* (Cambridge, MA: Harvard University Press, 2010), pp. 13, 56, 237.

115. Francis A. J. Ianni with Elizabeth Reuss-Ianni, *A Family Business: Kinship and Social Control in Organized Crime* (New York: Russell Sage Foundation, 1972), pp. 92–96; Harold Lasswell and Jeremiah McKenna, *The Impact of Organized Crime on an*

Inner City Community (New York: Policy Sciences Center, 1972); Don Liddick, *The Mob's Daily Number: Organized Crime and the Numbers Gambling Industry* (Lanham, MD: University Press of America, 1999), pp. 99–101, 161–63.

116. White, *Playing the Numbers*, pp. 237–38; FBI Report, Paul Joseph Correale, September 26, 1960, and FBI Report, Crime Conditions, May 15, 1962, both in RG 65 (NARA College Park).

117. Joseph Bonanno, *Man of Honor*, p. 153.

118. Bill Bonanno and Gary B. Abromovitz, *The Last Testament of Bill Bonanno: The Final Secrets of a Life in the Mafia* (New York: Harper, 2011), pp. 289–90.

119. Richard O. Davis and Richard G. Abram, *Betting the Line: Sports Wagering in American Life* (Columbus: Ohio State University Press, 2001), pp. 35–36, 41–42, 87.

120. Reuter, *Disorganized Crime*, pp. 14–40.

121. John Cummings and Ernest Volkman, *Goombata* (Boston: Little, Brown, 1990), p. 101, cited in Critchley, *Origin of Organized Crime*, pp. 237–38.

122. See chapter 7.

CHAPTER 3: THE MAFIA REBELLION OF 1928–1931 AND THE FALL OF THE BOSS OF BOSSES

1. Nick Gentile, *Vita di Capomafia* (Rome: Editori Riuniti,1963), p. 96; Joseph Bonanno with Sergio Lalli, *A Man of Honor: The Autobiography of Joseph Bonanno* (New York: Simon and Schuster, 1983), p. 87.

2. For examples of the conventional history of the Castellammarese War, see Selwyn Raab, *Five Families: The Rise, Decline, and Resurgence of America's Most Powerful Mafia Empires* (New York: St. Martin's Griffin, 2005), pp. 22–34; John Davis, *Mafia Dynasty: The Rise and Fall of the Gambino Crime Family* (New York: HarperCollins, 1993), pp. 36–43. By contrast, in his pioneering historical study of the conflict, David Critchley argues, "The War was predominantly a revolt by several U.S. Families against trends towards the informal consolidation of power that had built up, centered on the *capo di capi's* patronage powers." David Critchley, *The Origin of Organized Crime in America: The New York City Mafia, 1891–1931* (New York: Routledge, 2009), p. 165. However, Critchley still accepts much of the standard framing of "the Castellammare War of 1930–1931." David Critchley, "Buster, Maranzano, and the Castellammare War, 1930–1931," *Global Crime* 7, no. 1 (February 2006): 43–78. This book argues, moreover, that short-term ambitions and individual economic motives were more important factors than any revolt against patronage powers.

3. For more of a social-history approach, which uses census records to show the simi-larities of the Mafia leaders before and after the "Castellammare War" to rebut the myth of rapid Americanization, see Critchley, *Origin of Organized Crime*, pp. 202–206, 230–31.

4. Office of the Chief Medical Examiner, Autopsy of Salvatore D'Aquila, October 11, 1928 (NYMA); *Brooklyn Standard Union*, October 11, 1928; Mike Dash, *The First Family: Terror, Extortion and the Birth of the American Mafia* (New York: Simon and Schuster, 2009), pp. 291–92, 398.

5. Ibid., pp. 275, 325; *New York Times*, October 11, 1928; *Brooklyn Daily Eagle*, October 11, 1928.

6. Gentile, *Vita di Capomafia*, pp. 61, 76; FBI Report, Denver, La Cosa Nostra, March 29, 1964, in Records of the Federal Bureau of Investigation, Record Group 65, National Archives and Records Administration, College Park, MD (hereafter "NARA College Park").

7. *New York Times*, October 11, 1928; *Brooklyn Standard Union*, October 11, 1928; autopsy of D'Aquila, October 11, 1928 (NYMA); Dash, *First Family*, p. 362.

8. Critchley points out that the men first engaged D'Aquila in a discussion before killing him, and in 1968 an informant by the pseudonym "Jim Carra" claimed D'Aquila was killed by his own underboss. Critchley, *Origin of Organized Crime*, p. 289. On the other hand, Carra's version is uncorroborated, and other mob killings began with argu-ments with the victim, such as the January 1931 murder of Joseph Parrino in a restau-rant. *Brooklyn Daily Eagle*, January 20, 1931. Thanks to Rick Warner for this citation.

9. Gentile, *Vita di Capomafia*, p. 80.

10. Ibid., p. 96.

11. Critchley, *Origin of Organized Crime*, pp. 77, 157.

12. Dash, *First Family*, p. 320.

13. Thomas Hunt, "Profaci's Rise," *Informer: The Journal of American Crime and Law Enforcement* (January 2012): pp. 4–15; Critchley, *Origin of Organized Crime*, pp. 161–62.

14. Dash, *First Family*, pp. 364–66.

15. Critchley, *Origin of Organized Crime*, pp. 171–77; Dash, *First Family*, p. 328.

16. Gentile, *Vita di Capomafia*, p. 96; Bonanno, *Man of Honor*, p. 87.

17. *Brooklyn Daily Eagle*, February 27, 1930; Critchley, *Origin of Organized Crime*, p. 175.

18. Bonanno, *Man of Honor*, p. 106; Joseph Valachi, "The Real Thing: The Expose and Inside Doings of Cosa Nostra" (unpublished manuscript), pp. 339–40, in Boxes 1 and 2, Joseph Valachi Personal Papers, in John F. Kennedy Presidential Library and Museum, Boston, MA.

19. *Hearings before the Permanent Subcommittee on Investigations of the Committee on Government Operations: Organized Crime and the Illicit Traffic in Narcotics*, Senate, 88th Cong., 1st Sess. (1963), 163 (testimony of Joseph Valachi).

20. Gentile, *Vita di Capomafia*, p. 97; Critchley, *Origin of Organized Crime*, pp. 171, 178. Although Bonanno claimed Morello admitted his culpability in the Milazzo murder, there is no corroboration for this questionable story. Bonanno, *Man of Honor*, pp. 100, 103.

21. Bonanno, *Man of Honor*, p. 70.

22. Critchley, *Origin of Organized Crime*, pp. 144–45.

23. Bonanno, *Man of Honor*, p. 71; Peter Maas, *Valachi Papers* (New York: Putnam, 1968), p. 106.

24. Gentile, *Vita di Capomafia*, p. 109; Bonanno, *Man of Honor*, p. 103.

25. *Organized Crime*, 166 (testimony of Joseph Valachi); Salvatore Maranzano, quoted in Bonanno, *Man of Honor*, 86; Gentile, *Vita di Capomafia*, p. 97.

26. Critchley, *Origin of Organized Crime*, p. 173.

27. Gentile, *Vita di Capomafia*, p. 109.

28. Valachi, "The Real Thing," p. 287.

29. Bonanno, *Man of Honor*, p. 102; *Brooklyn Daily Star*, July 15, 1930.

30. Catania was killed on February 3, 1931 by Maranzano's hit men. *Organized Crime*, 188–89, 192 (testimony of Valachi).

31. FBI Report, Activities of Top Hoodlums in the New York Field Division, September 14, 1959 (NARA College Park); Peter Diapoulos and Steven Linakis, *The Sixth Family* (New York: Bantam, 1976), pp. 21–22; Valachi, "The Real Thing," p. 287.

32. Bonanno, *Man of Honor*, p. 86.

33. Office of the Chief Medical Examiner, Report of the Autopsy of Joseph Masseria, April 16, 1931 (NYMA); Office of the Chief Medical Examiner, Report of the Autopsy of Salvatore Maranzano, September 11, 1931 (NYMA); Thomas Hunt and Michael Tona, "Cleveland Convention Was to Be Masseria Coronation," *Informer: History of American Crime & Law Enforcement* (January 2010), p. 33 n. 62.

34. George Wolf with Joseph DiMona, *Frank Costello: Prime Minister of the Underworld* (London: Morrow, 1974), p. 83.

35. *New York Times*, August 15, 1930; *New York Sun*, August 16, 1930; *Brooklyn Standard Union*, August 16, 1930; Maas, *Valachi Papers*, p. 89.

36. Bonanno, *Man of Honor*, p. 107; Dash, *First Family*, p. 376.

37. *Organized Crime*, 164–66 (testimony of Valachi).

38. Ibid., 170; *New York Times*, November 6, 1930.

39. FBI Report, La Cosa Nostra, July 1, 1963, in RG 65 (NARA College Park); Gentile, *Vita di Capomafia*, p. 107.

40. Ibid., p. 108.

41. Bonanno, *Man of Honor*, p. 122.

42. *New York Times*, April 19, 1930, April 20, 1931; *Organized Crime*, 211 (testimony of Valachi).

43. Autopsy of Masseria (NYMA).

44. *New York Times*, April 16, 1931; *New York Sun*, April 16, 1931.

45. *Brooklyn Eagle*, April 17, 1931; autopsy of Masseria (NYMA); Critchley, "Castellammare War, 1930–1931," p. 64 n. 123.

46. Autopsy of Masseria (NYMA); *Daily Argus*, April 16, 1931.

47. *New York Times*, April 16, 1931; *New York Sun*, April 16, 1931.

48. It was unlikely Luciano was present at the Nuova. Luciano was not known as a hit man, no news accounts placed him in Brooklyn, and Nicola Gentile witnessed a calm Luciano in his residence shortly after the murder. Gentile, *Vita di Capomafia*, p. 112.

49. Critchley, *Origin of Organized Crime*, p. 302, n. 160 citing "Giuseppe Masseria, November 27, 1940," in Box 17, Murder, Inc. Collection, NYMA.

50. Confidential Memorandum, In Re: Anastasia Brothers, March 21, 1952, in Box 8, Albert Anastasia Closed Files (NYMA). The informant did not appear to have been a *mafioso* himself and made some farfetched claims. For example, he called Vito Genovese "the boss" of the Brooklyn mob, and he alleged that William O'Dwyer actively conspired in Abe Reles's murder. However, the informant was accurate about other waterfront matters, and his story about Giustra was corroborated. *New York Times*, December 12, 1930, September 12, 1932; *New York Sun*, May 15, 1931.

51. Gentile, *Vita di Capomafia*, p. 112.

52. Ibid., p. 113.

53. Bonanno, *Man of Honor*, p. 128.

54. Gentile, *Vita di Capomafia*, p. 115.

55. Bonanno, *Man of Honor*, pp. 126–27; Gentile, *Vita di Capomafia*, p. 115.

56. *New York Times*, June 6, 1931.

57. "Lucky Luciano Talks," *Esquire*, p. 128.

58. Humbert S. Nelli, *The Business of Crime: Italians and Syndicate Crime in the United States* (Chicago: University of Chicago, Press, 1976), pp. 205, 295 nn. 30–31.

59. *Organized Crime*, 217–18 (testimony of Valachi); Gentile, *Vita di Capomafia*, pp. 115–116.

60. Ibid.

61. *New York Times*, September 11, 1931; Bonanno, *Man of Honor*, p. 130; Gentile, *Vita di Capomafia*, p. 116.

62. *New York Times*, September 26, 1931; Bonanno, *Man of Honor*, p. 134.

63. Gaius Suetonius Tranquillus, *The Lives of the Twelve Caesars*, 121 CE.

64. FBI ELSUR Log, Steve Magaddino, June 3, 1963, in RG 65 (NARA College Park); FBI Memorandum, Subject: Steve Magaddino, March 31, 1965, in RG 65 (NARA College Park).

65. *Organized Crime*, 221, 226 (testimony of Valachi).

66. Dash makes no mention of their role in the Maranzano assassination. While noting their presence at Maranzano's office, Critchley concludes only that the Gaglianos "may have been involved in it." Critchley, *Origin of Organized Crime*, pp. 195, 305 n. 238, citing New York State Crime Commission, *Public Hearings (no. 4)* (November 1952), 111 (testimony of Lucchese).

67. *Organized Crime*, 226 (testimony of Valachi); FBI Memorandum, Thomas Lucchese, January 12, 1954, in FBI FOIA file of Thomas Lucchese (copy in possession of author).

68. Bonanno, *Man of Honor*, p. 139; Gentile, *Vita di Capomafia*, p. 117.

69. *New York Times*, September 11, 1931; *Public Hearings (no. 4)*, 95 (testimony of Lucchese).

70. Bonanno, *Man of Honor*, pp. 130, 137; *New York Times*, September 11, 1931.

71. Girolamo Santuccio, quoted in Maas, *Valachi Papers*, p. 115; *New York Times*, September 11, 1931.

72. Salvatore Maranzano, quoted in Maas, *Valachi Papers*, p. 115; Salvatore Maranzano, quoted in Gentile, *Vita di Capomafia*, p. 118.

73. *Organized Crime*, 228 (testimony of Valachi); Girolamo Santuccio and Sam Levine, quoted in Maas, *Valachi Papers*, p. 116.

74. *New York Times*, September 11, 1931; autopsy of Salvatore Maranzano, September 11, 1931 (NYMA).

75. *Organized Crime*, 231 (testimony of Valachi).

76. *Public Hearings (no. 4)*, 98 (testimony of Lucchese); *New York Times*, September 11, 1931; Maas, *Valachi Papers*, p. 116; *Organized Crime*, 224 (testimony of Valachi).

77. J. Richard Davis, "Things I Couldn't Tell till Now," *Collier's* (August 5, 1939): 12–13, 43–44.

78. Nelli, *Business of Crime*, pp. 179–84; Alan Block, *East Side, West Side: Organizing Crime in New York, 1930–1950* (Piscataway, NJ: Transaction Publishers, 1983), pp. 3–9.

79. Davis, *Mafia Dynasty*, p. 46.

80. Steven Runciman, *The Sicilian Vespers: A History of the Mediterranean World in the Later Thirteenth Century* (Cambridge: Cambridge University Press, 1958), p. 216; *The Godfather* (Paramount, 1972).

81. Critchley calculates thirteen casualties between May 1930 and April 1931. Critchley, "Castellammare War, 1930–1931," p. 65. Adding Salvatore D'Aquila (October 1928), Gaetano Reina (February 1930), and Salvatore Maranzano (September 1931), brings the total to sixteen casualties.

82. Nelli, *Business of Crime*, p. 172.

83. Gentile, *Vita di Capomafia*, pp. 101, 104.

84. Bonanno, *Man of Honor*, p. 97.

85. *Organized Crime*, 194 (Valachi testimony).

86. Magaddino, quoted in FBI Memorandum, Subject Steve Magaddino, January 24, 1964, RG 65 (NARA College Park).

87. Raab, *Five Families*, p. 28.

88. Critchley, *Origin of Organized Crime*, p. 206, citing *New York Times*, March 2, 1930.

89. Dash, *First Family*, pp. 117, 120.

90. *New York Times*, September 26, 1931.

91. Gentile, *Vita di Capomafia*, p. 119.

92. Ibid.; Bonanno, *Man of Honor*, p. 159.

93. Ibid., p. 141. Although some sources indicate Ciccio Milano of Cleveland also held a seat, he appears to have been removed shortly afterward. FBI Report, Anti-Racketeering Conspiracy, December 13, 1963 (NARA College Park).

94. *New York Times*, October 18, 1931.

CHAPTER 4: THE RACKETEER COMETH: HOW THE MOB INFILTRATED LABOR UNIONS

1. United States Census Bureau, *1920 Federal Population Census*, John Dioguardi, District 152, Manhattan, New York.

2. *New York Times*, September 2, 1934, January 16, 1979.

3. *Hearings before the Select Committee on Improper Activities in the Labor or Management Field: Investigation of Improper Activities in the Labor or Management Field: Part 10*, 85th Cong., 2d Sess. (1957), 3618–33 (opening presentation of Robert Kennedy), 3683–3718 (testimony of Lester Washburn).

4. Daniel Bell, *The End of Ideology: On the Exhaustion of Political Ideas in the Fifties* (New York: Free Press, 1960), p. 129.

5. Francis A. J. Ianni, *Black Mafia: Ethnic Succession in Organized Crime* (New York: Simon and Schuster, 1974), pp. 13–14.

6. Howard Abadinsky, *Organized Crime*, 9th ed. (New York: Cengage, 2009), pp. 27–35; Jeffrey Scott McIllwain, *Organizing Crime in Chinatown: Race and Racketeering in New York City, 1890–1910* (London: McFarland, 2004), p. 8.

7. Jay P. Dolan, *The Irish Americans: A History* (New York: Bloomsbury Press, 2010), pp. 110, 301.

8. *New York Times*, January 2, 1881, January 3, 1893.

9. Dolan, *Irish Americans*, p. 96.

10. Julius Drachsler, *Intermarriage in New York City: A Statistical Study of the Amalgamation of European Peoples* (New York: n.p., 1921), p. 44.

11. Tyler Anbinder, *Five Points: The 19th-Century New York City Neighborhood that Invented Tap Dance, Stole Elections, and Became the World's Most Notorious Slum* (New York: Plume, 2002), pp. 375, 497.

12. *New York Sun*, November 7, 1912, January 18, 1914; Anbinder, *Five Points*, pp. 284–89.

13. *New York Times*, December 27, 1925; *Brooklyn Daily Eagle*, January 10, 1926.

14. *Hearings before the Permanent Subcommittee on Investigations of the Committee on Government Operations: Organized Crime and the Illicit Traffic in Narcotics*, Senate, 88th Cong., 1st Sess. (1963), 148, 231 (testimony of Joseph Valachi); FBI Airtel, Harold Konigsberg, August 16, 1965, in Records of the Federal Bureau of Investigation, Record Group 65, National Archives and Records Administration, College Park, MD (hereafter "NARA College Park").

15. Report, Re: Casper Holstein, March 12, 1935, in FBI Freedom of Information Act File on Casper Holstein (copy in possession of author).

16. McIllwain, *Chinatown*, pp. 131–33.

17. New York State Advisory Committee, *Hometown Plans for the Construction Industry in New York* (New York: n.p., 1972), p. 1; Colin J. Davis, "'Shape or Fight?': New York's Black Longshoremen, 1945–1961," *International Labor and Working-Class History* 62, no. 62 (Fall 2002): 143–63.

18. Frank Lucas with Aliya King, *Original Gangster: The Real Life Story of One of America's Most Notorious Drug Lords* (New York: St. Martin's Press, 2010), p. 106.

19. *Organized Crime*, 254, 304 (testimony of Valachi); Robert A. Rockaway, *But He Was Good to his Mother: The Lives and Crimes of Jewish Gangsters* (New York: Gefen Publishing, 2000), pp. 24, 46.

20. Ira Rosenwaike, *Population History of New York City* (Syracuse, NY: Syracuse University Press, 1972), pp. 93–95.

21. Hadassa Kosak, *Cultures of Opposition: Jewish Immigrant Workers, New York City, 1881–1905* (Albany: State University of New York Press, 2000), pp. 16–18;

Samuel L. Baily, *Immigrants in the Lands of Promise: Italians in Buenos Aires and New York City, 1870 to 1914* (Ithaca, NY: Cornell University Press, 1999), pp. 65–66.

22. Moses Rischin, *The Promised City: New York's Jews, 1870–1914* (Cambridge, MA: Harvard University Press, 1977) pp. 59–66; Joshua M. Zeitz, *White Ethnic New York: Jews, Catholics, and the Shaping of Postwar Politics* (Chapel Hill: University of North Carolina Press, 2007), pp. 19–20, table 3.

23. Burton Turkus and Sid Feder, *Murder, Inc., the Story of "The Syndicate"* (London: Gollancz, 1951), pp. 28, 110–11.

24. Nicholas Pileggi, *Wiseguy: Life in a Mafia Family* (New York: Simon and Schuster, 1985), pp. 8–9.

25. Michael Franzese, *Blood Covenant* (New York: Whitaker House, 2003).

26. Jenna Weissman Joselit, *Our Gang: Jewish Crime and the New York Jewish Community, 1900–1940* (Bloomington: Indiana University Press, 1983), pp. 158–59.

27. Robert Orsi, "The Religious Boundaries of an Inbetween People: Street Feste and the Problem of the Dark-Skinned 'Other' in Italian Harlem, 1920–1990," *American Quarterly* 44, no. 3 (September 1992): 313–47.

28. *Proceedings of the Subcommittee of the Committee on Immigration of the Senate: Immigration Investigation—Part II*, 51st Cong, 2d Sess. (1892), 55 (testimony of James Buckley); Matthew Frye Jacobson, *Whiteness of a Different Color: European Immigrants and the Alchemy of Race* (Cambridge, MA: Harvard University Press, 1999), p. 56.

29. Herman Feldman, *Racial Factors in American Industry* (New York: Harper, 1931), pp. 156.

30. Table 4–1 is based on data and estimates from the following sources: Federal Writers' Project, *The Italians of New York* (New York: n.p., 1938), pp. 64–67; New York State Department of Labor, *Changing Employment Patterns in New York State, 1950 to 1964* (Albany, NY: n.p., 1966), pp. 5, 13; Charles P. Larrowe, *Shape-Up and Hiring Hall: A Comparison of Hiring Methods and Labor Relations on the New York and Seattle Water Fronts* (Berkeley: University of California, 1955), p. 5. There are no hard statistics for the percentage of Italians among the two thousand garbage workers. John McMahon and Herbert Gamache, *Refuse Collection: Department of Sanitation vs. Private Carting* (New York: n.p., 1970), p. 34. I selected 70 percent as a conservative estimate based on Reuter's observation that virtually all waste haulers were run by Italian families with relatives as employees. Peter Reuter, "The Cartage Industry in New York," in Michael Tonry and Albert J. Reiss Jr., eds., *Beyond the Law: Crime in Complex Organizations* (Chicago: University of Chicago Press, 1993), pp. 154–55. The historian David Critchley has also noted anecdotally the correlation of the Mafia with these workforces. *The Origin of Organized Crime: The New York City Mafia, 1891–1931* (New York: Routledge, 2008), p. 77.

31. Federal Writers' Project, *Italians of New York*, pp. 64–66, 70, 72; State of New York, *Provisions of Teamsters' Union Contracts in New York City* (New York: n.p., 1949), p. 3.

32. Caroline F. Ware, "Ethnic Communities," in Edwin R. Seligman, ed., *Encyclopedia of the Social Sciences*, vol. 5 (New York: Macmillan, 1937), p. 24.

33. David Roediger, *Working toward Whiteness: How America's Immigrants Became White: The Strange Journey from Ellis Island to the Suburbs* (New York: Basic, 2005), pp. 24, 82.

34. Joselit, *Our Gang*, p. 106.

35. Reuter, "The Cartage Industry," pp. 151–52; Critchley, *Origin of Organized Crime*, p. 77.

36. Sonny Montella, quoted in President's Commission on Organized Crime, *The Edge: Organized Crime, Business, and Labor Unions* (Washington, DC: GPO, 1986), p. 39.

37. Federal Writers' Project, *Italians of New York*, pp. 65–66; Ronald Goldstock, Director, and James B. Jacobs, Principal Draftsman, *Corruption and Racketeering in the New York City Construction Industry: Final Report* (New York: New York University Press, 1990), pp. 79–85.

38. See also chapter 6.

39. *Improper Activities*, 6752 (testimony of John Montesano).

40. Peter Reuter, "Cartage Industry," pp. 151–52.

41. Federal Writers' Project, *Italians of New York*, pp. 174–76; Peter Mass, *Underboss: Sammy the Bull Gravano's Story of Life in the Mafia* (New York: HarperCollins, 1997), pp. 75, 115.

42. *New York Times*, February 9, 1921; *Final Report of the Joint Legislative Committee on Housing* (Albany, NY: J. B. Lyon, 1923), pp. 9–12; Goldstock and Jacobs, *Construction Industry*, pp. 79–85.

43. John Dioguardi, quoted in Ovid Demaris, *The Last Mafioso: The Treacherous World of Jimmy Fratianno* (New York: Times Books, 1981), p. 81.

44. Daniel Tobin, quoted in Arthur M. Schlesinger Jr., *The Coming of the New Deal, 1933–1935* (New York: Houghton Mifflin, 1958), p. 411.

45. David Witwer, *Corruption and Reform in the Teamsters Union* (Chicago: University of Illinois Press, 2008), pp. 82–84, 119–20, 163–64.

46. Roy Williams, quoted in President's Commission on Organized Crime, *The Edge: Organized Crime, Business, and Labor Unions*, p. 83.

47. 29 U.S.C. §§ 151–69.

48. New York Department of Labor, *Trade Union Statistics* (Albany: n.p., 1909),

p. xxxvi; Joshua B. Freeman, *Working-Class New York: Life and Labor since World War II* (New York: New Press, 2000), pp. 41, 350.

49. Mediation Conference, Bush Terminal and BSEU Local 51B, November 5, 1934, in Box 9, Region II, New York, Case Files and Transcripts, 1933–35, Record Group 25 (NARA College Park); Mediation Conference, Case: Real Estate Board and BSEU Local 32B, October 17, 1934, and Case: Garment Center Building Owners #1093 and BSEU Local 32B, November 7, 1934, both in Box 22, RG 25 (NARA College Park); FBI Report, Anthony Carfano, June 18, 1958, in FBI FOIA File of Anthony Carfano (copy in possession of author).

50. Notice of complaint by Teamsters Local 202, Re: Blackford's, from Regional Labor Board, December 5, 1934, in Box 5, RG 25 (NARA College Park); Agreement with Teamsters Local 202, January 10, 1934, in Box 26, RG 25 (NARA College Park); *New York Sun*, January 8, 1941.

51. Report of Teamsters Strikes, Local 138, October 25, 1933, and Labor Board filing of Flour Truckmen's Association, December 20, 1933, both in Box 59, RG 25 (NARA College Park).

52. James B. Jacobs, *Mobsters, Unions, and Feds: The Mafia and the American Labor Movement* (New York: New York University Press, 2006), pp. 99–106; David Witwer, *Shadow of the Racketeer: Scandal in Organized Labor* (Chicago: University of Illinois Press, 2009), pp. 53–57, 223–26.

53. *Organized Crime: 25 Years after Valachi: Hearings before the Permanent Subcommittee on Investigations of the Committee on Government Affairs*, Senate, 100th Cong., 2d Sess. (1988), 236 (testimony of Vincent Cafaro); Jacobs, *Mobsters*, pp. 2, 24.

54. Stier, Anderson, and Malone, LLC, *The Teamsters: Perception and Reality* (Washington, DC: International Brotherhood of Teamsters, 2001), p. 151.

55. Trial transcript of *United States v. Campagna*, Cr. No. 114-101 (S.D.N.Y. 1943), quoted in Witwer, *Shadow of the Racketeer*, pp. 45, 268 n. 33.

56. FBI Office Memorandum, Criminal Rackets Activities, Los Angeles Division, March 27, 1957, in RG (NARA College Park); Demaris, *Last Mafioso*, pp. 81–82.

57. Howard Kimeldorf, *Reds or Rackets? The Making of Radical and Conservative Unions on the Waterfront* (Los Angeles: University of California Press, 1988), pp. 43–45.

58. Interview with Thomas E. Dewey (1966), pp. 383–84, in Columbia Center for Oral History.

59. Interview with Sam Madell, 1977, in Tamiment Library and Robert F. Wagner Labor Archives, New York, NY; *Public Hearings (No. 5) Conducted by the New York State Crime Commission Pursuant to the Governor's Executive Orders* (Albany, NY: n.p., 1953) (testimony of Marcy Protter), cited in Nathan Ward, *Dark Harbor: The War for*

the New York Waterfront (New York: Farrar, Straus and Giroux, 2010), pp. 3–18, 225. Thanks to Nathan Ward for discussing sources with me.

60. *Brooklyn Eagle*, May 4, 1940; *PM*, October 15, 1940; *Public Hearings (no. 5)* (testimony of Protter).

61. *Brooklyn Eagle*, May 4, 1940; *Public Hearings (no. 5)* (testimony of Protter).

62. *Brooklyn Eagle*, March 27, 1940.

63. Ibid.; *Public Hearings (no. 5)* (testimony of Protter).

64. Statement of Albert Tannenbaum in *Public Hearings (no. 5)* (testimony of E. A. Heffernan).

65. *Public Hearings (no. 5)* (testimony of Protter); FBI Report, William O'Dwyer, February 16, 1953, in FBI FOIA File on William O'Dwyer (copy in possession of author); *Amsterdam Evening Recorder*, March 26, 1940; *Brooklyn Eagle*, March 27, 1940.

66. Statement of Tannenbaum in *Public Hearings (no. 5)*; *New York Times*, December 3, 1941.

67. *Brooklyn Eagle*, January 30, 1941.

68. *PM*, October 10, 1940; *Brooklyn Eagle*, October 10, 1940.

69. *PM*, October 15, 1940.

70. *Brooklyn Eagle*, January 30, 1941, October 21, 1941; *New York Times*, February 7, 1941, November 13, 1941.

71. *United States v. Lanza*, 85 F.2d 544 (2d Cir. 1936).

72. *New York Sun*, April 10, 1931; *New York Times*, October 11, 1968.

73. *New York Times*, May 13, 1926.

74. *New York Times*, September 2, 1926; *New York Sun*, September 7, 1926.

75. *New York Sun*, June 3,1935, December 3, 1935.

76. *United States v. Lanza*, 85 F.2d at 545.

77. Ibid. at 545–46.

78. Ibid.

79. Ibid.

80. *United States v. Joseph Lanza, et. al.*, Case No. 382 (S.D.N.Y. 1935) (testimony of Waldman), in RG 276, Courts of Appeal, National Archives and Records Administration, New York, NY (hereafter "NARA New York").

81. *United States v. Lanza, et. al.*, RG 276 (NARA New York) (testimony of Seif).

82. Ibid. (testimony of O'Neil); *United States v. Lanza*, 85 F.2d at 546.

83. *United States v. Lanza, et. al.*, RG 276 (NARA New York) (testimony of Waldman).

84. Joselit, *Our Gang*, pp. 108–10, 147–48.

85. *New York Times*, October 28, 1936, November 9, 1936.

86. *New York Times*, April 8, 1941, November 30, 1941, December 3, 1941.

87. See chapter 3.

88. Witwer, *Teamsters Union*, pp. 92–93, 260.

89. *Organized Crime: 25 Years after Valachi*, 277 (testimony of Valachi).

90. *New York Times*, October 12, 1951.

91. *Brooklyn Eagle*, November 21, 1950, April 26, 1954; *Albany Knickerbocker News*, February 15, 1951; *Long Island Star-Journal*, May 3, 1954; *People against Benedict Macri*, Case No. 1405-49 (N.Y. Ct. Gen. Sess. 1951) (testimonies of Leo Greenberg, George Prince, and Edward Cohen), in Box 1, Collection No. 5780/170, International Ladies Garment Workers Union Papers, Kheel Center for Labor-Management Documentation and Archives, Cornell University, Ithaca, NY (hereafter "KC").

92. *People against Macri* (KC) (testimonies of Edward Cohen, Loreto Quintiliano, and Benedict Macri).

93. *New York Times*, May 13, 1949, May 19, 1949; *Brooklyn Eagle*, June 19, 1950.

94. *Brooklyn Eagle*, June 19, 1950; *New York Times*, December 10, 1952; *Long Island Star-Journal*, December 10, 1952.

95. *People against Macri* (testimonies of Samuel Blumenthal and Edward Weinberg) (KC).

96. Ibid. (statement of Judge Streit) (KC).

97. *New York Times*, March 4, 1952, March 8, 1952, December 13, 1952.

98. *Long Island Star-Journal*, January 13, 1953, May 3, 1954, October 26, 1957.

99. *New York Sun*, March 27, 1895 (thanks to Tom Hunt for this citation); Joseph Valachi, "The Real Thing" (unpublished manuscript), pp. 14–15, in Joseph Valachi Papers, Box 1, John F. Kennedy Presidential Library and Museum, Boston, MA.

100. *Queens Daily Star*, March 12, 1929.

101. *Improper Activities*, 6966–67 (testimony of Bernard Adelstein), 6691 (testimony of Robert Greene); *Brooklyn Eagle*, April 29, 1941; *United States v. International Brotherhood of Teamsters*, 998 F.2d 120 (2d Cir. 1993).

102. James B. Jacobs and Alex Hortis, "New York City as Organized Crime Fighter," *New York Law School Law Review* 42, nos. 3–4 (1998): 1069–92; *New York Times*, March 15, 1947, quoted in Jacobs, *Gotham Unbound*, pp. 80–95.

103. *Improper Activities*, 6746–47 (testimony of John Montesano).

104. Ibid.

105. Ibid., 6689 (testimony of Everett Doyle).

106. *Daily Argus*, July 17, 1941; *New York Times*, September 3, 1952, September 4, 1952; *Journal News*, August 25, 2002.

107. *Improper Activities*, 6693–94 (testimony of James Kelly), 6696–6701 (testimony of Everett Doyle), and 6714–15 (affidavit of Katherine Embree).

108. *Improper Activities*, 6700–6702 (testimony of Doyle).

109. Ibid.

110. Ibid.

111. Yonkers Police File on Homicide of John Acropolis, in Freedom of Information Law File on John Acropolis (copy in possession of author).

112. *Report from Chairman Maurice Hinchey to the New York State Assembly Environmental Committee on Organized Crime's Involvement in the Waste Hauling Industry* (Albany, NY: n.p., 1986), p. 17.

CHAPTER 5: THE MAFIA AND THE DRUG TRADE

1. Testimony of Charles Luciano in *People against Luciano* (N.Y. Ct. Spec. Sess. 1936), in Box 56, "Lucky" Luciano Closed Case Files, New York Municipal Archives, New York, NY (hereafter "NYMA"); Boylan Act, 1914 N.Y. Laws 1120 (1914); Harrison Narcotics Tax Act, 38 Stat. 785 (1914); *New York Times*, April 15, 1915, December 7, 1916.

2. *New York Times*, May 24, 1936, May 26, 1936.

3. *Time Magazine*, December 7, 1998. For example, an author writes: "Lucky was uninfluenced by any code of conduct, and certainly not by the so-called Sicilian Tradition. A trafficker in drugs and women, Luciano exploited cash sources that were frowned upon by his more uptight Sicilian conspirators." Mike La Sorte, "The Mafia Tradition, Camorra, Lucky Luciano" (October 2006), available at http://www.americanmafia.com/FeatureArticles364.html (accessed on July 9, 2013).

4. There has been little research on the American Mafia's role in the drug trade. As James Jacobs has observed, "Organized crime's involvement in drug dealing merits extensive study." James B. Jacobs with Christopher Panarella and Jay Worthington, *Busting the Mob: United States v. Cosa Nostra* (New York: New York University Press, 1994), p. 143. I am indebted to Philip Jenkins for highlighting the role of myth. Philip Jenkins, "Narcotics Trafficking and the American Mafia: The Myth of Internal Prohibition," *Crime, Law and Social Change* 18, no. 3 (1992): 303–18.

5. *The Godfather* (Paramount 1972) was based on the bestselling novel by Mario Puzo, *The Godfather* (New York: Penguin Books, 1969), pp. 303–309.

6. Peter Maas, *Underboss: Sammy the Bull Gravano's Story of Life in the Mafia* (New York: HarperCollins, 1997), p. 72.

7. Joseph Bonanno with Sergio Lalli, *A Man of Honor: The Autobiography of Joseph Bonanno* (New York: Simon and Schuster, 1983), pp. 149, 209.

8. *New York Times*, December 21, 1946, June 11, 1952.

9. Joseph Bonanno, *Man of Honor*, p. 209; Bill Bonanno, *Bound by Honor: A Mafioso's Story* (New York: St. Martin's Press, 1999), p. 56.

10. *Hearings before the Permanent Subcommittee on Investigations of the Committee on Government Affairs: Organized Crime: 25 Years After Valachi*, Senate, 100th Cong., 2d. Sess. (1988), 92–93, 548 (testimony of Angelo Lonardo).

11. Martin A. Gosch and Richard Hammer, *The Last Testament of Lucky Luciano* (Boston: Little, Brown, 1974), pp. 358–59.

12. Bonanno, *Man of Honor*, pp. 209–10.

13. Leroy Street, *I Was a Drug Addict* (New Rochelle, NY: Arlington House, 1953), pp. 13, 30.

14. David F. Musto, *The American Disease: Origins of Narcotic Control* (New Haven, CT: Yale University Press, 1973), pp. 3, 102–106.

15. Malcolm Delevinge, "Some International Aspects of the Problem of Drug Addiction," *British Journal of Inebriety* 32 (1935): 149, quoted in Richard Davenport-Hines, *The Pursuit of Oblivion: A Global History of Narcotics, 1500–2000* (New York: W. W. Norton, 2001), pp. 252–53.

16. Musto, *American Disease*, pp. 59–62, 151–63.

17. Legge 18 Febbraio 1923, N. 396 9 (GU N. 053 DEL 05/03/1923). Measures for the Suppression of the Abusive Trade of Poisonous Substances Having Stupefying Action. Published in the *Official Gazette of the Italian Republic*, no. 53 (March 5, 1923). I thank Professor Liliana Leone of Rome, Italy, for this reference.

18. *New York Times*, December 19, 1928, April 25, 1931, October 20, 1951; Elias Eliopoulos, New York Major Violator No. 63, in Box 175, Subject Files of the Bureau of Narcotics and Dangerous Drugs, 1916–1970, Record Group 170, National Archives and Records Administration, College Park, MD (hereafter "NARA College Park").

19. Carolyn Rothstein, *Now I'll Tell* (New York: Vintage Press, 1934), p. 172.

20. *New York Times*, December 11, 1928, December 22, 1928, March 6, 1929; Report on Joseph A. Doto, July 11, 1945, in FBI Freedom of Information Act File (hereafter "FOIA") of Joseph A. Doto (a.k.a. Joe Adonis) (copy in possession of author).

21. Alan A. Block, "The Snowman Cometh: Coke in Progressive New York," *Criminology* 17, no. 1 (1979): 75–99. This is not to suggest that all these Italian traffickers were affiliated with a Mafia family. However, the level of organization, and the presence of traffickers like Waxey Gordon, who worked with *mafiosi*, suggests some were

connected. See pp. 90–91. Additionally, as we have seen previously, the movement of Italian criminals into a field portended the Mafia's movement into it.

22. Trial transcripts in *People against Ciro Terranova*, Case No. 2472 (N.Y. Ct. Gen. Sess. 1918) and *People against Alessandro Vollero*, Case No. 226 (N.Y. Ct. App. 1918), cited in David Critchley, *The Origin of Organized Crime in America: The New York City Mafia, 1891–1931* (New York: Routledge Press, 2009), pp. 121, 277 nn. 150–55.

23. *New York Times*, January 25, 1917; oral history of Leroy Street (1980), quoted in David Courtwright, Herman Joseph, and Don Des Jarlais, *Addicts Who Survived: An Oral History of Narcotic Use in America before 1965* (Knoxville: University of Tennessee Press, 2012), p. 290. Cassette tapes of the oral histories by Courtwright, Joseph, and Des Jarlais are stored at the Columbia Oral History Center, New York, NY (hereafter "COHC").

24. Oral history of Charlie (1980), p. 186; Jack (1980), p. 110; Eddie (1980), p. 142; Curtis (1980), p. 192; Mel (1980), p. 88, all quoted in Courtwright, Joseph, and Des Jarlais, *Addicts Who Survived*.

25. Name Files of Suspected Narcotics Traffickers, 1923–1954, RG 59 (NARA College Park).

26. File of Vincenzo Di Stefano in Box 4, RG 59 (NARA College Park); FBN entries on Joseph Marino and Giuseppe Failla, in Wash. Confidential List, June 1, 1936, in Box 175, RG 170 (NARA College Park); Passport, Confidential Note, April 13, 1933, and Letter of U.S. Embassy in France, November 18, 1937, in File of Mariana Marsalisi, in Box 13, RG 59 (NARA College Park); FBN entries for Luigi Alabiso, Frank Caruso, and Mariano Marsalisi in "Washington Confidential List, March 15, 1932, July 1, 1933, & June 1, 1936," in Box 175, RG 170 (NARA College Park).

27. For examples of his East Harlem investigations, see FBN agent Max Roder's journal entries for January 28, February 1, 4–5, and 9, August 16 and 19, November 10, 21–22, and 29, 1938, in Journals of FBN Agent Max Roder, 1931–1959, Special Collections, Hesburgh Library, University of Notre Dame, South Bend, IN (hereafter "Roder Journals"). For examples of Little Italy investigations, see Roder journal entries for January 2–4 and 26, February 5–6 and 9–10, April 10, 16–17, and 23–26, 1940, Roder Journals; New York State Crime Commission, *Public Hearing (no. 4)* (November 1952), 216–17 (testimony of George White). For entries on Tramaglino and Marone, see Roder journal entries for October 26, 1940, November 2, and November 18, 1940, Roder Journals.

28. Report of Ernest Gentry to Major Garland Williams, January 2, 1941, in Box 1, George White Papers, Department of Special Collections, Stanford University, Stanford, CA.

29. FBN Binder for District No. 2, New York, NY, February 15, 1940, in Box 175, RG 170 (NARA).

30. FBI Airtel on Armone, July 2, 1959, in FBI FOIA File on Stephen Armone (copy in possession of author).

31. FBI Report on Ormento, December 26, 1957, in FBI FOIA File on John Ormento (copy in possession of author); FBN entry for Ormento, in International List of Persons Known to be or Suspected of Being Engaged in the Illicit Traffic in Narcotic Drugs, September 25, 1953, in Box 175, RG 170 (NARA College Park); Statement of Thomas Pennochio, February 3, 1936, in Box 34, "Lucky" Luciano Closed Case Files (NYMA); *New York Times*, October 7, 1938, June 13, 1939; *Public Hearing (no.4)*, 216–17 (testimony of White); FBI Record No. 269 969, April 1, 1987, in FBI FOIA File on Anthony Corallo (copy in possession of author); *New York Times*, August 16, 1957.

32. *New York Times*, January 25, 29, 30, 1934, February 2, 1934, October 19, 1937. For Rao's background, see FBN entry on Joseph Rao, in International List of Persons Known to be or Suspected of Being Engaged in the Illicit Traffic in Narcotic Drugs, February 15, 1940, in Box 175, RG 170 (NARA College Park).

33. Nicolo Gentile, *Vita di Capomafia* (Rome: Editori Riuniti, 1963), pp. 37, 42–45, 112–13; Momenta Sera (Rome), September 5, 1951, in Charles Luciano File in Box 12, RG 59 (NARA College Park).

34. Entry for Charles La Gaipa, No. 117, FBN, New York Major Violator, February 15, 1940, in Box 175, RG 170 (NARA College Park); entry for Calogero La Gaipa, in FBN's Washington Confidential List, June 1, 1936, in Box 175, RG 170 (NARA College Park); Gentile, *Vita di Capomafia*, pp. 150–53; *New Orleans Times-Picayune*, October 7 and 10, 1937, May 17, 1939; Critchley, *Origin of Organized Crime*, pp. 168, 294.

35. Oral history of Jack (1980), quoted in Courtwright, Joseph, and Des Jarlais, *Addicts Who Survived*, p. 111; United State Treasury Department, *Federal Bureau of Narcotics, Traffic in Opium and Other Dangerous Drugs for the Year Ended December 31, 1940* (Washington, DC: GPO, 1941), pp. 19–20.

36. Brief of Case Report Identified as SE-199-NY:S:4997-Helmuth Hartmann, et. al., in Box 1, George White Papers, Department of Special Collections, Stanford University, Stanford, CA.

37. *New York Times*, March 27, 1945, December 20, 1946, April 11, 1947.

38. *New York Times*, August 18, 1950, November 26, 1957.

39. Oral history of Arthur (October 31, 1980), quoted in Courtwright, Joseph, and Des Jarlais, *Addicts Who Survived*, p. 156.

40. FBI Report on Vincent Papa, March 23, 1978, in FBI FOIA File on Vincent Papa (copy in possession of author); State Commission of Investigation, *Narcotics Law Enforcement in New York City* (1972), p. 28; Report on Percent of Purity of Heroin Seized in Various Areas, 1949, in Box 46, RG 170 (NARA College Park).

41. Oral history of Abe D. (May 9, 1980) (COHC); oral history of Mel (July 3, 1980), p. 88, and Al (1980), quoted in Courtwright, Joseph, and Des Jarlais, *Addicts Who Survived*, p. 98.

42. *Hearings before the Permanent Subcommittee on Investigations of the Committee on Government Operations: Organized Crime and the Illicit Traffic in Narcotics*, Senate, 88th Cong., 1st Sess. (1963), 873 (testimony of Martin Pera).

43. FBN entry on Marseille Traffickers, No. 294, in Washington Confidential List, December 1, 1934, in Box 175, RG 170 (NARA College Park).

44. Oral history of Ralph Salerno (December 10, 1982), quoted in Courtwright, Joseph, and Des Jarlais, *Addicts Who Survived*, p. 201; *Hearings before the Permanent Subcommittee on Investigations of the Committee on Government Operations: Organized Crime and the Illicit Traffic in Narcotics*, 872–75 (testimony of Martin Pera).

45. See generally Name Files of Suspected Narcotics Traffickers, RG 59 (NARA College Park).

46. Oral history of Ralph Salerno (December 10, 1982), quoted in Courtwright, Joseph, and Des Jarlais, *Addicts Who Survived*, pp. 201–202.

47. Frank Lucas with Aliya S. King, *Original Gangster: The Real Life Story of One of America's Most Notorious Drug Lords* (New York: St. Martin's Press, 2010), pp. 133–53.

48. New York State Commission of Investigation, *Narcotics Law Enforcement*, p. 29.

49. Maurice Helbrant, *Narcotic Agent* (New York: Arno Press, 1953), p. 93.

50. Charles Siragusa, *The Trail of the Poppy: Behind the Mask of the Mafia* (Englewood Cliffs, NJ: Prentice-Hall, 1966), pp. 65–66, 79–80; Mayor's Committee on City Planning, *East Harlem Community Study* (New York: n.p., 1937), pp. 16–17.

51. FBN Case Report Identified as SE-199-NY:S:4997-Helmuth Hartmann, et. al., in Box 1, George White Papers, Department of Special Collections, Stanford University, Stanford, CA.

52. *New York Times*, December 20, 1946, April 9, 1947, April 11, 1947. In the late 1960s, police dubbed traffickers from the Genovese Family the "Pleasant Avenue Crew." David Durk and Ira Silverman, *The Pleasant Avenue Connection* (New York: Harper & Row, 1976).

53. Roder journal entries for March 27 and 29, April 10, 1946, and March 2, 4–5, 8–10, and 17, 1948, Roder Journals; FBN entries for John Ormento and Salvatore

Santoro, International List of Persons Known to Be or Suspected of Being Engaged in the Illicit Traffic in Narcotic Drugs, June 26, 1964, in Box 48, Subject Files of the Bureau of Narcotics and Dangerous Drugs, RG 170 (NARA College Park).

54. Testimony of John T. Cusack in *Joint Legislative Committee on Government Operations Regarding a Meeting at Apalachin, New York, November 14, 1957*, in FBI FOIA File on the Apalachin Meeting (copy in possession of author); FBI Report on Ormento, December 26, 1957, in FBI FOIA File on John Ormento (copy in possession of author).

55. Eric C. Schneider, *Smack: Heroin and the American City* (Philadelphia: University of Pennsylvania Press, 2011), p. 1; New York State Commission of Investigation, *Narcotics Law Enforcement*, p. 30; *Hearings before the Permanent Subcommittee on Investigations of the Committee on Government Operations: Organized Crime and the Illicit Traffic in Narcotics*, 877 (testimony of Martin Pera), 911–916 and Exhibit 3 (joint testimonies of Daniel Casey, George Belk, and Charles Ward).

56. FBN entries of James Roberts, Harold Jones, and Robert Frierson, in FBN's Suspected Negro Narcotic Traffickers, in Box 175, RG 170 (NARA College Park); William J. Spillard, *Needle in a Haystack: The Exciting Adventures of a Federal Narcotic Agent* (New York: McGraw-Hill, 1945), pp. 104–105, 122–26; Letter, Re: Vincent Gigante, March 8, 1960, in Federal Bureau of Prisons FOIA File on Vincent Gigante (copy in possession of author).

57. Oral history of Curtis (1980), quoted in Courtwright, Joseph, and Des Jarlais, *Addicts Who Survived*, p. 192.

58. Mayme Johnson and Karen E. Quinones Miller, *Harlem Godfather: The Rap on My Husband Ellsworth "Bumpy" Johnson* (Philadelphia: Oshun, 2008), p. 180.

59. Oral history of Ralph Salerno (December 10, 1982), quoted in Courtwright, Joseph, and Des Jarlais, *Addicts Who Survived*, pp. 201–202.

60. Durk and Silverman, *Pleasant Avenue Connection*, p. 49.

61. Entries for George Anderson and Herbert Drumgold in FBN's National List of Persons Known to Be or Suspected of Being Engaged in the Illicit Traffic in Narcotic Drugs, September 23, 1953, in Box 175, RG 170 (NARA College Park); Johnson, *Harlem Godfather*, p. 180.

62. Lucas, *Original Gangster*, p. 67.

63. FBI FOIA File on Ellsworth Johnson (copy in possession of author); Johnson, *Harlem Godfather*, pp. 22–23; John Johnson, *Fact Not Fiction in Harlem* (Glen Cove, NY: n.p., 1980), pp. 101–106; *New York Times*, July 12, 1968.

64. Claude Brown, *Manchild in the Promised Land* (New York: Signet Books, 1965), pp. 179–80; Welfare Council of New York City, *The Menace of Narcotics to the*

Children of New York: A Plan to Eradicate the Evil, Interim Report (New York: n.p., August 1951), pp. 8–13.

65. Oral history of Low (1981), quoted in Courtwright, Joseph, and Des Jarlais, *Addicts Who Survived*, p. 226.

66. Piri Thomas, *Down These Mean Streets* (New York: Vintage Books, 1997), pp. 115–16, 200–201.

67. Oral History of Ralph Salerno (December 10, 1982), quoted in Courtwright, Joseph, and Des Jarlais, *Addicts Who Survived*, p. 203.

68. Salvatore Mondello, *A Sicilian in East Harlem* (Youngstown, NY: Cambria Press, 2005), pp. 63–64.

69. Oral history of Dom Ambruzzi, quoted in Jeremy Larner, ed., *Addict in the Street* (New York: Penguin, 1966), pp. 42–44, 50–53.

70. Oral history of Eddie (1980), quoted in Courtwright, Joseph, and Des Jarlais, *Addicts Who Survived*, p. 142; Orsi, *Madonna of 115th Street*, p. 186; Eric C. Schneider, *Vampires, Dragons, and Egyptian Kings: Youth Gangs in Postwar New York* (Princeton, NJ: Princeton University Press, 1999), pp. 179–80, 230.

71. *Hearings before the Special Committee to Investigate Organized Crime in Interstate Commerce: Investigation of Organized Crime: Part 14*, Senate, 82nd Cong., 1st Sess. (1951), 356 (testimony of Charles Siragusa).

72. Kathryn Meyer and Terry Parssinen, *Webs of Smoke: Smugglers, Warlords, Spies, and the History of the International Drug Trade* (New York: Rowman and Littlefield, 2002), pp. 284–85; Papers of Harry Anslinger, Special Collections, Pennsylvania State University, College Station, PA.

73. Louis J. Freeh, *My FBI: Bringing Down the Mafia, Investigating Bill Clinton, and Fighting the War on Terror* (New York: St. Martin's Press, 2005), pp. 128–29.

74. Claire Sterling, *Octopus: How the Long Reach of the Sicilian Mafia Controls the Global Narcotics Trade* (New York: Simon and Schuster, 1990) (emphasis added), p. 85.

75. Gil Reavill, *Mafia Summit: J. Edgar Hoover, the Kennedy Brothers, and the Meeting That Unmasked the Mob* (New York: St. Martin's Press, 2013), pp. 82–83, 265.

76. Tim Shawcross and Martin Young, *Men of Honour: The Confessions of Tomasso Buscetta* (New York: HarperCollins, 1987); Pino Arlacchi, *Addio Cosa nostra: La vita di Tommaso Buscetta* (Milan, IT: Rizzoli, 1994). The so-called Pizza Connection from Sicily was not established until the mid-1970s. Jacobs, *Busting the Mob*, pp. 129–66. Recognizing this time lag after the *Hotel et des Palmes* 1957 gathering, Freeh offers an unconvincing explanation: "Other, equally infamous, meetings in Sicily and New York would be needed to nail things down. Still, this was the meeting that began to lay the framework for what would finally become known as the Pizza Connection." Freeh, *My FBI*, p. 129.

77. *Hearings before the Permanent Subcommittee on Investigations of the Committee on Government Operations: Organized Crime and the Illicit Traffic in Narcotics*, Exhibit 3 (joint testimonies of Daniel Casey, George Belk, and Charles Ward).

78. Government brief in *United States v. Reina*, Case No. 24321 (2d Cir. 1957), p. 24, in RG 276, United States Courts of Appeal, National Archives and Records Administration, New York, NY (hereafter "NARA New York").

79. This chart is based on: *United States v. Bentvena*, 319 F.2d 916 (2d Cir. 1963); *United States v. Reina*, 242 F.2d 302 (2d Cir. 1957); Appellate Briefs in *United States v. Agueci*, Case No. 27466 (2d Cir. 1962) and *United States v. Reina*, Case No. 24321 (2d Cir. 1957), in RG 276 (NARA New York); Maas, *Valachi Papers*, pp. 239–42; Gentile, *Vita di Capomafia*, pp. 151–52; *New Orleans Times-Picayune*, May 4, 1938.

80. Valachi detailed this scheme, for which he was never caught, in Maas, *Valachi Papers*, pp. 239–42.

81. Robin Moore, *The French Connection: The World's Most Crucial Narcotics Investigation* (Boston: Little, Brown, 1969); *The French Connection* (Twentieth Century Fox 1971).

82. FBN entry for Pasquale Fuca in FBN's Revision of International List Book, at New York, June 24, 1964, in Box 48, RG 170 (NARA College Park); Moore, *French Connection*, pp. 62–73.

83. Royal Canadian Mounted Police (hereafter "RCMP") reports of March 23, 1926, March 12, 1930, and March 25, 1931, cited in Antonio Nicaso, *Rocco Perri: The Story of Canada's Most Notorious Bootlegger* (Toronto: John Wiley, 2004), pp. 217–20.

84. Oral history of Ralph Salerno (December 10, 1982) (COHC).

85. RCMP entries for Frank Controni, Joseph Controni, and Vito Agueci in Revision of International List Book, at New York, June 24, 1964, in Box 48, RG 170 (NARA College Park).

86. Welfare Council, *Menace of Narcotics*, p. 14; *Committee on Government Operations, Permanent Subcommittee on Investigations: Organized Crime and the Illicit Traffic in Narcotics: Report*, Senate, 89th Cong., 1st Sess. (1965), 69; *Hearings before the Permanent Subcommittee on Investigations of the Committee on Government Operations: Organized Crime and the Illicit Traffic in Narcotics*, 270–71, 297 (testimony of Valachi).

87. Gentile, *Vita di Capomafia*, p. 150.

88. Maas, *Valachi Papers*, p. 222.

89. *New York Times*, September 26, 1931.

90. *United States v. Bentvena*, 319 F.2d 916 (2d Cir. 1963).

91. Joseph D. Pistone, *Donnie Brasco: My Undercover Life in the Mafia* (New York: Signet, 1989), p. 226.

92. Bill Bonanno, *Bound by Honor*, p. 78; *New York Times*, July 30, 1979, cited in David Amoruso, "The Story of Carmine Galante," November 24, 2010, available at Gangsters, Inc., http://gangstersinc.ning.com/profiles/blogs/death-in-the-afternoon-the (accessed on July 9, 2013).

93. FBI Memo, Natale Evola, January 29, 1958, in FBI FOIA File on Natale Evola (copy in possession of author); Joe Bonanno, *Man of Honor*, p. 142; Bill Bonanno, *The Last Testament of Bill Bonanno*, p. 70.

94. *Washington Post*, March 1, 1930; *New York Times*, February 20, 1930, March 1, 1930; Jill Jonnes, *Hep-Cats, Narcs, and Pipe Dreams: A History of America's Romance with Illegal Drugs* (Baltimore: Johns Hopkins University Press, 1999), p. 84.

95. Jack Kelly, *On the Street* (Chicago: Henry Regnery Co., 1974), p. 49; Tom Tripodi, *Crusade: Undercover against the Mafia and KGB* (New York: Brassey's, 1993), p. 25.

96. Kelly, *On the Street*, p. 49.

97. *New York Times*, June 15, 1951, September 26, 1951; Commission to Investigate Allegations of Police Corruption, *Commission Report* (New York: n.p., 1972), p. 92 (hereafter "Knapp Commission Report").

98. Oral history of Arthur (October 18, 1980), quoted in Courtwright, Joseph, and Des Jarlais, *Addicts Who Survived*, p. 156; Tripodi, *Crusade*, p. 161; Peter Maas, *Serpico* (New York: Viking Press, 1973), p. 156; Knapp Commission Report, p. 94.

99. Patrick V. Murphy, *Commissioner: A View from the Top of American Law Enforcement* (New York: Simon & Schuster, 1977), p. 245; FBI Report, Vincent Papa, March 23, 1978, in FBI FOIA File on Vincent Papa (copy in possession of author).

100. *Hearings before the Permanent Subcommittee on Investigations of the Committee on Government Operations: Organized Crime and the Illicit Traffic in Narcotics*, 319–20 (testimony of Valachi).

101. Wiretap conversation of Pussy Russo, quoted in Joseph Volz and Peter J. Bridge, eds., *The Mafia Talks* (Greenwich, CT: Fawcett, 1969), p. 98.

102. Tramunti report, October 23, 1973, in FBI FOIA File on Carmine Tramunti (copy in possession of author); Joseph O'Brien and Andris Kurins, *Boss of Bosses: The FBI and Paul Castellano* (New York: Dell, 1991), p. 153; Nicholas Pileggi, *Wise Guy: Life in a Mafia Family* (New York: Pocket Books 1985), p. 193.

103. Bill Bonanno, *Last Testament of Bill Bonanno*, p. 184.

104. Roder journal entries for October 21, 1942, February 4, 1944, October 30–31, 1944, Roder Journals; Maas, *Valachi Papers*, pp. 234–38; Gentile, *Vita di Capomafia*, pp. 149–50; Musto, *American Disease*, p. 201.

105. The table is based on the following sources: (1) Federal Bureau of Prisons'

responses to FOIA requests (copies in possession of author) (hereafter "BOP FOIA"); (2) FBI responses to FOIA requests (copies in possession of author) (hereafter "FBI FOIA"); (3) *New York Times* articles (hereafter "*New York Times*"); (4) *Hearings before the Permanent Subcommittee on Investigations of the Committee on Government Operations: Organized Crime and the Illicit Traffic in Narcotics*, Senate, 88th Cong., 1st Sess. (1963); and (5) FBN reports for District 2, New York, and the FBN's International List of Persons Known to Be or Suspected of Being Engaged in the Illicit Traffic in Narcotic Drugs, in Boxes 48 and 175, RG 170 (NARA College Park). This includes the following FBN lists: February 15, 1940, September 25, 1953, June 30, 1956, and June 26, 1964 (hereafter "FBN").

CHAPTER 6: THE MOB NIGHTLIFE

1. *New York Post*, September 6, 1946; Toni Carroll Terman, *Copacabana Sexcapades and Other Stories* (West Conshohocken, PA: Infinity Publishing, 2005), pp. 34–35.

2. *Hearings before the Permanent Subcommittee on Investigations of the Committee on Government Operations: Organized Crime and the Illicit Traffic in Narcotics*, Senate, 88th Cong., 1st Sess. (1963), 365 (testimony of Joseph Valachi); George Wolf with Joseph DiMona, *Frank Costello: Prime Minister of the Underworld* (Great Britain: Hodder & Stoughton Ltd., 1975), pp. 181–82; Mickey Podell-Raber with Charles Pignone, *The Copa: Jules Podell and the Hottest Club North of Havana* (New York: HarperCollins, 2007), pp. 34–42; FBI Memorandum on Frank Costello, November 24, 1944, in FBI Freedom of Information Act File (hereafter "FBI FOIA") on Frank Costello (copy in possession of author).

3. Stephen Fox, *Blood and Power: Organized Crime in Twentieth-Century America* (New York: William Morrow, 1989), pp. 78–87.

4. Vincent Teresa with Thomas C. Renner, *My Life in the Mafia* (New York: Doubleday, 1973), p. 118.

5. United States Constitution, Amendment XXI; *State Board of Equalization of California v. Young's Market Co.*, 299 U.S. 59 (1936).

6. New York State Liquor Authority, *ABC News* 8, no. 8 (March 1941), p. 20.

7. Commission to Investigate Allegations of Police Corruption and the City's Anti-Corruption Procedures, *Commission Report* (New York: n.p., 1972), p. 133 (hereafter "Knapp Commission Report").

8. Eddie Condon, *We Called It Music: A Generation of Jazz* (New York: Da Capo Press, 1992), pp. 123–25; FBI Memorandum, Owen Vincent Madden, May 15, 1953, in

FBI FOIA file on Owen Vincent Madden (copy in possession of author); Marion Moore Day and Francis "Doll" Thomas, quoted in Jeff Kisseloff, *You Must Remember This: An Oral History of Manhattan from the 1890s to World War II* (New York: Schocken Books, 1989), pp. 292, 310; Teddy Wilson, *Teddy Wilson Talks Jazz* (New York: Continuum, 1996), p. 16; Arnold Shaw, *52nd Street: The Street of Jazz* (New York: Da Capo Press, 1971), p. 66.

9. George Shearing with Alyn Shipton, *Lullaby of Birdland* (New York: Continuum, 2004), p. 84; Shaw, *52nd Street*, p. 66; Ralph Blumenthal, *Stork Club: America's Most Famous Nightspot and the Lost World of Café Society* (New York: Little, Brown, 2000), pp. 78–79; FBI Report, Francisca Castiglia, alias Frank Costello, January 8, 1959, reproduced in Charlie Carr, ed., *New York Police Files on the Mafia* (New York: Hosehead Productions, 2012), p. 54; Michael Franzese and Dara Matera, *Quitting the Mob: How the "Yuppie Don" Left the Mafia and Lived to Tell His Story* (New York: HarperCollins, 1992), p. 18.

10. Pops Foster with Tom Stoddard, *The Autobiography of Pops Foster: New Orleans Jazzman* (San Francisco: Backbeat Books, 2005), p. 170; Mezz Mezzrow, *Really the Blues* (New York: Citadel, 2001), p. 274; Louis Armstrong, quoted in Terry Teachout, *Pops: A Life of Louis Armstrong* (New York: Houghton Mifflin Harcourt, 2009), pp. 162–65, 194–95, 206–11.

11. FBI Airtel, May 9, 1962, Michelino Clemente, in Records of the Federal Bureau of Investigation, Record Group 65 (hereafter "NARA College Park"); Adrian Humphreys, *The Weasel: A Double Life in the Mob* (New York: Wiley, 2011), pp. 48–49; Terman, *Copacabana Sexcapades*, p. 11.

12. FBI Report, Anti-Racketeering, January 9, 1962, and FBI Report, Frank Bongiorno, November 30, 1961, both in RG 65 (NARA College Park); George Raft, quoted in Lewis Yablonsky, *George Raft* (New York: McGraw-Hill, 1974), pp. 29, 129.

13. FBI Memorandum, Francis Sinatra, September 29, 1950, in FBI FOIA file on Frank Sinatra (copy in possession of author); FBI Report, Frank Sinatra, July 20, 1973, in FBI FOIA file on Angelo DeCarlo (copy in possession of author); FBI Memorandum Re: Santo Trafficante Jr., March 9, 1967, in RG 65 (NARA College Park).

14. J. Randy Taraborrelli, *Sinatra: Behind the Legend* (New York: Carol, 1997), pp. 64, 88–89, 271–72, 392, citing *American Mercury* 72, no. 332 (August 1951): 29–36; *Hearings before the House Select Committee on Crime: Organized Crime in Sports*, House of Representatives, 92nd Cong., 2d. Sess. (1973), 731–55, 818–35, 1105–27 (testimonies of Joseph Barboza and Charles Carson).

15. Teresa, *My Life in the Mafia*, p. 123; George Jacobs and William Stadiem, *Mr. S: My Life with Frank Sinatra* (New York: HarperCollins, 2003), p. 82; Tina Sinatra, *My Father's Daughter: A Memoir* (New York: Simon and Schuster, 2000), p. 73.

16. *Hearings before a Subcommittee of the Committee on Interstate Commerce: Legalizing Transportation of Prize-Fight Films*, Senate, 67th Cong., 1st Sess. (1939); State of New York, *Report of the Joint Legislative Committee on Professional Boxing* (Albany, NY: n.p., 1963), pp. 11–13; Fox, *Blood and Power*, pp. 351–57; *Professional Boxing: Hearings before the Subcommittee on Antitrust and Monopoly of the Committee on the Judiciary: Part 3*, Senate, 87th Cong., 1st Sess. (1961), 1297–98 (testimony of Tommy Loughran) ("Senate Boxing Hearings").

17. New York State Crime Commission, *Public Hearings (no. 5)* (New York: n.p., 1953), 3667–70 (testimony of F. X. McQuade).

18. Ibid., 1343 (testimony of Melvin Krulewitch), 1394 (testimony of Abe Greene).

19. Senate Boxing Hearings, 104–13 (testimony of Frank Marrone).

20. Ibid., 62 (testimony of Lew Burston).

21. *Utica Observer-Dispatch*, August 10, 1958; FBI Report, Joseph Anthony Straci, RG 65 (NARA College Park).

22. *Life*, May 26, 1952; *Hearings before the Special Committee to Investigate Organized Crime in Interstate Commerce: Part 11*, Senate, 82nd Cong., 1st Sess. (1950), 261 (testimony of William Weisberg); Senate Boxing Hearings, 91, 104–11 (testimonies of Harry Stromberg and Frank Marrone).

23. Don Jordan, quoted in Peter Heller, *"In this Corner . . . !" 42 World Champions Tell Their Story* (New York: De Capo Press, 1994), p. 362.

24. Rocky Graziano, *Somebody up There Likes Me: The Story of My Life until Today* (New York: Simon & Schuster, 1955), pp. 160–62; Jake La Motta, *Raging Bull: My Story* (Englewood Cliffs, NJ: Prentice-Hall, 1970), p. 80; Marty Pomerantz, quoted in Allen Bodner, *When Boxing Was a Jewish Sport* (Westport, CT: Praeger, 1997), p. 37.

25. Danny Kapilow, quoted in Bodner, *When Boxing Was a Jewish Sport*, p. 135; Senate Boxing Hearings, 7–19 (testimony of Jake La Motta); La Motta, *Raging Bull*, pp. 159–62; *Brooklyn Eagle*, January 22, 1948.

26. Kapilow, quoted in Bodner, *When Boxing Was a Jewish Sport*, p. 136; Senate Boxing Hearings, 45–46 (testimony of Joe Louis).

27. *International Boxing Club of New York, Inc. v. United States*, 358 U.S. 242 (1959); Senate Boxing Hearings, 1394 (testimony of Abe Greene).

28. Kevin Mitchell, *Jacobs Beach: The Mob, the Fights, the Fifties* (New York: Pegasus Books, 2010), pp. 47–52.

29. *Life*, June 17, 1946, May 26, 1952; State of New York, *Report of the Joint Legislative Committee on Professional Boxing* (1963), p. 26.

30. Ibid., 80; Senate Boxing Hearings, 76 (testimony of Sam Richman), 570 (testi-

mony of James Norris); FBN File, Boxers and Managers, August 22, 1956, in Box 148, RG 170 (NARA College Park).

31. New York State Athletic Commission, *In the Matter of an Inquiry into Alleged Irregularities in the Conduct of Boxing* (December 12, 1955), copy in New York State Library, Albany, NY.

32. *New York Times*, September 20, 1953; *Brooklyn Eagle*, June 27, 1954; Angelo Dundee, *My View from the Corner: A Life in Boxing* (New York: McGraw Hill, 2008), p. 36.

33. *Brooklyn Eagle*, January 28, 1947; *Life*, February 10, 1947.

34. Senate Boxing Hearings, 114–15 (testimony of James P. McShane); *Hearings before the Permanent Subcommittee on Investigations of the Committee on Government Operations: Organized Crime and the Illicit Traffic in Narcotics*, 274 (testimony of Valachi); *Corruption in Professional Boxing: Hearings before the Permanent Subcommittee on Investigations of the Committee on Government Affairs*, Senate, 102nd Cong., 2d Sess. (1992), 97 (testimony of Michael Franzese); *Binghamton Press*, January 27, 1947; *Brooklyn Eagle*, January 28, 1947.

35. *New York Times*, February 11, 1947; Mitchell, *Jacobs Beach*, pp. 1–3.

36. *International Boxing Club of New York, Inc. v. United States*, 358 U.S. 242 (1959).

37. Senate Boxing Hearings, 302, 337 (testimony of Truman Gibson), 551–59 (testimony of Norris).

38. *New York Times*, July 25, 1958, October 31, 1959.

39. *International Boxing Club of New York, Inc. v. United States*, 358 U.S. at 246.

40. *New York Times*, September 23, 1959, May 31, 1961.

41. George Chauncey, *Gay New York: Gender, Urban Culture, and the Making of the Gay Male World, 1890–1940* (New York: Basic Books, 1995), pp. 336–44; Knapp Commission Report, pp. 133–42. Thanks to Lisa Davis and the website http://bitter queen.typepad.com for identifying FBI documents and other primary sources on gay bars cited in this chapter.

42. Stanley Walker, *The Night Club Era* (New York: Frederick A. Stokes, 1933), pp. 215–16; *New York Times*, November 30, 1967, March 23, 1970, August 1, 1977; Steve Ostrow, *Live at the Continental: The Inside Story of the World-Famous Continental Baths; Book One: Bette, Buns and Balls* (Bloomington, IN: Xlibris, 2007), pp. 123–24; interview of John Doe by John O'Brien (ca. 1984), tape AC0375 in ONE National Gay and Lesbian Archives, Los Angeles, CA.

43. Chauncey, *Gay New York*, pp. 72–86, 327, 450 n. 74.

44. FBI Report, David Petillo, August 30, 1968, and FBI Report, David Petillo,

September 27, 1963, both available at: http://bitterqueen.typepad.com/friends_of_ours/2010/12/the-fbi-files-david-petillo-did-it-in-drag.html (accessed May 21, 2013); *Life*, February 28, 1969; Martin Duberman, *Stonewall* (New York: Dutton, 1993), pp. 183–84, 297 n. 15; Donald Goddard, *Joey* (New York: Harper and Row, 1974), pp. 317, 333, 347–48; William Hoffman and Lake Headley, *Contract Killer: The Explosive Story of the Mafia's Most Notorious Hitman Donald "Tony The Greek" Frankos* (New York: Thunder's Mouth, 1993), p. 201.

45. *New York Times*, December 1, 1934, June 20, 1953; "Queer Doings Net Suspension for Vill. Clubs," *Billboard*, December 2, 1944; Buddy Kent and Gail, quoted in Lisa E. Davis, "Back in Buddy's Day: Drags Original Lesbians Reflect on Their Heyday," Xtra.ca, March 1, 2006, available at http://www.extra.ca/public/printStory.aspx?AFF_TYPE=4&STORY_ID=1427 (accessed May 21, 2013); Tommye and John, quoted in Joe E. Jeffreys, "Who's No Lady? Excerpts from an Oral History of New York City's 82 Club," *New York Folklore* 14, nos. 1–2 (1993): 185–202; *Brooklyn Daily Eagle*, October 29, 1937; see promotional piece for Howdy Club at Lesbian Herstory Archives, Brooklyn, NY; Alan Bérubé, *Coming Out Under Fire: The History of Gay Men and Women in World War Two* (New York: Free Press, 1990), pp. 113–16; Thaddeus Russell, *A Renegade History of the United States* (New York: Free Press, 2010), pp. 234–35.

46. Postcard of Tony Pastor's Downtown (in possession of the author); "Queer Doings Net Suspension for Vill. Clubs"; *New York Times*, February 27, 1944, November 30, 1967; FBI Report, Activities of Top Hoodlums, October 15, 1959, in RG 65 (NARA College Park).

47. "Queer Doings Net Suspension for Vill. Clubs"; Condon, *We Called It Music*, p. 8; *New York Times*, March 18, 1967.

48. Jack Lait and Lee Mortimer, *U.S.A. Confidential* (New York: Crown, 1952), p. 314.

49. Bertie, quoted in *Alison Owings, Hey, Waitress! The USA from the other Side of the Tray* (Los Angeles: University of California Press, 2002), pp. 193–94.

50. Buddy Kent and Gail, quoted in Lisa E. Davis, "Back in Buddy's Day"; Lyn, quoted in Lillian Faderman, *Odd Girls and Twilight Lovers: A History of Lesbian Life in Twentieth-Century America* (New York: Penguin Books, 1992), pp. 127, 332 n. 19.

51. *Hearings before the Permanent Subcommittee on Investigations of the Committee on Government Operations: Organized Crime and the Illicit Traffic in Narcotics*, 291–92 (testimony of Valachi); Peter Maas, *The Valachi Papers* (New York: Perennial, 2003), p. 231; *New York Times*, June 20, 1953; Davis, "Back in Buddy's Day."

52. Terry Noel, quoted in Morgan Stevens, "Special Feature on Terry Noel," 2005,

available at http://www.queermusicheritage.us/fem-terrynoel.html (accessed May 21, 2013); Tommye and John, quoted in Jeffreys, "Who's No Lady?" pp. 185–202.

53. Maas, *Valachi Papers*, pp. 210–12; *New York Times*, June 20, 1953; Charles Scaglione Sr., *Camelot Lost* (Pittsburgh: RoseDog Books, 2009), pp. 52–53.

54. *New York Times*, December 17, 1963, February 14, 1965, October 16, 1966, November 30, 1967, January 8, 1970, August 1, 1977; R. Thomas Collins Jr., News-Walker: A Story for Sweeney (Fairfax, VA: RavensYard, 2002), pp. 119–27; *United States v. Ianniello*, 808 F.2d 184 (2d Cir. 1986); FBI Report on Salvatore Granello, March 26, 1970, in FBI file on Salvatore Granello in RG 65 (NARA College Park), available at http://bitterqueen.typepad.com/friends_of_ours/2012/09/fbi-files-mob-boss-vito-genovese-protected-serial-child-rapist-salvatore-sally-burns-granello.html (accessed on May 21, 2013) (hereafter "FBI Report on Granello"); *New York Times*, October 7, 1970.

55. *People v. DeCurtis*, 331 N.Y.S.2d 214 (N.Y. App. Div. 2d Dept. 1970); Collins, *NewsWalker*, p. 107; *New York Times*, October 7, 1970; Jon Roberts and Evan Wright, *American Desperado: My Life—From Mafia Soldier to Cocaine Cowboy to Secret Government Asset* (New York: Crown, 2011), p. 96; FBI Report on Granello. For other gay bars controlled by the Mafia in the 1950s and '60s, see Duberman, *Stonewall*, pp. 183, 297 n. 15.

56. Interview of Chuck Shaheen by Martin Duberman (1991), in Martin B. Duberman Papers, 1917–1997, in New York Public Library, New York, NY; interview of Mary Crawford by Alan Bérubé, February 17, 1983, available at http://www.glbthistory.org (accessed May 21, 2013).

57. Public Broadcasting System, *The Stonewall Uprising* (2010); Kent, quoted in "Back in Buddy's Day."

58. FBI Airtel, Mattachine Society, Inc., Internal Security, June 11, 1959, and FBI Airtel, Subject: Mattachine Society, June 19, 1959, both in FBI FOIA File on the Mattachine Society (copy in possession of author); *New York Times*, November 30, 1967.

59. Duberman, *Stonewall*, pp. 183–85, 297 n. 11; Chuck Shaheen, quoted in David Carter, *Stonewall: The Riots that Sparked the Gay Revolution* (New York: St. Martin's, 2005), pp. 68, 281 n. 19; Lucian K. Truscott IV, "Gay Pride History: The Real Mob at Stonewall," available at http://www.throughyourbody.com/gay-pride-history-the-real-mob-at-stonewall/ (accessed May 21, 2013).

60. Carter, *Stonewall*, pp. 131–37, 262–64; Lincoln Anderson, *Villager*, June 16–22, 2004; *New York Daily News*, July 6, 1969.

61. Ray "Sylvia Lee" Rivera and Morty Manford, quoted in Eric Marcus, *Making Gay History: The Half-Century Fight for Lesbian and Gay Equal Rights* (New York: HarperCollins, 2002), pp. 127–29; protest leaflet available at http://www.pbs.org/wgbh/americanexperience/features/primary-resources/stonewall-leaflet/ (accessed May 21, 2013).

CHAPTER 7: THE LIVES OF WISEGUYS

1. State of New York, *1915 New York State Census*, Philip Albeniza, Assembly District 2, New York, NY; FBI Report, Philip Joseph Albanese, May 16, 1958, in Records of the Federal Bureau of Investigation, Record Group 65, National Archives and Records Administration, College Park, MD (hereafter "NARA College Park").

2. *Yonkers Herald-Statesmen*, August 13, 1953, April 15, 1955.

3. *United States v. Philip Albanese*, 224 F.2d 879 (2d Cir. 1955); *Yonkers Herald-Statesmen*, October 6, 1954.

4. For an overview of early Mafia memoirs, see Thomas A. Firestone, "Mafia Memoirs: What They Tell Us about Organized Crime," *Journal of Contemporary Criminal Justice* 9, no. 3 (August 1993): 197–220.

5. Joshua B. Freeman, *Working-Class New York: Life and Labor since World War II* (New York: New Press, 2001), pp. 7–18; United States Department of Labor Statistics, *100 Years of U.S. Consumer Spending: Data for the Nation, New York City, and Boston* (Washington, DC: n.p., 2006), p. 22, available at http://www.bls.gov/opub/uscs/ (accessed August 25, 2013).

6. Luciano, quoted in *New York Times*, June 19, 1936.

7. Rocco Morelli, *Forgetta 'bout It: From Mafia to Ministry* (Orlando, FL: Bridge-Logos, 2007), p. 35.

8. *Organized Crime: 25 Years after Valachi: Hearings before the Permanent Subcommittee on Investigations of the Committee on Governmental Affairs*, Senate, 100th Cong., 2d Sess. (1988), 203 (testimony of Joseph Pistone); Joseph D. Pistone with Richard Woodley, *Donnie Brasco* (New York: Signet, 1997), pp. 141–42. For additional examples of why men joined the Mafia, see Firestone, "Mafia Memoirs," pp. 200–15.

9. *Organized Crime: 25 Years after Valachi*, 236 (testimony of Vincent Cafaro); Tony Napoli, *My Father, My Don: A Son's Journey from Organized Crime to Sobriety* (Silver Spring, MD: Beckham, 2008), p. 47; Willie Fopiano, *The Godson: A True-Life Account of 20 Years Inside the Mob* (New York: St. Martin's Press, 1993), p. 8.

10. Antonio Calderone, Pino Arlacchi, and Marc Romano, *Men of Dishonor: Inside the Sicilian Mafia* (New York: William Morrow, 1993), p. 67; Peter Maas, *Underboss: Sammy the Bull Gravano's Story of Life in the Mafia* (New York: Harper Perennial, 1999), p. 88.

11. Charles Siragusa, *The Trail of the Poppy, Behind the Mask of the Mafia* (Englewood Cliffs, NJ: Prentice-Hall, Inc., 1966), p. 66; Joseph Bonanno with Sergio Lalli, *A Man of Honor: The Autobiography of Joseph Bonanno* (New York: Simon and Schuster, 1983), p. 158.

12. Joseph Cantalupo and Thomas Renner, *Body Mike: An Unsparing Exposé by the Mafia Insider Who Turned on the Mob* (New York: Villard Books, 1990), p. 24; Joe Barboza, *Barboza* (New York: Dell Publishing, 1975), p. 103.

13. Dennis N. Griffin and Andrew DiDonato, *Surviving the Mob: A Street Soldier's Life inside the Gambino Crime Family* (Las Vegas, NV: Huntington Press, 2010), p. 11; *Organized Crime: 25 Years after Valachi*, 203–204 (testimony of Joseph Pistone).

14. Tables 7–1 and 7–3 are based on the New York Family charts in *Hearings before the Permanent Subcommittee on Investigations of the Committee on Government Operations: Organized Crime and the Illicit Traffic in Narcotics*, Senate, 88th Cong., 1st Sess. (1963). To be consistent with Table 7–2, I have narrowed the population to those 162 soldiers for whom reliable background information was available. The McClellan Committee's charts were based on arrest records and FBI and FBN intelligence files. The charts roughly reflect the primary activities of the soldiers. I have made a few minor adjustments to the data. To be consistent with chapter 5, I have limited the "narcotics" category to those actually convicted of a narcotics crime. In addition, I have supplemented the activities for two soldiers: Joseph Gallo was involved in vending machines, and Joe Valachi was involved in multiple activities.

15. FBI Record Sheets reprinted in Charlie Carr, ed., *New York Police Files on the Mafia* (New York: Hosehead Productions, 2012), pp. 52, 94, 176, 184, 280.

16. DiDonato, *Surviving the Mob*, p. 6.

17. Peter Maas, *The Valachi Papers* (New York: G. P. Putnam's Sons, 1968), pp. 93, 129, 227, 232.

18. Maas, *Underboss*, p. 289 ("Sammy at once confessed to participating, in one way or another, in eighteen or nineteen murders").

19. Clinton Prison Classification Clinic, Report on Carmine Galante, February 1, 1944, in Records of the Department of Correctional Services, New York State Archives, Albany, NY (hereafter "NYSA").

20. *Organized Crime: 25 Years after Valachi*, 236 (testimony of Vincent Cafaro); Joseph Stassi, quoted in "Oldest Living Mafioso," *GQ* (September 2001), p. 376.

21. Tony Napoli with Charles Messina, *My Father, My Don*, p. 80.

22. Joseph Pistone, *The Way of the Wiseguy* (Philadelphia: Running Press, 2004), p. 24.

23. Sal Profaci, quoted in George Anastasia, *The Goodfella Tapes* (New York: Avon Books, 1998) p. 89.

24. Philip Leonetti, Scott Burnstein, and Christopher Graziano, *Mafia Prince: Inside America's Most Violent Crime Family and the Bloody Fall of La Cosa Nostra* (Philadelphia: Running Press, 2012), p. 25.

25. Maas, *Underboss*, p. 41; Peter Reuter, *Disorganized Crime: Illegal Markets and the Mafia* (Cambridge, MA: Massachusetts Institute of Technology Press, 1985), p. 99.

26. Theresa Dalessio with Patrick Picciarelli, *Mala Femina: A Woman's Life as the Daughter of a Don* (Fort Lee, NJ: Barricade Books, 2003), p. 40.

27. Maas, *Valachi Papers*, pp. 65, 79.

28. Pistone, *Donnie Brasco*, p. 115.

29. Louis Ferrante, *Unlocked: A Journey from Prison to Proust* (New York: Harper, 2008), p. 10.

30. Vincent Teresa with Thomas C. Renner, *My Life in the Mafia* (New York: Doubleday, 1973), p. 137.

31. *New York Age*, June 6, 1953; Thomas B. Ripy, *Federal Excise Taxes on Alcoholic Beverages* (Washington, DC: Congressional Research Service, 1999).

32. FBI, *Criminal Intelligence Digest*, February 11, 1965, in RG 65 (NARA College Park); case file on *United States v. Pillon and Gambino, et al.*, Case No. 38045 (E.D.N.Y. 1941), in Records of the District Court of the United States, RG 21, National Archives and Records Administration, New York, NY (hereafter "NARA New York").

33. Maas, *Valachi Papers*, p. 239.

34. Acknowledging the "wealth of testimony dealing with racketeering practices and organized crime involvement in the vending industry," in the 1950s, a later study found racketeering had dissipated by the early 1980s. Peter Reuter, Jonathan Rubin-stein, and Simon Wynn, *Racketeering in Legitimate Industries: Two Case Studies* (Washington, DC: National Institute of Justice, 1983), pp. 15–31. This change may be due to the entry of new public companies and video electronics. See ibid., pp. 21, 26–27.

35. *Hearings before the Select Committee on Improper Activities in the Labor or Management Field, Part 46*, Senate, 85th Cong., 2d. Sess. (1959) 16626–44 (testimony of Charles Lichtman), 16660–66 (testimony of Milton Green), 16667–79 (testimony of Benjamin Gottlieb).

36. President's Commission on Law Enforcement and Administration of Justice, *The Challenge of Crime in a Free Society* (Washington, DC: GPO, 1967), p. 189.

37. Donald R. Cressey, *Theft of the Nation: The Structure and Operations of Organized Crime in America* (Piscataway, NJ: Transaction Publishers, 2008), pp. 74–75.

38. Carl Sifakis, *The Mafia Encyclopedia*, 3rd ed. (New York: Checkmark Books, 2005), p. xv.

39. *Organized Crime: 25 Years after Valachi*, 301 (testimony of Joe Valachi); Joseph Volz and Peter J. Bridge, ed., *The Mafia Talks* (Greenwich, CT: Fawcett, 1969), p. 98.

40. David Critchley, *The Origin of Organized Crime in America: The New York City Mafia, 1891–1931* (New York: Routledge, 2009), pp. 238, 318 nn. 26–35.

41. In his otherwise well-researched book, Critchley relies on a skewed analysis of the income of mobsters: First, Critchley emphasizes mob boss John Gotti's "middle-class life-style" while conspicuously ignoring Gotti's predecessor, Paul Castellano. Castellano, the Gambino Family boss from 1976 through 1985, was a millionaire who lived in a mansion on Todt Hill, Staten Island (see below). Second, Critchley points to the 1953 divorce proceedings of Anna and Vito Genovese, noting that their house was assessed at only $55,000 and that Anna and the IRS were unable to prove Vito's illegal income. However, their $55,000 house in Atlantic Highlands, New Jersey, was worth more than four times the median house value in New Jersey in the 1950s (about $481,000 in 2013 dollars), which is not exactly middle class. United States Census Bureau, "Historical Census of Housing Tables Home Values," available at http://www.census.gov/hhes/www/housing/census/historic/values.html (accessed August 20, 2013). Furthermore, multiple underworld sources have since confirmed that Genovese was in fact receiving cash income through hidden interests in nightclubs, narcotics, and other illegal funds. *Organized Crime: 25 Years after Valachi*, 291–92 (testimony of Valachi); FBI Memorandum, Salvatore Granello, October 5, 1960, and FBI Report, La Cosa Nostra, August 21, 1964, both in RG 65 (NARA College Park); *United States v. Aviles*, 274 F.2d 179 (2d Cir. 1960). Third, Critchley cites a study of "a sample of wills or probates left by deceased Mafia figures in New Jersey-Pennsylvania" that "uncovered their generally leaving few or no assets." Critchley, *Origin of Organized Crime*, p. 238 (citing Michael Libonati and Herbert Edelhertz, *Study of Property Ownership and Devolution in the Organized Crime Environment* [1983]). But that study relied on a small sample of legal estate filings for mostly low-level men (twelve of the fifteen men). As the authors themselves acknowledge, "estate probate laws and tax requirements are not taken seriously by organized crime figures," and organized crime figures often hold a range of "non-legal property interests" that do not show up in estate filings. Libonati and Edelhertz, *Study of Property Ownership*, pp. 18–20, 38–40, available at https://www.ncjrs.gov/pdffiles1/Digitization/95269NCJRS.pdf (accessed August 25, 2013). Fourth, Critchley focuses on bookmaking, with "strikingly little mention of numbers." Shane White et al., *Playing with Numbers: Gambling in Harlem between the Wars* (Cambridge, MA: Harvard University Press, 2010), p. 283 n. 13. However, the numbers lottery was more territorial with higher potential profits (see chapter 2).

42. Joseph "Joe Dogs" Iannuzi, *Joe Dogs: The Life and Crimes of a Mobster* (New York: Pocket Books, 1993), p. 10.

43. Annelise Graebner Anderson, *The Business of Organized Crime: A Cosa Nostra Family* (Stanford, CA: Hoover Institution Press, 1979), pp. 113–14; John Kroger, *Convictions: A Prosecutor's Battles against Mafia Killers, Drug Kingpins, and Enron Thieves* (New York: Farrar, Straus and Giroux, 2009), p. 139.

44. Martin Booth, *Opium: A History* (New York: Thomas Dunne Books, 1998), pp. 331–32; Peter Reuter and John Haaga, *The Organization of High-Level Drug Markets: An Exploratory Study* (Santa Monica, CA: RAND Corporation, 1989). The Mafia's move to the wholesaling level made economic sense: another study showed that wholesale distributors and drug-gang leaders made far higher incomes than street-level dealers. Steven D. Levitt and Sudhir Alladi Venatesh, "An Economic Analysis of a Drug-Selling Gang's Finances," *Quarterly Journal of Economics* 115, no. 3 (2000): 755–89.

45. See chapter 4.

46. *Organized Crime: 25 Years after Valachi*, 225 (statement of Vincent Cafaro), quoted in James B. Jacobs, *Mobsters, Unions, and Feds: The Mafia and the American Labor Movement* (New York: New York University Press, 2006), p. 40.

47. Jacobs, *Mobsters, Unions, and Feds*, pp. 33–34; David Witwer, *Shadow of the Racketeer: Scandal in Organized Labor* (Champaign: University of Illinois Press, 2009), pp. 56–57.

48. Nicholas Pileggi, *Wiseguy: Life in a Mafia Family* (New York: Simon and Schuster, 1985), p. 46.

49. Salvatore Mondello, *A Sicilian in East Harlem* (Youngstown, NY: Cambria Press, 2005), p. 64.

50. See also Frances A. J. Ianni with Elizabeth Reuss-Ianni, *A Family Business: Kinship and Social Control in Organized Crime* (New York: Russell Sage Foundation, 1972), pp. 75–82.

51. During this era, Queens, Staten Island, and the outer Bronx were largely residential, middle-class, suburban areas. Although Queens is different today, during the 1950s, it had the newest housing stock and the second-highest median income of the boroughs. The surrounding counties of Westchester County (north of New York City) and Nassau County (on Long Island) were among the most upwardly mobile counties in the nation. In suburban New Jersey, Essex, Bergen, and Union Counties each had per-capita incomes above the New York metropolitan region. The Commission on Governmental Operations of the City of New York, *New York City in Transition* (New York: n.p., 1960), pp. 63–69; Andrew Hurley, *Diners, Bowling Alleys, and Trailer Parks: Chasing the American Dream in Postwar Consumer Culture* (New York: Basic Books, 2001), p. 51; Kenneth T. Jackson, *Crabgrass Frontier: The Suburbanization of the United States* (New York: Oxford University Press, 1985), pp. 237, 277, 284.

52. This statistic is calculated from table 7–3.

53. *Organized Crime: 25 Years after Valachi*, 277 (testimony of Valachi).

54. Joseph Valachi, "The Real Thing" (unpublished manuscript), pp. 2–8, 11–12, 21–22, 78–79, in Boxes 1 and 2, Joseph Valachi Papers, in John F. Kennedy Presidential Library and Museum, Boston, MA; Letter of Federal Bureau of Prisons, Wife of

Prisoner Joseph Valachi, December 7, 1962, in Box 1, Records of the Senate Permanent Subcommittee on Investigations, National Archives and Records Administration, Washington, DC (hereafter "NARA Washington").

55. FBI Report, John Franzese, October 6, 1960, in RG 65 (NARA College Park); Michael Franzese with Dary Matera, *Quitting the Mob: How the "Yuppie Don" Left the Mafia and Lived to Tell His Story* (New York: HarperCollins, 1992), pp. 31, 74; Michael Franzese, *Blood Covenant* (New Kensington, PA: Whitaker House, 2003), pp. 28–29, 33.

56. *Organized Crime: 25 Years after Valachi*, 301 (testimony of Valachi).

57. FBI Memorandum, Michael Coppola, Top Hoodlum Coverage, Aril 16, 1954, and FBI Memorandum, Michael Coppola, July 22, 1957, both in FBI FOIA File on Mike Coppola (copy in possession of author); *Brooklyn Eagle*, February 7, 1939; Hank Messick, "What Goes On Inside Mafia Life," *Miami Herald*, December 8, 1968; Hank Messick with Joseph L. Nellis, *The Private Lives of Public Enemies* (New York: P. H. Wyden, 1973), p. 197.

58. FBI Memorandum, Ruggiero Boiardo, May 12, 1954, in FBI FOIA File (copy in possession of author); FBI Memorandum, The Criminal Commission; Angelo Bruno, December 27, 1962, in RG 65 (NARA College Park); Richard Linnett, *In the Godfather Garden: The Long Life and Times of Richie "The Boot" Boiardo* (New Brunswick, NJ: Rutgers University Press, 2013), pp. 2–4.

59. FBI Report, Crime Conditions in the New York Division, December 27, 1963, in RG 65 (NARA College Park); *People v. Brown*, 80 Misc.2d 778 (Sup. Ct. N.Y. Cnty. 1975); *New York Times*, April 20, 1978, April 11, 1989, July 29, 1992; testimony of Angelo Lonardo, quoted in James B. Jacobs, Christopher Panarella, and Jay Worthington, *Busting the Mob: United States v. Cosa Nostra* (New York: New York University Press, 1994), pp. 197–98.

60. *New York Times*, August 16, 1957, July 27, 1968, February 18, 1985, September 1, 2000; FBI Report, Michelino Clemente, May 3, 1961, in RG 65 (NARA College Park).

61. Paul Castellano on an electronic surveillance recording, quoted in President's Commission on Organized Crime, *Edge*, pp. xx, 200–208, 240; Joseph F. O'Brien and Andris Kurins, *Boss of Bosses: The FBI and Paul Castellano* (New York: Island Books, 1991), pp. 28–30, 69–72, 205–206, 261; Ronald Goldstock, Director, and James B. Jacobs, Principal Draftsman, *Corruption and Racketeering in the New York City Construction Industry* (New York: New York University Press, 1990), p. 84.

62. Chicago Heights banker's report, quoted in Matthew Luzi, *The Boys in Chicago Heights: The Forgotten Crew of the Chicago Outfit* (Charleston, SC: History Press, 2012), p. 51; Louis Ferrante, *Mob Rules: What the Mafia Can Teach the Legitimate Businessman* (New York: Penguin, 2011), p. 67; Henry Hill, *Gangsters and Goodfellas: The Mob, Witness Protection, and Life on the Run* (Lanham, MD: M. Evans, 2004), pp. 35, 78.

63. Teresa, *My Life in the Mafia*, pp. 70, 130; Hill, *Gangsters and Goodfellas*, pp. 35, 78; Pistone, *Way of the Wiseguy*, p. 34.

64. President's Commission on Organized Crime, *Organized Crime and Money Laundering: Record of Hearing II, March 14, 1984* (Washington, DC: GPO, 1984), 30–31, 40, 44–45 (testimony of Jimmy Fratianno).

65. Jimmy Fratianno, quoted in Ovid Demaris, *The Last Mafioso: The Treacherous World of Jimmy Fratianno* (New York: Times Books, 1981), p. 105.

66. Lynda Milito with Reg Potterton, *Mafia Wife: My Story of Love, Murder, and Madness* (New York: HarperCollins, 2003), p. 131.

67. Briefs in *United States vs. Frank Costello*, Case No. 382 (2d Cir. 1936) in Records of the United States Courts of Appeal, RG 276 (NARA New York); *United States v. Costello*, 221 F.2d 668 (2d. Cir. 1955); *Costello v. United States*, 350 U.S. 359 (1956).

68. *Organized Crime: 25 Years after Valachi*, 249 (testimony of Cafaro).

69. Maas, *Underboss*, p. 73.

70. Philip Carlo, *Gaspipe: Confessions of a Mafia Boss* (New York: HarperCollins, 2008), p. 95.

71. Pileggi, *Wiseguy*, p. 90.

72. Pistone, *Way of the Wiseguy*, p. 53.

73. *Brooklyn Daily Eagle*, October 17, 1929.

74. Teresa, *My Life in the Mafia*, p. 118.

75. Sal Polisi and Steve Dougherty, *The Sinatra Club: My Life Inside the New York Mafia* (New York: Gallery Books, 2012), p. 25.

76. Gene Mustain and Jerry Capeci, *Mob Star: The Story of John Gotti* (Indianapolis: Alpha Books: 1988), p. 162.

77. Pileggi, *Wiseguy*, pp. 54, 80.

78. *New York Daily News*, January 29, 2012; "Reputed Mafia Boss John Gotti Says He's Not Living High-Life in Jail," Associated Press, February 9, 1992; *Time*, September 29, 1986.

79. Charles Luciano, quoted in *American Weekly* interview reprinted in Sid Feder and Joachim Joesten, *The Luciano Story* (New York: Da Capo Press, 1994), p. 309.

80. Teresa, *My Life in the Mafia*, p. 62.

81. Henry Hill, quoted in Pileggi, *Wiseguy*, p. 55.

82. Mario Puzo, *The Godfather* (New York: G. P. Putnam's Sons, 1969), p. 88.

83. Joseph Pistone and Charles Brandt, *Donnie Brasco: Unfinished Business* (Philadelphia: Running Press, 2007), p. 34.

84. *Donnie Brasco* (Mandalay Pictures, 1997).

85. Pistone, *Unfinished Business*, pp. 71–72; Sifakis, *Mafia Encyclopedia*, pp. 45–46; Pistone, *Donnie Brasco*, p. 115.

86. *Organized Crime: 25 Years after Valachi*, 270–71 (testimony of Valachi); Bonanno, *Man of Honor*, pp. 105–108; Sifakis, *Mafia Encyclopedia*, pp. 45–46. This estimated homicide total for the 1930s is based on Eric Monkonnen, *Murder in New York City* (Los Angeles: University of California Press, 2000), pp. 9, 15–16, appendix.

87. Peter Davidson, *Bones on the Beach: Mafia, Murder, and the True Story of an Undercover Cop Who Went under the Covers with a Wiseguy* (New York: Berkley, 2010), p. 39.

88. Thomas Hunt and Martha Sheldon, *Deep Water: Joseph P. Macheca and the Birth of the American Mafia* (Hartford, CT: iUniverse, 2007), p. 219. I thank Tom Hunt and Rick Warner for helping identify many of these informants.

89. Report of the Questore, August 3, 1900, in *Archivio central dello Stato*, cited in Salvatore Lupo, *History of the Mafia* (New York: Columbia University Press, 2009), pp. 108–11, 293 n. 72.

90. Mike Dash, *The First Family: Terror, Extortion, and the Birth of the American Mafia* (New York: Simon and Schuster, 2009), pp. 274, 396 (citing Secret Service Dailies, RG 87, NARA College Park).

91. Thomas Hunt and Michael A. Tona, "The Good Killers: 1921's Glimpse of the Mafia" (2007), available at http://www.onewal.com/a014/f_goodkillers.html (accessed August 4, 2013).

92. Nick Gentile, *Vita di Capomafia* (Rome: Editori Riuniti, 1963), pp. 160–62; Cable to Mr. Fuller, March 29, 1940, and Telegram from American Embassy in Rome, December 19, 1940, in Gentile File, Box 7, Name Files of Suspected Narcotics Traffickers, 1923–54, RG 59 (NARA College Park).

93. Daily Report of Agents, Detroit, May 16, 1922, in Secret Service Dailies, RG 87, NARA College Park. Thanks to Angelo Santino and Rick Warner for this citation.

94. Testimony of Melchiorre Allegra (1937), *L'Ora* articles transcribed by Extra-Legal Governance Institute (ExLEGI), University of Oxford, available at http://www.exlegi.ox.ac.uk/resources/allegra.asp (accessed August 25, 2013) (cited in Critchley, *Origin of Organized Crime*, p. 62).

95. See chapter 9; *Final Report of the Select Committee on Improper Activities in the Labor or Management Field*, Senate Report No. *1139*, Senate, 86th Cong., 2d Sess. (1960), 500.

96. *New York Crime Commission, Public Hearing (no. 4)* (1952), 222 (testimony of George White); Maas, *Valachi Papers*, pp. 200, 219–21.

97. Charles Siragusa, *The Trail of the Poppy: Behind the Mask of the Mafia* (Englewood Cliffs, NJ: Prentice-Hall, 1966), pp. 70–71; Maas, *Valachi Papers*, pp. 212–14.

98. *Binghamton Press*, July 19, 1958; *New York Times*, July 20, 1958.

99. FBI Special Summary Report: Angelo Bruno, July 28, 1962 (copy in posses-sion of author). My thanks to David Critchley for supplying this document.

100. 5 U.S.C. § 552(b)(7); Anthony Villano, *Brick Agent: Inside the Mafia for the FBI* (New York: Ballantine Books, 1977), p. 91.

101. *The Godfather Part III* (Paramount Pictures 1990); "Members Only," *The Sopranos* (HBO, 2006).

102. *Organized Crime: 25 Years after Valachi*, 270–71 (testimony of Valachi).

103. FBI Interview with William Medico, June 25, 1959, in RG 65 (NARA College Park); *Lockport Union-Sun and Journal*, April 3, 1970. I thank David Critchley for bringing the FBI interview of Medico to my attention.

104. New York FBI Report, La Cosa Nostra, September 26, 1968, in RG 65 (NARA College Park); *Organized Crime: 25 Years after Valachi*, 302 (testimony of Shanley); San Diego FBI Report, La Cosa Nostra, August 22, 1968, in RG 65 (NARA College Park).

105. Gentile, *Vita di Capomafia*, p. 173.

106. Calderone, *Men of Dishonor*, p. 156.

107. This list is drawn from soldiers identified in *Hearings before the Permanent Subcommittee on Investigations of the Committee on Government Operations: Organized Crime and the Illicit Traffic in Narcotics*, Senate, 88th Cong., 1st Sess. (1963) ("McClellan Committee charts"). For their backgrounds, I cross-referenced the names of soldiers with genealogical records from Ancestry.com, newspaper articles, FBI reports, and the 1950s versions of the FBN's International List of Persons Known to Be or Suspected of Being Engaged in the Illicit Traffic in Narcotics Drugs, June 30, 1956, in Box 175, RG 10 (NARA College Park). I eliminated names from the charts if the soldier died before 1955, there was insufficient information on his background, or he was based outside of New York City. For example, while James Colletti is listed as a Bonanno Family soldier, he was effectively the boss of Pueblo, Colorado.

CHAPTER 8: MOUTHPIECES FOR THE MOB: CROOKED COPS, MOB LAWYERS, AND DIRECTOR HOOVER

1. Contrary to initial reports, Ciro Terranova was not present. *New York Times*, December 13 and December 17, 1929, and February 16, 1930; *Brooklyn Standard Union*, December 30, 1929; *New York Sun*, January 20, 1930.

2. *New York Times*, December 8 and December 24, 1929.

3. *New York Times*, September 29, 1929, December 22, 1929, and March 13 and March 14, 1930.

4. *New York Times*, June 25, 1930, August 21, 1931.

5. *Report and Proceedings of the Senate Committee Appointed to Investigate the Police Department of the City of New York* (Albany, NY: J. B. Lyon, 1895); *Commission to Investigate Allegations of Police Corruption and the City's Anti-Corruption Procedures, Commission Report* (New York: n.p., 1972).

6. Nicholas Pileggi, *Wiseguy: Life in a Mafia Family* (New York: Simon and Schuster, 1985), pp. 50, 107.

7. Robert Leuci, *All the Centurions: A New York City Cop Remembers His Years on the Street, 1961–1981* (New York: HarperCollins, 2004), pp. 219–20.

8. Brian McDonald, *My Father's Gun: One Family, Three Badges, One Hundred Years in the NYPD* (New York: Penguin, 1999), p. 177.

9. Peter Maas, *Serpico* (New York: Viking Press, 1973), pp. 306–307.

10. Harold R. Danforth and James D. Horan, *The D. A.'s Man* (New York: Crown, 1957), p. 47.

11. Henry Hill, *Gangsters and Goodfellas: The Mob, Witness Protection, and Life on the Run* (Lanham, MD: M. Evans, 2004), p. 53.

12. John Harlan Amen, *Report of Kings County Investigation, 1938–1942* (New York: n.p. 1942); Alan Block, *East Side, West Side: Organizing Crime in New York, 1930–1950* (Piscataway, NJ: Transaction Publishers, 1983), pp. 84–85.

13. Leuci, *All the Centurions*, p. 176.

14. *New York Times*, December 6, 1972.

15. George P. LeBrun, *It's Time to Tell* (New York: William Morrow, 1962), pp. 145–46.

16. *New York Times*, December 11, 1970, September 25, 1972.

17. FBI criminal record of Antonio Corallo, October 18, 1962, and NYPD criminal record of Alex Di Bruzzi [*sic*], December 31, 1958, reprinted in Charlie Carr, ed., *New York Police Files on the Mafia* (New York: Hosehead Productions, 2012), pp. 84–85, 232–33.

18. Richard H. Rovere, *Howe & Hummel: Their True and Scandalous History* (New York: Farrar, Straus and Giroux, 1947), p. 79.

19. *New York Times*, February 28, 1924.

20. Samuel Leibowitz, quoted in Quentin Reynolds, *Courtroom: The Story of Samuel S. Leibowitz* (New York: Farrar, Straus and Giroux, 1999), pp. 417–18.

21. Evan Thomas, *The Man to See: Edward Bennett Williams; Ultimate Insider; Legendary Trial Lawyer* (New York: Touchstone, 1991), pp. 96, 188.

22. Frank Ragano and Selwyn Raab, *Mob Lawyer* (New York: Scribners, 1994), p. 362.

23. Interview with Thomas E. Dewey (1959), in Columbia Center for Oral History (hereafter "COHC"); *New York Times*, January 1, 1970.

24. *Collier's*, July 22, 1939.

25. Interview with Dewey (1959) (CCOH), p. 440.

26. *New York Times*, February 25, 1939, January 27, 1940, January 1, 1970.

27. *New York Times*, September 10, 1973; FBI Report, Frank DeSimone, June 10, 1958, Airtel to New York, Re: La Cosa Nostra, April 27, 1964, and FBI Report, Los Angeles, May 12, 1965, both in Records of the Federal Bureau of Investigation, Record Group 65, in National Archives and Records Administration, College Park, MD (hereafter "NARA College Park").

28. Robert Cooley with Hillel Levin, *When Corruption Was King: How I Helped the Mob Rule Chicago Then Brought the Outfit Down* (New York: Carroll & Graf, 2004), p. 126.

29. Robert F. Simone, *The Last Mouthpiece: The Man Who Dared to Defend the Mob* (Philadelphia: Camino Books, 2001), p. xi.

30. Oscar Goodman with George Anastasia, *Being Oscar: From Mob Lawyer to Mayor of Las Vegas, Only in America* (New York: Weinstein Books, 2013), p. 9.

31. Thomas Hunt, *Deep Water: Joseph P. Macheca and the Birth of the American Mafia* (North Charleston, SC: CreateSpace, 2010); *Utica Observer-Dispatch*, August 19, 1958, June 5, 1959.

32. *Niagara Falls Gazette*, December 15, 1959.

33. *Buffalo Courier-Express*, July 23, 1960; Bill Bonanno and Gary Abromovitz, *The Last Testament of Bill Bonanno: The Final Secrets of a Life in the Mafia* (New York: William Morrow, 2011).

34. Dennis Griffin, *Mob Nemesis: How the FBI Crippled Organized Crime* (New York: Prometheus Books, 2002), p. 36.

35. *New York Times*, September 5, 1970, June 29, 1971.

36. Marchi, quoted in Griffin, *Mob Nemesis*, p. 38.

37. Edward Bennett Williams, *One Man's Freedom* (New York: Atheneum, 1962), pp. 107–108; *Costello v. Immigration and Naturalization Service*, 376 U.S. 120 (1964).

38. *United States v. Bufalino*, 285 F.2d 408, 419–20 (2d Cir. 1960) (Clark, J., concurring).

39. Luciano, quoted in Sid Feder and Joachim Joesten, *The Luciano Story* (New York: Da Capo Press, 1954), p. 311.

40. James B. Jacobs, Coleen Friel, and Robert Radick, *Gotham Unbound: How*

New York City Was Liberated from the Grip of Organized Crime (New York: New York University Press, 2001), pp. 18, 229–30.

41. Anthony Summers, *Official and Confidential: The Secret Life of J. Edgar Hoover* (New York: Putnam, 1993).

42. Athan Theoharis, *J. Edgar Hoover, Sex, and Crime: An Historical Attitude* (Chicago: Ivan R. Dee, 1995), pp. 23–55; Peter Maas, "Setting the Record Straight," *Esquire* (May 1993): 56–58.

43. *Miami Herald*, April 8, 2001; David K. Johnson, *The Lavender Scare: The Cold War Persecution of Gays and Lesbians in the Federal Government* (Chicago: University of Chicago Press, 2004), p. 12.

44. This section is adapted in part from Alex Hortis, "'Plagued Ever Since': Late in His Life, FBI Director J. Edgar Hoover Reflects on His Mafia Denials," *Informer: The History of American Crime and Law Enforcement* (July 2011): 5–19.

45. Curt Gentry, *J. Edgar Hoover: The Man and the Secrets* (New York: W. W. Norton, 1991), pp. 82–83.

46. Rhodri Jeffreys-Jones, *The FBI: A History* (New Haven, CT: Yale University Press, 2007), p. 121.

47. Tim Weiner, *Enemies: A History of the FBI* (New York: Random House, 2012), pp. 119–20, 152–57; John Earl Haynes, Harvey Klehr, and Alexander Vassilev, *Spies: The Rise and Fall of the KGB in America* (New Haven, CT: Yale University Press, 2009), pp. 84–85.

48. Jeffreys-Jones, *FBI*, pp. 161–62.

49. Herbert Brownell, *Advising Ike: The Memoirs of Attorney General Herbert Brownell* (Lawrence: University Press of Kansas,1993), p. 235.

50. Interview of Robert Kennedy, quoted in Edwin Guthman and Jeffrey Shulman, eds., *Robert Kennedy in His Own Words: The Unpublished Recollections of the Kennedy Years* (New York: Bantam, 1988), p. 121; Weiner, *Enemies*, pp. 203–26.

51. *New York Times*, September 22, 1936.

52. Although I disagree with several of his conclusions about Hoover, the unpublished thesis of Aharon W. Zorea, "Plurality and Law: The Rise of Law Enforcement in Organized Crime Control" (Ph.D. dissertation, St. Louis University, 2005), does a good job of describing some of the politics of federal law enforcement. Thanks to David Critchley for informing me of it.

53. Robert A. Caro, *The Passage of Power: The Years of Lyndon Johnson, vol. 4* (New York: Vintage, 2013), pp. 9–10, 65, 459.

54. Charles Morgan Jr., quoted in Ovid Demaris, *The Director: An Oral Biography of J. Edgar Hoover* (New York: Harper's Press, 1975).

55. Gentry, *Hoover*, pp. 116, 380, 445.

56. The Mafia was prosperous and growing after World War II, and it reopened "the books" to allow more members in the mid-1950s. See chapter 7.

57. *Washington Post*, March 19, 1949.

58. *Washington Post*, September 22, 1949.

59. *New York Times*, April 2, 1950.

60. *New York Times*, April 9, 1950; FBI Report, La Cosa Nostra, Kansas City Division, June 7, 1964, in RG 65 (NARA College Park). The requests continued after the Kefauver Committee Hearings. For example, in August 1953, Sheriff Ed Blackburn of Tampa Bay, Florida (home of the Santo Trafficante Family of the Mafia), playing to Hoover's sensibilities, urged the FBI "to declare the Mafia a subversive, un-American group threatening the internal security of the nation." *New York Times*, August 14, 1953.

61. *Brooklyn Eagle*, April 17, 1950; *New York Times*, April 18, 1950.

62. Arthur M. Schlesinger Jr. and Roger Bruns, eds., *Congress Investigates, 1792–1974* (New York: Chelsea House, 1975), pp. 352–82.

63. *Third Interim Report of the Special Committee to Investigate Organized Crime in Interstate Commerce*, Senate, 82nd Cong., 1st Sess. (1951), 149.

64. *New York Times*, May 14, 1950, January 21, 1951.

65. Estes Kefauver, *Crime in America* (Garden City, NY: Doubleday, 1951), p. 25; Michael Woodiwiss, *Organized Crime and American Power* (Toronto: University of Toronto Press, 2001), pp. 242, 251.

66. Ronald Radosh and Joyce Milton, *The Rosenberg File*, 2nd ed. (New Haven, CT: Yale University Press, 1997), pp. 40, 499.

67. *Hearings before the Special Committee to Investigate Organized Crime in Interstate Commerce: Investigation of Organized Crime in Interstate Commerce*, Senate, 82nd Cong., 1st Sess. (1951), 350–57 (testimony of Charles Siragusa, FBN), 3–11 (testimony of M. H. Goldschein, Department of Justice), 532, 537, 540–41 (testimony of J. Edgar Hoover).

68. Hoover's insistence that local authorities could simply clean up corruption and deal with organized crime was proven wrong by almost a century of local impotence against the Mafia. The paralyzing effect of corruption on local law enforcement is one of the best justifications *for* federal intervention. Richard A. Posner, *Economic Analysis of Law* (New York: Aspen, 1992), p. 637; Charles F. C. Ruff, "Federal Prosecution of Local Corruption: A Case Study in the Making of Law Enforcement Policy," *George Washington Law Journal* 65 (1977): 1171, 1212–15. Moreover, Hoover was motivated much more by the goal of increasing counterintelligence than he was by factors like federalism and local autonomy.

69. *Hearings before the Special Committee* (testimony of Hoover), 537 (emphasis added).

70. Neil J. Welch and David W. Marston, *Inside Hoover's FBI: The Field Chief Reports* (Garden City, NY: Doubleday, 1984), pp. 80–85.

71. The CAPGA investigation was shut down by Attorney General Tom Clark because the FBI was using wiretaps of dubious legality. This may have also frustrated the FBI from investigating organized crime. William E. Roemer Jr., *Roemer: Man against the Mob* (New York: Ballantine, 1989), pp. 19–22.

72. Robert Kennedy, quoted in Edwin Guthman and Jeffrey Shulman, eds., *Robert Kennedy in His Own Words: The Unpublished Recollections of the Kennedy Years* (New York: Bantam, 1988), p. 120.

73. *Binghamton Press*, November 21, 1957, quoted in Gil Reavill, *Mafia Summit: J. Edgar Hoover, the Kennedy Brothers, and the Meeting That Unmasked the Mob* (New York: Thomas Dunne, 2013), pp. 140–41; *Binghamton Press*, August 13, 1959.

74. FBI Report, Activities of Top Hoodlums in the New York Field Division, January 8, 1959, in FBI FOIA File on Top Hoodlum Program (copy in possession of author).

75. William C. Sullivan, *The Bureau: My Thirty Years in Hoover's FBI* (New York: Norton, 1979), pp. 120–21

76. Cartha D. "Deke" DeLoach, *Hoover's FBI: The Inside Story by Hoover's Trusted Lieutenant* (Washington, DC: Regnery Publishing, 1997), p. 303.

77. Oliver "Buck" Williams, *A G-Man's Journal: A Legendary Career Inside the FBI—From the Kennedy Assassination to the Oklahoma City Bombing* (New York: Pocket Books, 1998), pp. 4–7.

78. Ed Reid, *The Grim Reapers: The Anatomy of Organized Crime in America* (Chicago: Henry Regnery, 1969). Reid's *Grim Reapers* is an early journalistic book on the Mafia, which is *not* critical of Hoover. Hoover's recommendation of this book further reflects genuine regret that the FBI missed the Mafia.

79. The FBI's official historian Dr. John Fox discovered Hoover's handwritten note. Although we disagree on Hoover's record on the Mafia, I thank Dr. Fox for supplying me the note without any preconditions.

80. Unfortunately, Mr. Rosen died in 2005 before I could interview him. Mr. Rosen had a distinguished career in the FBI, and led key investigations of civil rights violations and murders in the South. *Society of Former Special Agents of the FBI* (Washington: Turner Publishing, 1997), p. 217.

81. William Hundley, quoted in Demaris, *Director*, p. 142.

82. *Hearings before the Select Committee on Improper Activities in the Labor or*

Management Field: Investigation of Improper Activities in the Labor or Management Field, 85th Cong., 2d Sess. (1958), 12223 (testimony of Martin Pera).

83. *FBI Law Enforcement Bulletin*, January 1962.

84. *FBI Law Enforcement Bulletin*, September 1963; *New York Times*, August 31, 1963.

85. *New York Times*, November 16, 1957.

86. Gordon Hawkins, "God and the Mafia," in *National Affairs* 14 (Winter 1969): 24–51. For other examples, see Richard Warner, "The Warner Files: God and the Mafia," *Informer: The Journal of American Crime and Law Enforcement* (April 2013): 69–71.

87. As David Critchley had pointed out, Joe Valachi's thousand-page handwritten memoirs in prison are consistent with his testimony, and they have been substantially corroborated by other *mafiosi*. David Critchley, *Origin of Organized Crime*, pp. 167, 293.

CHAPTER 9: THE ASSASSINATIONS OF 1957

1. New York Police Department DD5, Files of the Central Intelligence Bureau, May 17, 1957, in Box 5, Office of the District Attorney (Manhattan) Albert Anastasia Files, 1954–1963 (hereafter "Anastasia Files") in New York Municipal Archives, New York, NY (hereafter "NYMA"); *New York Times*, March 6, 1956, May 3, 1957.

2. *Hearings before the Permanent Subcommittee on Investigations of the Committee on Government Operations: Organized Crime and the Illicit Traffic in Narcotics*, Senate, 88th Cong., 1st Sess. (1963), 291–92 (testimony of Joseph Valachi); Peter Maas, *The Valachi Papers* (New York: Perennial, 2003), pp. 210–12; *New York Times*, October 10, 1963.

3. *People against Genovese* correspondence files in Box 12, in District Attorney (Kings County), Murder, Inc. Case Files (hereafter "Murder, Inc. Files") (NYMA); *New York Times*, February 15, 1969.

4. Selwyn Raab, *Five Families: The Rise, Decline, and Resurgence of America's Most Powerful Mafia Empires* (New York: St. Martin's Press, 2005), p. 61; Investigative Case File on Vito Genovese, 1950–51 (statement of Anna Genovese), in Box 87, in Record Group 46, Records of the Special Committee to Investigate Organized Crime in Interstate Commerce, National Archives and Records Administration, Washington, DC (hereafter "NARA Washington"); *New York Times*, March 17, 1932; *New York Sun*, June 25, 1932; *Schenectady Gazette*, March 17, 1932. See Lennert Van't Riet, David Critchley, and Steve Turner, in *Informer: The History of American Crime and Law Enforcement* (January 2014): 52–96.

5. Raab, *Five Families*, p. 82; NYPD Report, Death of Material Witness, Peter LaTempa, February 10, 1945, and Letter of Chief Deputy Sheriff to Acting District

Attorney, December 7, 1944, in *People against Genovese*, Box 12, in Murder, Inc. Files (NYMA) (documents posted by author, May 28, 2013, at https://groups.yahoo.com/neo/groups/americanmafia/files/La%20Tempa%20Investigation); *New York Times*, February 10, 1945; *Brooklyn Eagle*, June 6, 1946.

6. *Collier's*, April 12, 1947.

7. FBI Memorandum, La Cosa Nostra, August 8, 1963, in Records of the Federal Bureau of Investigation, Record Group 65, National Archives and Records Administration, College Park, MD (hereafter "NARA College Park").

8. Memorandum, Interview with Commissioner Cavanagh, Re: Richard W. Hoffman, March 8, 1951, in Box 77, Investigative Files, Special Committee to Investigate Organized Crime in Interstate Commerce, National Archives and Records Administration, Washington, DC (hereafter "NARA Washington").

9. *United States v. Frank Costello*, 511 U.S. 1069 (1956).

10. *New York Times*, May 3 and May 4, 1957; John Johnson Jr. and Joel Selvin with Dick Cami, *Peppermint Twist, The Mob, the Music, and the Most Famous Dance Club of the '60s* (New York: St. Martin's Press, 2012), p. 62; Paul David Pope, *The Deeds of My Fathers: How My Grandfather and Father Built New York and Created the Tabloid World of Today* (New York: Philip Turner Books, 2010), pp. 81–82, 247–48.

11. *New York Times*, May 4 and May 5, 1957.

12. Ibid.

13. *New York Times*, May 3, 1957, May 16, 1958.

14. *New York Times*, August 20, 1957; *Long Island Star-Journal*, May 3, 1957.

15. Valachi, quoted in Mass, *Valachi Papers*, p. 243; Bill Bonanno and Gary B. Abromovitz, *The Last Testament of Bill Bonanno: The Final Secrets of a Life in the Mafia* (New York: HarperCollins, 2011), p. 172.

16. *Hearings before the Permanent Subcommittee on Investigations of the Committee on Government Operations: Organized Crime and the Illicit Traffic in Narcotics*, 252 (testimony of John Shanley); FBI Report, Crime Conditions in the New York Division, December 3, 1962, in RG 65 (NARA College Park).

17. FBI Memorandum, La Cosa Nostra, August 8, 1963, in RG 65 (NARA College Park).

18. Joseph Bonanno with Sergio Lalli, *A Man of Honor: The Autobiography of Joseph Bonanno* (New York: Simon and Schuster, 1983), p. 184.

19. Bill Bonanno, *Last Testament of Bill Bonanno*, p. 173.

20. George Wolf with Joseph DiMona, *Frank Costello: Prime Minister of the Underworld* (New York: Morrow, 1974), pp. 258–60.

21. *New York Times*, May 4, 1957.

22. *New York Times*, May 21, 1958.

23. *New York Times*, May 28, 1958.

24. Ibid.

25. Wolf, *Frank Costello*, p. 260.

26. New York State Crime Commission, *Public Hearings (no. 5)* (Albany, NY: n.p., 1953), 1698 (testimony of Umberto Anastasio).

27. Bonanno, *Man of Honor*, pp. 166, 169; Nicolo Gentile, *Vita di Capomafia* (Rome: Editori Riuniti, 1963), p. 136.

28. *Brooklyn Daily Eagle*, April 20 and April 27, 1951.

29. Bonanno, *Man of Honor*, p. 171; FBI Report, The Criminal "Commission," December 19, 1962, in RG 65 (NARA College Park).

30. Gentile, *Vita di Capomafia*, pp. 116–17.

31. Ibid.; Bonanno, *Man of Honor*, p. 121.

32. Gentile, *Vito de Capomafia*, p. 117.

33. Bonanno, *Man of Honor*, p. 141.

34. *Hearings before the Permanent Subcommittee on Investigations of the Committee on Government Operations: Organized Crime and the Illicit Traffic in Narcotics*, 296–97 (testimony of Valachi).

35. FBI Memorandum, *Criminal Intelligence Digest*, February 11, 1965, in RG 65 (NARA College Park).

36. See chapter 2.

37. *Life*, July 1, 1957.

38. *New York Times*, June 18, 1957 and April 7, 1959; *Albany Knickerbocker News*, June 18, 1957.

39. FBI Memorandum, *Criminal Intelligence Digest*, February 11, 1965, and FBI Report, La Cosa Nostra, Newark Division, October 3, 1967, both in RG 65 (NARA College Park).

40. General Investigative Intelligence File, Albert Anastasia, February 25, 1954, and General Investigative Intelligence File, Albert Anastasia, March 31, 1955, in FBI Freedom of Information Act File (hereafter "FBI FOIA File") on Anastasia (copy in possession of author); United States Treasury Department, Bureau of Narcotics, *Mafia* (New York: Collins, 2007), pp. 287, 289, 292; *New York Times*, October 26, 1957.

41. NYPD Report, List of Property on A. Anastasia, October 1957, NYPD Report, Christening at Essex House, Albert Anastasio, May 13, 1957, and NYPD DD5, Interview of Albert Anastasio Jr., November 1, 1957, all in Box 2, Anastasia Files (NYMA).

42. NYPD DD5, Interview of Albert Anastasio Jr., November 1, 1957, in Box 2,

Anastasia Files (NYMA); Kenneth C. Wolensky, Nicole H. Wolensky, and Robert P. Wolensky, *Fighting for the Union Label: The Women's Garment Industry and the IGLWU in Pennsylvania* (University Park, PA: Penn State University Press, 2002), pp. 52–53, 84, 180–182.

43. NYPD DD5, Interview with Members of Deceased's Family, October 25, 1957, in Box 2, Anastasia Files (NYMA).

44. Joe Valachi, quoted in Maas, *Valachi Papers*, p. 249.

45. NYPD DD5, Subject: Investigation of Anastasia's Mortgage, November 5, 1957, in Box 2, Anastasia Files (NYMA); *New York Times*, October 26, 1957.

46. NYPD DD5, Interview with Harry "Champ" Segal, June 4, 1957, in Box 2, Anastasia Files (NYMA); *New York Times*, October 29, October 30, 1957, February 1, 1958.

47. NYPD Notes of Interview with Joe Silesi, October 9, 1961, and November 6, 1961, in Box 2, Anastasia Files (NYMA).

48. *Hearings before the Permanent Subcommittee on Investigations of the Committee on Government Operations: Organized Crime and the Illicit Traffic in Narcotics*, 348–49 (testimony of Valachi).

49. NYPD Notes of Interview with Joe Silesi, October 9, 1961, and November 6, 1961, in Box 3, Anastasia Files (NYMA); FBI Memorandum, American Gambling Activities in Cuba, February 28, 1958, and FBI Report, Tampa Office, Santo Trafficante Jr., September 22, 1960, both in RG 65 (NARA College Park).

50. *Hearings before the Permanent Subcommittee on Investigations of the Committee on Government Operations: Organized Crime and the Illicit Traffic in Narcotics*, 349 (testimony of Valachi); Joe Valachi, quoted in Maas, *Valachi Papers*, p. 249.

51. FBI Report from Los Angeles Office, La Cosa Nostra, December 13, 1963, in RG 65 (NARA College Park).

52. See chapter 3.

53. NYPD Notes of Interview with Joe Silesi, October 9, 1961, and November 6, 1961, and NYPD DD5, Subject: Santo Trafficante, November 13, 1959, both in Box 2, Anastasia Files (NYMA); FBI Memorandum, American Gambling Activities in Cuba, Top Hoodlum Program, February 28, 1958, in RG 65 (NARA College Park).

54. NYPD Notes of Interview with Anthony Coppola, October 25, 1957, in Box 2, Anastasia Files (NYMA); *New York Times*, October 26, 1957.

55. NYPD DD5, Interview of Albert Anastasio Jr., November 1, 1957, in Box 2, Anastasia Files (NYMA); *New York Times*, October 26, 1957.

56. NYPD Report, Subject: Albert Anastasia, September 1963, in Box 2, Anastasia Files (NYMA); FBI Memorandum, Gambling Activities in Cuba, January 17, 1958, in RG 65 (NARA College Park).

57. NYPD Notes of Interview with Anthony Coppola, October 25, 1957, in Box 2, Anastasia Files (NYMA); *New York Times*, October 26, 1957.

58. Ibid.

59. NYPD DD5, Subject: Andrew Alberti, November 5, 1957, and NYPD DD5, Subject: Interrogation of Johnny Busso, November 5, 1957, both in Box 2, Anastasia Files (NYMA), in RG 65; FBI Report, NY-92-632, Activities of Top Hoodlums in the New York Field Division, September 14, 1959, and FBI Report, NY 92-2300, Anti-Racketeering-Conspiracy, Gambino Family, July 1, 1963, both in RG 65 (NARA College Park); *Hearings before the Select Committee on Improper Activities in the Labor or Management Field: Part 32*, Senate, 85th Cong., 2d Sess. (1958), 12246 (testimony of Martin Pera); *Yonkers Herald Statesmen*, March 17, 1954; Bureau of Narcotics, *Mafia*, pp. 334, 347, 360.

60. *New York Times*, October 26, 1957.

61. NYPD Notes of Interview with Joseph Saloney, October 29, 1957, in Box 1, Anastasia Files (NYMA); *New York Times*, October 26, 1957.

62. NYPD Notes of Interviews with Arthur Grasso, Joseph Saloney, and Anthony Arbisi, October 29, 1957, each in Box 1, Anastasia Files (NYMA).

63. Ibid.; NYPD DD5, Subject: Autopsy Report, October 27, 1957, and NYPD DD5, Homicide Report, October 28, 1957, both in Box 2, Anastasia Files (NYMA); *New York Daily News*, October 26, 1957; *New York Times*, October 26, 1957. Although news reports erroneously stated that the gunmen wore scarves, most of the employees said they wore hats and aviator glasses.

64. NYPD Notes of Interview with Joseph Saloney, October 29, 1957, and NYPD Notes of Interrogation of Joseph Saloney, October 25, 1957, both in Box 1, Anastasia Files (NYMA); FBI Teletype, Criminal Intelligence Program, January 3, 1963, in RG 65 (NARA College Park).

65. NYPD DD5, David Mazer, October 25, 1957, NYPD DD5, Subject: Recovery of Gun, October 25, 1957, and NYPD DD5, Subject: Test Specimens, October 28, 1957, each in Box 2, Anastasia Files (NYMA).

66. NYPD Notes of Interrogation of Joseph Saloney, October 25, 1957; NYPD Report, Subject: Albert Anastasia, September 1963, both in Box 2, Anastasia Files (NYMA); Arthur Nash, *New York City Gangland* (Chicago, IL: Arcadia, 2010), p. 90.

67. *New York Times*, October 26, 1957.

68. Barber's Names, Chairs, Customers–Polygraph Exams, March 27, 1963, in Box 3, Anastasia Files (NYMA).

69. NYPD DD5, Subject: Vincent J. Squillante, September 30, 1958, in Box 2, Anastasia Files (NYMA); *New York Times*, October 1, 1958.

70. NYPD Teletype Alarm, October 25, 1957, and NYPD DD5, Charles Davis, October 26, 1957, both in Box 2, Anastasia Files (NYMA).

71. *Hearings before the Permanent Subcommittee on Investigations of the Committee on Government Operations: Organized Crime and the Illicit Traffic in Narcotics*, 348–49 (testimony of Valachi).

72. Vincent Teresa with Thomas C. Renner, *My Life in the Mafia* (New York: Doubleday, 1974), p. 178.

73. Bonanno, *Man of Honor*, p. 207.

74. Wolf, *Frank Costello*, pp. 262–63.

75. In April 1958, the NYPD received an alternative tip about the Patriarca Family of New England. The NYPD contacted the Providence, Rhode Island, police department: "This department is in receipt of information that [Raymond] Patriarca might be involved in the killing of Albert Anastasia." The NYPD then requested information on Providence mobsters. Nothing came of it though, and the lead was shelved. NYPD DD5, Subject: Request Communication, April 11, 1958, in Box 2, Anastasia Files (NYMA).

76. NYPD DD5, Subject Santo Trafficante, November 13, 1959, in Box 2, Anastasia Files (NYMA).

77. Sidney Slater and Quentin Reynolds, "My Life Inside the Mob," *Saturday Evening Post*, August 24, 1963, pp. 38–55.

78. Peter Diapoulos and Steven Linakis, *The Sixth Family* (New York: Bantam, 1976), p. 22.

79. Slater, *Saturday Evening Post*, p. 40.

80. Jerry Capeci, "The Men Who Hit Albert Anastasia," October 18, 2001, available at http://www.ganglandnews.com (accessed July 20, 2013); *New York Times*, October 8, 2008.

81. Jerry Capeci, *The Complete Idiot's Guide to the Mafia* (New York: Penguin, 2004), p. 290; *New York Times*, June 23 and July 30, 1965, and October 8, 2008.

82. The informant does *not* identify Wittenberg as the second gunman. As for the plotters, the informant stated that a cabal of *mafiosi*, including Joseph Biondo, Charles Dongarra, and Joseph Riccobono, formed after they learned that Anastasia was planning to have them killed. The informant said that these three individuals, "plus Andrew Alberti, Joseph Gallo, Steve Grammatula [*sic*]" and the second gunman, planned the assassination. FBI Teletype from SAC, New York, 92-632, Criminal Intelligence Program, January 3, 1963 (NARA College Park). Capeci relates that researcher Andy Petepiece also found the January 3, 1963, report.

83. In the newspapers, Alberti was briefly identified, as follows: "Detectives investigating the Anastasia slaying yesterday questioned Andrew Alberti, a suspended prize

fight manager. He operates a bakery at 441 East Twelfth Street and Lives at 2675 Henry Hudson Parkway." *New York Times*, November 13, 1957.

84. NYPD DD5, Subject: Interrogation of Johnny Busso, November 5, 1957, in Box 2, Anastasia Files, (NYMA).

85. Ibid.

86. *Kingston Daily Freeman*, November 10, 1964.

87. FBI Teletype, To Director, FBI, From SAC, New York, Criminal Intelligence Committee, January 3, 1963, in RG 65 (NARA College Park). FBI Report, La Cosa Nostra, Gambino Family, August 21, 1964, in RG 65 (NARA College Park); *New York Times*, June 23, 1965; *Long Island Star-Journal*, July 9, 1966. As for Grammauta's physical appearance, see the FBI photo reprinted in Jerry Capeci, "The Men Who Hit Albert Anastasia," October 18, 2001, available at http://www.ganglandnews.com (accessed July 20, 2013); *New York Times*, June 23, 1965.

88. Again, there is no indication that Busso was involved in the plot. Johnny Busso fought in a bout at Madison Square Garden that Friday night, October 25, 1957. *New York Times*, October 26, 1957.

89. *New York Times*, October 26, 1957.

90. Raab, *Five Families*, p. 115.

91. Bonanno, *Man of Honor*, p. 208.

92. *Hearings before the Permanent Subcommittee on Investigations of the Committee on Government Operations: Organized Crime and the Illicit Traffic in Narcotics*, 425 (chart of Gambino Family); Maas, *Valachi Papers*, p. 229.

93. Armand "Tommy" Rava, one of the few Anastasia loyalists, was known to harbor enmity toward Carlo Gambino. After attending the Apalachin meeting in November 1957, Rava disappeared and was believed murdered. FBI Report, La Cosa Nostra, September 26, 1968, in RG 65 (NARA College Park).

94. FBI AIRTEL, From SAC to Director, FBI, August 7, 1962, in FBI FOIA File of Anthony Anastasia, available at http://www.thesmokinggun.com/file/brotherly-love-fuhgeddaboutit-0 (accessed July 20, 2013); Bill Bonanno, *Last Testament of Bill Bonanno*, pp. 132, 156.

95. Bonanno, *Man of Honor*, p. 208.

96. *Hearings before the Permanent Subcommittee on Investigations of the Committee on Government Operations: Organized Crime and the Illicit Traffic in Narcotics*, 389 (testimony of Valachi).

CHAPTER 10: APALACHIN

1. Testimony of Edgar D. Croswell (1957), in Box 9, Master Case Files of the New York State Temporary Commission of Investigation (hereafter "COI"), New York State Archives, Albany, NY (hereafter "NYSA"). This chapter draws principally on the COI files of the public inquiry into the Apalachin meeting, and the trial testimony in *United States v. Bufalino* (S.D.N.Y. 1959), National Archives and Records Administration, Northeast Region, New York, NY (hereafter "NARA NY").

2. *Binghamton Press*, December 13, 1957; *New York Times*, November 3, 1959, November 21, 1990.

3. Testimony of Croswell (1957), in Box 9, COI (NYSA).

4. FBI Report, Joseph Barbara, November 19, 1957, in FBI Freedom of Information Act File (hereafter "FBI FOIA File") on Joseph Barbara Sr. (copy in possession of author); testimony of Croswell (1957), in Box 9, COI (NYSA).

5. *Hearings before the Select Committee on Improper Activities in the Labor or Management Field*, Senate, 85th Cong., 2d. Sess. (1958), 12202–12209 (testimony of Croswell); *United States v. Bonanno*, 180 F.Supp. 71, 73–75 (S.D.N.Y. 1960).

6. *United States v. Bufalino* (S.D.N.Y. 1959) (testimony of Croswell) (NARA NY); *Binghamton Press*, June 14, 1959.

7. *Binghamton Press*, June 14, 1959.

8. Testimony of Croswell (1957), in Box 9, COI (NYSA); *Binghamton Press*, June 14, 1959.

9. Weather records available at http://www.farmersalmanac.com/weather-history/13732/ 1956/10/18/ (accessed July 25, 2013).

10. Testimony of Frederick Leibe (1957), in Box 9, COI (NYSA).

11. FBI Memorandum, Re: Carmine Galante, January 24, 1958, in FBI FOIA File on Carmine Galante (copy in possession of author); testimony of Croswell, in Box 9, COI (NYSA).

12. *United States v. Bufalino* (S.D.N.Y. 1959) (testimony of Croswell) (NARA NY).

13. Record of Interview with Edgar Croswell, in Box 9, COI (NYSA); *New York Times*, January 7, 1958, July 24, 1959; *Binghamton Press*, February 11, 1958.

14. Testimony of Richard Klausner (1958), in Box 9, COI (NYSA).

15. *United States v. Bentvena*, 319 F.2d 916 (2d Cir. 1963); Memorandum of Edward Kirk to Chief Investigator Joseph Milenky, Suspected Attendees at Hoodlum Meeting, March 19, 1959, in Box 5, COI (NYSA).

16. *Binghamton Press*, October 25, 1957.

17. Testimony of Marguerite Russell (1958), in Box 9, COI (NYSA).

18. *Organized Crime and Illicit Traffic in Narcotics: Hearings before the Committee on Government Operations, Permanent Subcommittee on Investigations*, Senate, 88th Cong., 1st Sess. (1963), 389 (testimony of Joseph Valachi); *Binghamton Press*, January 26, 1958, November 14, 1977.

19. Testimony of Croswell (1957), in Box 9, COI (NYSA).

20. Joseph Bonanno with Sergio Lalli, *A Man of Honor: The Autobiography of Joseph Bonanno* (New York: Simon and Schuster, 1983), p. 203.

21. Testimony of Joseph Barbara Jr. (1957), in Box 9, COI (NYSA); *United States v. Bufalino* (S.D.N.Y. 1959) (testimony of Helen Schroeder) (NARA NY).

22. *New York Times*, November 15, 1957; testimony of Croswell, in Box 9, COI (NYSA).

23. Interview with Croswell (1957), in Box 9, COI (NYSA).

24. *United States v. Bufalino* (S.D.N.Y. 1959) (testimonies of Croswell and Schroeder) (NARA NY).

25. Ibid. (testimonies of Croswell and Brown) (NARA NY).

26. Testimony of Croswell (1957), in Box 9, COI (NYSA); *Hearings on Organized Crime: 25 Years after Valachi: Hearings before the Permanent Subcommittee on Investigations of the Committee on Governmental Affairs*, Senate, 100th Cong., 2d Sess. (1988), 530–33 (testimony of Angelo Lonardo); Ovid Demaris, *The Last Mafioso: The Treacherous World of Jimmy Fratianno* (New York: Bantam, 1981), pp. 105–106, 188–89.

27. Testimony of Russell (1959), in Box 9, COI (NYSA); weather records available at http://www.farmersalmanac.com/weather-history/13732/1957/11/14/.

28. Testimony of Russell (1959), in Box 9, COI (NYSA).

29. For a list of the attendees, see table 10–1. For their transportation to Apalachin, see Report to Governor Averell Harriman, November 27, 1957, in Box 1, COI (NYSA), and Arthur L. Reuter, Acting Commissioner of Investigation, *Report on the Activities and Associations of Persons Identified as Present at the Residence of Joseph Barbara, Sr., at Apalachin, New York, on November 14, 1957, and the Reasons for Their Presence* (1958) (hereafter "Reuter Report").

30. *United States v. Bufalino* (S.D.N.Y. 1959) (testimony of Russell) (NARA NY); testimony of Russell (1959), in Box 9, COI (NYSA); testimony of Vincent Rao (1959), in Box 7, COI (NYSA); *Binghamton Press*, July 1, 1959.

31. *United States v. Bufalino*, 285 F.2d 408, 412 (2d Cir. 1960); testimony of Russell (1959), in Box 9, COI (NYSA).

32. Report of Trooper Vincent Vasisko, November 23, 1957, in Box 1, COI

(NYSA); testimony of Rao (1959), in Box 7, COI (NYSA); *New York Times*, November 15, 1957; *Binghamton Press*, December 21, 1959.

33. Interview with Croswell, in Box 1, COI (NYSA); *United States v. Bufalino* (S.D.N.Y. 1959) (testimony of Vincent Vasisko) (NARA NY).

34. *Hearings on Organized Crime: 25 Years after Valachi*, 389 (testimony of Valachi); *Bufalino*, 285 F.2d at 412.

35. *United States v. Bufalino* (S.D.N.Y. 1959) (testimony of Croswell) (NARA NY); testimony of Croswell (NYSA). In contrast, Gil Reavill asserts that "Croswell had done a sly thing," consciously trying to "lull those at the estate into a false sense of confidence, that they could leave the estate without being stopped." Gil Reavill, *Mafia Summit: J. Edgar Hoover, the Kennedy Brothers, and the Meeting That Unmasked the Mob* (New York: St. Martin's Press, 2013), p. 95. This is one of multiple points in which *Mafia Summit* is at variance with the eyewitness statements or investigative records of the State Commission of Investigation and *United States v. Bufalino* (S.D.N.Y. 1959).

36. Interview with Croswell, in Box 1, COI (NYSA); *United States v. Bufalino* (S.D.N.Y. 1959) (testimony of Croswell) (NARA NY).

37. Report of Vincent Vasisko, November 23, 1957, in Box 1, COI (NYSA); *United States v. Bufalino* (S.D.N.Y. 1959) (testimony of Croswell) (NARA NY).

38. Report of Lt. K. E. Weidenborner, November 16, 1957, in Box 1, COI (NYSA).

39. Report to Governor Harriman, November 27, 1957, and Report of Trooper Cohen, November 15, 1957, both in Box 1, COI (NYSA).

40. *Hearings on Organized Crime: 25 Years after Valachi*, 350 (testimony of Valachi); *New York Times*, November 22, 1957.

41. *United States v. Bufalino* (S.D.N.Y. 1959) (testimony of Croswell) (NARA NY); *Hearings on Organized Crime: 25 Years after Valachi*, 308 (testimony of John Shanley).

42. Report to Governor Harriman, November 27, 1957, in Box 1, COI (NYSA).

43. Reuter Report, p. 16 and appendix.

44. Rocco Morelli, *Forgetta 'bout It: From Mafia to Ministry* (, FL: Bridge-Logos, 2007), p. 74; Report to Governor Harriman, November 27, 1957, in Box 1, COI (NYSA).

45. FBI Report, Joseph Civello, August 31, 1961, in Records of the Federal Bureau of Investigation, Record Group 65, National Archives and Records Administration, College Park, MD ("NARA College Park").

46. Report to Governor Harriman, November 27, 1957, in Box 1, COI (NYSA); *United States v. Bufalino* (S.D.N.Y. 1959) (testimony of Croswell) (NARA NY).

47. *United States v. Bufalino* (S.D.N.Y. 1959) (testimony of Croswell) (NARA NY).

48. Also in the Falcone car were Dominick D'Agostino and Samuel Lagattuta of Buffalo. Ibid.

49. *Hearings on Organized Crime: 25 Years after Valachi*, 386 (testimony of Valachi); *Utica Press*, July 2, 1958.

50. *Utica Press*, February 8, 1958; May 20, 1959; May 24, 1963.

51. *United States v. Bufalino* (S.D.N.Y. 1959) (testimonies of Kenneth Brown and Arthur Ruston); Report of Vasisko, November 23, 1957 (NYSA).

52. Report of B. Muthig, November 15, 1957, in Box 1, COI (NYSA); *United States v. Bufalino* (S.D.N.Y. 1959) (testimony of Brown) (NY NARA).

53. Reuter Report, p. 41 and App. C; *New York Times*, November 3, 1959.

54. Testimony of Kenneth Brown, in Box 1, COI (NYSA); Reuter Report, appendix C, p. 6a; Report of Trooper B. Muthig, November 15, 1957, in Box 1, COI (NYSA).

55. Bonanno, *Man of Honor*, p. 216.

56. Report to Governor Harriman, November 27, 1957, in Box 1, COI (NYSA). This matches Bonanno's number in the Social Security Death Index, http://ssdmf.info/ (accessed July 25, 2013).

57. *Binghamton Press*, November 14, 1984.

58. *United States v. Bufalino* (S.D.N.Y. 1959) (joint stipulation on Trafficante airline tickets) (NARA NY); Report of Trooper F. A. Tiffany, November 15, 1957, in Box 1, COI (NYSA).

59. Report on Discharge of Firearms by Trooper F. A. Tiffany, November 15, 1957, in Box 1, COI (NYSA).

60. *United States v. Bufalino* (S.D.N.Y. 1959) (testimony of Glenn Craig) (NARA NY); Report of Trooper T. G. Sackel, November 14, 1957, in Box 1, COI (NYSA).

61. Testimony of Croswell, in Box 1, COI (NYSA); Appellee's Brief, *United States v. Bufalino* (2d Cir. 1960), in RG 65 (NARA College Park).

62. Report to Governor Harriman, November 27, 1957, in Box 1, COI (NYSA).

63. United States Census Bureau, *1920 Federal Population Census*, James Colletti, District 133, Ouray, CO; United States Census Bureau, *1920 Federal Population Census*, Frank Zito, District 174, Springfield, IL.

64. FBI Report, James Colletti, June 8, 1959, and FBI Report, Frank Zito, June 5, 1959, both in RG 65 (NARA College Park).

65. Reuter Report, appendix C, pp. 15, 62; Report to Governor Harriman, November 27, 1957, in Box 1, COI (NYSA); Report of Trooper Smith, November 15,

1957, in Box 1, COI (NYSA); *United States v. Bufalino* (S.D.N.Y. 1959) (testimony of Joseph Smith) (NARA NY).

66. David Witwer, *Corruption and Reform in the Teamsters Union* (Chicago: University of Illinois Press, 2008), p. 171.

67. Report of Muthig, November 15, 1957, and Report to Governor Harriman, November 27, 1957, both in Box 1, COI (NYSA).

68. Report of Trooper C. F. Erway, November 14, 1957, Report of Trooper C. M. Dobbs, November 15, 1957, Report of Trooper M. Capozzi, November 15, 1957, all in Box 1, COI (NYSA).

69. Testimony of Croswell (1957), in Box 1, COI (NYSA); Report of Erway, November 14, 1957, in Box 1, COI (NYSA).

70. Memorandum of Eliot Lumbard to Edward Kirk, December 4, 1958, in Box 5, COI (NYSA); Report of Special Agent Patrick Collins, New Orleans Field Office, La Cosa Nostra, July 11, 1967, in RG 65 (NARA College Park).

71. Testimony of Russell, in Box 9, COI (NYSA).

72. Testimony of Joseph Benenati (1959), in Box 7, COI (NYSA).

73. Memorandum of Lumbard to Kirk, December 4, 1958, in Box 5, COI (NYSA).

74. FBI Memorandum, Subject: Samuel M. Giancana, January 18, 1966, in RG 65 (NARA College Park).

75. William F. Roemer Jr., *Accardo: The Genuine Godfather* (New York: Ballantine Books, 1995), pp. 166–67, 194–96; William F. Roemer Jr., *Roemer: Man against the Mob* (New York: Ballantine Books, 1989), pp. 114–19; Antoinette Giancana, *Mafia Princess: Growing up in Sam Giancana's Family* (New York: William Morrow, 1984), pp. 156–57.

76. Memorandum of Agent Skinner, Re: Neil Migliore, September 18, 1958, in Box 5, COI (NYSA); Reuter Report, appendix A–3. The driver of the other car told police that he saw two passengers in Migliore's car. To settle the case, Neil Migliore and his father Americo Migliore signed a release saying they were passengers in the car, and Neil forged the signature of Peter Valenti, as the third passenger. None of these three men was likely to have been invited to attend the Apalachin meeting. FBI Report of Albany Field Office, August 14, 1959, in RG 65 (NARA College Park); *Binghamton Press*, July 24, 1959.

77. Memorandum, Suspected Attendees, March 19, 1959, in Box 5, COI (NYSA). Joe Bonanno claimed "Lucchese, I later learned from my own sources, had avoided police detection by ... grabbing a ride with a soda delivery truck." Bonanno, *Man of Honor*, p. 215. This may be another face-saving story by Bonanno.

78. Testimony of Croswell, in Box 1, COI (NYSA).

79. Despite speculation, there is no reliable proof for the attendance of Milwaukee boss Frank Balistrieri; New England boss Raymond Patriarca; St. Louis boss John Vitale; former Boston boss Philip Buccola; Rockford, Illinois, underboss Joseph Zammuto; Detroit *caporegime* Anthony Giacalone; the Controni brothers of Montreal; or Giuseppe Settacase of Sicily.

80. The FBI investigated allegations that other Floridians were present at Apalachin. However, they discovered that Bartola Failla of Miami had traveled to New Jersey for a denaturalization proceeding. FBI Memorandum, Meeting of Hoodlums, December 12, 1958, in RG 65 (NARA College Park). Although an informant reported Joe Silesi, Trafficante's gambling partner, was present, the FBI found no corroborating evidence. FBI Report, Activities of Top Hoodlums, September 14, 1959, in RG 65 (NARA College Park). The Commission and the FBI also investigated two associates of Northeastern Pennsylvania boss Russell Bufalino. They suspected Modesto "Murph" Loquasto, but an FBI informant saw him operating a craps game in Pittston, Pennsylvania, on the evening of November 14, 1957. FBI Report on Russell Bufalino, May 16, 1958, in RG 65 (NARA College Park). They also looked hard at William Medico of Pittston, but uncovered only a summer trip to Apalachin. FBI Memorandum, William Medico, June 24, 1959, in RG 65 (NARA College Park).

81. Reavill, *Mafia Summit*, pp. 5, 146.

82. Testimony of Russell, in Box 9, COI (NYSA). At most, Russell conceded, it could "possibly" have been more, but she gave no higher numbers. Ibid.

83. *Binghamton Press*, August 5, 1963.

84. Report of Trooper Greer, November 15, 1957, and Report of Trooper Cohen, November 15, 1957, both in Box 1, COI (NYSA).

85. Interview with Croswell, in Box 1, COI (NYSA); *United States v. Bufalino* (S.D.N.Y. 1959) (testimony of Croswell) (NARA NY).

86. Testimony of Croswell, in Box 1, COI (NYSA).

87. Interview with Croswell, in Box 1, COI (NYSA).

88. *Chicago Tribune*, November 15, 1957; *San Francisco Chronicle*, November 15, 1957; *New York Times*, November 15, 1957; *New York Daily News*, November 15, 1957.

89. *Binghamton Press*, November 18 and 21, 1957; *New York Times*, November 26, 1957.

90. *Life*, December 9, 1957.

91. Bonanno, *Man of Honor*, p. 211.

92. *Life*, December 9, 1957, p. 57.

93. Bonanno, *Man of Honor*, p. 212.

94. *Albany Knickerbocker*, October 16, 1961; *Utica Press*, April 12, 1962; *New York Herald Tribune*, November 4, 1959.

95. *United States v. Bufalino*, 285 F.2d 408, 419 (2d Cir. 1960) (Clark, J., concurring); *Binghamton Press*, November 13, 1977.

96. Since the appellate court reversed the convictions for insufficient evidence, it did not reach the trial court's ruling on the legality of the detention. The concurring judge, however, noted that the detention and search were "highly dubious" and that the admission of the resulting statements into evidence was of "doubtful validity." *United States v. Bufalino*, 285 F.2d at 420 n. 3. These actions would likely be considered unconstitutional today. *Brown v. Texas*, 443 U.S. 47, 53 (1979).

97. *United States v. Bufalino* (S.D.N.Y. 1959) (testimony of Croswell) (NARA NY).

98. Dennis Eisenberg, Uri Dan, and Eli Landau, *Meyer Lansky: Mogul of the Mob* (New York: Paddington Press, 1979), p. 248.

99. Robert Lacey, *Little Man: Meyer Lansky and the Gangster Life* (New York: Little, Brown, 1991), p. 35. Croswell denied having any advanced knowledge of the meeting. Interview of Croswell, in Box 1, COI (NYSA).

100. *Hearings on Organized Crime: 25 Years after Valachi*, 387–88 (testimony of Valachi); FBI Report, Meeting of Hoodlums, Apalachin, NY, October 31, 1958, in RG 65 (NARA College Park).

101. FBI Report, Meeting of Hoodlums, Apalachin, NY, November 20, 1959, and FBI Report, Santo Trafficante, January 17, 1958, both in RG 65 (NARA College Park).

102. Testimony of Roy Williams, quoted in James B. Jacobs, Christopher Panarella, and Jay Worthington, *Busting the Mob: United States v. Cosa Nostra* (New York: New York University Press, 1994), p. 187.

103. Bonanno, *Man of Honor*, p. 209.

104. Selwyn Raab, *Five Families: The Rise, Decline, and Resurgence of America's Most Powerful Mafia Empires* (New York: St. Martin's Press, 2005), pp. 118–19.

105. Reavill, *Mafia Summit*, pp. 90, 206–207, 275.

106. Reuter Report, p. 24; *New York Times*, July 10–11 and July 23, 1956.

107. See chapter 4.

108. Testimony of Joseph Profaci (1959), in Box 7, COI (NYSA); testimony of Joseph Magliocco (1958), in Box 9, COI (NYSA).

109. Colloquy of Robert Kennedy and John Montana in *Hearings before the Select Committee on Improper Activities*, 12312–14.

110. Testimony of Rao (1959), in Box 7, COI (NYSA); *United States v. Bufalino* (S.D.N.Y. 1959) (testimony of Croswell) (NARA NY).

111. *United States v. Bufalino*, 285 F.2d at 412–19 (Clark, J., concurring). Given Croswell's prior wiretapping, defense lawyers cross-examined Croswell concerning whether he was tipped off by a wiretap that day. Croswell testified that he had not listened to a wiretap on Barbara's house in some time, and the defense had no contrary evidence. *United States v. Bufalino* (S.D.N.Y. 1959) (testimony of Croswell) (NARA NY).

112. *Binghamton Press*, June 22, 1959.

113. Wiretap conversation quoted in *Saturday Evening Post*, November 9, 1963.

114. Bonanno, *Man of Honor*, p. 215.

115. Joseph Valachi, "The Real Thing" (unpublished manuscript), p. 922, in Boxes 1–2, Joseph Valachi Personal Papers, John F. Kennedy Presidential Library and Museum, Boston, MA.

116. Nicholas Pileggi, *Wiseguy: Life in a Mafia Family* (New York: Simon and Schuster, 1985), p. 22.

117. President Eisenhower's Daily Appointment Schedule, Friday, November 15, 1957, available at http://millercenter.org/scripps/archive/documents/dde/diary, Dwight D. Eisenhower Presidential Library and Museum, Abilene, KS; Daily Logs of the Director of the FBI, November 15, 1957, in RG 65 (NARA College Park).

118. *New York Times*, November 16, 1957.

119. Interview of Robert Kennedy, quoted in Edwin Guthman and Jeffrey Shulman, eds., *Robert Kennedy in His Own Words: The Unpublished Recollections of the Kennedy Years* (New York: Bantam, 1988), p. 120.

120. William C. Sullivan, *The Bureau: My Thirty Years in Hoover's FBI* (New York: W. W. Norton, 1979), pp. 117–22.

121. FBI Report, MAFIA, July 9, 1958, in FBI FOIA File on Mafia Monograph, available at http://vault.fbi.gov/Mafia%20Monograph (accessed July 25, 2013).

122. Ibid., p. 2 (underline in original). The report's evidence was weak by today's standards

123. Sullivan, *Bureau*, p. 121.

124. Roemer, *Man against the Mob*, p. 24.

125. Letter of J. Edgar Hoover, March 14, 1961, reprinted in *Everything Secret Degenerates: The FBI's Use of Murderers as Informants: House Rep. 108–414*, House of Representatives, 108th Cong., 2d Sess. (2004), 1–15, 38–40, 126–29, 452–57; *Hearings on Organized Crime: 25 Years after Valachi*, 238–392 (testimony of Valachi).

126. This table is derived from (1) Reports of Troopers, November 15, 1957, in Box 1, COI (NYSA); (2) Memorandum of Lumbard to Kirk, December 4, 1958, in Box 5, COI (NYSA); and (3) the Reuter Report. The attendees' positions are based on FBI reports and Mafia family charts in *Organized Crime and Illicit Traffic in Narcotics:*

Hearings before the Committee on Government Operations, Permanent Subcommittee on Investigations, Senate, 88th Cong., 1st Sess. (1963).

127. Although Joseph Barbara Sr. and Russell Bufalino were technically under the Magaddino Family of Buffalo, for all practical purposes Barbara was the boss of Endicott, New York, and Bufalino was the boss of northeastern Pennsylvania. FBI Report, The Criminal "Commission;" Buffalo Division, January 14, 1963, and FBI AIRTEL, La Cosa Nostra AR–Conspiracy, April 1, 1969, both in RG 65 (NARA College Park).

SELECT BIBLIOGRAPHY

Archival Sources

John F. Kennedy Presidential Library and Museum, Boston, MA
  Joseph Valachi Papers, 1964
  Records of Robert F. Kennedy, 1957–1963
John Jay College of Criminal Justice, Lloyd Sealy Library, New York, NY
  Trial Transcripts of the County of New York, Court of General Sessions, 1883–1927
Kheel Center for Labor-Management Documentation and Archives, Ithaca, New York
  Records of International Ladies' Garment Workers' Union, Transcript in *People against Macri*
National Archives and Records Administration, College Park, MD
  Records of the Department of State, Files of Suspected Narcotics Traffickers, 1923–1954
  Records of the Federal Bureau of Investigation, 1896–1996
  Records of the Federal Bureau of Narcotics, 1915–1946
  Records of the Federal Bureau of Prisons, Case Files of Notorious Offenders, 1919–1975
  Records of the United States Secret Service, Daily Reports of Agents, 1875–1936
National Archives and Records Administration, New York, NY
  Records of the United States Court of Appeals for the Second Circuit
  Records of the United States District Court for the Southern District of New York
National Archives and Records Administration, Washington, DC
  Records of the Special Committee to Investigate Organized Crime in Interstate Commerce
  Records of the Senate Permanent Subcommittee on Investigations
New York Municipal Archives, New York, NY
  Kings County District Attorney, Murder, Inc., Case Files, 1940–1945
  Lucky Luciano Closed Case File, 1936
  New York Police Department Files on Albert Anastasia Case, 1954–1963
  New York County District Attorney Records, Closed Case Files, 1895–1966

Office of the Chief Medical Examiner, Death Records, 1918–1946
Records of Mayor Fiorello LaGuardia, Subject Files, 1934–1945
New York State Archives, Albany, NY
   Master Files of the New York State Temporary Commission of Investigation on
      Apalachin
   Records of the Department of Correctional Services
Stanford University, Department of Special Collections, Stanford, CA
   Federal Bureau of Narcotics Agent George White Papers, 1932–1970
University of Notre Dame, Rare Books and Special Collections, Notre Dame, IN
   Federal Bureau of Narcotics Agent Max H. Roder Journals, 1931–1959
University of Rochester, Department of Special Collections, Rochester, NY
   Governor Thomas E. Dewey Papers, Prison Reports of Charles Luciano
Wisconsin Historical Society, Madison, Wisconsin
   International Brotherhood of Teamsters, Chauffeurs, Warehousemen and Helpers
      of America Records, 1904–1952

Books

Abadinsky, Howard. *Organized Crime*, 10th ed. (Belmont, CA: Wadsworth, 2013).

Anderson, Annelise. *The Business of Organized Crime: A Cosa Nostra Family* (Stanford, CA: Hoover Institution Press, 1979).

Bell, Daniel. *The End of Ideology* (New York: Collier Books, 1961).

Block, Alan A. *East Side, West Side: Organizing Crime in New York, 1930–1950* (Piscataway, NJ: Transaction Publishers, 1983).

Bonanno, Joseph, with Sergio Lalli. *A Man of Honor: The Autobiography of Joseph Bonanno* (New York: Simon and Schuster, 1983).

Capeci, Jerry, and Gene Mustain. *Mob Star: The Story of John Gotti* (Indianapolis: Alpha, 1988).

Carter, David. *Stonewall: The Riots That Sparked the Gay Revolution* (New York: St. Martin's, 2010).

Courtwright, David, et al. *Addicts Who Survived: An Oral History of Narcotic Use in America, 1923–1965* (Knoxville: University of Tennessee Press, 1989).

Critchley, David. *The Origin of Organized Crime in America: The New York City Mafia, 1891–1931* (New York: Routledge, 2009).

Dash, Mike. *The First Family: Terror, Extortion, Revenge, Murder, and the Birth of the American Mafia* (New York: Simon and Schuster, 2009).

Dickie, John. *Cosa Nostra: A History of the Sicilian Mafia* (New York: Palgrave Mac-Millan, 2004).

Federal Writers' Project. *New York City Guide* (New York: Random House, 1939).

Fiorentini, Gianluca, and Sam Peltzman, eds. *The Economics of Organised Crime* (Cambridge: Cambridge University Press, 1995).

Flynn, William J. *The Barrel Mystery* (New York: J. A. McCann, 1919).

Fox, Stephen. *Blood and Power: Organized Crime in 20th-Century America* (New York: Penguin Books, 1990).

Gambetta, Diego. *Codes of the Underworld: How Criminals Communicate* (Princeton, NJ: Princeton University Press, 2011).

Gentile, Nicola. *Vita di Capomafia* (Rome: Editori Riuniti, 1963).

Goldstock, Ronald, Director, and James B. Jacobs, Principal Draftsman. *Corruption and Racketeering in the New York City Construction Industry: The Final Report of the New York State Organized Crime Taskforce* (New York: New York University Press, 1991).

Griffin, Joe, with Don DeNevi. *Mob Nemesis: How the FBI Crippled Organized Crime* (Amherst, NY: Prometheus Books, 2002).

Hunt, Thomas, and Michael A. Tona. *DiCarlo: Buffalo's First Family of Crime*, vols. 1 and (Raleigh, NC: lulu, 2013).

Ianni, Francis A. J. *A Family Business: Kinship and Social Control in Organized Crime* (New York: Russell Sage Foundation, 1972).

Jacobs, James B. *Mobsters, Unions, and Feds: The Mafia and the American Labor Movement* (New York: New York University Press, 2003).

Jacobs, James B. Coleen Friel, and Robert Radick. *Gotham Unbound: How New York City Was Liberated from the Grip of Organized Crime* (New York: New York University Press, 1999).

Joselit, Jenna Weissman. *Our Gang: Jewish Crime and the New York Jewish Community, 1900–1940* (Bloomington: Indiana University Press, 1983).

Lerner, Michael A. *Dry Manhattan: Prohibition in New York City* (Cambridge, MA: Harvard University Press, 2007).

Levitt, Steven D., and Stephen J. Dubner. *Freakonomics: A Rogue Economist Explores the Hidden Side of Everything* (New York: William Morrow, 2009).

Maas, Peter. *The Valachi Papers* (New York: G. P. Putnam's Sons, 1968).

Meyer, Kathryn, and Terry Parssinen. *Webs of Smoke: Smugglers, Warlords, Spies, and the History of the International Drug Trade* (New York: Rowman and Littlefield, 2002).

Mitchell, Kevin. *Jacobs Beach: The Mob, The Fights, The Fifties* (New York: Pegasus, 2010).

Nelli, Humbert. *The Business of Crime: Italians and Syndicate Crime in the United States* (New York: Oxford University Press, 1976).

Pileggi, Nicholas. *Wiseguy: Life in a Mafia Family* (New York: Simon and Schuster, 1985).

Pistone, Joseph D. with Richard Woodley. *Donnie Brasco: My Undercover Life in the Mafia* (New York: Penguin Putnam, 1989).

Raab, Selwyn. *Five Families: The Rise, Decline, and Resurgence of America's Most Powerful Mafia Empires* (New York: Thomas Dunne Books, 2006).

Reuter, Peter. *Disorganized Crime: Illegal Markets and the Mafia* (Cambridge, MA: Massachusetts Institute of Technology Press, 1985).

Schatzberg, Rufus, and Robert J. Kelly. *African American Organized Crime: A Social History* (New Brunswick, NJ: Rutgers University Press, 1997).

Schneider, Eric C. *Smack: Heroin and the American City* (Philadelphia: University of Pennsylvania Press, 2011).

Turkus, Burton B., and Sid Feder. *Murder, Inc.: The Story of the Syndicate* (New York: Farrar, Straus and Young, 1952).

United States Treasury Department, Bureau of Narcotics. *Mafia: The Government's Secret File on Organized Crime* (New York: Collins, 2007).

Varese, Frederico. *Mafias on the Move: How Organized Crime Conquers New Territories* (Princeton, NJ: Princeton University Press, 2013).

Valentine, Douglas. *The Strength of the Wolf: The Secret History of America's War on Drugs* (New York: Verso, 2004).

White, Shane, et al. *Playing the Numbers: Gambling in Harlem between the Wars* (Cambridge, MA: Harvard University Press, 2010).

Witwer, David. *Corruption and Reform in the Teamsters Union* (Champaign: University of Illinois Press, 2003).

———. *The Shadow of the Racketeer: Scandal in Organized Labor* (Champaign: University of Illinois Press, 2009).

Wolf, George, with Joseph DiMona. *Frank Costello: Prime Minister of the Underworld* (New York: William Morrow, 1974).

Woodiwiss, Michael. *Organized Crime and American Power: A History* (Toronto: University of Toronto Press, 2001).

INDEX

AAMONY. *See* Associated Amusement Machine Operators of New York (AAMONY)

Abbattemarco, Frank, 205

Abbattemarco, Tony, 205

Abbrescia, Angelo, 148

Abraham Lincoln Independent Political Club, 179

Abruzzi, Dom, 140

Accardi, Settimo, 202

Accardo, Anthony ("Tony"), 267, 280

Acropolis, John ("Little Caesar"), 121–22

Adelstein, Bernard ("Bernie"), 120, 121–22

Adonis, Joe, 56, 90, 235

Adonis Social Club, 101

Agone, Joseph, 202

Agueci, Albert, 143

Agueci, U.S. v., 142

Agueci, Vito, 143

Aiello, Joseph, 71, 76, 77, 87

Aiello Family, 76, 77

Alabiso, Luigi, 132, 148

Alaimo, Dominick, 257, 280

A. L. A. Schechter Poultry Corporation, 32–33

Albanese, Philip ("Philly Katz"), 149, 177–78, 202

Albasi, John, 149

Albero, Charles ("Little Bullets"), 137, 149, 202

Alberti, Andrew ("Andy"), 200, 240, 241, 245–46, 247

alcohol. *See* bootlegging

Alcohol and Tobacco Tax Division. *See* Treasury Department

Alescia, James, 90, 95, 145, 149

Allegra, Melchiorre, 197

Allied Truckmen's Mutual Association, 99

Allocco, Dominick, 149

Alo, Vincent, 216

Aloi, Sevastian ("Buster"), 189

Altimari, Michael, 149

Amalgamated Meat Cutters Union, 32, 38–39

Ameli, Salvatore, 149

Amen, John Harlan, 209

Amendola, Frank, 149

American Civil Liberties Union, 217

American-Italian Club in San Diego, CA, 199

American Mercury (magazine), 158

Anaclerio, Germaio, 149, 200

Analyze This (film), 269–70

Anastasia, Albert ("The Executioner"), 12, 25, 26, 56, 75, 87, 105, 111, 112, 117, 119, 120, 133, 209, 230, 231–40, 240, 241–47, 242, 243–44, 247, 253, 260, 263, 272

Anastasia Family, 62, 133, 234, 235–36, 238, 240, 244

Anastasio, Albert, Jr., 236, 239
Anastasio, Anthony ("Tough Tony"),
    24–25, 26, 102, 106, 242, 247
Anastasio, Gerardo ("Jerry"), 24–25, 106
Anastasio, Joseph, 24–25, 106
Anastasio, Salvatore, 236
Anastasio, Umberto. *See* Anastasia,
    Albert ("The Executioner")
Anderson, George, 139
Angelicola, Alfred, 255
Angiulo, Gennaro ("Jerry"), 192
Annicchiarico, Anthony, 149
Anslinger, Harry, 140
Apalachin, NY, 12, 129, 137, 185, 194,
    199, 213, 215–16, 221, 222, 224, 248,
    249–81
    attendees, Nov. 14, 1957 Mafia
        Meeting, 277–81
    map of Barbara estate, 261
Arcel, Ray, 164, 166
Ardito, John, 149, 202
Arlington Hotel, 252, 253, 267
Armone, Joseph ("Joe Piney"), 145, 149,
    200, 246
Armone, Stephen ("Steve"), 132, 133,
    145, 149, 240, 245, 246, 247
Armour and Company, 254
Armstrong, Louis, 157
Aronica, Eduardo, 200
Arra, Frank, 204
assault and battery. *See* strongarm tactics
Associated Amusement Machine Opera-
    tors of New York (AAMONY), 185
Atlanta Federal Penitentiary, 11, 46, 47,
    56, 73, 90
Atlantic City, NJ, 209
Attardi, Alfonso, 149

Auburn, NY, 259, 278
Aviles, U.S. v., 142
Avola, Mario, 149
Azores, The (restaurant), 38

Ball, Lucille, 157
Baltimore, MD, 19, 138
Baratta, Peter, 200
Barbara, Josephine Vivona, 249, 253,
    256, 266, 273
Barbara, Joseph, Jr., 254–55, 260, 278
Barbara, Joseph, Sr., 65, 248, 249–51,
    252, 253–54, 255, 266, 268, 270, 273,
    274, 278
    map of estate, 261
Barbato, Arnold, 149
Barbato, Salvatore, 149
Barbella, Rocco. *See* Graziano, Rocky
Barboza, Joe ("The Animal"), 180
Barcellona, Charles, 149, 200
Barese, Ernesto, 200, 235
Barra, Joseph, 202
Barrasso, Albert, 202
Barzini, Don (fictional character), 127, 128
Bayer (company), 129, 130
BCI. *See* New York State Police, Bureau
    of Criminal Investigation
Bell, Daniel, 100
Bellanca, Sebastiano, 149, 200, 235
Belloise, Steve, 163
Belmont, Al, 276
Bendenelli, Joseph, 204
Bennett, Harry, 33
Bentvena, U.S. v., 142
Berkshire Downs horse track, 158
Bernava, Joseph, 202
Bilko, Sergeant (fictional character), 155

Billingsley, Sherman, 157

Binaggio, Charles, 219

Biondo, Joseph, 240, 244, 245, 247

"Black Handers," 35

Black Mafia: Ethnic Succession in Organized Crime (Ianni), 100

Block, Alan, 131

Block, Max ("The Butcher"), 32, 38–39

Blood Covenant (Franzese), 103

Blumenthal, Sam, 118–19

Boardwalk Empire (TV series), 12, 45, 81, 283

Boccia, Ferdinand ("The Shadow"), 197, 226, 227

Boggs-Daniel Act, 272–73

Boiardo, Anthony, 202

Boiardo, Ruggiero ("Richie the Book"), 190

Bonadio, Paul, 202, 235

Bonanno, Bill (son of Joseph), 66, 128, 145–46, 148, 283

Bonanno, Joseph ("Joe"), 12, 28, 33, 34, 49, 52, 64, 66, 71–72, 76, 78, 79, 81, 91, 94, 96, 97, 98, 146, 179, 209, 225, 230, 232, 233, 244, 247, 252, 262–63, 270, 272, 274, 277, 283
    and drugs, 125, 127, 128, 129, 130, 140, 144, 145

Bonanno, William (food distributor in Tucson, AZ), 214

Bonanno Family, 59, 62, 96, 97, 142, 144, 145, 146, 170, 180, 195, 200, 253, 259, 277

Bonasera, Cassandros, 205

Bonfiglio, Frank, 228

Bongiorno, Frank ("Frankie Brown"), 158

Bonina, Nicholas, 204

Bonventre, John, 252, 262, 277

Bonventre, Vito, 76, 81

bookmaking. *See* gambling

Booth Fisheries, 115

bootlegging, 25, 46, 49, 51–53, 55–56, 65, 67, 71, 72, 75, 77, 79, 81, 82, 88, 94, 101, 127, 155, 156, 157, 171, 180, 181, 184–85, 190, 194, 250–51

Boston, MA, 85, 164, 179, 220, 238, 256, 259

Boston Garden, 164

"Bottle Alley Gang," 64

Bound by Honor (Bonanno), 145–46

Bove, Joseph, 149

boxing, 160–66

Boxing Managers Guild, 34, 162, 164

Brando, Marlon, 20, 126, 127

Brescia, Lorenzo, 202

bribery, 8, 46, 109, 165, 181, 187, 191, 208, 209–210, 213, 270

Brindell, Robert, 106

Bronfman, Samuel, 51

Bronx, 38, 39, 52, 58, 76, 80, 83, 130, 160, 170, 189, 197, 207, 209, 234
    Belmont, 58
    Central Bronx, 58, 75, 117, 188, 200, 234
    East Bronx/Pelham Bay, 188, 200, 201, 203
    Little Italy in, 234
    North Bronx, 177, 188, 201–205
    South Bronx, 188, 202, 203, 204

Bronx, Upper Manhattan, and Brooklyn Fish Dealers Association, 114

Bronx Terminal Market, 39

Brooklyn, 19, 20, 23, 24, 25, 26, 27, 29, 30, 38, 39, 42, 47, 55, 56, 58, 71, 72,

77, 78, 79, 80–81, 83, 87, 96, 103,
  105–106, 127, 131, 147, 184, 188,
  189, 197, 200–206, 209, 228, 232
    Bensonhurst, 179
    Central Brooklyn, 66, 75, 76
    Coney Island, 76, 86, 88–89
    Fort Greene, 39
    Red Hook, 23, 25, 58, 110, 111
    South Brooklyn, 23, 75, 76, 80, 101,
      106, 109–113, 188, 209
    Williamsburg, 49, 58, 179
Brooklyn Fish Dealers Association, 34
Brooklyn Trade Waste Removers Associa-
  tion (BTWRA), 120
Brown, Harry, 95
Brown, Kenneth, 255, 256–57, 260, 262
Browne, Claude, 139
Brownell, Herbert, 217
BTWRA. *See* Brooklyn Trade Waste
  Removers Association (BTWRA)
Buchalter, Louis ("Lepke"), 38, 107, 116,
  130
Buckeye Cigarette Service Company, 255
Bufalino, Russell, 198, 236, 258, 267, 280
Bufalino Family, 198–99, 257
Buffalo, NY, 76, 77, 96, 97, 248, 255,
  256, 262, 266, 267, 279
Buia, Angelo, 149
Buia, Matildo, 149
Building Services Employees Local 51B,
  107
burglary. *See* criminal receiver of stolen
  goods
Buscetta, Tomasso, 141
Busso, Johnny, 240, 245–46
Buzzeo, Philip, 149

Cafaro, Vincent ("Fish"), 59, 108, 182,
  187, 193
Calderone, Antonio, 179, 199
Callace, Frank, 149, 204
Callinbrano, Sally, 59
Calloway, Cab, 157
Cal-Neva Lodge, 158
Camarda, Emil, 24, 105, 110
Camden, NJ, 188, 204
Camorra gang, 39, 47, 131
Campisi, Charles, 149
Campisi, Thomas, 149, 202
Canada Dry bottling company (Endicott,
  NY), 254
Cannone, Ignatius ("Nat"), 257, 258, 278
Cantalupo Realty, 179
Capalbo, Gaetano, 149
Capeci, Jerry, 245
Capeheart, Homer, 219
CAPGA (code name for reactivation of
  Capone gang), 221
Capone, Alphonse ("Al," "Scarface"), 12,
  23, 46, 49, 71, 76, 77, 87–88, 88, 90,
  95, 96, 97, 101, 157, 191, 209, 211,
  215, 221
Caponigro, Antonio, 202
Capuzzi, Nick, 76, 83
Carbo, Paolo ("Frankie" a.k.a. Mr. Gray),
  38, 158, 160–62, 163, 164, 165, 166,
  204
Carfano, Anthony ("Little Augie
  Pisano"), 56, 107, 225, 238
Carillo, Anthony, 202
Carlisi, Roy, 266, 279
Carminati, Anthony, 149, 200
Carter, David, 172
Carting, Rex, 122

Caruso, Frank, 132, 149, 202

Casablanca, James, 149, 200

Casablanca, Joseph, 149

Casablanca, Vincent, 149

Casella, Peter, 149

Casertano, Steve, 149

Casso, Anthony ("Gaspipe"), 59–60, 193–94

Castellammarese clan, 55, 72, 75, 76, 77, 78, 79, 80, 81, 88, 90, 96, 270

Castellammarese War of 1930–1931, 7, 71–98

Castellano, Paul, 148, 181, 191, 199, 258, 277

Castiglia, Francesco. *See* Costello, Frank

Cataldo, Joseph ("Joe the Wop"), 169

Catania, James, 207

Catania, Joseph ("Joe the Baker"), 76, 81, 207

Catena, Gerardo ("Gerry"), 230, 258, 277

Cavalieri, Samuel, 149, 205

Celambrino, Salvatore, 202

Celi, Arthur, 149

Centore, Lawrence, 202

Cerrito, Joseph, 267, 281

Chauncey, George, 166–67

Chicago, IL, 49, 62, 76, 83, 87–88, 95, 96, 108, 138, 157, 164, 165, 191, 201, 202, 203, 209, 215, 221, 248, 257, 267, 272, 280

Chicago Outfit, 67, 76, 77, 95, 97, 108, 213, 267, 276
    See also Capone, Alphonse ("Al," "Scarface")

Chicago Stadium, 165

Chicago Tribune (newspaper), 269

Chiri, Charles Salvatore, 259, 279

Ciccone, Anthony, 150

Ciccone, Ralph, 150

Cinquegrana, Bendetto, 150

Cirillo, Dominick ("Quiet Dom"), 144

City Democratic Club, 24

Civella, Nick, 265, 272, 280

Civello, Joseph, 259, 272, 281

Clemente, Michelino ("Loader Mike"), 25–26, 202

Clemente, Salvatore, 196

Cleveland, OH, 87, 128, 138, 255, 258–59, 265–66, 272, 280

Club 82 (gay nightclub), 170

Club Abbey (speakeasy), 167

Club Durant (speakeasy), 157

Club Richman (speakeasy), 157

Coast Guard, 50, 51

Coca-Cola, 129

Coco, Eddie, 105, 162, 165

Coll, Babyface, 157

Coll, Vincent ("Mad Dog"), 93, 101, 211

Colletti, James ("Black Jim"), 264–65, 281

Collier's (magazine), 93

Colombo, Joseph ("Joe"), 179, 214

Colorado Cheese Company, 265

"Combination, The" (underworld's commission on boxing), 160–62

Commission, the (Cosa Nostra), 64, 95–98, 182, 198, 221, 230, 232, 234, 238, 248, 253, 267, 271, 272

Communist Party USA (CPUSA), 22, 109, 116, 217

Coney Island. *See* Brooklyn

Congress Plaza Hotel, 87–88

Consolo, Michael, 200

Contaldo, Thomas, 150

Controni, Frank, 143

Controni, Joseph, 143

Cooley, Robert, 212–13

Copacabana, the "Copa" (night club), 7, 155, 158–60, 211

Coppola, Anthony ("Cappy"), 236–37, 238, 239

Coppola, Francis Ford, 11–12, 93, 127

Coppola, Michael ("Trigger Mike"), 66, 190

Corallo, Anthony ("Tony Ducks"), 107, 132, 144, 150, 191, 210

Coralluzzo, Earl, 202

Corleone, Don Vito (fictional character), 126–27, 146, 195

Corleone, Michael (fictional character), 94, 198

Corleone, Sonny (fictional character), 195

Corona, Frank, 150

Corozzo, Nicholas ("Nicky"), 180

Corrao, Vincent, 150, 205

Corsaro, Michael, 150

Costello, Frank, 7, 50–52, 56, 65, 82, 90, 108, 127, 147, 155, 157, 158, 181, 192–93, 211, 214, 219, 225–32, 237, 244, 266

Costello, Loretta, 228

Cotton Club (night club), 157

counterfeiting, 11, 46, 73, 76, 95, 181, 196, 197, 200, 201, 203, 205, 206, 251

Court of Appeals, 215, 274

CPUSA. *See* Communist Party USA (CPUSA)

Craig, Glenn, 264

Crime Commission of Greater Miami, 218

criminal receiver of stolen goods, 22, 41–42, 43, 52, 65, 80, 81, 90, 94, 113, 147, 180, 183, 218

Crisci, Anthony, 150

Criscuolo, Alfred, 150, 202

Croswell, Edgar D., 249–51, 252–53, 254–55, 256–57, 258, 260, 262, 266, 268, 269, 270–71

Cuba, 158, 237, 238, 244, 256, 263, 272

Cucchiara, Frank, 259, 272, 279

Cuomo, Matthew, 200

Cupola, Alfred, 202

Curb Exchange, 53, 137

Cusamono, James, 149

D'Agostino, Dom, 279

Daily News (newspaper), 269

Dalessio, John, 183

Dalitz, Moe, 102

Dallas, TX, 259, 281

Dallesio, Alex, 201

Dallesio, John, 201

Dallesio, Mike, 201

D'Ambrosio, Al, 205

D'Ambrosio, Salvatore, 206

D'Aquila, Salvatore ("Totò"), 46–47, 72–73, 74, 76, 77, 80, 95

D'Argenio, Edward, 150, 205

Davis, John H., 93

Davis, J. Richard ("Dixie"), 93, 207, 212

De Brizzi, Alex, 201

DeCarlo, Angelo ("Gyp"), 158

DeCavalcante Family, 147–48, 259, 263–64

DeCurtis, Edward ("Eddie Toy"), 170

De Feo, Pete, 202

De George, James, 150

Della Femina, Jerry, 58

Delmonico's (restaurant), 30

DeLoach, Cartha ("Deke"), 221

Delta Fish Company, Inc., 114

De Lutro, Charles, 201

DeMarco, John, 255, 265–66, 280

DeMartino, Anthony, 202

DeMartino, Benjamin, 202

DeMartino, Theodore, 150, 203

DeMartino, William, 150

Democratic political machines, 209

Dempsey, Jack, 160

De Niro, Robert, 270

Dennis, Blackie, 168

Dentico, Joseph, 150

D'Ercole, Joseph, 150

DeSimone, Frank, 212, 264, 281

DeSimone, Tommy, 194

Detroit, MI, 33, 74, 76, 77, 78, 126, 157, 164, 165, 197, 266, 280

Detroit Olympia Arena, 165

Dewey, Thomas E., 109–110, 209, 212, 216

Diamond, Jack ("Legs"), 52, 157

Diapoulos, Peter ("The Greek"), 245

DiBene, Nicholas, 201

Di Brizzi, Alex ("The Ox"), 26–27, 210

DiDonato, Andrew, 181

DiGregorio, Gaspar, 49, 262

Dillinger, John, 218

DiNota, Andrew, 180

Dioguardi, Giovanni ("Johnny Dio," "John"), 99, 106, 107, 108, 117, 205

Dioguardi, Thomas ("Tommy" "Tommy Dio"), 117, 205

Dioguardo, Louis, 150

DiPalermo, Charles, 205

DiPalermo, Joseph, 150, 184, 205, 252

DiPasqua, Anthony, 150

DiPietro, Cosmo, 203

Di Pietro, Vincent, 150

Di Stefano, Vincenzo ("Vincent"), 131–32, 150

DiTrapani, Frank, 32

Dolan, Jay, 100

Domingo, Sebastiano ("Buster"), 76, 83

Donaato, Frank, 150

Donato, Anthony, 150

Donnie Brasco (film), 195

Dorsey, Tommy, 159

Downtown (gay nightclub), 168–69

Doyle, Everett, 122

Dragna, Louis, 166

Dreiser, Theodore, 217

drug trade, 7, 13, 64, 65, 90, 125–53, 177, 180, 181, 187, 189, 197, 200–206, 215, 218, 225, 245, 246, 252, 259, 266, 272–73, 283, 284

Drumgold, Herbert, 139

Dubinsky, David, 107–108, 116–17

Dundee, Angelo, 164

Durk, David, 139

Dutchess County, NY, 188, 190, 204

Dwyer, William ("Big Bill"), 49, 51, 101, 209

Eagle Building Corporation, 89–90

East Harlem, 58, 63, 188, 189, 190

Eboli, Tommy, 170, 229

Edelbaum, Maurice, 231

"Eighteen Street Gang," 64

Eliopoulos, Elias, 130

Eliopoulos, George, 130

Elizabeth Street, 58

Ellington, Duke, 157
Embarrato, Alfred, 150
Endicott, NY, 248, 249, 250, 254, 266, 270, 278
Endicott-Johnson Shoe factory, 250
Erickson, Frank, 225
Essex House Hotel, 236
Evola, Natale ("Diamond Joe"), 144, 146, 150, 259, 277
extortion. *See* strongarm tactics

Falcone, Joseph, 199, 260, 279
Falcone, Salvatore, 199, 260, 279
Farulla, Rosario, 150
Federal Bureau of Investigation (FBI), 8, 12, 28, 59, 61, 63, 108, 140, 167, 191, 198, 199, 208, 213, 214, 216–18, 219, 220–24, 229, 238, 244, 245, 268, 272, 275, 276–77
Federal Bureau of Narcotics (FBN), 132, 135, 136, 138, 139, 140, 144, 146, 148, 197, 215, 220, 221, 223, 269, 275
Federal Communications Act of 1934, 64–65
Fein, Benjamin ("Dopey Benny"), 116
Feinglass, Abe, 30
Ferraco, James ("Jimmy"), 111
Ferrante, Louis, 183, 192
Ferrara, Clara, 59
Ferrigno, Bartolo, 206
Ferrigno, Stephen ("Steve"), 76, 83
Ferro, Anthony, 203
Fiaschetti, Michael, 196
Filardo, Joseph, 265, 281
Fiore, Vincent, 260
Firpo, Luis, 160
Five Families (Raab), 95, 226

Flegenheimer, Arthur. *See* Schultz, Dutch (a.k.a. Arthur Flegenheimer)
Floyd, Pretty Boy, 218
FOIA. *See* Freedom of Information Act (FOIA)
Fontana, Bartolo, 196
Fopiano, Willie, 179
Ford Motor Company's Internal Security Department, 33
forgeries. *See* counterfeiting
Forlano, Nicholas ("Jiggs"), 145, 150
Fort Leavenworth prison, 259
Foster, Pops, 157
Fox, Billy, 163
Franco, Cosmo, 150
Franse, Steve, 168, 169, 170
Franzese, John ("Sonny"), 157, 189
Franzese, Michael, 61, 103
Frasca, Cosmo, 206
Fratelli Berio Distributing Company, 273
Fratianno, Jimmy, 61, 65, 192
Freedom of Information Act (FOIA), 198
French Connection, The (film), 143
French Connection case, 13, 135, 143, 144, 147
Friedkin, William, 143
Fuca, Joe, 143
Fuca, Pasquale ("Patsy"), 143
Fuca, Tony, 143
Fulton Fish Market, 25, 113
Fulton Market Watchmen and Patrol Association, 113
Futterman, George ("Muscles"), 119

Gagliano, Joseph ("Pip the Blind"), 137, 150

Gagliano, Tomasso ("Tom"), 75, 76, 77, 78, 83, 90–91, 93, 96, 97

Gagliano Family, 96, 97, 116

Gagliardi, Frank, 201

Gagliodotto, Charles, 150, 167, 201

Galante, Carmine ("Lilo"), 140, 144, 145, 146, 150, 182, 184, 252–53, 266, 270, 277

Galgano, Michael, 201

Gallo, Albert ("Kid Blast"), 63, 206

Gallo, Joseph ("Crazy Joe," "Joey," "Jukebox King"), 12, 63, 167, 185, 206, 244–45

Gallo, Lawrence ("Larry"), 63, 198, 206, 245

Galluccio, Frank, 203

Gambetta, Diego, 61

Gambino, Carlo, 39, 184, 198, 234, 244, 245, 247, 248, 258, 277

Gambino Family, 39, 62, 106, 132, 145, 170, 180, 181–82, 184–85, 191, 192, 200–202, 246, 247, 277

gambling, 7, 27, 46, 65, 66–67, 75, 81, 101, 108, 126, 160, 164–65, 180, 183, 185, 186–87, 190, 191, 192, 194–95, 200–206, 210, 212, 218–19, 236–37, 251, 260, 263, 265, 272, 284
    bookmaking, 46, 66–67, 162, 180, 182, 187, 210
    numbers lottery, 66–67, 75, 81, 101, 180, 190, 210, 212, 284
    sports betting, 66–67, 180, 237

Garbo, Greta, 170

Gargotta, Charles ("Mad Dog"), 219

Garland, Judy, 170

Garofalo, Frank, 252

Garufi, Agatino, 150

Geiger Products Corporation, 114

Genese, Pasquale, 201

Gennaro, Joseph, 150

Genovese, Anna, 170

Genovese, Michael ("Mike"), 267, 268, 280

Genovese, Vito, 56, 76, 90, 107, 144, 145, 148, 150, 168, 169, 186, 189, 197, 198, 226–27, 237, 244, 245, 247, 248, 257, 258, 271, 277

Genovese Family, 25, 26, 62, 142, 144, 167, 169, 170, 171, 190, 202–204, 209, 248, 258, 277–78

Gentile, Nicola, 49, 64, 71, 73, 74, 80, 88, 89, 91, 94, 96, 133, 145, 148, 197, 199

Gentry, Elmer, 132

Geoghan, William, 209

Geraghty, Tom, 49

Giancana, Sam, 158, 267, 274, 280

Giannini, Eugenio ("Eugene," "Gene"), 151, 197

Gibson, Truman K., Jr., 165–66

Gigante, Mario, 203

Gigante, Olympia, 231

Gigante, Vincent ("The Chin"), 102, 144, 203, 229, 230–31

Giglio, Salvatore, 151

Gillespie, Dizzie, 157

Gioielli, Joseph ("Joe Jelly"), 245

Giuliani, Rudolph, 216

Giusto, John ("Scarface"), 118

Giustra, Anthony, 110

Giustra, John ("Silk Stockings"), 87, 110

Gleason, Jack, 95

Gleason, Teddy, 105

Gleitsmann, Chris, 252–53

Godfather, The (films), 11–12, 93–94, 126–27, 128, 283

Godfather Part III, The, 198
Godfather, The (Puzo), 195
Goldstock, Ronald, 59
"Good Killers, the," 196
Goodman, Oscar, 213
Goodman Hat Company, 44
Gopher Gang (Irish gang), 101
Gordon, Waxey, 216
Gosch, Martin, 128
Gotti, John, 12, 186, 194
Grammauta, Stephen ("Steve" a.k.a.
    "Stevie Coogan"), 245, 246, 247
Granello, Salvatore ("Solly Burns"), 171,
    205
Granza, Anthony, 151, 201
Grasso, Arthur, 239, 240, 242
Gravano, Sammy ("The Bull"), 106, 127,
    179, 181–82, 183, 193
Graziano, Rocky, 105, 159, 162, 164–65
Great Gatsby, The (Fitzgerald), 158
Greenwich Village, 156, 168, 178
    East and West Village, 201, 202, 203
    South Village, 24, 49, 52, 58
Griffin, Dennis, 214
Grim Reapers, The (Reid), 222
Guarnieri, Anthony ("Guv"), 251, 259,
    278
Guccia, Bartolo, 257, 278
Guido, Alfred, 151

Hackman, Gene, 143
Half Moon Hotel, 112, 114
Haller, Mark, 65
Hammer, Richard, 128
Harlem, 11, 52, 59, 66, 76, 101, 131, 138,
    139, 157, 190, 212, 284
East Harlem, 27, 35, 47, 50, 58, 59, 63,
    73, 75, 80, 82–83, 131, 132, 134–35,
    136–37, 139–40, 188, 189, 190, 191,
    200, 203, 204, 205, 259
Little Italy in, 59, 131
Harlem Renaissance, 157
Harriman, Averell, 269
Harrison Narcotics Act of 1914, 130
Hartman, Helmuth, 134
Havana, Cuba, 158, 237, 256, 272, 281
Hawkins, Gordon, 224
Hawks, Howard, 11
Helblock, Joe, 157
Helbrant, Maurice, 136
Hennessy, David, 213
heroin. *See* drug trade
hijacking. *See* criminal receiver of stolen
    goods
Hill, Henry, 38, 60, 61, 103, 187, 192,
    194, 195, 208, 209, 275
Hill, Karen, 194
Hines, James ("Jimmy"), 212
Hoffa, Jimmy, 99, 107
Hogan, Frank, 209
Holstein, Casper ("Bolito King"),
    101–102
Home Box Office (HBO), 45, 81
homicide. *See* murder/homicide
Hoover, J. Edgar, 8, 108, 207, 208, 216–
    18, 219, 220–24, 249, 275, 276–77
Horan, James, 209
Hortis, Alex, 7–8
Hotel Casey, 267
Hotel et des Palmes, 140–41
Howdy Club (gay nightclub), 168, 169
Howe & Hummel (law firm), 210
Hudson Dusters (Irish gang), 101
Hundley, William, 222

Iamascia, Daniel, 207

Ianni, Francis, 100

Ianniello, Matthew ("Matty the Horse"), 170, 171–72

Iannuzi, Joseph ("Joe Dogs"), 186

IATSE. *See* International Alliance of Theatrical Stage Employees (IATSE)

IBC. *See* International Boxing Club (IBC)

IBT. *See* International Brotherhood of Teamsters (IBT)

Ida, Joseph ("Joe"), 258, 280

ILA. *See* International Longshoremen's Association (ILA)

ILGWU. *See* International Ladies' Garment Workers' Union (ILGWU)

Il Progresso (newspaper), 228

Incendiarism in Greater New York (New York Fire Commissioner), 34–35

Indelicato, Al ("Sonny Red"), 208

informants, 196–98

Internal Revenue Service (IRS), 177, 192

International Alliance of Theatrical Stage Employees (IATSE), 108

International Boxing Club (IBC), 162, 165–66

International Brotherhood of Teamsters (IBT), 38, 99, 107, 108, 119–23, 190, 265, 272

International Ladies' Garment Workers' Union (ILGWU), 33–34, 107–108, 116–19, 236

International Longshoremen's Association (ILA), 22, 23–24, 25, 26–27, 102, 105–106, 109–113, 242

Irish Potato Famine of 1845–1852, 100

IRS. *See* Internal Revenue Service (IRS)

Isabella, Florio, 151

"Italian-American Civil Rights League," 214

It Happened in Brooklyn (film), 155

I Vespri Siciliani (Verdi), 93

Jacobs, George, 158

Jacobs, James B., 7–8, 108

Jacobs, Michael ("Uncle Mike"), 163

Jersey City, NJ, 19, 188, 203

Johnson, Ellsworth ("Bumpy"), 138, 139

Johnson, Enoch ("Nucky"), 209

Jordan, Don, 162, 166

Joselit, Jenna Weissman, 103, 105

Joseph Lanza, et. al., United States v., 114

Justice Department, 192, 214, 218, 219, 220, 222, 273

Kansas City, MO, 108, 133, 219, 256, 265, 272, 280–81

Kansas City Star (newspaper), 219

Kapilow, Danny, 163

Kastel, Phillip ("Dandy Phil"), 65

Katzenberg, Yasha, 130

Kefauver, Estes, 219

Kefauver Committee hearings, 219, 220, 222–23, 227, 276

Kelly, Jack, 146–47

Kelly, Paul. *See* Vaccarelli, Paolo (aka "Paul Kelly")

Kennedy, John F., 17

Kennedy, Robert F., 217, 221, 269, 273, 275, 276

Kennedy, Sergeant, 257

Kennedy, William, 228, 229

Kent, Buddy, 169, 171

Kingsley, Sidney, 155

Kiselik, Jerome, 114, 115–16
Knapp Commission, 36, 147, 156, 167, 208

labor racketeering, 8, 99–123, 181, 187, 190
    See also strongarm tactics
La Cascia, Charles, 151
La Duca, James, 255, 266, 279
La Gaipa, Charles ("Big Nose"), 133
La Gaipa, U.S. v., 142
Lagattuta, Samuel, 279
Lagatutta, Pietro ("Pete the Bum"), 42, 43
La Guardia, Fiorello, 39–40
Laietta, August, 203
L'Aiglon Restaurant, 228
LaMare, Chester, 76, 78, 197
La Motta, Jake, 163, 165
Lansky, Meyer, 102, 216, 271
Lanza, James, 281
Lanza, Joseph ("Socks"), 25, 107, 113–16, 267
Lapi, Joseph, 203
LaRasso, Louis ("Fat Lou"), 263–64, 280
LaRocca, John, 267, 280
Last Testament of Lucky Luciano, The (Gosch and Hammer), 128–29
Las Vegas, NV, 65, 138, 190, 213, 255
LaTempa, Peter ("Pete," "Petey Spats"), 197, 227
La Verdi, Leon, 169
lawyers for the Mob, 207–224
Lay Fish Company, 114
Lazzara, Ernest, 203
LeBrun, George, 210
Leibe, Fred, 252
Leibowitz, Samuel S., 211
Leitsch, Richard, 171

Leonard, Jackie, 166
Leonetti, Philip, 182
Lerner, Michael, 50
Lessa, Daniel, 151
Leuci, Robert, 208, 209–210
Levey, Edgar, 29–30
Levine, Sam ("Red"), 92–93
Lexow Committee, 21, 35–36, 208
Licchi, Benjamin, 151
Licchi, Joseph, 151
Lichtman, Charles, 185
Lido Restaurant, 189, 209
Life (magazine), 269, 270
Life of a Mafia Boss (Gentile), 133, 199
Linardi, John, 151
liquor. *See* bootlegging
Liquori, Ralph, 132, 151
Lisi, Anthony, 151, 205
Little Italy. *See* specific areas, Bronx, Harlem, Manhattan
Livorsi, Frank ("Cheech"), 76, 86, 134, 151, 203
loansharking, 27, 65, 180, 182–83, 189, 190, 200–206
LoCascio, Peter, 151
Lockwood Committee, 106
Loiacano, Angelo, 151
Lombardino, Andrew, 203
Lombardino, Paul, 151, 203
Lombardo, Philip, 151, 203
Lombardozzi, Carmine, 263, 277
Lonardo, Angelo, 128, 144
Lonergan, Richard ("Pegleg"), 101
Long Island, 18, 50, 137, 170, 177, 188, 189, 194, 200, 202–205
LoPiccolo, Giuseppe ("Joseph"), 151, 201
Lo Proto, Salvatore, 205

Los Angeles, CA, 65, 108, 138, 166, 212, 238, 256, 264, 281

Louis, Joe ("Brown Bomber"), 163, 165

Lucania, Salvatore. *See* Luciano, Charles ("Lucky," a.k.a. Charles Ross, a.k.a Salvatore Lucania)

Lucas, Frank, 102, 136, 139

Lucchese, Thomas ("Tommy"), 38, 75, 76, 77, 78, 83, 90–91, 93, 127, 197, 198, 236, 247, 267, 272

Lucchese Family, 60, 63, 103, 132, 137, 138, 141, 142, 143, 144, 145, 147, 148, 162, 163, 165, 181, 187, 191, 192, 197, 204–205, 208, 212, 259, 267, 273, 275, 278

Luciano, Charles ("Lucky," a.k.a. Charles Ross, a.k.a. Salvatore Lucania), 42, 44–46, 56, 71, 72, 76, 77, 85, 86, 87, 90, 93, 95, 96, 97, 108, 109, 116, 125, 128–29, 132, 140, 144, 151, 158, 167, 177, 178, 194–95, 196, 215, 219, 233, 283

Luciano, Frank, 201

Luciano, Ron, 270

Luciano Family, 66, 96, 97, 141, 147, 155, 177, 181, 190, 225, 226, 229, 230, 231, 232

Lucky, Charley. *See* Luciano, Charles ("Lucky")

Lupo, Ignazio ("The Wolf"), 11, 46, 47

Lurye, Willie, 117–18

Macri, Benedict, 117–19

Macri, Vincent, 117, 119

Macri-Lee Corporation, 117

Madden, Owney ("The Killer"), 49, 52, 101, 157

Madell, Steve, 22

Madison Square Garden, 162, 163, 164, 165

Mafia Dynasty (Davis), 93

Mafia II (video game), 283

Magaddino, Antonio ("Anthony"), 262, 279

Magaddino, Stefano ("Steve," "Stephen"), 76, 77, 90, 94, 96, 97, 196, 248, 253, 267, 274, 279

Magaddino Family, 76, 96, 97, 260, 262

Magic Touch (restaurant), 170

Magliocco, Joseph, 75, 258–59, 273, 278

Magliocco Family, 145

Magnasco, Joseph, 206

Maimone, Salvatore, 151

Maione, Michael, 203

Majuri, Frank ("Fat Frank"), 263–64, 279

Malin, Jean, 167

Malizia, John, 151

Manca, John, 28

Mancino, Francesco, 151

Mancuso, Rosario, 260, 279

Mandelbaum, Frederika ("Mother"), 210

Maneri, Salvatore, 151, 205

Manford, Morty, 172

Manfredi, Joseph ("Jo Jo"), 145, 201

Manfredonia, Richard, 151

Mangano, Philip, 25, 87, 231, 232, 247

Mangano, Vincent, 24, 25, 56, 75, 90, 96, 97, 105, 145, 209, 231–33, 247

Mangano Family, 25, 27, 96, 97, 120, 133, 142, 231

Manhattan, 19, 25, 27, 28–29, 30–31, 35, 37, 43–44, 47, 48, 53–54, 62, 76, 87, 90, 106, 109, 114, 118–19, 156, 158, 166, 168, 183, 185, 188, 193, 194, 195, 214, 216, 220, 228–29, 237, 238

East Side, 23, 25–26, 131, 171
    Lower East Side, 23, 27, 34–35, 42, 43, 47, 53–54, 56, 73, 125, 160, 177, 200, 201, 202, 203, 205
    Upper East Side, 139, 201
Hell's Kitchen, 49, 52
Little Italy in, 27, 41–44, 53–54, 58, 59, 99, 104–105, 108, 125, 132, 139
Lower Manhattan, 18, 20, 30–31, 39, 42, 66, 76, 80, 106, 116, 139, 188
Midtown, 155, 161, 225, 239–42
Upper Manhattan, 114
West Side, 23, 49, 101
    Upper West Side, 54, 201, 228
See also Greenwich Village; Harlem
Mannarino, Gabriel, 268, 280
Mannino, Vincent, 24
Man of Honor, A (Bonanno), 12, 71, 79, 127, 145, 262
Marangello, Nicholas, 200
Maranzano, Salvatore, 49, 52, 72, 76, 77, 79–82, 83, 85, 87–93, 94, 95, 96, 101, 145, 232, 233, 238, 247
Marcello, Carlos, 211, 218, 219, 266
Marcello, Joseph, 266, 281
Marchi, John, 214
Marchitto, Anthony, 203
Mari, Frank, 200
Marone, Joseph ("Joe"), 132, 151
Marsalisi, Mariano, 132, 151
Martello, Nicholas, 151
Martino, Gaetano, 203
Marzano, Alfonso, 203
Masseria, Giuseppe ("Joe the Boss"), 41–44, 50, 53–56, 71–72, 74–75, 76, 77, 78, 79–82, 83, 85–87, 88, 89, 90, 94, 95, 116, 232, 233, 238, 283
Masseria Family, 55–56, 63, 72, 74, 76, 77, 80–81, 82, 83, 85, 95
Massi, James, 151, 201
Masters, Viola, 166
Matranga, Charles ("Millionaire Charlie"), 196
Mattachine Society, 171
Mauro, Vincent, 151, 203
Mazzie, Pete, 112
Mazzie, Rocco, 145, 151
McClellan, John, 178, 185, 217
McClellan Committee (U.S. Senate), 17, 39, 178, 180, 185, 187, 188, 217, 269, 273, 275
    list of soldiers of the New York families identified at hearings, 200–206
McCormack, William J., 160
McFall Road. *See* Apalachin, NY
McGrath, J. Howard, 218, 219
Medico, William ("Bill"), 198–99
Medico Industries, 198, 199
Merman, Ethel, 155
Messina, Gaspare, 85
Metropolitan New York Dry Wall Contractors Association, 34
Metropolitan Restaurant and Cafeteria Owners Association, 37
Meyer, Kathryn, 140
Mezzrow, Mezz, 157
Miami, FL, 65, 190, 199, 218, 271
Miami Beach, FL, 95, 190
Migliore, Neil, 205, 267

Milazzo, Gaspare, 76, 77, 78, 80
Milazzo Family, 76
Milk Dealers' Protective Association, 38
Milo, Louis, 203
Milo, Sabato, 203
Milo, Thomas, Sr., 203
Milto, Lynda, 192
Mineo, Alfred, 75, 83
Mineo Family, 75, 76
Miniaci, Al, 228
Miraglia, Lester, 151
Miranda, Barney, 203
Miranda, Michele, 263, 278
Mission Beverage Company, 250
Mitchell, John, 214
Mob Candy (magazine), 283
Mob Wives (TV series), 283
Moccardi, Frank, 201
Moccio, Pasquale, 151, 203
Monachino, Patsy, 259, 278
Monachino, Sam, 259, 278
Mondello, Salvatore, 59, 139–40, 188
money laundering, 192
Monsignore Restaurant, 228
Montana, Charles, 279
Montana, John C. ("The Arm"), 256, 262, 273, 279
Montella, Sonny, 105
Montemurro, Samuel, 151
Montesano, John, 32, 105–106
moonshining. *See* bootlegging
Morahan, John, 52
Morelli, Rocco, 178
Morello, Giuseppe ("The Clutch Hand"), 11, 42, 46–47, 55–56, 73, 76, 82–83, 94, 95, 283
    death of, 95

Morello Family, 11, 39, 46–47, 56, 64, 82, 95, 196, 215
Moretti, Willie, 158, 219, 226
Morton, Tommy, 38
"Moustache Petes," 72, 94–95
murder/homicide, 25, 74, 76, 78, 83, 87, 93, 95, 114, 116, 118, 148, 160, 170, 179, 180, 181–82, 183, 197, 212, 219, 225–29, 232, 233, 242, 244, 246, 247, 250, 260
    "made my bones" myth, 195–96
Murphy, Ed ("The Skull"), 171–72
Murphy, Patrick, 147
Mussolini, Benito, 79, 226

Nani, Sebastiano, 151, 206
Napoli, Anthony ("Tony Nap"), 59, 182
narcotics. *See* drug trade
National Archives, 12, 245
National Fascist Party, 226
National Industrial Recovery Act, 33
Newark, NJ, 19, 184, 188, 190, 202, 203, 259
New Jersey
    suburban New Jersey, 188, 200–206
    See also Camden, NJ; Hoboken, NJ; Jersey City, NJ; Newark, NJ
New Orleans, LA, 65, 157, 196, 213, 218, 266, 272, 281
New York City, 7–8
    economics, 28–30
    fragile industries, 37–40
    Irish population, 7, 8, 49, 50, 57, 95, 102, 105, 106, 107, 177, 271
    Jewish population, 7, 8, 11, 35, 44, 49, 50, 56, 57, 95, 100, 105, 106, 107, 271

nightlife in, 155–73
population, 27
   demographic trends and immi-
     gration, 57–58
   Irish population, 100–101
   Jewish population, 102–103
   Sicilian immigrants in the
     workforce, 103–106
   Port of New York, 18–19, 20–22,
     23–27, 130
   during Prohibition, 41–67
   unemployment rate, 178
   See also specific areas and neighbor-
     hoods, i.e., Bronx, Harlem, Man-
     hattan, Staten Island, etc.,
New York City Fire Commissioner, 34–35
New York City Police Department
   (NYPD), 41–44, 48, 53, 61, 86, 87,
   135, 144, 167, 172, 207, 215, 229, 235,
   236, 242–44, 245, 246
   and corruption, 21, 35–36, 146–47,
     172, 208–209
New York Clearing House, 66
New York Daily News (newspaper), 172
New York Evening Telegram, 41
New York Municipal Archives, 245
New York State Appellate Division, 208
New York State Athletic Commission
   (NYSAC), 160, 165, 240
New York State Commission of Investi-
   gations, 120, 267, 268, 269, 273
New York State Crime Commission, 127,
   267, 268
New York State Department of Com-
   merce, 17
New York State Joint Legislative Com-
   mittee on Crime, 210

New York State Liquor Authority
   (NYSLA), 51–52, 156, 167, 168, 169
New York State Organized Crime Task
   Force, 59
New York State Police, 216, 249–51,
   256–57, 263, 270–71
   Bureau of Criminal Investigation
     (BCI), 254, 268
New York Times (newspaper), 88, 146,
   219, 247, 269
Night of the Sicilian Vespers, 93
Nobile, George, 151, 203
Noel, Terry, 170
Norris, James, 165, 166
numbers lottery. *See* gambling
Nuova Villa Tammaro (restaurant), 86,
   88–89
Nutt, Levi, 146
NYPD. *See* New York City Police
   Department (NYPD)
NYSAC. *See* New York State Athletic
   Commission (NYSAC)
NYSLA. *See* New York State Liquor
   Authority (NYSLA)

*Octopus: How the Long Reach of the
   Sicilian Mafia Controls the Global Nar-
   cotics Trade* (Sterling), 140–41
O'Dwyer, William, ("Bill"), 22, 112, 120
*Official and Confidential: The Secret Life
   of J. Edgar Hoover* (Summers), 216
Ofrica, Sebastian, 203
Oliveto, Dominick, 258, 280
omertà, Mafia code of silence, 196–98, 274
181 Club (gay nightclub), 169, 170, 171
On the Waterfront (film), 20
Onxy (night club), 157

Orchid Room (tavern), 189
Orlando, Lorenzo, 151
Ormento, John ("Big John"), 132, 137–38, 145, 152, 259, 272, 278
Orsi, Robert, 59, 103
Orsini, Joseph, 141–42
Orzo, Theodore, 152
Osticco, James, 268, 280

Pacella, Louis, 203
Pagano, Joseph, 203
Pagano, Pasquale, 204
Pagano, Pat, 170
Pagliarelli Family, 197
Palermo, Frank ("Blinky"), 158, 160, 162, 163, 164, 165, 166
Palermo, Sicily, 24, 44, 72, 75, 140, 234
Palmer, A. Mitchell, 217
Palmotto, Nicholas, 184
Panebianco, Vincent, 152
Panica, Vic, 205
Panto, Peter, 110–13, 247
Paoli, Orlando, 152
Papa, Vincent ("Vinnie Papa"), 147, 152
Pappadia, Andinno, 152, 205
Paramount Vending (company), 228
Parisi, Joe, 120, 121–22
Parker, Charlie ("Bird"), 157
Park Sheraton Hotel, 240, 245, 246
Parkway Motel, 254, 255, 265, 266
Parrino, Sam, 78
Parsons, Freddie, 139
Parssinen, Terry, 140
Pascale, Pete, 59
Pastor, Tony, 168–69
Patriarca, Raymond ("Ray"), 179–80, 259

Patriarca Family, 159, 238, 259
Paul Kelly Association, 23
Peck, Charles, 276
Pecoraro, Michael, 201
Peloso, Anthony, 152
Pennochio, Thomas ("The Bull"), 132, 152
People against Benedict Macri, 118
Perillo, Armando, 152
Perrano, Joseph, 82
Perretti, Joseph, 152
Perretti, Peter, 152
Perri, Rocco, 143
Persico, Carmine, 204
Petillo, David, 167, 204
Petrilli, Dominick ("The Gap"), 134, 152, 197
Petrone, John, 200
Pettigrew, Nat, 139
Philadelphia, PA, 19, 115, 138, 162, 164, 182, 228, 258, 280
Phil Silvers Show, The (TV show), 155
Picarelli, James, 152, 204
Pieri, Salvatore, 152
Pine, Seymour, 172
Pinzolo, Joseph, 76, 78, 80, 83
Pisciotta, Rosario, 152
Pistone, Joseph, 59, 61, 62, 180, 182, 183, 192, 194, 195
Pistone, Lawrence, 201
Pittsburgh, PA, 87, 133, 267, 268, 280
"Pizza Connection" heroin prosecution, 141
Polisi, Sal, 194
Polizzano, Carmine, 152
Pollaro, Gaspar, 82
Pope, Generose, 228

Port of New York, 18–19, 20–22, 23–27, 130

Posner, Richard, 65

Potenza, Vincent, 205

President's Commission on Law Enforcement, 186

Presinzano, Angelo, 200

Presinzano, Frank, 152, 200

Presta, Mario, 281

Prisco, Rudolph, 204

Profaci, Frank, 206

Profaci, Joseph, 75, 76, 81, 96, 97, 198, 245, 258–59, 273, 278

Profaci Family, 63, 75, 76, 96, 97, 189, 198, 205–206, 244, 245, 259, 278

Prohibition, 41–67

Prosser, Monte, 155

Provenzano, Anthony ("Tony Pro"), 158

Provenzano, Joe, 196

Puco, Stephen, 152

Pueblo, CO, 264–65, 281

Purple Onion (gay bar), 167

Puzo, Mario, 93, 127, 195

Queens, 188, 189, 191, 200–206

Raab, Selwyn, 95, 226, 227, 272

Rabito, Anthony ("Fat Tony"), 170–71

Raft, George, 158

Ragano, Frank, 211

Ragone, Joseph, 152

Rao, Charlie, 205

Rao, Joseph ("Joey"), 59, 132–33, 204

Rao, Vincent, 259, 273, 278

Rastelli, Philip, 200

Rattenni, Nicholas ("Nick," "Cockeyed Nick"), 121–22, 123, 204

Rava, Armand ("Tommy"), 258, 277

Reavill, Gil, 141, 272, 273

Regional Labor Boards, 107

Reid, Ed, 222

Reina, Gaetano, 75, 77–78, 80

Reina, Giacomo, 152

Reina, U.S. v., 142

Reina Family, 63, 75, 76, 77–78, 80, 83, 90

Reles, Abe ("Kid Twist"), 112–13

Republican political machines, 209

Reuter, Arthur, 269

Reuther, Walter, 33, 108

Revell, Oliver ("Buck"), 222

Ricca, Paul ("The Waiter"), 96, 108, 219

Riccardulli, John, 152

Riccobono, Joseph ("Staten Island Joe"), 199, 258, 277

Rickard, Tex, 160

Riela, Anthony, 200, 259, 279

Riis, Jacob, 29

Rinaldi, Rosario, 152

Rivera, Ray ("Sylvia Lee"), 172

Roche Guard (Irish gang), 101

Rochester, NY, 122, 260, 279

Rockland County, NY, 188

Roder, Max, 132

Roemer, William, 221, 267, 276

Rofrano, Peter, 35

Rogers, William P., 275

Romano, Arnold, 152

Romano, Nunzio, 152

Romero, Anthony, 111

Rosato, Joseph ("Joe Palisades"), 197, 259, 278

Rosedell Manufacturing Company, 117

Roselli, John, 61

Rosen, Alex, 222
Rosen, Harry ("Nig"), 95
Rosen, Joseph, 116
Rosenberger, Julius and Ethel, 220
Rosenstiel, Susan, 216
Rosenwaike, Ira, 57
Rosner, Edmund, 210
Ross, Charles. *See* Luciano, Charles ("Lucky" a.k.a. Charles Ross, a.k.a. Salvatore Lucania)
Rossi, Hugo, 152, 201
Rothstein, Arnold, 51, 116, 130, 146, 208
Rubino, Cristoforo, 197, 206
Ruffino, Giuseppe and Salvatore, 42, 80
Ruggiero, Benjamin ("Lefty Guns"), 178–79
Runyon, Damon, 157
Rupolo, Ernest ("The Hawk"), 197
Russell, Marguerite, 256, 266, 268
Ruston, Arthur, 255, 256–57, 260
Ryan, Joseph P. ("King Joe"), 22, 24, 25, 26, 27

Sabella, Michael, 200
Sackel, T. G., 260, 262
St. Louis Arena, 165
Salemi, Leonard, 152
Salerno, Angelo, 152, 204
Salerno, Anthony ("Fat Tony"), 66, 144, 152, 158, 190–91, 204
Salerno, Ferdinand, 204
Salerno, Ralph, 135–36, 138, 139, 143
Salli, Salvatore, 152
Salvo, Batisto, 204
Samuels, Francis, 91, 93
San Carlos Hotel, 238, 239

San Francisco Chronicle (newspaper), 269
San Jose, CA, 267, 281
Sansone, Carmelo, 152
Santagata, Aniello, 152
Santoro, Salvatore ("Tom Mix"), 134, 138, 145, 152
Santuccio, Girolamo ("Bobby Doyle"), 76, 83, 84, 91, 93
Saturday Evening Post (magazine), 244–45
Savino, John, 204
Scalici, Giacomo, 201
Scalici, Salvatore, 201
Scalise, Frank ("Cheech"), 62, 232, 233–34, 237
Scalise, George, 107
Scalise, Jack, 234
Scalise, Joseph, 234
Scalish, John, 255, 265–66, 280
Scandifia, Mike, 201
Scara-Mix Concrete Company, 191
Scarcelli, Paul. *See* Presta, Mario ("Paul Scarcelli")
Scarface (film), 11
Scarpato, Gerardo, 86
Scarpulla, Giacomo, 201
Schechter brothers, 32–33
Schiavo, Giovanni, 224
Schillaci, Giovanni, 152, 204
Schipani, Joseph, 152, 206
Schiro, Nicola ("Cola"), 75, 76, 79, 81
Schneider, Eric, 138
Schroeder, Helen, 254, 255
Schultz, Dutch (a.k.a. Arthur Flegenheimer), 37, 52, 90, 157, 167, 185, 212
Sciandra, Angelo, 268, 280
Sciortino, Patsy, 259, 278

Scorsese, Martin, 11

Scotto, Anthony, 105

Scozzari, Simone, 264, 281

Seagram's (liquor conglomerate), 51

Secret Service, 11, 46, 64, 196, 197, 215

Serpico, Frank, 36, 61, 147, 209

Serritella, Anthony, 62

Shaheen, Chuck, 171

Shank, Reuben ("Cowboy"), 164–65

Shapiro, Jacob ("Gurrah"), 116

Shearing, George, 157

Sherman Antitrust Act, 113, 114, 115, 116, 166

Shillitani, Salvatore ("Sally Shields"), 141–42, 152, 205

Shor, Toots, 155

Siano, Fiore, 170, 204

Sica, Joe, 166

Siegel, Benjamin ("Bugsy"), 52

Siino, Francesco, 196

Siino Family, 63

Silesi, Joe, 237

Silvers, Phil, 155

Simone, Bobby, 213

Simpson's pawnbrokers, 42, 43

Sinatra, Frank, 155, 158–60

Sing Sing (prison), 44, 53, 116, 161, 182, 189, 252

Siragusa, Charles, 136, 140, 179

Slater, Sidney, 245

Smith, Tom, 95

Smurra, George, 204

Sobel, Irving, 130

Sopranos, The (TV series), 12, 198, 227, 283

Spadaro, Joseph, 200

sports betting. See gambling

Springfield, IL, 264, 265, 280

Squillante, Vincent ("Jimmy"), 120, 121, 239, 240, 243

Stacher, Joseph ("Doc"), 271

Stallone, Joseph, 152

Stassi, James, 201

Stassi, Joseph ("Hoboken Joe"), 182, 201

Staten Island, 18, 26–27, 58, 106, 183, 188, 191, 201, 202, 205

Statler Hotel, 258

Sterling, Claire, 140–41

Stillman's Gym, 161, 164–65

Stone, Paula, 155

Stonewall Inn, 167, 171–72, 173

Stonewall riots of 1969, 13

Stopelli, John, 152, 204

Stork Club (night club), 157, 189

Stracci, Joseph ("Joe Stretch"), 59, 76, 86, 106, 158, 204

Street, Leroy, 129, 131

Strollo, Anthony ("Tony Bender"), 170, 197

strongarm tactics, 39, 43, 116, 177, 180, 181–82, 200–206, 210, 260

    assault and battery, 43, 180, 181–82, 185, 210, 260

    extortion, 21, 27–28, 34, 35, 37, 43, 46, 104, 109, 164, 180, 181–82, 189, 208, 255

    See also labor racketeering

Stutz, Joe, 59

suburbs, Mafia's move to, 187–91

Sullivan, William, 221, 276

Summers, Anthony, 216

Tacoma, Anthony, 153

Tamberlani, John, 152

Tambone, Peter, 153
Tammany Hall, 8, 207, 209, 212
Tampa, FL, 237, 238, 244, 263, 281
Tantillo, Enrico, 153
tax evasion, 88, 96, 119, 146, 177, 181, 184–85, 190, 191
    avoiding fixed assets, 191–93
Tepacanoe Democratic Club, 207
Teresa, Dominick, 60
Teresa, Vincent ("Fat Vinnie"), 60, 155, 156, 159, 183, 193, 194, 195, 238, 244
Terranova, Ciro ("the Artichoke King"), 39–40, 46, 59, 86, 196, 208
Terranova, Nick, 46, 196
Terranova, Vincenzo, 46, 196
Tessalone, James, 153
theft. See criminal receiver of stolen goods
Thomas, Piri, 139
Thompson, Henry, 95
Thurmond, Strom, 218
Tieri, Frank, 204
Time (magazine), 125
Times Square, 158, 170
Tobin, Daniel, 107
Tocco, Joseph, 153
Toledo, OH, 164
Tolentino, Nicholas ("Big Nose"), 137, 153, 205
Tolson, Clyde, 275
Top Echelon Criminal Information Program of FBI, 277
Top Hoodlum Program, 276
Tornabe, Salvatore, 259, 278
Tortorella, Arthur, 202
Tortorella, Peter J., 202
Tortorici, Joseph, 204
Touhy, Roger, 49

Tourine, Charles, Sr., 204
Trafficante, Santo, 211, 237, 238, 239, 244, 263, 272, 281
Tramaglino, Eugene, 132, 153
Tramunti, Carmine, 148, 181, 267
Treasury Department, 215, 255, 256–57, 260
    Alcohol and Tobacco Tax Division, 185, 216, 255
    See also Federal Bureau of Narcotics (FBN)
Tripodi, Tom, 146
Troia, Vincenzo, 80, 87
Tuminaro, Angelo ("Little Angie"), 143, 153, 205
Turrigiano, Patsy, 251, 255, 258, 278
Twentieth Century Sporting Club, 163

Uale, Frankie, 56
UAW. See United Automobile Workers (UAW)
Union Pacific Produce Company, 39, 40
United Automobile Workers (UAW), 108
United Hebrew Trades (union), 116
United Seafood Workers, 25, 113–16
United States. See individual departments and agencies, i.e., Federal Bureau of Narcotics, Justice Department, etc.,
Utica, NY, 199, 260, 279

Vaccarelli, Paolo (a.k.a. "Paul Kelly"), 23–24, 106, 119
Vadala, Anthony, 205
Valachi, Joseph ("Joe" a.k.a. "Joe Cago"), 28, 37, 62, 65, 76, 78, 80, 83, 86, 90, 94, 95, 101, 117, 119, 144, 145, 147, 148, 150, 153, 157, 170, 177, 181, 183,

185, 189–90, 196, 197, 198, 204, 209, 224, 226, 229, 233–34, 236, 238, 244, 272, 275, 277

Valachi scheme, 142

Valenti, Constenze, 260, 279

Valenti, Frank, 260, 279

Valenti, Umberto, 41

Vario, Paul ("Paulie"), 60, 61, 103, 148, 187, 208, 209

Vasisko, Vincent, 252, 254–55, 256–57, 262, 268, 270

vending machines, 180, 181, 185, 189, 201–206

Vento, Joseph, 153, 205

Verdi, Giuseppe, 93

Verdiccio, Joseph, 27

Vernotico, Anna, 226–27

Vernotico, Gerard, 226, 227

Villano, Anthony, 198

Vintaloro, James, 205

Vita di Capomafia (Gentile), 133, 199

Vitale, Albert H., 207–208

Vitale, Salvatore, 153

Vittorio Castle (banquet hall), 190

Volpe, Louis, 252

Waldorf Astoria Hotel, 225

Walker, Jimmy, 22

Warner Brothers, 270

Warwick Hotel, 238, 239

Washington Post (newspaper), 275

Washington Star (newspaper), 275

Weinberg, Abe ("Bo"), 92–93

Weinberg, Morris, 118–19

Weiss, Emanuel ("Mendy"), 111, 112

Welch, Neil, 220

Welfare Island Penitentiary, 132

Westchester County, NY, 119–23, 188, 189, 201–205

"Westies, the," 62

White, George, 132

White Hand gang (Irish gang), 101

Williams, Edward Bennett, 211, 214

Williams, Roy, 107, 272

Wilson, Teddy, 157

Wirtz, Arthur, 165

Wittenberg, Arnold ("Witty"), 245

Yo Gotti (rap music), 283

Youngstown, OH, 164

Zaluchi, Don (fictional), 126, 128

Zerilli, Joseph, 266, 280

Zicari, Emanuel ("Manny"), 251, 256, 257, 258, 266, 278

Zito, Frank, 264–65, 280

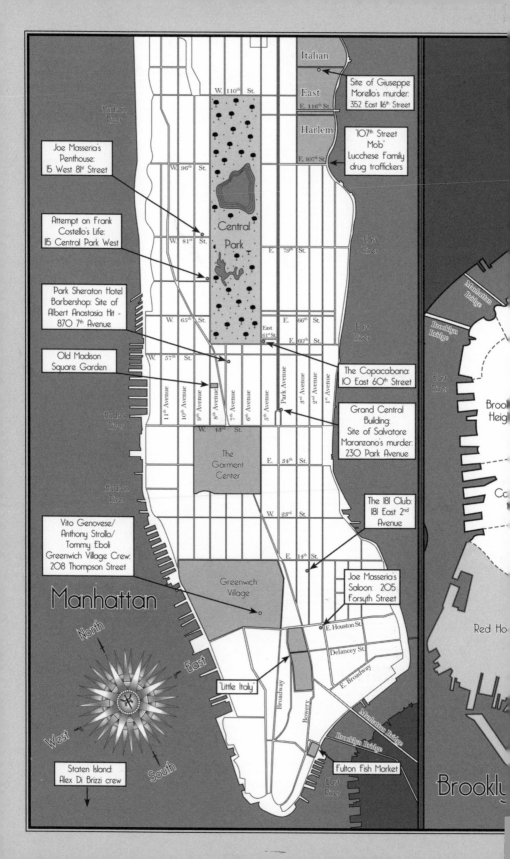

Italian

East
E. 116th St.

Harlem
E. 107th St.

Site of Giuseppe Morello's murder: 352 East 116th Street

"107th Street Mob" Lucchese Family drug traffickers

W. 110th St.

Joe Masseria's Penthouse: 15 West 81st Street

W. 96th St.

Hudson River

Central Park

East River

Attempt on Frank Costello's Life: 115 Central Park West

W. 81st St.

E. 79th St.

Park Sheraton Hotel Barbershop: Site of Albert Anastasia Hit - 870 7th Avenue

W. 65th St.

E. 66th St.

E. 60th St.

East River

Old Madison Square Garden

W. 57th St.

East 61st St.

The Copacabana: 10 East 60th Street

11th Avenue
10th Avenue
9th Avenue
8th Avenue
7th Avenue
6th Avenue
5th Avenue
Park Avenue
3rd Avenue
2nd Avenue
1st Avenue

Grand Central Building: Site of Salvatore Maranzano's murder: 230 Park Avenue

W. 43rd St.

The Garment Center

E. 34th St.

Hudson River

The 181 Club: 181 East 2nd Avenue

W. 23rd St.

Vito Genovese/ Anthony Strollo/ Tommy Eboli Greenwich Village Crew: 208 Thompson Street

E. 14th St.

Manhattan

North

East

Greenwich Village

Joe Masseria's Saloon: 205 Forsyth Street

E. Houston St.

Delancey St.

West

South

"Little Italy"

Broadway

E. Broadway

Bowery

Manhattan Bridge

Staten Island: Alex Di Brizzi crew

Brooklyn Bridge

Fulton Fish Market

East River

Manhattan Bridge

Brooklyn Bridge

Brooklyn Heights

Co

Red Ho

Brookly

East River

Hudson River